Mature Christianity

Mature Christianity

*The Recognition and Repudiation
of the Anti-Jewish Polemic of the New Testament*

Norman A. Beck

Selinsgrove: Susquehanna University Press
London and Toronto: Associated University Presses

© 1985 by Associated University Presses, Inc.

Associated University Presses
440 Forsgate Drive
Cranbury, NJ 08512

Associated University Presses
25 Sicilian Avenue
London WC1A 2QH, England

Associated University Presses
2133 Royal Windsor Drive
Unit 1
Mississauga, Ontario
Canada L5J 1K5

The paper used in this publication meets the minimum requirements of the
American National Standard for Permanence of Paper for Printed Library
Materials Z39.48-1984.

Library of Congress Cataloging in Publication Data

Beck, Norman A., 1933–
   Mature Christianity.

   Bibliography: p.
   Includes index.
   1. Jews in the New Testament.   2. Bible.   N.T.—Criticism, interpretation, etc.   3. Judaism—Controversial
literature—History and criticism.   I. Title.
BS2545.J44B43   1985   261.2'6   83-51047
ISBN 0-941664-03-1   (alkaline paper)

Printed in the United States of America

To Esther
and to our children
Matthew, David, and Laura

Contents

Preface

One of the essentials for the continued health and vitality of a religion is sincere and responsible self-criticism. During the infancy, childhood, and adolescence of a religion, however, there is generally insufficient ego security to allow anything other than positive evaluations from within.

Early in its development, in what in this study is considered to be the adolescence of a religion, the time typically when the normative literature of a religion is being formulated, sincere and responsible self-criticism is usually notably lacking. As religious self-identity is being established and as attempts are being made to prove the superiority of the new religion over its older relatives, polemic against others rather than criticism of self is deemed desirable. In fact, any self-criticism is likely to be used against the new community by its competitors and is therefore carefully suppressed. Religious self-criticism at this stage of development is not considered to be edifying. It does not have the possibility through broad, popular usage to rise to the status of sacred Scripture. Only when a religious community attains a significant level of maturity is serious self-criticism permitted.

Among the religions that originated in the Near East and their derivatives that have become important in Western civilization, there is an exception to the observation that the sacred Scriptures of a religious tradition do not permit significant self-criticism. By adding to its collection of authoritative religious literature material from a variety of oral and written sources over an exceptionally long period of time, thereby incorporating into its sacred canon the writings of many of its prophetic traditions, Judaism made this important step during the centuries prior to the beginning of the common era and gave evidence of its growing maturity. We are not to assume that this acceptance of prophetic self-criticism was accomplished easily or completely—the prophets in the narrow sense or in the broader designation of the *nebi'im* were not given equal status with the basic Torah—and the Samaritans, the Sadducees, the Karaites, and others with similar sympathies never have been able to grant much authority to the self-critical prophetic traditions. In this sense these particular Jews may be said figuratively to have "killed the prophets and stoned those sent to them" by refusing to accept the authority of these innovations.

The self-criticism that Judaism did permit, as might have been expected, made Judaism particularly vulnerable to the polemical attacks of its off-spring and later competitors. Christianity, Islam, Mormonism, and Moon-ism, whose polemic is surveyed in the introduction and later sections of this study, each mercilessly utilized Judaism's prophetic self-criticism against it. The prophetic self-criticism was distorted when used not as self-criticism but as a weapon against Judaism in the heat of religious competi-tion.

Perhaps we can postulate at this point that the distortion of this self-criticism of Judaism occurred in part when Jewish figurative, symbolic language was taken literally whenever such literalism was to the advantage of the antagonists. The irony of the situation is particularly striking when we observe that early Christianity was able to interpret Jewish prophetic self-criticism literally against Judaism and still manage to retain the Jewish Scriptures as the earlier and larger portion of its Bible. It was able to refute Judaism from Judaism's own sacred writings while at the same time claim-ing ownership of the Jewish literature being used as evidence in its polemic!

Religious self-criticism, if taken seriously, implies that necessary and appropriate modifications of the religion will follow. The fact that Jewish groups for the most part were able to incorporate the self-critical prophetic traditions into their authoritative canon is an indication that they were willing to permit modifications to their theology and to their praxis. The ability of Jewish groups during the years since 70 C.E. to permit new inter-pretations to move through oral and written stages and to give them valid-ity as Talmudic and Responsa literature is evidence of the continued health and vitality of Judaism.

The purpose of the present study is not, however, to advocate the con-tinuing self-criticism and appropriate modification of Judaism. Instead, it is an attempt from within the Christian tradition to examine an aspect of the Christian use of Jewish self-criticism, namely, the anti-Jewish polemic of the Christian New Testament. It is one attempt among many in our time being made by those who are of the opinion that Christianity as a religion is sufficiently mature and self-confident during the last two decades of the twentieth century to be critical of itself and of its own distinctive sacred Scriptures, the New Testament. It is an attempt being made by one who lives within the Christian tradition and who for many years has been keenly interested in its origin, development, and growth, and desires to see its acceptance of some carefully made and appropriate modifications essential for the continued health and vitality of the Christian tradition in the future. In order for this to occur, self-criticism of the New Testament and of contemporary Christianity is necessary.

To many readers this self-criticism will appear irresponsibly radical, far more radical, for example, than the demythologizing of the language of biblical and liturgical material advocated during the past half century by

Rudolf Bultmann and others. In this study not only will there be efforts to "crack the code" of the ancient texts in order to perceive their original meaning and then to express that meaning in terminology understandable and appropriate to our time, but also there will be the possibility of the repudiation of the content of some texts. Although New Testament texts during the past three centuries have been removed from both the Greek and the version editions on text-critical grounds when there was convincing evidence that they were lacking in reputable early manuscripts, texts have not generally been rejected on the grounds that continuing their authoritative validity was harmful to ethnic and religious groups outside the Christian community. In practice, however, each member of a religious community, through usage or lack of usage of specific texts, is involved in determining their authoritative validity, as can be seen, for example, in the use or lack of use of the so-called Old Testament Apocrypha as Christian canonical Scripture. Past reformers such as Martin Luther have reduced the authoritative status of certain portions, even of entire books, both of Old Testament and New Testament material, while emphasizing others. Following in this tradition, the present study makes literary critical evaluations of segments of the New Testament writings that may be considered damaging to Jewish people, dehumanizing to Christians, and detrimental to Christianity.

During the course of this study, as the authority of portions of the sacred Scriptures of Christianity over us is questioned, inevitably we become involved in matters of Christology. It is an assumption within this study that Christianity is sufficiently mature at this time that Christology may be discussed and that it will not be required that God, Jesus, the New Testament, and the church each be understood in precisely the same way by all members of the Christian fellowship. This effort is made in the hope that together we may participate in delivering to the next generation a live, dynamic, and healthily self-critical religious tradition.

Acknowledgments

The research and the writing of this book have been supported by generous grants and I am happy to express my gratitude to the following individuals and the agencies that made them possible: to Rabbi Solomon S. Bernards and the Anti-Defamation League of B'nai B'rith for books, articles, and other bibliographic assistance; to Dr. Frank Giesber and Texas Lutheran College for Faculty Research Grants during the summers of 1977, 1979, and 1981; to the Rev. S. Philip Froiland and the Division for College and University Services of The American Lutheran Church for a Graduate Study Grant during the summer of 1980; and most of all to Mr. Marvin Selig and the Structural Metals, Inc. Foundation of Seguin, Texas, for major Research Grants during the years 1978–1983.

Numerous scholars read extensive parts of the manuscript during its earlier stages and provided invaluable responses and suggestions. Among the most noteworthy of these are the following: Dr. M. Sharon Burns, RSM, Dr. Herbert W. Cassell, Dr. Moshe Davis, Dr. H. J. Flanders, Jr., Dr. John E. Groh, the Rev. David B. Kaplan, Dr. Gerard J. Kuiper, Dr. William L. Lane, Dr. Saul Lerner, Dr. T. W. Lewis III, Dr. Gerald W. McCulloch, Dr. Samuel M. Stahl, Dr. Zwi Werblowsky, and my colleagues at Texas Lutheran College Dr. Peter Ansorge, Dr. Kent Boynton, and Dr. Paul Scheie. Especially helpful in providing encouragement and impetus for this work from the time that I presented a paper on this subject at the Jewish-Lutheran Concerns Consultation sponsored by The American Lutheran Church and the Anti-Defamation League at Madison, Wisconsin, during November of 1976, have been Trudy Rogness Jensen and Rabbi Bernards. Further stimulation has come from students in classes at Texas Lutheran College, from pastors in the Victoria, Texas, Lutheran Church in America Pastors' Retreat, and in Wartburg Theological Seminary Extension Courses for pastors in Austin and in Cuero, Texas, and from other people in Lay Schools of Theology in various churches and synagogues.

Finally, for the careful typing and proofreading of the typescript I am grateful to Sherri Almquist, the executive secretary to the Vice President for Academic Affairs at Texas Lutheran College.

Abbreviations of Periodicals

ATR	Anglican Theological Review
CBQ	Catholic Biblical Quarterly
CC	Christian Century
CCAR	Central Conference of American Rabbis Journal
ET	Expository Times
HTR	Harvard Theological Review
Interp	Interpretation
JAAR	Journal of the American Academy of Religion
JBL	Journal of Biblical Literature
JES	Journal of Ecumenical Studies
JR	Journal of Religion
JRJ	Journal of Reform Judaism
JTS	Journal of Theological Studies
NT	Novum Testamentum
NTS	New Testament Studies
RB	Revue biblique
RL	Religion in Life
TS	Theological Studies
ZAW	Zeitschrift für die alttestamentliche Wissenschaft
ZNW	Zeitschrift für die neutestamentliche Wissenschaft und die Kunde des Urchristentums
ZTK	Zeitschrift für Theologie und Kirche

Mature Christianity

Introduction:
The Role of Polemic in the Sacred Scriptures
of Religious Communities

Polemic against other religious groups is common in the sacred Scriptures of religious communities. This polemic ranges from the subtle and abstruse to the overt and bitter. It is directed primarily against those other religious groups which are the most closely related to the new religious communities from which they set themselves apart. This is to be expected, because the religious groups from which we have written records have had their inception at least in part as a reaction against other religious traditions that were prior to and contemporary with themselves.

Just as in the life of an individual the adolescent breaks away from the parent, sometimes with much scorn and contempt for the values and practices of the parent and of the parent's generation, so too in the history of religions the new community strikes out verbally against the parent community. The futile attempts of the older generation to retain the younger by argument or by force only increase the bitterness and animosity. Mutual rejection intensifies. Usually the closer the family ties had been, the greater is the viciousness of the denunciations. The verbal attack is directed against the religious community that gave birth to and nurtured the new group, while virtually nothing is said against distant faith communities not directly involved nor simultaneously competing for the allegiance of the same persons. Indeed, this polemic is helpful in our attempts to reconstruct the religious scenario of periods early in the development of religious communities.

A. Polemic in the Hebrew Scriptures

In the Hebrew Scriptures polemic includes subtle degradation of Babylonian and Egyptian celestial and terrestrial deities (the greater light, the lesser light, the stars, and the sea monsters) in the Priestly creation account, Gen. 1:1–2:4a, followed by admonitions in Deut. 4:19 and Zeph. 6:5 against worship of the sun, the moon, the stars, all the hosts of heaven, material things that the Lord God has provided. The Tower of Babel account in Gen. 11 is apparently in part polemic against Mesopotamian city cultures with their gateway-to-heaven towers at the summits of their ziggurats. Anti-Egyptian polemic is inherent in Israel's basic confession of faith that Yahweh delivered Israel from Egyptian bondage.

Polemic against the nearer neighbors of the Israelites, the Canaanites, and against their cultic practices is much more common. Canaan is personified and cursed; a slave of slaves shall he be to his brothers because of his sexual perversions (Gen. 9:20–27). The serpent, a phallic symbol within the Canaanite fertility cults, is the agent for the seduction of Eve (Gen. 3). In the Yahwistic creation account there may be skillfully subtle polemic against fertility cult practices of intercourse with animals when it is recorded that among all of the cattle, the birds of the air, and the beasts of the field there was not found a helper fit for the man; instead, the Lord God made from a rib of the man a woman and brought her to the man to be a helper fit for him (Gen. 2:18–25).[1]

There was a time when the use of household gods had been customary among the ancestors of the Israelites. In the Jacob story in Gen. 31 the use of such objects was put down when Rachel was said to have stolen her father's household deities, placed them in the camel's saddle in her tent, and sat upon them. She refused to get up while her father searched the tent for them, claiming that she was in the midst of her menstrual cycle, thus covering them with her uncleanness. Within Yahwism in its national stage in the Shechemite Dodecalogue, in the Decalogue in Exod. 20 and Deut. 5, and elsewhere, there are the well-known prohibitions against making graven images in the form of any figure, male or female, of any beast, bird, reptile, or fish.[2] Beyond this there are vitriolic denunciations of the various Baal cults and their worship practices. To cite only one example, in Deut. 12:1–3, 29–31 it is commanded that the places where the nations that the Israelites would dispossess had served their gods upon the high mountains and the hills and under every green tree must all be destroyed. The Canaanite altars must be torn down, their pillars dashed into pieces, and their Asherim burned. The graven images of their gods must be cut down and the name of their holy ones destroyed. It is said that these antecedents of the Israelites have done every abominable thing, even burning their own sons and daughters in the fire of their gods.[3]

These instances of polemic are indications that the Israelite cult developed alongside of, to some extent out of, and in opposition to the local fertility and weather deities whose worship was widespread in agricultural Canaan. Certainly the political conquest of the land was no easy task, as the records in Judges and 1 Samuel indicate, and the religious conquest of the agricultural deities was an equally long and frustrating struggle.[4]

As a result of the extensive military achievements of David and the establishment of the Empire, large numbers of non-Israelites were brought into the nation and into the royal court. Elijah, a few generations later, is said to have felt that he alone remained as one who would speak for the Lord; he had to be reassured that the Lord would leave seven thousand in Israel who had not bowed to Baal and kissed him (1 Kings 19). In Hos. 2:2–13 we read that although it was the Lord who gave Israel its grain, wine, oil, silver, and gold, these precious gifts were all too frequently offered as oblations to the Baals. During Josiah's reform, vessels made for Baal, for Asherah, and for all the hosts of heaven were brought out of the temple of the Lord and burned outside Jerusalem. The priests were deposed whom the kings of Judah had ordained to burn incense to Baal, to the sun, and the moon, the constellations, and all the hosts of the heavens, and Josiah is commended for defiling the high places that Solomon had built for Ashtoreth, for Chemosh, and for Milcom (2 Kings 23:4–14). The polemic against the making of idols and against the cult of idols continues in Isa. 40:19–20; 41:6–7; 42:17; 44:9–20; 45:16–17, 20b; 46:5–8; 48:22; Ps. 97:7; and many other places, most graphically in the Bel and the Dragon Additions to Daniel.

B. Polemic in the Greek New Testament

Polemic in the New Testament is subtle against Persian Zoroastrianism and Mithraism in the account of the adoration of the infant Jesus by the magi from the east in Matt. 2,[5] more apparent against various forms of incipient Gnosticism in John, Colossians, 1 John, and elsewhere, and most overt and bitter against the complex Judaism of the first century of the common era, in which context more than any other early Christianity developed. This New Testament polemic against its parent Judaism is the subject of the present study.

To assist us in gaining a better perspective of the problem of the New Testament polemic against the Jewish sources and competition of Christianity, let us turn also to some of the remarks included some six centuries later in the Koran about the Jewish and the Christian predecessors of Islam, and then look in addition at similar material in the Book of Mormon and in the Divine Principle of Moonism.

C. Polemic in the Koran

Extensive portions of the Koran are devoted to anti-Jewish polemic. Only a few key examples can be cited here. It is written in Surah 2:40–145 that humiliation and wretchedness were stamped upon the Jews and that they were visited with wrath from Allah because they disbelieved in Allah's revelations and killed their prophets wrongfully. In 4:46 it is taught that Allah has cursed the Jews because of their disbelief. Only a few of them believe in Allah as Allah is revealed through his prophet Muhammad. In 4:161 it is said that because of their taking usury when they were forbidden it and their devouring people's wealth by false pretenses, for those of them who do not believe in Allah a painful doom has been prepared. In 59:3–4 it is written that for those Jews who are opposed to Allah and to his messenger Muhammad there will be in the hereafter the punishment of fire. The volume and the vehemence of the anti-Jewish material in the Koran is ample evidence of the degree of Jewish background in Islamic thought and of the vitality of the Jewish religion in the milieu in which Islam was developed.

Jews and Christians together (the people of the Scripture) are accused in Surah 2:109 of trying because of envy to make the followers of Allah and of Muhammad his prophet disbelieve what they have been taught and follow them instead. These people of the Scripture say according to 2:111 that no one enters Paradise unless he is a Jew or a Christian. In 2:113 it is written that the Jews and the Christians each claim that the other follows nothing true; yet both are readers of the Scripture. They are people who have passed away (2:134, 141). If they had observed the Torah and the Gospel and all that has been revealed to them from their Lord, they would surely have prospered. There are those among them who are moderate, but many of them are evil (5:66–68). Believing followers of Allah are advised not to take the Jews and Christians as friends, for they are friends to each other. Those who take them as friends become one with them. Allah does not guide those who do wrong and make a jest and sport of the religion of his followers when they call to prayer (5:51, 57).

Christians are said to have forgotten part of their covenant. It is for this reason that enmity and hatred have been stirred up among them until the Day of Resurrection, when Allah will inform them of their handiwork (5:14). Muhammad, the messenger of Allah, has come, making clear much of that which the people of the Scripture used to hide, forgiving much, and bringing light from Allah and a Scripture clearly understandable, so that those who seek Allah's good pleasure are guided into paths of peace, out of darkness into light, and led on a straight path (5:15–16). They surely disbelieve who say that Allah is the Messiah, the son of Mary. The Messiah himself said, "Worship Allah, my Lord and your Lord." Whoever appoints partners for Allah, for him Allah has forbidden Paradise. They surely disbelieve who say that Allah is the third of three, when there is no God except Allah, the One God. The Messiah, the son of Mary, was only a messenger like those who had passed away before him. His mother was a saintly woman, and they both used to eat earthly food (5:17, 72–75; 9:30).

Nevertheless, the polemic in the Koran is much stronger against the Jews than against the Christians. For example, in 5:82–83 it is written that the most vehement of mankind in hostility to the Muslims are the Jews and the idolaters. On the other hand, those who are nearest to the Muslims in affection are those who say that they are Christians. These have among them priests and monks who are not proud, who recognize the truth in that which has been revealed to Muhammad the prophet. On the contrary, the likeness of those who have been entrusted with the Law of Moses (62:5), yet apply it not, is as the likeness of an ass carrying books!

D. *Polemic in the Book of Mormon*

When we move to the nineteenth century and to the Book of Mormon we find similar invectives.[6] The two principal objects of this polemic are the Jews and "the church of the devil." Only representative examples of the attacks can be cited here.

Nephi testifies that when his father, Lehi, filled with the Spirit of the Lord, prophesied against Jerusalem during the reign of Zedekiah, the Jews were angry with him, mocked him, and sought his life, as they had the prophets of old, whom they had cast out, stoned, and slain (1 Nephi 1:1–10:3). It is foretold that the Gospel will be preached among the Jews. The Jews, however, will not believe, and will dwindle in unbelief. They will slay the Messiah. The house of Israel is compared to an olive tree, whose branches will be broken off and scattered over the earth until the Gentiles have received the fullness of the Gospel. Only then will the remnants of the house of Israel come to the knowledge of the true Messiah, their Lord and their Redeemer, and be grafted again into the olive tree (1 Nephi 10:11–14). When the day comes that the Only-begotten of the Father will manifest himself in the flesh to the Jews, they will reject him because of their iniquities and the hardness of their hearts and the stiffness of their necks. They will crucify him. After he has been raised from the dead and has revealed himself to those who will believe in him, Jerusalem will be destroyed again, an altogether appropriate affliction for those who fight against God and against the people of the church (2 Nephi 25:12–20; Alma 33:14–17).

Continuing in the style of Jewish and of Christian apocalyptic, it is said that then the house of Israel is seen to have gathered together to fight against the twelve apostles of the Lamb. Like the fall of a great and spacious building will be the destruction of all who fight against the twelve apostles of the Lamb. Those who reject the Lamb will dwindle in unbelief and become a dark, loathsome, and filthy people, full of idleness and of every kind of abomination (1 Nephi 11:35–36; 12:1–23).[7]

When we turn to the other major object of Book of Mormon polemic, we see that the devil is considered to be the foundation of a great and detestable church which is seen to have taken away from the Gospel of the Lamb many parts that are plain and most precious, and many covenants of the Lord, that it might pervert the ways of the Lord and blind the eyes and harden the hearts of the children of men (1 Nephi 13). There are only two churches, the church of the Lamb of God and the church of the devil. The numbers of those in the church of the Lamb of God are few because of the wickedness and abominations of the church of the devil. The church of the devil is the whore of all the earth. It gathers multitudes to fight against the Lamb of God. However, the wrath of God is poured out against that great and detestable church to destroy it, to fulfill the covenants that God has made with his people who are truly of the house of Israel[8] (1 Nephi 14).

In other places polemic is directed against various churches within Christianity. For example, in Mormon 8:32 it is written that there will come a day when there will be churches built up that will say, "Come to me, and for your money you shall be forgiven your sins." He who says that little children need baptism denies the mercies of God, and is in danger of death, hell, and endless torment (Moroni 8:19–21). It will come to pass that churches will be built up and not unto the Lord, each claiming that it alone belongs to the Lord. They and their priests will contend with one another, teaching what they have learned and denying the revelation of the Holy Spirit (2 Nephi 28:3–6).

Gentile Christians are denounced for claiming that they have a Bible and for claiming that there cannot be any more Bible than that which they have. These Gentile Christians are reminded that it was because of the Jews that they "obtained" a Bible. It is said that instead of expressing their gratitude to the people through whom they obtained a Bible these Gentile Christians have cursed and hated the Jews. Therefore these Gentile Christians are said to be under the condemnation of the Lord, who has not forgotten the people of the Lord. In addition, the Gentile Christians are told that just because they have a Bible they should not suppose that it contains all of God's words. They should not suppose that God has not caused more words to be written (2 Nephi 29:3–10).

E. Polemic in the Divine Principle

In the Divine Principle[9] of Moonism it is taught that Christianity has superseded Judaism and it in turn is being superseded by those who gather around the "Lord of the Second Advent."[10] The Israelites have opposed God's will. They did not believe the testimony of John the Baptist that Jesus was the Messiah.[11] Instead, after waiting for the Messiah for such a long time, when he came they crucified him. Jesus grieved over the treachery of the Jewish people. He wept over Jerusalem and cursed it so that it would be destroyed so utterly that not one stone would be left upon another. On another occasion (Matt. 23:13–36), he cursed the Jewish people in great indignation, prophesying that they would suffer. Because of the Jewish people's disbelief in Jesus, they all were destined to hell. As Jesus foretold, the chosen nation of Israel declined after his death. They have lost their qualification as the chosen people and have been scattered and persecuted through the present day.[12] Indeed, their failure to accept Jesus as their

Messiah was consistent with their failure, through faithlessness and rebellion, throughout their history to follow the will of God, as recorded in their own Scriptures. Therefore the foundation of their tabernacle was invaded by Satan.[13]

When the Jews did not believe Jesus and delivered him up for crucifixion, his body was invaded by Satan. Consequently, when Christians believe in Jesus and become one body with him whose body was invaded by Satan, their bodies remain subject to Satan's invasion and regardless of how devout Christians may be, they cannot fulfill physical salvation by redemption through Jesus' crucifixion alone. Their physical sin has not been annihilated. Their salvation through redemption by the cross of Christ is spiritual salvation only. It will be necessary for Christ to return to the earth to provide the physical in addition to the spiritual salvation.[14]

Today's Christianity is attached to the authority and rites of the church. Its inner concepts are corrupt. Its leaders, including its priests and ministers, are becoming spiritually darker every day. Innumerable Christians of today are dashing down a road that is apt to lead them into Hell. At the time of the coming of the Lord of the Second Advent, Christian laymen and those without any religious faith but who are very conscientious may be the ones to accept the Lord's words rather than the leading class of Christianity. Christian leaders today, the Second Israel, who are captive to scriptural words, will surely criticize the words and conduct of the Lord of the Second Advent. They can be expected to persecute him and brand him a heretic.[15] If this happens, God will have to abandon the Christians when they persecute the Lord of the Second Advent, just as God abandoned the Jewish people who rejected Jesus. Those who serve the Lord of the Second Advent will become the Third Israel, the chosen nation.[16]

According to Moonism, the Bible should be read with a knowledge of Divine Principle in order that the Bible may be understood.[17] With the coming of the Lord of the Second Advent, the Bible will be fulfilled. Christianity will be superseded and its leaders cast away. All other religions will be superseded as well. When earthly saints attend the Lord of the Second Advent and devote themselves to the will of God through the cooperation of the spirit-men descending to them from Paradise, Christianity is destined to reach its unification. The Lord of the Second Advent, coming as the central figure of Christianity, will also play the role of Buddha, of the "True Man" of the Confucianists, of "Chung Do Ryung" whom the Koreans anticipate, and of the central figure whom people in all other religions await.[18] Then all will be one. It could therefore be said that Moonism is attempting to do to Christianity and to the specifically Christian sacred writings the same things that the early Christians did to their satisfaction to Judaism and to the Jewish Scriptures.

Summary

Polemic against other religious groups to which the new religious communities are closely related and from which they are derived has been apparent in a survey examination of sacred writings of Judaism, Christianity, Islam, Mormonism, and Moonism, a related grouping of religions, each of which established its identity, partially at least, by literary attack upon its antecedents.[19]

Among the sacred Scriptures surveyed, the Hebrew Bible contains by far the most self-criticism. Its composition covered a lengthy period of time compared to the others. During much of its history Judaism has permitted great diversity. The Jewish self-criticism has been utilized profusely against the Jewish people by each subsequent group, beginning with Christianity. The Christian polemic against the Jews has been used against Christianity itself in the Koran, the Book of Mormon, and the Divine Principle.

Notes

1. In the Shechemite Dodecalogue intercourse with any kind of beast is forbidden along with the prohibitions against incest (Deut. 27:20–23).

2. The bronze serpent account in Num. 21:8–9 is a fascinating exception to these prohibitions.

3. See Gen. 22:1–14, 19 regarding, among other things, polemic against such practices.

4. See Gerhard von Rad, *Old Testament Theology*, vol. 1 (New York: Harper & Row, 1962). For an example of Jewish sensitivity of the harsh anti-Canaanite polemic of the Torah, see Eric L. Friedland, "What of the Canaanites?" *JRJ* 27 (1980): 77–81.

5. This account may also be an echo of the Num. 24:17b word of Balaam, a magus from the East who saw a star rise out of Jacob. See Raymond E. Brown, *The Birth of the Messiah* (Garden City, N.Y.: Doubleday, 1979), pp. 36, 168–69, 190–200.

6. For initial work done on this subject I am indebted to one of my students, Stephen P. Schrank.

7. See also Mosiah 3:7; 13:28–35; Alma 5:38–41; Helaman 8:12–28. The anti-Jewish polemic of the Book of Mormon, though condemnatory of the Jews, is basically secondhand polemic, derived largely from the New Testament and from Christianity. Its firsthand polemic, developed from bitter experience in its nineteenth century rural American context, is against what it depicts as "the church of the devil."

Because Mormons identify themselves genealogically by means of the Book of Mormon with ancient Israel and consider themselves to *be* Israel in a new stage of its history and because some Mormon writers denounce all enemies of Israel, W. D. Davies in "Israel, the Mormons and the Land," *Reflections on Mormonism: Judaeo-Christian Parallels*, ed. T. G. Madsen (Provo, Utah: Religious Studies Center, Brigham Young University, 1978), pp. 79–97, expresses the opinion that Mormonism "is as far removed from anti-Semitism and even anti-Judaism as it can be." He finds that in some Mormon writers "There is instead what one might almost call a pro-Semitism." Krister Stendahl in "The Sermon on the Mount and Third Nephi,"

Reflections on Mormonism: Judaeo-Christian Parallels, ed. T. G. Madsen (Provo, Utah: Religious Studies Center, Brigham Young University, 1978), pp. 139–54, and *Meanings: The Bible as Document and as Guide* (Philadelphia: Fortress, 1984), pp. 99–113, concurs with Davies and observes that the word *Pharisee* does not occur in the Book of Mormon. Therefore Stendahl finds it "truly refreshing and welcome and unique" that "the Christian habit of using the term *Pharisees* as a symbol for the wrong attitude toward God is not part of the Mormon tradition."

The nonoccurrence of the terms *Pharisee* and *Pharisees* in the Book of Mormon can be attributed to its nineteenth-century rural American context. Unlike the life situation in which the documents that were to become the New Testament were formulated, there were no groups of people in nineteenth-century rural America who were primarily designated as "Pharisees." Therefore, the term *Pharisees* would have had little meaning in that life situation. It remained in the New Testament documents, but it was not employed in the redaction of earlier documents and in the composition of new material that was to become the Book of Mormon, and that is, as Stendahl says, "refreshing."

Because Mormons consider themselves to *be* Israel in a new stage of its history, when Mormon writers identifying themselves in accordance with Book of Mormon terminology as Israel and as "the church of the Lamb of God" denounce what the Book of Mormon designates as "the church of the devil" and all other enemies of Israel, they are basically denouncing all who have been adversaries of Mormon people and only secondarily denouncing all adversaries of the Jews. Consequently, what may appear to be "pro-Semitism" in Mormon literature is primarily "pro-Mormonism." The literature of each religious community is understandably positive about itself, particularly during the adolescence of that religious community. However, when a new religious community considers itself to *be* an older religious community in a new stage of its history and preempts both the name and the claims for validity of the older religious community, the members of the older religious community do not perceive the statements of the community that claims to have superseded it to be positive toward themselves even when the name of the older religious community is honored within the new religious community.

8. Here the community that produced this writing that became sacred to itself, like others before and after it, appropriated the designation "house of Israel" for itself.

9. *Divine Principle* (Washington, D.C.: The Holy Spirit Association for the Unification of World Christianity, 1973).

10. Mary Jo Geisler, "Polemic in the Divine Principle," unpublished paper, Texas Lutheran College, Seguin, Texas, 1978.

11. According to the Divine Principle, God's plan of salvation was thwarted when John the Baptist failed to declare himself to be Elijah returned to the earth and, after his own imprisonment by Herod, doubted that Jesus was the Messiah. Even before his imprisonment John made a serious blunder in continuing to baptize people separately from Jesus, thus confusing the Jewish people, including their chief priests. *Divine Principle,* pp. 157–63, 349.

12. *Divine Principle,* pp. 143–47. See also pp. 200, 232, 357–59, 510, 518, 533.

13. Ibid., pp. 293–342.

14. Ibid., pp. 147–49.

15. Ibid., pp. 532–35.

16. Ibid., pp. 364, 521.

17. Ibid., p. 149.

18. Ibid., pp. 188–91, 528–29. More specific polemic in Divine Principle is directed against the ecclesiastical authority, predestination, and unconditional grace teachings of classical Roman Catholic, Reformed, and Lutheran Christianity. Much

of the anti-Jewish polemic and the polemic against certain groups of Christians within Divine Principle is a heritage from the work of Presbyterian missionaries in Korea prior to 1960. The teachings of the Presbyterian missionaries regarding predestination are in turn criticized through their reinterpretation in Divine Principle.

19. A similar pattern could be traced in the sacred writings of the Hindu, Jain, and Buddhist traditions and their derivatives, and in other groupings of related religious communities. Normative writings of other groups that were developed within the Jewish and Christian environment, such as the Church of Christ Scientist and the Jehovah's Witnesses, not covered in this brief survey, include the same kind of polemic.

1

Focusing on the Issue

In many instances in the history of religion, within a century or two of their inception new religions virtually eliminate their antecedents. After a bitter struggle, Zoroastrianism became the official religion of the Persian Empire and few traces of the religion of the earlier Iranians remain. Islam almost completely replaced the other religions that were native to the Arabian peninsula, absorbing what it did not destroy and destroying what it did not absorb of the native cults. Of course, other factors in addition to the purely religious ones are involved. Political upheaval and external conquest cause tribal and national religious groups to be dispersed and dissipated. In this way countless religious groups have become extinct, succumbing to others more capable of adaptation and modification. Although dealing with polemic that is directed against religious groups that are no longer extant is of interest as an academic exercise, such polemic is not the primary issue in this study. If there are no identifiable Kenizzites, Kadmonites, or Perizzites living in the world today, no harm is being done to them by polemic still aimed in their direction!

In other instances the earlier religion continues to exist alongside of the newer religious community that was derived largely from it. When this occurs, as it has in the case of Judaism and of the religions developed from Judaism and from Jewish and Christian antecedents as surveyed in the Introduction above, the polemic against the parent religion can contribute over a period of time to deplorable, unspeakably horrendous injustice. Particularly is this the case when adherents of the derived religion outnumber those of the antecedent one and exercise political control over them, as Christians have over Jews in Western civilization since the fourth century of the common era—directly during the period of that great medieval synthesis of religion and culture known as Christendom and in varying degrees indirectly since the crumbling of that synthesis. Although there were obviously political, social, and economic as well as religious factors involved, the anti-Jewish polemic in the Christian New Testament over a

31

period of many centuries has contributed to the development of prejudices and actions that have been extremely detrimental to Jewish life and community. As Christians, we are concerned about what has happened to Jewish people during the intervening centuries because of this polemic in the New Testament and the prejudices and oppressive actions for which it has provided theological justification. Beyond that, we are concerned about our own attitudes and responsibilities today. The central issue of this study, therefore, can be stated as follows: What are we who live as Christians during the latter decades of the twentieth century going to do about the anti-Jewish polemic in the New Testament,[1] which has provided the theological basis for oppressive, unjust, and extremely hurtful anti-Semitism?[2]

A. The Question of Authority

This leads us into the more specific question: Should we stand in judgment over our own scriptural traditions, perhaps even repudiating a few portions as damaging to the Christian position and harmful to Jews? The question obviously becomes one of authority. Do our scriptural traditions have authority over us, or do we have authority over our Scriptures? What relationship of authority between our scriptural traditions and ourselves is most desirable?

In 2 Tim. 3:14–16 we have a statement that for many Christians provides an unequivocal answer to the question of authority. According to these verses Timothy is instructed to continue in that which he has learned and accepted, knowing from whom he learned it, and that since his childhood he has been familiar with the sacred writings that are able to prepare him intellectually for salvation through his faith, which is in Christ Jesus. It is added that every portion of scripture is *"theopneustos"* (literally, "God-breathed") and is useful for instruction, for reproof, for correction, for training in righteousness, so that the man of God may be perfect, thoroughly equipped for every good thing. In addition, according to 2 Peter 1:19–21, we have the prophetic word as something that is entirely reliable, to which it is well to pay close attention, as to a lamp shining in a dark place, until the time when the day dawns and the morning star rises in our hearts, since we know this as of prime importance that every prophecy of Scripture does not come into being as one's own explanation, for not by the will of man was any prophecy ever produced, but, moved by the Holy Spirit, men spoke from God. One can hardly doubt that these verses make strong claims for the authority of scriptural traditions over us.

Incorporated into the Nicene Creed is the statement that Jesus Christ was raised from the dead "in accordance with the Scriptures." In more recent times we have established for ourselves statements of confession and subscription such as those in which we say that we accept all of the canonical books of the Old and New Testaments as a whole and in all their parts as the divinely inspired, revealed, and inerrant Word of God, and submit to this as the only infallible authority in all matters of faith and life.[3]

It should be noted that the matrix of the formation of statements of confession and subscription such as that to which reference has been made above was one of intense controversy against other Christian groups in which it was felt that support from an inerrant and infallible authority was necessary. The opponents in this controversy in turn felt compelled to claim an inerrant and infallible ecclesiastical authority.

The use of words such as *inerrant* and *infallible* forces us in our deliberations to the question not merely of significant and helpful authority, but to the question of *ultimate* authority. When we come to realize finally, with some assistance from Paul Tillich,[4] that every type of faith has the tendency, particularly under the pressures of controversy, to elevate its concrete symbols to the level of absolute validity, we see that it is idolatrous of us to attribute inerrant, infallible, ultimate authority either to scriptural traditions or to ecclesiastical institutions. Scriptural traditions and ecclesiastical institutions point to the ultimate, they participate in that to which they point, and they open up levels of reality otherwise closed to us,[5] and as such they have been assigned *significant* authority over us by us during various periods of our history. It is apparent, therefore, that the people of any religious traditions may through usage and decree determine that their scriptural traditions and their institutions have significant authority among them. In theistic religious systems the members of the community claim divine inspiration and divine revelation not only as we have it in 2 Tim. 3:14–16 and in 2 Peter 1:19–21 above for the origin of the tradition and of the institutions, but also for each step of the process by which authority is attributed to them.

Subscription to the significant authority of scriptural traditions and of institutions is appropriate and essential in order that there may be proper accountability within a religious community. Subscription to them as infallible and ultimate authority, however, is idolatrous.

A relationship of mutual authority and mutual responsibility is desirable. In such a situation we are accountable under the ultimate divine authority to be responsible for our own scriptural traditions. This accountability involves our subscription to our scriptural traditions as having significant authority over us and the necessity of our having significant authority over them as well. This necessity of ours to have significant authority over our own scriptural traditions means that we shall stand in significant judgment over our scriptural traditions just as they stand in significant judgment over us.

In practice we have stood in significant judgment over our scriptural traditions throughout our history. The early church boldly reinterpreted the Jewish Scriptures to meet its needs, pressing them into service as messianic prophecies and typologies of Jesus' life. Allegorical interpretations were commonly employed. Large portions of the Jewish scriptures, though retained canonically by the early Christians, were virtually ignored in practice. Animal sacrifices, for example, were rejected with the theological basis for the rejection provided most fully in the Epistle to the Hebrews. Likewise the religious requirement of circumcision and dietary regulations was dropped at an early date, as can be seen already in the Galatians, 1 Corinthians, Romans, Acts, and the Gospel accounts.

Reinterpretations by Christians of scriptural traditions have not been limited to the Jewish portion. Segments of the specifically Christian canonical literature have been largely ignored in practice by most Christians— segments such as the suggestion to remain unmarried,[6] the stipulations concerning hair styles and head coverings,[7] the role of women in the churches,[8] and the ceremony of footwashing commanded in John 13. Such portions of New Testament literature were not repudiated officially; they simply have been reinterpreted allegorically or otherwise, or progressively ignored in Christian praxis by large numbers of people. In our own time there are attempts in various ways to repudiate some of the New Testament suggestions and stipulations concerning the role of women in the churches. When this is done in various denominations and synods, it is not without great difficulty.

B. The Basic Presupposition of This Study

The basic presupposition of this study, therefore, is that since it is patently idolatrous to suppose that any entity except God is truly ultimate, inerrant, and infallible, and since in practice we are responsible for our own scriptural traditions and have stood in judgment over them throughout our history, *we can carefully and deliberately, repudiate[9] portions of our scriptural traditions that have proved to be deleterious to persons either within or outside of the Christian community.* The repudiation, wherever it may be found to be necessary, will take a variety of forms, depending upon the content of the scriptural material and the reasoned judgment of those involved in the self-criticism.

Our present concern, an issue raised forcibly by Rosemary Ruether in calling into question the "left hand of Christology" in *Faith and Fratricide,* is this: For the sake primarily of persons outside of our own religious community, are we willing to take the risks involved in a drastic repudiation of a portion of the New Testament record, namely, its anti-Jewish polemic? Can a religion that is built upon the concept of sacrifice of self for the sake of others and of God's vindication of that self-sacrifice make a substantial self-sacrifice itself for the sake of others? Can Christian theology survive this major surgery self-administered, this repudiation of a part of its scriptural tradition? Is there adequate strength and maturity, and is there enough creativity within Christianity and in Christian theology at the present time to accomplish this? Can we stop being anti-Jewish in our scriptural traditions and in our practice and still remain Christian? What would be the shape of a late twentieth-century Christianity that would have severed its anti-Jewish "left hand of Christology"? What effect would this action have upon the closely related issues of

a. Christianity's claim to have abrogated Judaism;
b. Christianity's assertion that it has the universal, one way for all people, including Jewish people;[10] and
c. Christianity's teaching of fulfilled messianism?[11]

As suggested above in the Preface to this study, there is precedent in Christian history for attempts at drastic repudiation of substantial portions of the scriptural, even the New Testament scriptural, traditions. I think, as a prime example, of Martin Luther's attempt during the sixteenth century to repudiate the Epistle of James on the theological grounds that it was an unacceptable contradiction to Paul's theology of grace in Galatians and Romans.

It is my opinion, as stated in the Preface above, that the Christian tradition—in fact any religious tradition—should be encouraged to be critical of itself. Such self-criticism may not be acceptable during the youth and adolescence of a religious tradition. Mormonism, for example, is probably a long way from the time when its adherents will be permitted to be critical of it. Islam has given little evidence of significant self-criticism. The Roman Catholic Church would not tolerate it during the sixteenth century, and is experiencing difficulty in handling it during our own time. Most of the other sections of Christianity find self-criticism equally difficult. Nevertheless, I think that radical self-criticism is essential to the health and vitality of the church, and the ecumenical movements of the twentieth century have provided a climate in which efforts can be diverted from intra-Christian criticism to Christian self-criticism.

C. The Methodology to Be Employed

Finally, in this focusing on the issue, there should be some explanation of the methodology followed in this study. Obviously, a careful methodological approach is needed, involving the best possible textual, literary, redactional, source, and form critical analyses. If this is to be done, it must be done conversant with the literature that has been developed around these texts—an enormous exegetical and hermeneutical task! There can be no doubt that specialists in each area of biblical text study will find much to improve upon what can be done here.

Some writers do not distinguish polemic material in the New Testament from that which is apologetic. Although the two are related somewhat as offense and defense are related in a sports event, the concentration here will be upon that which is polemic against the Jewish religion and its adherents during the first century rather than upon early Christian apologetic of itself. This study differs considerably, therefore, from Barnabas Lindars's study of the way in which Jewish scriptural traditions were quoted in the New Testament.[12]

The methodology employed varies somewhat from one type of New Testament literature to another. This is considered to be necessary because the investigation should be appropriate to the various types of literature under scrutiny. Also, there is some variety in the manner in which the results of the investigation are presented, for the sake of those who read and the one who writes.

Basically, the study is a survey of anti-Jewish polemic beginning with the epistles of Paul, and beyond them with the greater Pauline corpus. The largest sections relate to the Synoptic Gospels, Acts, and the Fourth Gospel, simply because they are the writings with the heaviest concentration of anti-Jewish material. The survey continues with the Johannine Epistles, the Apocalypse, Hebrews, The Epistle of James, 1 Peter, Jude, and 2 Peter. This sequence has been selected to conform roughly with the sequence in which it is thought that these documents were developed within the early Christian communities. It is probable that many were in process of development concurrently.

After this extensive survey, there is a brief chapter of conclusions, implications, and future agenda for a mature Christianity.

Notes

1. Among the more significant attempts to identify this polemic are the following: Philip Deever, "Anti-Judaism of the New Testament in the Light of Its Biblical and Hellenistic Context," Th.D. diss., Union Theological Seminary 1958; James Parkes, *The Conflict of the Church and the Synagogue* (New York: Meridian Books, 1961); Jules Isaac, *The Teaching of Contempt: Christian Roots of Anti-Semitism* (New York: Holt, Rinehart and Winston, 1964); E. Grässer, "Die antijudische Polemik im Johannesevangelium," *NTS* 11 (1964): 77–90; Gregory Baum, *Is the New Testament Anti-Semitic?* (New York: Paulist, 1965); Dominic M. Crossan, "Anti-Semitism and the Gospel," *TS* 26 (1965): 189–214; Joseph Fitzmyer, "Anti-Semitism and the Cry of 'All the People,'" *TS* 26 (1965): 667–71; Gerald O'Collins, "Anti-Semitism in the Gospel," *TS* 26 (1965): 663–66; A. Roy Eckardt, *Elder and Younger Brothers* (New York: Scribner, 1967); W. Eckert, et al., ed., *Antijudaismus im Neuen Testament? Exegetische und systematische Beiträge*, Abh. z. christl. jüd. Dialog 1 (Munich, 1967); Markus Barth, "Was Paul an Anti-Semite?" *JES* 5 (1968): 78–104; Rosemary Radford Ruether, "Theological Anti-Semitism in the New Testament," *CC* 85 (1968): 191–96; Bruce Vawter, "Are the Gospels Anti-Semitic?" *JES* 5 (1968): 473–87; Joseph Grassi, "Are the Roots of Anti-Semitism in the Gospels?" *Root and Branch* (New York: Roth, 1973), pp. 71–88; Rosemary Radford Ruether, *Faith and Fratricide: The Theological*

Roots of Anti-Semitism (New York: Seabury, 1974), pp. 64–116; Massey H. Shepherd, "The Jews in the Gospel of John," *ATR* suppl. 34 (1974): 95–112; Eldon Jay Epp, "Anti-Semitism and the Popularity of the Fourth Gospel in Christianity," *CCAR* 22 (1975): 35–57; Paul J. Kirsch, *We Christians and Jews* (Philadelphia: Fortress, 1975); Reginald Fuller, "The 'Jews' in the Fourth Gospel," *Dialog* 16 (1977): 31–37; Eugene Fisher, "Are the Gospels Anti-Semitic?" *Faith Without Prejudice; Rebuilding Christian Attitudes Toward Judaism* (New York: Paulist, 1977), pp. 54–75; Samuel Sandmel, *Anti-Semitism in the New Testament?* (Philadelphia: Fortress, 1978); John Koenig, *Jews and Christians in Dialogue: New Testament Foundations* (Philadelphia: Westminster, 1979); Alan T. Davies, ed., *Antisemitism and the Foundations of Christianity* (New York: Paulist, 1979); Daniel J. Harrington, *God's People in Christ: New Testament Perspectives on the Church and Judaism* (Philadelphia: Fortress, 1980); John T. Pawlikowski, *What Are They Saying About Christian-Jewish Relations?* (New York: Paulist, 1980); John G. Gager, *The Origins of Anti-Semitism* (New York: Oxford University Press, 1984).

2. It has become the practice of many to write the word *anti-Semitism* without capitalization and with no hyphen, in accordance with the suggestion of James Parkes, "Judaism and the Jewish People in Their World Setting at the End of 1973," pamphlet distributed by the Canadian Council of Christians and Jews (Toronto, 1974). A. Roy Eckardt, "The Nemesis of Christian Antisemitism," in *Jewish-Christian Relations in Today's World*, ed. J. E. Wood (Waco, Texas: Baylor University Press, 1971), pp. 45–62, used the word in this form, but credited Parkes with sharing the idea in a conversation that the word is entitled to neither a hyphen nor a capital. Alan T. Davies had earlier used the word in this way in *Antisemitism and the Christian Mind* (New York: Seabury, 1969), as had Eckardt still earlier in "The Theology of Antisemitism," *RL* 31 (1962): 552–62.

3. *United Testimony on Faith and Life*, 3. The Means of Grace, as quoted in *The Constitution and Bylaws of The American Lutheran Church* 3.10.

4. Paul Tillich, *Dynamics of Faith* (New York: Harper & Row, 1957).

5. Ibid., pp. 41–43.

6. 1 Cor. 7.

7. 2 Cor. 11:4–16; 1 Tim. 2:9, Acts 18:18.

8. 1 Cor. 14:33b–36; 1 Tim. 2:11–15. But see also Mark 15:40–41, 47; 16:1–8; Matt. 27:55–61; 28:1–10; Luke 23:49, 55–56; 24:1–11; John 19:25–27; 20:11–18; Acts 9:36–39; Rom. 16:1–16; 1 Cor. 11:5; 16:19; Gal. 3:27–28; Eph. 5:22–33; Phil. 4:2–3; Col. 3:18–19; 2 Tim. 1:5; 4:19; 1 Peter 3:1–7; and Rev. 2:20–23.

9. *Repudiate* rather than *reject* is the terminology employed here in accordance with the directives of the Division of Theological Studies of the Lutheran Council in the U.S.A. and of the Seventh General Convention of The American Lutheran Church (see below, pp. 48–50). The sense of the word *repudiate* as used in this study is that we "refuse to accept as valid or binding," "disown," and "separate ourselves from" certain expressions rather than that we "reject" them, that is that we "deny" them, "refuse to recognize" them, or "expel" them. We can repudiate something that is in our heritage, but we cannot deny it or refuse to recognize that it is there. For this reason I have chosen as the subtitle of this work "The Recognition and Repudiation of the Anti-Jewish Polemic in the New Testament."

10. For numerous viewpoints by Christians and by Jews regarding this assertion, see the articles on the subject of "Christian Mission and Jewish Witness" in *Face to Face: an Interreligious Bulletin* 3–4 (Fall/Winter, 1977).

11. See Ruether, *Faith and Fratricide*, esp. pp. 246–51. See also Hans Küng, *On Being a Christian* (Garden City, N.Y.: Doubleday, 1976), pp. 166–74, and chap. 11, Conclusions, Implications, and Future Agenda for a Mature Christianity, below, pp. 283–286, where I distinguish defamatory polemic from supersessionistic polemic and from christological polemic. For a more detailed sketch of a mature

approach to Christian theology that repudiates its anti-Jewish elements, see Paul M. van Buren, *Discerning the Way: A Theology of the Jewish Christian Reality* (New York: Seabury, 1980). In addition, see Robert S. Frey, "Issues in Post-Holocaust Christian Theology," *Dialog* 22 (1983): 227–35, and Carl E. Braaten, "Jesus Among Jews and Gentiles," *Currents in Theology and Mission* 10 (1983): 197–209.

12. Barnabas Lindars, *New Testament Apologetic* (London: SCM Press, 1961).

2

Anti-Jewish Polemic in the Epistles of Paul

This present study of anti-Jewish polemic in the epistles of Paul operates with the following four presuppositions:

1. Seven epistles of Paul are extant and incorporated into the New Testament canon; the remainder that carry Paul's name in the canon are for the most part heavily redacted or actually written by followers and admirers of Paul.
2. It is probable that some redaction was done also on the seven basic epistles of Paul after he had died. By careful form-critical and theological analyses of evidence in the texts, we can detect the hand of redactors in certain instances in the seven basic epistles.[1]
3. Paul's thought as we have it in his epistles was dynamic. He enjoyed paradox. But it is not likely that he blatantly contradicted himself on the important issue of the relationship between the early Christian communities and the Jewish people in other groups.
4. Acts of Apostles represents a theological position from a period several decades after Paul's death.

In accordance with presupposition one above, the seven basic epistles of Paul are examined in this chapter; anti-Jewish polemic in later Pauline traditions will be the subject of chapter 3.

As presuppositions one and two indicate, the line between the writings of Paul and those of his admirers cannot be drawn sharply in the Pauline corpus. The writings of the disciples blended with those of the master whom they followed, as frequently occurs in religious literature. That a specific item was included within the New Testament canon is an indication that its content was acceptably orthodox to the majority of users regardless of who may have written it originally. Nevertheless, for the purposes in this study, because I am attempting to trace as clearly as possible the development of the anti-Jewish argumentation, it makes a difference whether pejorative statements were expressed against Jewish people by Paul early in the 50s of the first century, or by Gentile Christians several decades later.

Presuppositions one through three are intended to show that the study is open to the possibility that we can recover a reasonably coherent picture of what Paul himself wrote, and likely also taught, about Jews who did not consider Jesus to have been the Messiah who would usher in the age of peace and happiness. The seven basic epistles of Paul appear to be the oldest portions of the New Testament in the form in which the writings have come to us. Moreover, it is generally agreed that Paul was a highly significant theologian of early Christianity from whose writings a well-developed Christology can be formulated. Whatever Paul wrote about the Jews is of great value, therefore, for all who are interested in a Christology for contemporary Christianity that will not encourage bigotry and prejudice against Jews.

The inclusion of presupposition four shows that in this study the document Acts of Apostles will be examined almost entirely separately from Paul's epistles. Perhaps it would be more adequate to state that although Paul's writings may be utilized to some extent to assist us in our understanding of Acts, there will be conscious efforts to prevent Acts from coloring our interpretation of Paul's epistles. Since Paul wrote first, let us attempt to hear him first. We shall hear him first of all in 1 Thessalonians.

A. 1 Thessalonians

Within 1 Thessalonians as we have used it at least since the time of the earliest extant manuscripts of that epistle, there is included what is by far the most vitriolic anti-Jewish segment of the entire Pauline corpus, 1 Thess. 2:13–16. One's attitude toward these four verses is of critical importance in any study of anti-Jewish polemic in the New Testament, since the position that a person takes with regard to these verses will determine how they will influence that person's understanding of all other anti-Jewish portions of the New Testament.

This report of the current study of the place of 1 Thess. 2:13–16 in that epistle will involve form-critical, theological, and practical considerations.

1. Form-Critical Considerations

In the opinion of some, for example, William G. Doty in *Letters in Primitive Christianity*,[2] 1 Thess. 2:13–16 functions as an eschatological conclusion to Paul's appeal to the Thessalonians in 2:1–12, and is, presumably, the second of three similar eschatological conclusions in the epistle, the others being 1:10 and 3:13. If 2:13–16 functions as an eschatological conclusion by Paul, however, it constitutes a vindictive eschatology that contrasts sharply with the comforting assurance in 2:12b that "God calls you continually into his own kingdom and glory." The comforting assurance in 2:12b seems to provide an appropriate conclusion to Paul's train of thought in 2:1–12a. On the other hand, the vindictive statement in 2:13–16 is not directly related to Paul's concern for the Thessalonian congregation, a concern that continues in 2:17. In addition, if 2:13–16 is one of three eschatological conclusions intended as such by Paul, it is unlike the other two. It differs not only because of its vindictive tone, but also because it lacks any mention of the coming of Jesus with all his saints, which is basic to the other two in 1:10 and 3:13 and to the dominant concern later in the epistle, that is, proper behavior for those who anticipate the parousia of Jesus, the nature of that parousia, and the time when the Day of the Lord will come. If there are three eschatological conclusions in the first half of the letter, therefore, the second comes not in 2:13–16, but in 2:19–20, at the end of the chapter, where there is reference to the expected coming of Jesus. Accordingly, each of the first three chapters ends with an eschatological conclusion, as apparently was seen by those who made the chapter divisions that we use. Verses 19–20 at the end of chapter two interrupt the apostolic travelogue, as that is defined by Robert W. Funk,[3] but interruptions of thought with eschatological statements are common in Paul's writings.

Initially, the first portion of 2:13 appears to be no worse than a redundancy of 1:2, a second thanksgiving emphasis that is to be echoed again even more briefly in 3:9. The remainder of 2:13 is largely repetitious of 1:2–2:12 and consistent with Paul's claim in Gal. 1:11–12, functioning as a springboard for the denunciation of the Jews in 2:14–16, but otherwise adding little. Verses 14–16 are connected with the rest of the epistle only by the tenuous thread of the *mimesis* motif, tenuous because elsewhere Paul always writes about imitation of himself and of his co-workers, and through them of Christ the Lord, never about imitation of the churches that are in Judea. The vicious denunciation of the Jews has no point of contact elsewhere in the epistle, nor anywhere else in Paul's epistles for that matter.

On the basis of form-critical considerations, 1 Thess. 2:13–16 is extraneous. If it is from Paul, it is a self-contained excursus with a thanksgiving, an apologia, a commendation of the Thessalonians for imitating the churches in Judea, and a vindictive condemnation of the Jews for killing Jesus and the prophets,[4] displeasing God, and opposing all men. If it is the work of a redactor, the opening words of verse 13, "And because of this we also thank . . . ," were probably composed as a connecting link, as Hendrikus Boers has suggested.[5] That the word received from Paul and his fellow-workers is called "truly the word of God" later in verse 13 is a claim more explicit than is made elsewhere in Paul, a claim similar to the claims made later in 2 Tim. 3:14–16 and 2 Peter 1:19–21. In any case, 2:13–16 does not fit into the structure of the epistle. When attempts are made to include these verses in a structural analysis of the epistle, these verses invariably befuddle the analyst and make a coherent picture impossible.

When these four verses are treated as an excursus by Paul or as a redactional interpolation, a coherent form-critical analysis can be obtained. Using the terminology of Paul Schubert,[6] Jack T. Sanders,[7] William G. Doty,[8] Hendrikus Boers,[9] and others, we may say that 1 Thess. 1:1 is the opening or prescript and 1:2–10 the thanksgiving, which, not atypically of Paul, includes extended reminiscences punctuated by much concern for the theological development of those for whom the letter is intended. Chapter 2:1–3:13, minus 2:13–16, is the body of the epistle. It includes apologia and reminiscences, and at 2:17 becomes an extended apostolic travelogue (apostolic parousia). Chapter 4:1–5:22 is the parenesis, and 5:23–28 the closing, whch includes fraternal greetings, requests, and benedictions.

In summary, form-critically, 2:13–16 would be acceptable as an excursus, even by Paul himself—though more likely a redactional interpolation after Paul's death—if we were not also to entertain theological considerations.

2. Theological Considerations

The theological considerations that make these verses unacceptable even as a tangential excursus by Paul himself were explained more than a century ago by F. C. Baur[10] and others, more recently by K.-G. Eckart,[11] and most explicitly by Birger Pearson.[12] Because the present study led to the same conclusion that Pearson had reached earlier, a conclusion accepted and supported by Hendrikus Boers,[13] Helmut Koester,[14] and Gerhard Krodel,[15] theological considerations will be presented briefly here.

It is written in 1 Thess. 2:14 that the Thessalonians became imitators of the churches of God that are in Judea in Christ Jesus because they suffered the same things at the hands of their fellow-countrymen as the Judean Christians suffered at the hands of the Jews. It is hardly possible that Paul himself would have written in this detached way about the churches in Judea suffering at the hands of the Jews, since according to Gal. 1:13–14 Paul himself had formerly within Judaism persecuted the church and tried to destroy it. It becomes even more remarkable that Paul would have written in this way about "the Jews who killed the Lord Jesus," when we read in 1 Cor.2:8 that Paul laid the responsibility for the crucifixion upon "the *rulers* of this age." Since Paul continued to identify himself as a Hebrew, a Jew, even in his later letters,[16] it is unlikely that he charged that the Jews are opposed to all men, a phrase used politically by outsiders against the Jews during the Greco-Roman period.

The persons addressed in 1 Thessalonians must for the most part have been non-Jews, for in 1:9 Paul wrote about what a welcome he and his companions had received among them, and how they had turned from idols to serve the living and true God. The shameful treatment and suffering at Philippi mentioned in 2:2 may have been caused by Judaizing Christians or by those who continued to worship idols made by hand. When we read 1 Thessalonians, omitting the virulent defamation in the 2:13–16 excursus and without the framework provided later by the book of Acts, we find much pastoral love and concern, but nothing to indicate that Paul's position was unquestionably that of anti-Judaism.[17]

Without the virulent defamation of 2:13–16, the chronological contradiction is removed between the "wrath which has come" upon the Jews at last in 2:16c (understandable only after the siege and fall of Jerusalem in 70 C.E.) and the "wrath which is coming" in 1:10.

Any theological consideration of the anti-Jewish polemic in 1 Thess. 2:13–16 must be made in the light of Paul's prolonged deliberation over the condition of the Jews in his Epistle to the Romans, for it is in Romans, as Krister Stendahl points out in *Paul Among Jews and Gentiles*,[18] that Paul writes about Jews, not about Judaizing Christians or hostile Gentiles. If we are to interpret our scriptural traditions from our scriptural traditions, and specifically Paul from Paul, we look to Paul's *magnum opus*.

Paul wrote in Rom. 1:16 that the Gospel is the way in which God accomplishes salvation for all who believe, for the Jew first and then also the Greek, and in 2:10 that there will be glory and honor and peace for everyone who does that which is good, the Jew first and then the Greek. In Rom. 3:1–2 he asks, "What is the advantage of the Jew?" "What is the value of circumcision?" and answers, "Much in every respect. First of all, the Jews have been entrusted with the sayings of God." In Rom. 3:9 it seems likely that Paul is identifying himself with the Jews. With strong feelings he wrote in 9:1–5, "I wish that I myself were accursed and away from Christ for the sake of my brethren, my kinsmen by race. They are the Israelites, of whom are the sonship, and the glory and the covenants, and the giving of the Torah and the worship and the promises. The fathers are theirs, and of them is the Christ, as a human person. May God who is over all be blessed for ever."

Although in Rom. 10:1–3 Paul wrote that they (Israel) are unaware of the righteousness that is of God and are trying to establish their own, and in 10:21 the quotation from Isa. 65:2 that "All day long I have held out my hands to a people who are disobedient and contrary," he continued in 11:1–5, "I ask then, has God rejected God's people? Certainly not . . . ! God has not rejected God's people whom God foreknew." So also we read in Rom. 11:25–31, "A hardening has come upon a part of Israel, until the full number of the Gentiles has come in, and thus all Israel will be saved." "On the one hand, with respect to the gospel they are estranged because of you, but with respect to election they are loved because of the fathers, for the freely given gifts and the calling of God are irrevocable." It is hardly possible that the same Paul who wrote these things would, even in a sudden burst of anger, have written 1 Thess. 2:13–16, particularly 2:16c, "Wrath has come upon them at last!" Apart from 2:13–16 there is no indication in 1 Thessalonians that Paul was angry against anyone, not even against his opposition in 2:2, 3:3–4, and 3:7, nor against Satan in 2:18 or the tempter in 3:5.

In view then of form-critical and theological considerations, it seems almost certain that a redactor, from a theological and political position similar to that expressed in the Luke-Acts or the Matthean tradition, inserted what we call 2:13–16 into 1 Thessalonians. Christian interpreters, during centuries of reading Paul and understanding his work within the framework provided later in the book of Acts, have accepted 1 Thess. 2:13–16 as Paul's own composition and permitted this redactional excursus to color their perception of Paul.[19]

3. Practical Considerations

From these form-critical and theological considerations we turn finally to practical considerations, where, if the evidence and conclusions above are accepted, the questions are now focused. What continued use should we make of 1 Thess. 2:13–16? How determinative shall form-critical and theological considerations be in our continued use of these verses? If by such analyses we conclude that what we have before us is almost certainly a redactional interpolation that contradicts Paul's own expressions concerning Jews, how far should we go in reducing or eliminating usage of this bitter polemic, which is, as Jules Isaac[20] calls it, obsolete, and which we late in the twentieth century might label "X-rated," harmful with no redeeming social value? Lacking the autograph of this epistle or any manuscript from the first century that might not include these verses, what can we, and should we, as late twentieth-century Christians, do with these verses?

Although without manuscript support our carefully determined principles of textual criticism may not permit us to reduce 1 Thess. 2:13–16 to the status of variant readings in the critical apparatus of Greek editions, it is incumbent upon us, I think, to indicate in some manner within the text and in the critical apparatus of future Greek editions that on form-critical and theological grounds many scholars conjecture that 2:13–16 is a redactional interpolation after Paul's death.

When we prepare translations for popular usage, our possibilities for diversity in theological interpretation are expanded. Frequently during the translation process we "water down" or eliminate material that seems offensive to us. It might be feasible here to retain 2:13–16, but to render "the Jews" of verse 14 as "their political leaders," parallel to "your own fellow-countrymen" earlier in the verse, so that we would have in verses 14–16 something like: "For you became imitators of the churches of God which are in Judea in Christ Jesus, because you suffered the same sort of things from your own fellow-countrymen as they did from their political leaders, who killed both the Lord Jesus and the prophets and have been driving us out, and are not pleasing to God, and are against all men, hindering us as we attempt to speak to the nations in order that they might be saved, in order as always to fill up the measure of their sins. But the wrath has come upon them at last!" The "Jews" and possibly also the "Pharisees" in anti-Jewish polemic elsewhere in the Greek New Testament might be translated with similar circumlocutions for use in our time, even though the meaning would obviously be altered somewhat.

A second possibility would be to retain the literal translation "Jews," but place parentheses or brackets around verses 13–16 and explain in a footnote that, because verse 13 appears to be redundant and verses 14–16 contrary theologically to what Paul wrote elsewhere in the New Testament collection, verses 13–16 were almost certainly added to the epistle after Paul's death, and are an indication of how some Christians felt about some Jews late in the first century.

A third possibility would be to relegate the verses themselves to a footnote in small italicized letters with an explanation as above appended.

As a fourth possibility the verses could be eliminated entirely from the translation, with or without an explanation provided for those who would miss them or would notice the lacuna of four verses in the verse numeration.

My own choice would be the third possibility above. A precedent has been rather firmly established during the present century for relegating verses or portions of verses to small italicized letters in a footnote whenever it can be shown that they are not present in some of what textual critics consider to be the best early manuscripts available and that reasons can be adduced as to how or why the longer readings came into the scriptural tradition. Therefore, to relegate 1 Thess. 2:13–16 to an italicized footnote on form-critical and theological grounds would merely be an extension—though admittedly an important one—of a present policy. Some future discovery of a library of an early Pauline Christian community may vindicate our decision to relegate these four verses to a footnote, just as the judgment of Johann J. Griesbach that on the basis of patristic and versional evidence the shorter form of the Lord's Prayer in Luke 11:3–4 was to be preferred was confirmed a few years later when the readings of codex Vaticanus became available for publication and it was seen that all of Griesbach's omissions were supported by that early manuscript.[21]

At any rate, the presence or absence of these four verses in 1 Thessalonians has a decisive effect upon the tenor of the entire letter, as anyone who has read the epistle without them and then with them has surely seen.

Finally, liturgically we can avoid usage of these four verses if they remain in the text. If we do use them we can explain homiletically and didactically our aversion to them on form-critical and theological grounds in our ex-

egesis of the epistle, and our distaste for them on social and humanistic
grounds today. As long as they remain in any way, these four verses are an
embarrassment to us as Christians when we consider our scriptural traditions to be authoritative for our faith and life. To prune them from our
scriptural tradition, or at least to identify them as redactional interpolation,
would in my opinion be beneficial theologically and practically both to
Christians and to Jews during these final decades of the twentieth century
and as we move into the twenty-first.

Excursus: On Freedom from a Written Code for New Life in the Spirit

Undoubtedly most Christians will reason that it is unwise to tamper with
the biblical text of 1 Thess. 2:13–16. What right do we have to repudiate a
text that has been canonical and authoritative for many centuries? Will not
a repudiation of even this small segment of scriptural tradition irreparably
undermine confidence in the unchanging Word of God? If a precedent is
established by which portions of the biblical account that include teachings
that have become objectionable to certain modern thinkers can summarily
be rejected, will not our grandchildren be left with no more than a torso of
what our parents considered scriptural?

Certainly these objections are to be taken seriously. No one should arbi-
trarily remove that which many generations of people in our religious
tradition have found to be of great value. Our biblical traditions have
significant authority over us. But we also have significant authority over
them. Checks and balances are desirable for any system, even for a religious system, to operate effectively.

What is involved is obviously the "Theology of the Word." We are dealing with the interaction between permanent and changing factors within
the Word of God. The Word of God is one of our most basic symbols of God
in our religious system. Nevertheless the Word of God is not God! It must
not be worshiped as if it were God. There are permanent factors in the
Word, but changing factors are also operative.

Each year we become increasingly aware of the dynamic nature of all of
life and of the dynamic nature of the Word of God as an important element
in life. The Hebrew Scriptures were developed gradually over long periods
of dynamic interaction between God and mankind. Some portions of the
Hebrew Scriptures have been valued much more highly than others by
Jewish people. So also for Christian people not all parts of what is commonly called Scripture is of equal value. There is not even agreement upon
whether the Old Testament Apocrypha should be an integral part of the
Christian Bible. And among those portions about which there is canonical
agreement, there are obviously personal preferences, a canon within a
canon.

Within the Judaism of the first century C.E. and within Judaism today
there was and is far more freedom of interpretation than most Christians

realize. It can be said that Judaism has thrived theologically upon discussion of interpretations of the Word. Whenever more than one interpretation is possible, there is freedom. The writers in the early church whose work eventually was incorporated into the New Testament were not exceptions to the Jewish pattern. Even a casual reading of the New Testament reveals the freedom that the early Christians exercised over the written code that they utilized as authoritative. Paul made a point of this in his controversy with the Judaizing Christians. He made it most explicitly in 2 Cor. 3:6 and Rom. 7:6 in his references to freedom from a written code for the sake of new life in the spirit.[22] The writers of Mark, Matthew, Luke-Acts, and the Epistle to the Hebrews frequently quoted their written code (the Hebrew Scriptures or a Greek translation of Hebrew Scriptures tradition) with amazing freedom.[23] Our continuing quest for the historical Jesus indicates to us that Jesus also, as a reformer within the Palestinian Judaism of the first century C.E. may have exhibited considerable freedom from the written code of his time for the sake of new life in the spirit, particularly in regard to ritual cleanness and to divorce possibilities.[24]

Christianity claims to be a religion of the spirit of God, characterized by dynamic interaction with God, freedom from the letter of the law, and love for all people in grateful response to God's grace. Does this not suggest that we who live within this tradition during these last decades of the twentieth century may carefully in the spirit, in dynamic interaction with God, express some freedom within *our* written code and from that written code for the sake of new life in the spirit today and in the future?

The changing factor in the "Theology of the Word" is the change that has occurred from the late first century C.E. to the late twentieth century. During the latter decades of the first century there were expulsions of Christians from Jewish synagogues[25] and sporadic persecutions of Christians by Roman government authorities. Persecutions of Christians late in the first century apparently did not always cause dismay to Jewish religious leaders. It is an accepted presupposition in the form-critical study of the New Testaments accounts that animosity between Christians and Jews during the latter decades of the first century had an effect on the early Christian proclamation and teaching. A portion of the early Christian proclamation and teaching became our New Testament. Hardly anyone would deny today that whatever direct or indirect Jewish contributions there may have been to the suffering of Christians during the first few centuries C.E. have been repaid with centuries-long compounded interest in direct and indirect Christian contributions to the sufferings of Jews since that time. In a period in which animosity between Christians and Jews cannot be justified, my purpose is to identify as carefully as I can the effect that animosity between Christians and Jews during the latter decades of the first century had upon the early Christian proclamation and teaching that became the New Testament.

The majority of ecclesiastical Christians still hold a "theology of Israel" based on what Harold Ditmanson calls a theory of rejection and substitution.[26] This traditional view of the relationship between Judaism and Christianity was formulated early in the development of the church. In it Jews are regarded as stubborn and perverse unbelievers for whom compulsory exposure to Christian teachings is appropriate. For some who hold this view the misfortunes and suffering of Jews are considered to be equitable punishment for their self-incriminating crime of deicide. For many centuries there were accusations of illegal usury, of poisoning of the water used by Christians, and even of ritual murder of Christian babies, which led to the imprisonment, torture, explusion, and execution of entire populations of Jews. Anti-Jewish legal actions by both church and state were simply translation into statutory form of what the biblical and theological tradition suggested. Even though most Christians have repudiated the charges of deicide and of ritual murder, relatively few have fully renounced the theory of rejection and substitution that supplies the theological basis for anti-Jewish attitudes and actions. As long as it is denied that Jewish faith is a valid and living form of spirituality, it is not likely that anti-Semitism among Christians will be eradicated.

As Ditmanson points out, the traditional "theology of Israel" and its theory of rejection and substitution have been undermined since World War II and the Holocaust by a series of official church declarations repudiating anti-Semitism. In 1948 the World Council of Churches denounced anti-Semitism as absolutely irreconcilable with the profession and practice of the Christian faith. The Lutheran World Federation meeting in 1964 urged itself and its member churches

> to examine their publications for possible anti-Semitic references, and to remove and oppose false generalizations about Jews. Especially reprehensible are the notions that Jews, rather than all mankind, are responsible for the death of Jesus the Christ, and that God has for this reason rejected his covenant people. Such examination and reformation must also be directed to pastoral practice and preaching references. This is our simply duty under the commandment common to Jews and Christians: "Thou shalt not bear false witness against thy neighbor."[27]

During the same year the House of Bishops of the Protestant Episcopal Church renounced the charge of deicide as a tragic misunderstanding of the inner significance of the crucifixion. A year later the Second Vatican Council stated that

> Although the Church is the new people of God, the Jews should not be presented as repudiated or cursed by God, as if such views followed from the Holy Scriptures.[28]

Among the statements expressed in a document prepared by the Division of Theological Studies, Lutheran Council in the U.S.A., at the request of the Council's Executive Committee, and forwarded to its member churches in 1971, it is said that in order that conversations between Lutheran Christians and Jews may be honest and fruitful

> Christians should make it clear that there is no biblical or theological basis for anti-Semitism. Supposed theological or biblical bases for anti-Semitism are to be examined and repudiated. Conscious or unconscious manifestations of discrimination are to be opposed.[29]

In response, an *ad hoc* committee appointed by the general president of The American Lutheran Church at the request of its 1972 Church Council noted in its report that in reference to the basis for anti-Semitism

> as a matter of fact there can be such a basis in some biblical texts. For example: Matthew 27:25 ("His blood be on us and on our children!") and Revelation 2:9 and 3:9 ("synagogue of Satan"). What needs to be said is that while these expressions are there in the New Testament and have been used in terrible ways, in the light of the message of the New Testament as a whole there can be no justification or excuse for anti-Semitism.[30]

The Lutheran Council in the U.S.A. document was commended to the congregations of The American Lutheran Church along with the elaborative paper, "The American Lutheran Church and the Jewish Community," prepared by the *ad hoc* committee and by a unanimous vote of the Seventh General Convention of The American Lutheran Church in 1974, transmitted to its congregations as a statement of comment and counsel.[31]

There is indeed "a basis" for anti-Semitism "in some biblical texts." The clarifying comment by the *ad hoc* committee is appropriate; in the light of the message of the New Testament as a whole there can be no justification or excuse for anti-Semitism. In the statement in "Some Observations and Guidelines" that "Supposed theological or biblical bases for anti-Semitism are to be examined and repudiated" there is a mandate for what is being done here.

How serious, however, are we about repudiation of scriptural traditions? Although in recent years there has been a noticeable cleansing of anti-Semitic reference from the parish education materials of many denominations[32] and Martin Luther's infamous treatise "On the Jews and Their Lies" has been renounced repeatedly from within the Lutheran tradition in our time,[33] repudiation of liturgical[34] and of biblical traditions is not easily accomplished.

How shall we interpret the admonition of the Lutheran World Federation to itself and to its member churches to examine their publications for possible anti-Semitic references and to remove and oppose false generalizations about Jews, and that especially reprehensible are the notions that Jews, rather than all mankind, are responsible for the death of Jesus and that God has for this reason rejected his covenant people? When repudiation of specific anti-Semitic content is being advocated, do we consider translations of the New Testament into modern languages to be excluded from consideration? Shall we exclude from consideration the pejorative generalizations about the Jews in Matthew, Luke-Acts, and the Fourth Gospel? Shall the notion in Matthew, Luke-Acts, the Fourth Gospel, and 1 Thess. 2:13–16 that Jews rather than all mankind were responsible for the death of Jesus be exempt from this admonition because these are documents within sacred Scriptures?

There is a difference, of course, between the *preparation* of parish educatin material for contemporary use and the *republication* of biblical materials, since there is far more flexibility in the composition of the former. But can the latter be exempted when new translations of the biblical material are being prepared for contemporary use? It would appear that if directives such as the one received from the Lutheran World Federation in 1964 are to be taken seriously, our denominations have a responsibility to commission new translations of biblical material in which there is a careful sensitivity to anti-Semitic references, to pejorative generalizations about the Jews, and to statements about responsibility for the death of Jesus and rejection of the God-Israel covenant. If the commissioning of new translations is not feasible, at least new translations that exhibit this kind of sensitivity should be prepared by committees of qualified and sensitive scholars and marketed through our denominational publishing houses.

The recognition and repudiation of biblical anti-Semitic references, of pejorative generalizations about the Jews, and of statements about responsibility for the death of Jesus and about the God-Israel covenant will occur not in debate and "win-lose" voting in church conventions and councils, but in practical popular usage. When translations of the New Testament that exhibit the sensitivities listed above are sold, used, and accepted, attitudinal changes will occur. Ecclesiastical administrators and legislators are attuned to the trends among the people whom they serve and represent. Translations of the New Testament that are sensitive to the recognition and repudiation of the anti-Jewish polemic of the New Testament should be prepared and distributed now in order that the Lutheran World Federation directive may be implemented and so that parish teaching will reverse a long tradition of promoting a climate for anti-Semitism in our churches and in our homes. If the Apostle Paul and most likely also the Jesus of history exercised some freedom from their written code for the sake of new life in the Spirit, cannot we also carefully and prayerfully follow in their tradition?

B. Galatians

Polemic in the epistle of Paul to the Galatians is not directed against Jews or Judaism or Israel *per se*, but against Christians of the "circumcision party," who wanted to require Gentile followers of Jesus to observe the Mosaic codes and contemporary Jewish customs.[35] Although Paul claimed in 1:13–14 that earlier in his life he had been a zealous adherent of Judaism, because of a revelation of Jesus the Christ he was now proclaiming the good news of the resurrection of Jesus, God's Son, among the Gentiles. Paul was adamantly opposed to the "circumcision party," as we can see not only in Galatians but also in 1 and 2 Corinthians, Phil. 3:2–11, and in Romans. From indications in Paul's letters and in the oldest portions of the later pseudo-Clementine literature,[36] the Judaizing Christians and their second-century c.e. successors were equally intransigent.[37]

Certainly Paul's theological position was not the sole factor in the separation of emerging Christianity from its Jewish milieu. To his Judaizing opponents, however, Paul's teaching and practice deviated excessively from that of the earlier Jerusalem apostles. They seem to have considered Paul to have been born out of due time; they thought that he was immature and unreasonable; and in their opinion the Spirit-derived character of his ministry was much too dependent upon visions and revelations.[38] To Paul, the attack upon his apostolic credentials was an annoyance that persisted for several years. According to Galatians and Romans the real issue for Paul, however, was the unfettered proclamation of the good news that God's grace is appropriated not through a comprehensive observance of the Torah as interpreted by various Jewish groups during the first century c.e., but by the gift of faith in what God had done uniquely and thoroughly in Jesus perceived to be *the* Messiah.

From our standpoint we can appreciate the sincerity and the strength of conviction of each party in the dispute. Each doubtless considered itself to be acting in conformity to the will of God. The human struggle between emphasis upon right actions and adequate faith, evidenced already in the Hebrew Scriptures and elsewhere in the New Testament documents, continues in Jewish and in Christian thought. That the grace of God is operative in either instance is frequently lost sight of in the controversy.

Although we cannot change the past, our understanding of it undergoes constant revision. Strictly speaking, the past does not exist. What does exist abundantly is evidence of previous human activity. Succinctly defined, history according to Walter Bauer is "present human thought about past human thought."[39] The polemic in the Epistle to the Galatians can be seen, therefore, to be "past human thought," motivated by divine revelation. Our reaction and response to it is "present human thought," motivated also by divine revelation, the quality of which is yet to be tested. What shall be our reaction and response today to this segment of first-century polemic?

Since more than nineteen centuries have passed and since it was Paul's credentials and not ours being questioned, we can afford to take a somewhat dispassionate view of the situation. Regardless of whether the Judaizers were Gentile Christians who attempted to live in the Jewish way or

Jewish Christians who wished to continue and to promulgate Jewish customs within the church—their ranks may have included some of each—what we read in the literature concerning the Epistle to the Galatians is the word *Judaizers* spoken about in what is obviously a disparaging way. Since the word *Judaizers* suggests Judaism and the Jews, and for some perhaps even Judas, the depreciatory association is inevitable. Both accuracy and humanistic concerns would indicate, therefore, that our references should be to "Judaizing Christians" rather than to "Judaizers" in all of our discussions, proclamations, and teachings.

As we look at the content of Galatians, we find in 1:13–14 reference to Paul's former conduct "within Judaism" associated with his overly zealous persecution of the church of God in an effort to destroy it. The basic military-training motif of the necessity and justification of killing the enemy in order that the enemy may not be able to kill you has probably been operative consciously and subconsciously among Christians whenever these verses are read. Although there is no textual evidence that the words *in Judaism* were inserted at a later date, when the process of separation of Christianity from Judaism would have been substantially complete, it should be noted that although references to "the Jews" abound in the New Testament writings, *in Judaism* occurs nowhere else in the New Testament.[40] In view of recent emphasis upon Paul's experiences as constituting a call rather than a conversion,[41] and in line with our growing awareness that both Jews and Christians are "people of God," it would be appropriate in new and in revised translations of 1:13–14 to omit *in Judaism* as tautologous after "my conduct formerly," which adequately expresses the thought in this context. *En tō Ioudaïsmō* obviously would remain in the Greek text.

In 2:13 the sense of "also the remaining Jews acted hypocritically with him" in this context is clearly "the remaining Jewish Christians," and it should for accuracy and fairness be translated accordingly. When Paul wrote about addressing Peter directly in 2:14, *ei su Ioudaios hyparchōn* should be expressed as "If you, though born as a Jew" in the light of 2:15a. These translation suggestions would improve precision and result in greater accuracy, in addition to disassociating for Christian readers the concepts of "Jew" and "hypocrisy."[42]

It should be seen that in 3:10 Paul's quotation of the vivid curse formula from the conclusion of the Shechemite Dodecalogue of Deut. 27 was applied to the Christians of the circumcision party, who are the object of his argumentation in this epistle. He went so far as to write in 3:13 that Christ became a curse for us. When the Epistle to the Romans is taken into consideration along with Gal. 3, Christians should not rationalize contempt for the Jews[43] or for anyone else by recourse to Paul's writings. While Paul in 3:24–25 labeled the Torah our "child-leader" until the coming of the Christ, he saw the Torah itself also as holy and just and good (Rom. 7:7–25).

Nevertheless, Paul objected vehemently to the successful attempts of the Christians of the circumcision party to induce the Gentile Christians of Galatia to observe Jewish days, and months, and times, and years (Sabbaths, calendar months, festivals, and probably jubilee years).[44] In Paul's allegorical interpretation of Abraham's two sons in 4:25, the "present Jerusalem" was the Jerusalem base of the circumcision party of Judaizing Christians that Paul opposed, rather than Jerusalem as the religious and cultural center of Judaism. The Jerusalem above, which is free (4:26), is the source of the spiritual revelation that Paul claimed for himself. The controversy is clearly between Paul and the circumcision party of Christians, not between Christianity and Judaism. Nevertheless, generation after generation of Christians have heard Paul's allegory as a disparagement of Judaism, and moved to "cast out the slave and her son" (4:30), thinking that by removing the Jews from their lands they were doing the will of God.

Finally, the contrast between the catalogues of the works of the flesh and the fruits of the Spirit in 5:16–26 is a contrast also between Paul's view of freedom through the spiritual revelation that he had received and the legalistic requirements taught by his Christian opponents. In Paul's opinion his adversaries from within the circumcision party of the church wished to have the Gentile Christians of Galatia circumcised primarily in order that they might boast in their flesh (6:13).

Paul's epistle to the Galatians provides for us keen insight into the apostle's visceral-level thinking. It was of great value to the monk Luther in his sixteenth-century ecclesiastical and political struggle. Paul's conviction that in Christ Jesus there is neither Jew nor Greek, slave nor free, male nor female is unsurpassed elsewhere in Christian thought. It is exceedingly regrettable, however, that this epistle has been used within Christian traditions as a divine authorization for the contempt and deplorable mistreatment of our Jewish brethren. Every effort should be expended now to translate, interpret, and teach this epistle in ways that will reflect its original purpose of resolving problems of life-style within Christianity, rather than to misuse it as a weapon against Jews.

C. 1 Corinthians

The problems that Paul addressed in 1 Corinthians differed markedly from the controversy with the Judaizing Christians that he faced in Galatians. The point of continuity, however, is that in both instances life-style within emerging Christianity was the issue. Whereas in Galatians Paul claimed revelations of the Spirit in his refutation of Christian legalists, in 1 Corinthians Paul's most persistent problem was to restrain the influence of spirit-filled enthusiasts who claimed, as in the mystery cults and in Gnosticism, that they had attained a state of perfection that allowed them to share in divine wisdom and liberated them from the powers of fate and death in this world.[45] As a result, in 1 Corinthians Paul took a stance somewhere between the Jew and the Greek (9:20–23), and did not hesitate to use the Torah as he interpreted it (9:8–10; 7:19) as his base wherever necessary in renouncing the libertinism of the enthusiasts. Consequently, this epistle is not a source for overtly anti-Jewish polemic.

It is not that Paul merely assumed a Jewish position. His strong emphasis on the proclamation of Christ crucified would preclude that. He wrote that the proclamation of Christ crucified and resurrected is a *skandalon* to the Jews, who ask for signs of proof (1:22–23). But to the Jews who are called, this Christ is the power of God and the wisdom of God (1:24). Not the Jews specifically but the "rulers of this age" (2:8) crucified the Lord of glory. Jewish examples and illustrations were used in the letter. Christ crucified was called our paschal lamb who has been sacrificed (5:7). The festival is to be celebrated with the unleavened bread of purity and truth (5:8). "Our fathers" (10:1–4) all were under the cloud and passed through the sea and were "baptized" into the covenant of Moses in the cloud and in the sea. All of our fathers[46] ate the same spiritual bread and drank the same spiritual drink, for they drank from the spiritual rock that followed them.[47] That rock was the Christ. The people of Israel eat the sacrifices as participants at the altar (10:18). Offense should not be given to Jews or to Greeks or to the church of God (10:32). Love *(agape)* is the way to go.

D. Philippians

Anti-Jewish polemic in the imprisonment epistles Philippians and Philemon will be examined next, before continuing with 2 Corinthians. The sequence of Paul's letters conjectured here is influenced by those who find a period of confinement in Ephesus implied by these epistles even though in the Acts account there is no mention of an incarceration in that city. Since a detailed discussion of evidence from Paul's letters and Acts by which we can attempt to reconstruct Paul's itinerary lies beyond the scope of this study, it will be mentioned here only that the ease of communication between Paul and the recipients of Philippians and Philemon implies a location relatively close to Philippi and to Colossae, for which Ephesus would qualify much better than would Caesarea or Rome.[48] 1 Cor. 15:32 and 2 Cor. 1:8–11 report intense affliction in Ephesus along with despair of life and the feeling of the sentence of death before divine deliverance came in Asia. Because 2 Cor. 1:8–11 indicates the end of the experience in Asia, we shall wait until later to consider this remaining Corinthian correspondence. This delay has the added advantage of allowing some time for further events to have transpired in Corinth.

If the conjecture is correct that the Epistle to the Philippians and that which is called 2 Corinthians are compilations later in the first century, each from portions of what had been several letters of the historical Paul, we shall not be able to determine the precise sequence of these epistles. What we can do is to study the configurations that we have in these epistles and try to determine why the documents were given the arrangements that have come down to us.

Among the segments identified by Günther Bornkamm,[49] the only portion of Philippians in which blatant anti-Jewish material occurs[50] is in what he calls "the very sharply polemical section of the book, 3:2–4:9." Even here in 3:2–9, however, the polemic as in Galatians is directed against Judaizing Christians, the circumcision party members whom Paul labels as evil-workers and dogs because they would mutilate the flesh. Over against this group of the followers of Jesus who would require all Christians to live a Jewish life-style, Paul outlined his own background of living in accordance with a righteousness of his own based on the Torah, a way of living that Paul had rejected for the sake of faith in Jesus the Christ as his Lord. The polemic in Philippians was not aimed at Jews who did not claim to be participants in the emerging Christian community. The polemic here is a warning, a precautionary move; it has the ring of a preemptive strike. It serves as a basis for Paul's call to his readers to follow his example of striving for the prize of attaining the resurrection from the dead through association with the suffering, death, and resurrection of Jesus the Christ.

Paul's claim that he and those who think the way he does are the true circumcision (3:3) can be considered to be not only a refutation of the Judaizing Christians, but also an effort to supersede the parent religion. Paul does claim to have something better than what he had formerly as a Pharisee, but his personal attack is not against the Pharisees; it is against circumcision party Christians. Our translations of Philippians should make this clear.

E. Philemon

Other than the usual witness of Paul that Jesus is the Christ, the only even subtle anti-Jewish materials in this brief personal letter are the references to Paul's current condition as a prisoner (1) for Christ Jesus and for the gospel (13).[51] There is no complaint or blame expressed for anyone explicitly related to Paul's imprisonment.

F. 2 Corinthians

In this analysis of the anti-Jewish polemic in 2 Corinthians, the various segments of material identified in compilation theories will first be considered separately, followed by a summary evaluation of the epistle as a whole.[52] The sequence in which the segments will be considered is somewhat arbitrary; no certain knowledge of their chronological order of composition is assumed.

Mature Christianity

Regardless of whether 6:14–7:1 was written by Paul in this place or in a previous letter or whether it is a portion of Qumran-like material written by someone else and inserted subsequently,[53] it adamantly opposes Belial, darkness, idolatry, iniquity, uncleanness, and unbelief. It advocates Christ, light, the temple of the living God, righteousness, holiness, and belief. The Lord God Almighty will welcome and mingle with his sons and daughters who separate themselves from evil and touch nothing unclean. Although the passage may be sectarian, it is not anti-Jewish, except possibly if Christ or Messiah is seen in a Christian anti-Jewish sense. The concept of Messiah, after all, has a long Jewish background. Only in narrow sectarian thought today would the account be considered anti-Jewish.

The "beautiful" portion (2:14–6:13 and 7:2–4)—beautiful because of the preponderance of words meaning fragrance, aroma, splendor, glory, treasure, new, reconciliation, acceptable, open, and joy—is anti-Jewish in the sense that the life-style that Paul promotes is proclaimed to be superior to that of Moses and of the earlier Israelites. Here Paul sets his ministry in Christ apart from that of the earlier written code of his own tradition, carved in letters on stone. For Paul this new ministry supersedes the old; it is the ministry of a new covenant, which in the Spirit of the living God gives life. However, as R. H. Strachan points out,[54] in Paul's sharp antithesis between the old religion and the new the contrast between "letter" and "spirit" was applicable in Paul's time but is not applicable for us today. For many centuries Christianity has possessed a written code of its own, a collection of documents for use in the church. In Paul's time the Gospel was not yet exposed to the exigencies that come to a "book" religion. It was a spoken word living on the lips and in the lives of the believers. At the most there may have been a few brief collections of sayings of Jesus and stories about his life. Today Christianity is susceptible to the same indictment that Paul applied to book-centered Judaism, that "the written code kills, but the Spirit gives life."

As we evaluate this section of 2 Corinthians we might wish that Paul had expressed his enthusiasm for the new ministry he claimed in words less disparaging of his own religious background, for to us the beauty of the section is marred by Paul's excessively enthusiastic put-down of his own religious tradition. We see this also in the "Law-Gospel" dialectic in the Epistle to the Romans.[55] Is devaluation of that which is older and earlier essential for the successful promotion of the newer and more recent in theology or in any other segment of our economy? More particularly, what should we, with the perspective which the intervening centuries of time have given to us, do with this portion of the epistle?

The "life-death" comparison between the new and the earlier covenants seems unfair from our perspective. The spirit of what Paul wrote would seem to be that we should not let our religion be solidified and determined absolutely by what has come down to us in a written code, even in the written code of Paul himself. The Spirit of God gives life also today and that life has more splendor than that which is seen only in the written code from the past. Nevertheless, we should not disregard the great and precious God-given traditions from the past. God will speak to us and through us as the written traditions from the past are used among us. Since even religious fundamentalists do not consistently interpret the biblical account literally but are more concerned about correspondence to external reality, as James Barr has shown,[56] our translation interpretation of this segment of 2 Corinthians, particularly of 3:6–18, can be done in the life-giving Spirit about which Paul wrote. It is not that we would practice cunning or tamper with the word of God, as Paul himself indicated in 4:2, but that the word of God may be heard clearly and freely today. A few suggestions, therefore, regarding translation interpretations of portions of the 3:6–18 text follow.

In 3:6 the sense of what Paul wrote would seem to be that God has made us able to be ministers of a new covenant, not of a covenant rigidly bound by what has been written in the distant past but of a covenant that is open to new insights from the Spirit of God. For the covenant rigidly bound by what has been written in the distant past does not produce new life today, but the covenant that is open to new insights from the Spirit of God is fruitful and life-giving.[57]

In view of what Paul wrote elsewhere about the value of the written word of God, particularly in Rom. 7:7–25, that the written word of God is holy and just and good, a realistic translation of *hē diakonia tou thanatou en grammasin entetupōmenē lithois* in 3:7 would be "the ministry of the word of God written in the distant past and carved in letters in stone which does not produce new life today."

In 3:9 if there was splendor in the ministry that condemns sin and idolatry, much more rich in glory is the ministry that declares what is just and righteous. In this case (3:10) that which was and is glorious has less splendor now in the light of the exceedingly great splendor of new life in the Spirit of God. The glow on Moses' face from his having been in the presence of God was veiled from the children of Israel so that they might not look closely at the vestiges of that which was fading away as the minutes, hours, and days passed since Moses has been in God's presence (3:13). But the minds of the Israelites were petrified by the glow from Moses' face (3:14). One of the purposes of the Torah text was to emphasize the magnificence of the divine glory. The gist of 3:14b–18 is that Christ the Lord is the Spirit of God who takes away the veil that separates God's people from God.

Obviously, in this segment of the epistle Paul was enthusiastically promoting a new relationship between God and God's people, a relationship in which Jesus Christ as Lord is of paramount importance in removing every impediment. It is a ministry of reconciliation that Paul was advocating. The views of Judaizing Christians and of Jews who would not accept

Jesus as *the* Christ and Lord as Paul was proclaiming him to be were considered passé by Paul.

Whatever may be our opinion about Paul's position, we do well to be open to what the Spirit of God is saying today just as Paul was open to the Spirit of God in his time. Our ministry of reconciliation today implies that we shall proceed with an appreciation of both the ministry that Paul proclaimed and of the ministry that he hoped to supersede. With the passage of time and with the maturity given to Christian theology in this generation, we no longer are compelled to disparage the Jewish expression of the biblical covenant. In so doing we act in accordance with the Christian faith as it has developed since the period of Paul. Even though the Jewish Scriptures are often quoted in the New Testament and in other Christian literature with little or no regard for their context and original intent in order to show that they give specific witness to the coming of Jesus as the Christ, the Jewish Scriptures have been retained within the canonical writings of the Christian faith. Today in much of Christian scholarship there is an increasing appreciation of the Jewish Scriptures in their own right.[58] One of the most significant results of this changing attitude is a new ministry of reconciliation in which the righteousness of God may be seen.

The section of 2 Corinthians that includes the greeting, blessing, and extended apostolic travelogue of the letter as we have it now (1:1–2:13, 7:5–16) is not virulently anti-Jewish. Paul wrote about affliction in Asia without indicating who was the cause of it. The "sentence of death" of 1:9 may imply the Roman government, especially in conjunction with "fighting with beasts at Ephesus" in 1 Cor. 15:32, rather than Jewish opposition. The greatest afflictions about which Paul wrote in this pastoral section of the letter concern his agony over his apostolic relationship with the congregation in Corinth, agony related much more to his Judaizing Christian opponents than to non-Christian Jews. Non-Christian Jews are refuted only christologically, as in 1:20, in which it is stated that the promises of God, as many as there are, have a positive affirmation in God's son, Jesus the Christ.

The separate chapters 8 and 9, in their concern for the offering for the relief of the saints, are devoid of specifically anti-Jewish material.

Although in chapters 10–13 five times Paul is said to have received from Jews the customary thirty-nine lashes (11:24), and although he wrote about being in danger from his own people (11:26), the same recital of perils includes references to similar sufferings at the hands of false Christian brethren and of Roman government officials, not to mention natural catastrophies common in antiquity to anyone who would travel as much as Paul journeyed during his ministry. The Jews are mentioned only incidentally in this section. Paul's concerns were for the people of the Corinthian congregation, over against the Christians who suspected Paul and accused him of acting in a worldly fashion. Paul was opposed to Christian false apostles who had invaded his mission congregations with a different Gospel and another Jesus. He had nothing except scorn for those whom he called "superlative apostles," fellow Christians who persistently attempted to disqualify him among the Corinthians.

When Paul defended his apostleship in 11:22–23a, he claimed that he also was numbered among the Hebrews, the Israelites, descendants of Abraham, and servants of Christ. His struggle, therefore, was against fellow followers of Jesus as the Christ who were of Jewish tradition and heritage. It is unfortunate that in 11:23b–33 sufferings received at the hands of Jews seem to stand out so as to be accessible readily to be used later as rationalizations by Christians inflicting sufferings upon Jews. The term *Jews* in 11:24 has a specific reference for Christians today, unlike its counterpart, *Gentiles,* which is vague and unspecific in current Christian usage. Our vernacular translations of 2 Cor. 11 should represent "Jews" as "people of my own background" and identify the false brethren who brought danger upon Paul (11:26) as Christians. Also specific dangers and hardships caused by the Roman government officials should be identified as such in our translations. Although it may have been unwise and not safe for Paul to mention harassment by Roman government officials at the time he wrote his letters, there is no reason today why such identifications should not be made when we translate Paul's letters. The result would be translations that would indicate more accurately the political situation when Paul wrote his letters to the Corinthians.

In conclusion, our examination of anti-Jewish material in 2 Corinthians has shown it to be, apart from the epistle to the Romans, our most important source of information about Paul's attitude toward the Jews who did not accept Jesus as the Messiah. Paul claimed in this epistle a new ministry, which to him was superior to the ministry of his ancestors and of his own earlier experiences. It was a ministry that in his opinion superseded the ministry revealed by God through Moses. Nevertheless, Paul did not resort to virulent attacks or name-calling against those who maintained the ministry of his fathers, even though allegedly the opposition of some of them against Paul included acts of violence.[59]

G. Romans

Until recently, most New Testament scholarship has considered Paul's Epistle to the Romans to be a theological treatise that rather incidentally happens to have come down through time to us in the form of a letter, with Rom. 16 added to the treatise in order to give it the appearance of a letter.

Now, however, we are engaged in a "great Romans debate,"[60] which focuses on the question of identifying as clearly as possible the specific group to which Paul wrote this epistle. Were they predominantly Jewish Christians or Gentile Christians? What were their concerns, their attitudes, their problems? What did Paul hope to accomplish in writing this epistle? Was Paul's original epistle extensively expanded to include interpolations that would make the document more valuable for general Christian use, to move it in the direction of making it into a timeless theological treatise for the church? As methodologies tested on other New Testament materials are applied to Romans, is it possible that soon we shall be enriched by having in a sense not one epistle but two, one the Romans that we have been reading all of these years, and the other a conjectural shorter form more specifically applied to a first-century congregation?[61] What are the implications of this debate for our examination of the anti-Jewish polemic in the epistle and for our translation and use of the document today?

As this examination of the anti-Jewish polemic of this epistle begins, it is essential that the presuppositions with which it proceeds be established and expressed, since the presuppositions chosen will have a significant effect upon any such study.

First of all, Karl P. Donfried's basic methodological principles, that "Any study of Romans should proceed on the initial assumption that this letter was written by Paul to deal with a concrete situation in Rome" and that "any study of Romans should proceed on the assumption that Rom. 16 is an integral part of the original letter,"[62] are followed. It is assumed further that there is value in the conjecture of Paul Minear that in Romans Paul was concerned about a conflict between Jewish Christians and Gentile Christians in Rome,[63] and of Willi Marxsen that this conflict developed when Jewish Christians who had been expelled from Rome along with other Jews by Claudius in 49 C.E. returned to Rome after the death of Claudius five years later.[64] Finally, the suggestion of Wolfgang Wiefel is followed that after the death of Claudius the right of free assembly was denied to the synagogue congregations in the capital city and that this made a different organizational structure, the house church, necessary for the Gentile Christians in Rome. Wiefel thinks that in these house churches Jewish Christians were in a minority status within a spiritual outlook and organizational structure different from that which had existed earlier within the Jewish synagogues. According to Wiefel, therefore, the *Sitz im Leben* of the epistle is that it was written to urge the Gentile Christian majority who are the primary addressees of the letter to cooperate with the Jewish Christians and welcome them, since the Gospel is the power of God for salvation to everyone who has faith, to the Jews first and also to the Greeks. Paul exhorted the Gentile Christians not to rise self-gloriously against the olive tree, historic Israel, that supports them. Paul was trying to impress upon the Gentile Christians his own conviction that the people of Israel have their place irrevocably within God's master plan and that Gentile Christians should graciously acknowledge their spiritual descent from Israel. In Romans, as in most of his previous letters, Paul wrote concerning life-style within the congregations. Therefore he was addressing an intra-Christian situation. Nevertheless, in this epistle he related in some detail also his understanding of Israel's past, its present position, and its future destiny, all from the perspective of *Heilsgeschichte*.[65] With Ernst Käsemann we could say that in Romans salvation history is guaranteed by the faithfulness of God. Its continuity is dependent upon God's power. God's grace transcends all human possibilities and expectations. Justification by faith for Paul in Romans, consequently, is not merely individualistic and forensic; it is also universal in scope, as it is in Jewish apocalyptic thought.[66] Romans 9–11 and the entire epistle are to be understood in this context.

If the historical situation in Rome at mid-first century and the contributions of Jewish apocalyptic thought to biblical *Heilsgeschichte* are important keys to our understanding of Romans, how shall we evaluate what is written in this epistle about the Jews and Judaism? Can we agree with W. Wiefel that in this epistle Paul developed a theology of history in which he acknowledged the people of his own heritage and, although he parted company with the overwhelming majority of Jews who rejected his proclamation of Jesus as the Christ, he assigned to Israel, even to the Israel that rejected his proclamation, an important place at the end of history? Can we see in Paul's olive-tree analogy in Rom. 11:16–24 an indication that for Paul the cultivated olive tree (Israel) is both essential and precious in God's plan of salvation?

Regardless of whether Rom. 1:2–4 is a primitive Christian creedal statement known to Christians in Rome and to Paul before he wrote this epistle, or whether Paul composed these verses to provide an expanded doctrinal emphasis in his greeting section, or whether this segment is an interpolation into Paul's letter after his death, in these verses Jesus is proclaimed to be more than that which is feasible for any man to be within a Jewish community. Paul here, as in the epistolary salutation of his letter to the Philippians, is a servant not of God but of Jesus Christ. In addition, the recipients of the letter are called of, by, in relation to, or to belong to Jesus the Christ. Although messiahs, messiahship, and the messianic age were commonly expected within certain segments of the Judaism of the first century c.e., the exclusive designation of Jesus as not only "the Son of God" but also "the Lord of us" sets this document apart from Judaism. The designation of Jesus as Lord accomplishes the separation even if the Lordship is perceived in the sense of "our boss." It is made more sharply if Lord is recognized as a translation of the Hebrew divine tetragrammaton. Furthermore, the prophets of God in the Jewish sacred writings are here said to have proclaimed the good news of God concerning Jesus who appeared from the line of Davidic descent according to the flesh and was declared to be established with power as the Son of God according to the Spirit of holiness on the basis of his resurrection from the dead. The Jewish sacred writings are said to testify of the Gospel of God, which as defined here goes beyond the scope of these same Jewish sacred writings.

Rom. 1:2–4 in its context, therefore, is patently anti-Jewish, but not virulently anti-Jewish. In condensed form it is an expression of the essentials of Christian dogma. It presents something new and different from Judaism.[67] It is anti-Jewish in that it uses a Jewish chassis in developing a vehicle that is no longer Jewish. The new creed is patently anti-Jewish in that it is to Jewish theology something like what the first automobile was to a horse-drawn carriage; the vehicle now moved with the horse in a strikingly different form under the hood! This analogy is made with no attempt to place a value judgment upon either vehicle, but with the realization that much of our concern stems from the claims of superiority made by the users of the newer means of transportation.

There is a certain priority for the Jews in much of this epistle, though this priority is not always to their advantage. It is said that the Gospel is the power of God for salvation for everyone who believes, to the Jew first and also to the Greek (1:16), but "distress and a difficult place will be the plight of every individual who does that which is bad, the Jew first and also the Greek" (2:9). In the same sequence "glory and honor and peace will come to everyone who does that which is good, to the Jew first and then to the Greek" (2:10). The prominent position of the Jew because of the Jewish life-style prescribed in the Jewish written code can become a cause for boasting. Also, if this life-style is accepted but not maintained, God is dishonored and God's name profaned among non-Jews (2:17–24). Circumcision is profitable if the life-style of the written code is observed perfectly. But if it is not, it is of no value in Paul's opinion. God's praise comes to the Jew who is one privately, internally, which is of greater value than are externals such as circumcision (2:18–29).

Nevertheless, there is much that is extraordinary about the Jew; there is a profitable advantage in circumcision. To the Jews have been entrusted the sayings of God. Moreover, the unfaithfulness of some—even if all were to be unfaithful—does not cancel out the faithfulness of God (3:1–8).

It is possible that Paul counted himself among the Jews in an interrogative *proechometha* ("Are we as Jews at any advantage at all?") in 3:9. Perhaps more likely, at that point in the presentation of his reasoning he was identifying himself with the members of the house church congregations in Rome to whom he addressed his words. Therefore, he asked, "Are we (as Christians) at any advantage at this point?" "Are we ourselves any better off?" "Have we anything that we can hold up before us to protect ourselves?" And the answer clearly was, "No! Not at all!" For as he wrote, "We have already established the point that both, Jews and Greeks (Jewish Christians and Gentile Christians), are subjected to sin." It should be noted here that the recent trend in the study of Romans toward an awareness of the possibility of locating the basic concerns of this epistle in the life-style problems of house church congregations in mid-first-century Rome and in

Paul's efforts to establish a *modus vivendi* among them does much to move the argument of the epistle out of the Jewish vs. Christian arena and into an inter-Christian problem area. This reduces the anti-Jewish polemic level of the epistle while simultaneously enhancing the practical value of the epistle for Christian use today. Particularly will this be the case if we can move this new awareness beyond the scholarly research level into the pastor's study and pulpit and into the home studies of our fellow Christians.

The basic Jewish Scriptures (the Torah and the prophets) affirm the righteousness of God, even though that righteousness has now been revealed in a new way through faith in Jesus as the Messiah (3:21–26). Even here there is no basis for us as Jewish Christians and as non-Jewish Christians to boast. Both are declared just by God on the basis of faith, which does not eliminate the value of the Torah in its proper place. It even sustains it (3:27–31).

The transition to a consideration of Abraham in chapter 4 is not a smooth one in any of the textual variants in 4:1. Perhaps the best that we can do in English is something like "What then shall we say that Abraham our physical forefather experienced?" In the midst of Paul's reflections concerning salvation history as it pertains to groups of Christians of both Jewish and non-Jewish background, it is not surprising that he would turn to the experiences of father Abraham, perceived as having been the common ancestor of many nations. As Paul explained it, the promise given to Abraham or to his descendants that he, and through him they, would inherit the world was graciously established for all the future descendants of Abraham, both Jews and non-Jews (4:13, 16). At the same time Paul insisted that as he perceived it, the Jewish life-style as prescribed in the written code was not so important as God's gracious promise, since the promise preceded the written code in time and transcended it in scope. The written code even induces God's anger, since there is Torah-breaking only when there is a Torah to break (4:15). Abraham's faith in God was considered to be the correct response to God in Jewish tradition (Gen. 15:6); it was essential for right relationships. As Paul saw it in his time, faith in God was still the correct and all-important response to God and the basis for right relationships. What was added according to Paul was that Jesus is the Lord of Paul and of the Jewish Christians and non-Jewish Christians whom Paul was trying to unite more closely within the house church congregations in Rome. Paul stressed that Jesus' death had been a substitutionary atonement and that belief in God, who had raised Jesus from the dead, was now a further basis for right relationships (4:22–25).

Paul continued, in a way not possible within Judaism, to claim that it is through "our Lord Jesus Christ" that we have peace with God and access to the grace of God in which we stand (5:1–11). The Sinai revelation slipped in on the side, so to speak,[68] in order that the number of obvious sins might become more apparent. But to the extent that sin became more apparent, so also God's grace became even more apparent (5:20).

Baptism "into Christ Jesus" in order to be united with him in death and in resurrection is also patently anti-Jewish, although not virulently anti-Jewish (6:1–11). If 6:12–23 is isolated from the full context of the epistle and perceived as addressed only to Christians of Jewish background, its emphasis on their previous life-style under the law, sin, and death as opposed to their present situation under grace, righteousness, and eternal life becomes particularly disparaging and offensive to Jews.[69] On the assumption that Paul was writing primarily to non-Jewish members of house church congregations in Rome and only secondarily to those who had formerly lived as Jews, statements such as that in 6:19 that Paul's hearers had once offered parts of their bodies to be subject to immoral activities without restraint can be seen as having been directed not primarily at Jewish Christians but at Christians of Gentile background. Our father Abraham was viewed as the father of many nations, all of whom are sinful. If the sins of Israel stood out in any way, it is only because the Sinai revelation made them more apparent. God's entire creation is ungodly and sinful; no one is righteous (1:18–2:16; 3:9–26; 8:18–25). The freely given gift of God of eternal life in Jesus Christ our Lord is offered to all (6:23). In our translation into languages currently being used it may be necessary to include interpretative elaborations in places such as Rom. 6:19 in order that it may be clear that statements such as "you who once offered parts of your bodies to immoral activities without restraint" were not addressed exclusively or even primarily to Christians who had formerly lived as Jews.

In the text of the epistle it is difficult to determine which group Paul was addressing at any given time. The greeting was addressed "to all who are in Rome beloved by God, called to be holy" (1:7a), which implies a community or grouping of communities that would be composed of persons of both Jewish and non-Jewish backgrounds. There is some evidence within the epistle that Paul may have addressed Gentile Christians separately in comparatively impersonal terms such as "O man, everyone who judges" (2:1, 3), and "Who are you, O man, to answer back to God?" (9:20),[70] while speaking to Christians from Jewish backgrounds more warmly as "brothers." For example, it is written in 7:1 "Or are you ignorant, brothers—for I am speaking to ones who know the Torah," in 7:4 "So that, my brothers, you have died with respect to the Torah," and most of all in 9:3 "For I often wish that I myself could be anathema and separated from the Christ for the sake of my brothers, my relatives in human terms." But there are other instances in which "brothers" is used in which both Jewish Christians and non-Jewish Christians appear to be addressed. Perhaps when Paul perceived them as together in house churches, he perceived them together as "brothers." The conjectured distinction between the designations "the weak" and "the strong" for Jewish Christians and for Gentile Christians respectively in Rom. 14:1–15:13 is also not entirely convincing.[71]

Nevertheless, there may be an indication in 7:1 that Paul was turning to some extent from addressing Gentile Christians in chapter 6 to speaking to Christians from Jewish backgrounds ("I speak now to those who know the Torah").

Perhaps we are nearing the point in which we as Christians, even as Christians within the Lutheran tradition, can recognize objectively that in Romans Paul overreacted in his insistence that in the community that claims that Jesus is *the* Christ there remains no obligation or relationship to the Jewish Torah. Paul wrote as he did because of circumstances within his own personal and communal experiences. In his opinion at that time a complete break from the Torah was essential in order that the message of the Gospel might be clearly expressed. Yet, in spite of this, Paul continued to utilize the written code as supportive evidence when it was to his advantage in his argumentation.[72]

Much of the ambivalence and ambiguity of Paul and of the church regarding the Torah is evident in Rom. 7. The Torah is no longer in effect for those who belong to the body of the Christ. However, the Torah is not sin, though apart from the Torah sin is dead (7:7–8). The Torah is holy and the commandment is holy and just and good, but the commandment that was meant to be life-giving was found to result in Paul's death (7:9–12). Actually, it was sin that caused Paul's death, for the Torah is spiritual while Paul is physical and subject to sin and death (7:13–25). The Torah is good, but it "kills" Paul by indicating Paul's sin and weakness. Only God through Jesus the Messiah as Lord rescues Paul from his wretched condition. The Torah could not help him.

In our translation and use of Romans we would do well to clarify that it was only certain aspects of the Torah, such as circumcision as a religious rite and the observance of the Jewish dietary regulations as a requirement, that were abrogated by the church. The Torah, in the broader sense of the Jewish Scriptures, was the Bible of the early church and was retained as the "First Testament" of the church. It is simply that this "First Testament" has been demythologized and reinterpreted in Christian preaching and teaching to meet the needs of the ongoing life of the church. In our own time we are beginning to do more of the same to the specifically Christian Scriptures so that, to apply Paul *mutatis mutandis* from Rom. 7:6, we now serve "in the newness of the spirit and are not restricted in every way to the old limitations of the written code."[73]

Indeed, according to 8:1–39 "the Torah of the spirit of life in Christ Jesus has set Paul free from the Torah of sin and death." For Paul's hearers who are in Christ Jesus there is no longer any condemnation. Their sin has been condemned and the spirit of God lives in them.

As we enter into a consideration of the recognition and repudiation of anti-Jewish polemic in Rom. 9–11, the climax of the epistle,[74] it is appropriate to begin with the insights of Krister Stendahl regarding Paul's panoramic view of how his ministry to the Gentiles fits into the *Heilsgeschichte* of God. Stendahl notes that this heart of Romans is concerned with the question of the relationship between the church and the Jewish people and their mutual coexistence in the mysterious plan of God. Paul did not write that when God's kingdom is fully consummated all of Israel will accept Jesus as the Messiah.[75] It is rather that the time will come when all Israel will be saved (11:26). As Stendahl has indicated, the whole section of Rom. 10:18–11:36, including the final doxology in 11:33–36, was written without using the name of Jesus Christ. In Romans Paul's fundamental focus was on the relationship between Jews and Gentiles, not on justification, or predestination, or on any other abstract theological concept. Paul affirmed a God-willed coexistence between the church and the synagogue in which the Christian missionary urge to convert Israel is held in check. In Christian usage, however, after Paul's death Romans became a theological tractate on the nature of the Christian faith. Justification no longer justified the status of Gentile Christians, but became the timeless answer to the plights and pains of the introspective conscience of many people in the West.[76]

In Rom. 9:1–5 Paul, the Christian missionary to the Gentiles, expressed with much emphasis his concern about Israel and the Jewish people.[77] "I speak the truth in Christ," he wrote. "I am not lying. My conscience testifies with me in the Holy Spirit that there is great sorrow and unceasing pain in my heart for my brothers, the Israelites." Paul would have been willing to have been anathema from Christ for their sake, which is an extremely strong statement for one to whom Christ was so important. Paul would have been willing to do this because "they are the ones to whom belongs the inheritance as the people of God. Theirs is the glory and the covenant(s), the revelation of the Torah, the worship of God, and the promise(s). The fathers are theirs and from them physically has come the Messiah." Such thoughts led Paul into a blessing of God who is to be blessed forever.

Election, selection, predestination, justice, indeed the entire matter of *Heilsgeschichte* is a matter of God's mercy, guaranteed by God's faithfulness. Both Jewish-background Christians and Gentile-background Christians are called by God to respond in faith to God's faithfulness, as clearly indicated in the quotations from the prophetic traditions of Hosea and Isaiah. Neither Jewish-background Christians nor Gentile-background Christians have any right to criticize God's mercy and God's faithfulness, even though there are people in each group who try without success to do everything themselves, in their own way. The proper response for both Jewish-background Christians and Gentile-background Christians is to surrender self and to call upon the name of the Lord. For Paul this involved the confession that Jesus is Lord and the belief that God raised Jesus from the dead (10:9), a confession and a belief that obviously was causing a separation between the church and the synagogue.

This brings us to a crucial point in our evaluation of anti-Jewish polemic in the writings of Paul. In Rom. 10 Paul employed a technique characteristic of religious polemical writings; he used what had been internal Jewish prophetic self-criticism against Israel from the outside. Because of the candor of the classical Jewish prophets and their followers who recorded prophetic tradition and because these prophetic traditions were preserved and respected by most Jewish groups, Judaism has been particularly susceptible to this kind of external criticism not only from Christian writers such as Paul, but also from those who compiled the Koran, the Book of Mormon, and the Divine Principle of Moonism, as indicated briefly in the introduction of the present study. Nevertheless, Paul did not conclude that God had rejected his people Israel (11:1). This sets Paul apart from the writers of the Koran, the Book of Mormon, and the Divine Principle. If we as Christians recognize this, and if we wish to be consistent with Paul, we will acknowledge that we are bound to the Jews much more closely than are the adherents of Islam, of Mormonism, and of Moonism. Our translations and our use of Romans should make this clear, especially in places such as Rom. 10:19, 21. Since Paul claimed his identity as an Israelite in this same context (11:1), and since the Israel involved in each instance is clearly the Israel of the past, it would be appropriate to translate "Israel" in 10:19, 21 as "our fathers." The result would be, "Did our fathers not know?" and "But to our fathers he said, 'The whole day long I held out my hand to a people who were disobedient and obstinate.' " With this translation Christian readers would more appropriately see the continuity of the people of God, would have their own egoistic tendencies identified in the text, and would not so easily be able self-righteously to place themselves in a superior and bigoted position in relation to their Jewish contemporaries.

Similarly sensitive translations of "Israel" should be made in 9:31 and 11:2. Since the "Israel" involved in 9:31 is again the Israel of the past, "our fathers pursuing the Torah as a written code of behavior for their righteousness did not attain their righteousness via the Torah" would be an accurate and appropriate interpretative translation. The "Israel" of 11:2 is "the people of the Northern Kingdom," as is apparent from the context of the reference in 1 Kings 19:10, 14. There is no reason for us any longer to blame the Jews of all times for the situation in Elijah's complaint about the people of the Northern Kingdom who were at that time under the control of the "wicked" queen Jezebel, the daughter of the king of the Sidonians, who induced her husband, Ahab, to worship and serve her Baal and provoke Yahweh, the God of Israel, by tearing down Yahweh's altars and killing Yahweh's prophets. Incidentally, this complaint of Elijah in 1 Kings

19:10, 14 contributed to the impression fostered in the 1 Thess. 2:13–16 interpolation, discussed earlier in this chapter, that the Jews habitually killed their own prophets. Instead of a literal but misleading translation of "Israel" in 11:2b such as "or do you not know what the scripture says in respect to Elijah, how he appealed to God against Israel?" it would be much more accurate and appropriate to consider the context of the use of the reference to "Israel" in the 1 Kings setting and provide a sensitive interpretative translation such as "or are you not aware of what is written (in 1 Kings 19:10, 14) about Elijah, how he appealed to God against the people of the Northern Kingdom, who were dominated by Jezebel, the wicked queen?" The most literal translation does not always most accurately reproduce the original situation.

Again in 11:7 "Israel" is the Israel of the past, not Israel contemporary with Paul or with us. It should be rendered as "Our fathers did not obtain what they were seeking. Some of them, the ones selected, obtained it, but the rest were hardened." "Our fathers" accurately represents the situation of the writer and of the Christians of Jewish background who were being addressed in this portion of Romans. A few verses later in 11:13 Paul turned his attention from them to the Christians from Gentile backgrounds.

For those who question the propriety of using a sensitive interpretative translation technique in order to represent accurately the sense of the original situation as well as to reduce the force of the anti-Jewish polemic that has come to us from the first-century religious competition between the emerging church and its Jewish parentage, it must be stated that a sensitive interpretative translation technique at least is far better than an insensitive one that increases the force of the anti-Jewish element in the New Testament. Surprising as it may seem to many Christians today, most of the commonly used translations of the Greek New Testament into English made since 1920 have insensitive interpretative translations in this crucial section, Rom. 11:11–32, which result in English language texts that are much more anti-Jewish than is the Greek original, as the following sketch indicates.

In the Greek text of 11:28, in which there are no significant textual variants, the adjectives *echthroi* and *agapētoi* are rather sharply contrasted. Therefore a literal translation would be something such as "With respect to the Gospel they are *not loved* (estranged, hostile, enemies, opposed, etc.) because of you, but with respect to the election they are *beloved* because of the fathers." The antecedent of the two adjectives here contrasted would seem, from the context of this portion of Romans 11, to be Jews contemporary with Paul who had heard the Gospel of Jesus as *the* Messiah but refused to join with Paul and with the Jewish Christians and the Gentile Christians of Rome.[78] The Greek text is not explicit about by whom with respect to the Gospel they are "not loved" because of you, though with respect to the election they are "beloved" because of the fathers. Martin Luther's German translation (1522), the *Douay-Rheims* edition (1610, 1750), and the *King James Version* (1611) all retain the ambiguity of the Greek text as to by whom Jews contemporary with Paul are said to be "not loved" and "beloved." Since 1920, however, most of the commonly used English-language translations add some form of interpretative qualifier "of God" to *echthroi*, as indicated in the following excerpts:

James Moffatt, 1922	they are enemies of God
Edgar J. Goodspeed, 1935	they are treated as enemies of God
The Revised Standard Version, 1946, 1971	they are enemies of God
J. B. Phillips, 1958	they are at present God's enemies
The New English Bible, 1961	they are treated as God's enemies
William F. Beck, 1963	God's rule in telling the good news is to treat them as His enemies
The Amplified Bible, 1965	they [the Jews, at present] are enemies [of God][79]
Good News for Modern Man, 1966	the Jews are God's enemies
The Jerusalem Bible, 1966	The Jews are enemies of God
The New American Bible, 1970	the Jews are enemies of God.

The Living Bible, 1971, is somewhat a special case. Its interpretation in 11:28 is as follows:

> Now many of the Jews are enemies of the Gospel. They hate it. . . . Yet the Jews are still beloved of God because of his promises to Abraham, Isaac, and Jacob.

Among the post-1920 English translations available when this comparison was made, only the *New American Standard Bible,* 1960, the *Modern Language Bible,* 1969, and the *New International Version,* 1978, do not include the heightened anti-Jewish emphasis that the others examined cause by adding some form of qualifying "of God" to their translation of *echthroi* in 11:28. The *New American Standard Bible* adds an interpretative qualifier that is slightly positive to the Jews by saying "from the standpoint of God's choice they are beloved," and shows some sensitivity to the issue involved here.

A comparison of these translations in the larger segment of Romans under consideration (11:11–32) indicates that again there is no evidence of a heightened anti-Jewish bias in Martin Luther's German edition, in the *Douay-Rheims* edition, the *King James Version,* or the *New American Standard Bible.* All of the others, however, replaced pronouns or unexpressed subjects of verbs in the Greek text with the specific noun "Jews" or "Israel"[80] in pejorative situations in at least one instance in 11:11–32, as the following listing indicates:

James Moffatt, Edgar J. Goodspeed, J. B. Phillips, *The New English Bible*, the *Modern Language Bible*, and the *New International Version*	once
The Revised Standard Version	twice
William F. Beck	three times
The Jerusalem Bible and *The New American Bible*	four times
The Amplified Bible	five times
Good News for Modern Man	eight times
The Living Bible	thirteen times.

The result is an unnecessary and constant bombardment of the reader of this crucial New Testament text with the idea that the Jews are people who stumble, are jealous, disobedient, do not believe God, have left God, have set themselves as enemies against the Gospel, are full of ungodliness, refuse God's gifts, are rebels, etc. According to *The Living Bible*

> think how much greater a blessing the world will share in later on when the Jews, too, come to Christ (11:12c)

> And how wonderful it will be when they become Christians! When God turned away from them it meant that he turned to the rest of the world to offer his salvation: and now it is even more wonderful when the Jews come to Christ. It will be like dead people coming back to life (11:15).

What is given above is no longer a translation, but a commentary on the text.[81] Such comments should be reserved for separate publication apart from the biblical text.

A sensitive interpretative translation of 11:11–32 would involve for the most part no more than a literal translation of the Greek text. In the only instance in the entire section in which either "the Jews" or "Israel" is mentioned specifically in the Greek text—"Israel" once in 11:25 and once in 11:26—"a partial hardening," or "a hardening in some respects has come to Israel" could be translated as ". . . has come to my people," which is what Israel is in respect to Paul. "Thus all Israel will be saved" could be represented as "Thus all my people will be saved." Neither of these instances of the word *Israel* in the Greek text, however, puts Israel in a particularly unfavorable position, since, biblically speaking, hardening of certain people is accomplished by God as part of God's amazing plan of salvation. The reflections by which Paul was inspired to write the magnificent conclusion (11:33–36) to Romans 9–11 were not brought about by his concentration upon Jewish intransigence, but by his understanding of God's glorious plan of salvation. Insensitive interpretative translations of 11:11–32 such as those cited above obscure the reason for Paul's exclamation "O the depth of the riches and wisdom and knowledge of God . . ." that follows it, or, even worse, give the false impression that Paul was praising God for condemning Paul's own people.

This analysis of the anti-Jewish polemic in Romans 9–11 is concluded, therefore, with the observation that when the Greek text is permitted to speak without an exaggeration of whatever anti-Jewish polemic there may be in it, these three chapters, which more than any other portion of the New Testament relate directly[82] to the Jews and Judaism, are not virulently anti-Jewish. After all, in them the good olive tree is Jewish and the Deliverer will come from Zion.

After Paul had reached and expressed his great insights regarding God's plan of salvation for both Israel and the church, he concluded his epistle with appropriately tender admonitions for peace and harmony among the Jewish Christian and the Gentile Christian members of the house church congregations in Rome. He appealed to them together as brothers in one body to think with sober judgment, to be genuine in love, and to be patient in tribulation, overcoming evil with good (12:1–21). Accordingly, each of them is to live in conformity to the God-given authority of the government (13:1–7),[83] obedient to the commandments of God, particularly in view of the imminence of the end (13:8–14). Those who are strong in faith should welcome and be patient with the peculiarities of the weak. Jewish dietary and festival practices should be respected, though not required, within the house church communities. Each person and group should welcome and accept the other. Gentile Christians and Jewish Christians are to rejoice together and with one voice glorify God. Paul's desire is to be a minister in the priestly service of the Gospel of God in order that the Gentile Christians may be an offering acceptable to God (14:1–15:21). The mention of the Gentile Christians as an offering seems to trigger the thought of Paul's apostolic travelogue, with his impending journey to Jerusalem to accompany those who were bringing the money gifts to the poor among the saints in Jerusalem as a physical manifestation of God's plan of salvation for both Jews and Gentiles (15:22–33). The identity of the disbelievers who may cause difficulties for Paul in Judea (15:31) is vague in the Greek manuscripts and in most English translations, except again in *The Living Bible* in which they are identified as "those who are not Christians." The disbelievers could be "those who are not Christians," but in view of Paul's concerns throughout Romans and elsewhere in his letters, it is more likely that they are Christians who disbelieve that Gentile Christians can be welcomed into fellowship with Jewish Christians in one body in the church. In these final chapters of Romans Paul emphasized the death and resurrection of Jesus as Lord and Christ, so what he wrote was not acceptable on confessional grounds to Jews who remained Jews, but, as elsewhere in this epistle, Paul was in no instance virulently anti-Jewish.

Conclusion

Although Paul was consistently partial to the Gospel as he understood it, and strongly partisan for the blend of Jewish and Gentile Christianity that he was advocating, Paul as known to us from his letters[84] maintained his identity as a Jew and his kinship with all Jewish people. Moreover, he expected to share along with them, in a common destiny, in God's amazing plan of salvation. We as Christians late in the twentieth century are true to Paul and to the Word of God in Paul's letters when we show a recognition of this kinship with Jews and a sensitivity to this common destiny as we translate and as we employ what Paul wrote in our proclamation, in our teaching, and in our lives.

Notes

1. For an example of the view that scribes, commentators, and editors added short comments and explanatory glosses as well as lengthy interpolations to Paul's originally much shorter Epistle to the Romans in order to supplement the epistle and make it more suitable for general use, see J. C. O'Neill, *Paul's Letter to the Romans* (Baltimore, Md.: Penguin, 1975).

2. William G. Doty, *Letters in Primitive Christianity* (Philadelphia: Fortress, 1971), p. 36.

3. Robert W. Funk, *Language, Hermeneutic, and Word of God* (New York: Harper & Row, 1966), pp. 265–74.

4. The trend toward additional anti-Jewish polemic in the textual tradition is shown in that late manuscripts followed Marcion in adding *"idious"* before "prophets" so that the text would read that the Jews killed *their own* prophets.

5. Hendrikus Boers, "The Form-Critical Study of Paul's Letters: I Thessalonians as a Case Study," *NTS* 22 (1975–76): 151–52. See also James A. Fischer, "Pauline Literary Forms and Thought Patterns," *CBQ* 39 (1977): 209–23.

6. Paul Schubert, *Form and Function of the Pauline Thanksgivings*, Beih. *ZNW*, 20 (Berlin, 1939).

7. Jack T. Sanders, "The Transition from Opening Epistolary Thanksgiving to Body in the Letters of the Pauline Corpus," *JBL* 81 (1962): 348–62.

8. Doty, *Letters in Primitive Christianity.*

9. Boers, "The Form-Critical Study of Paul's Letters."

10. F. C. Baur, *Paulus, der Apostel Jesus Christi* (1845), ET *Paul, the Apostle of Jesus Christ,* trans. from the 2d German ed. by A. Menzies (London, 1875).

11. K.-G. Eckart, "Der zweite echte Brief des Apostels Paulus an die Thessalonicher," *ZTK* 58 (1961): 32–34.

12. Birger Pearson, "I Thessalonians 2:13–16: A Deutero-Pauline Interpolation," *HTR* 64 (1971): 79–94. Daryl Schmidt, "I Thess 2:13–16: Linguistic Evidence for an Interpolation," *JBL* 102 (1983): 269–79, adds from linguistic analysis evidence that these four verses are built around a conflation of Pauline expressions, each found somewhere in the Pauline corpus, but that the final combination is not typical of Paul's own syntax.

13. Boers, "The Form-Critical Study of Paul's Letters," pp. 151–58.

14. Helmut Koester, *Introduction to the New Testament,* (Philadelphia: Fortress, 1982), 2:113.

15. Gerhard Krodel, "2 Thessalonians," in *Ephesians, Colossians, 2 Thessalonians, The Pastoral Epistles,* Proclamation Commentaries, ed. G. Krodel (Philadelphia: Fortress, 1978), pp. 77–79.

16. 2 Cor. 11:22; Rom. 9:1–3; 11:1; Phil. 3:4–6.

17. Contrary to the opinion of Rosemary Radford Ruether, *Faith and Fratricide: The Theological Roots of Anti-Semitism* (New York: Seabury, 1974), pp. 95–107. For detailed, extended reviews of Ruether's book, see John M. Oesterreicher, *Anatomy of Contempt: A Critique of R. R. Ruether's "Faith and Fratricide"* (South Orange, N.J.: The Institute of Judaeo-Christian Studies, Seton Hall University, Institute paper no. 4, 1975), and Thomas A. Idinopulos and Roy Bowen Ward, "Is Christology Inherently Anti-Semitic? A Critical Review of Rosemary Ruether's *Faith and Fratricide,*" *JAAR* 45 (1977): 193–214.

18. Krister Stendahl, *Paul Among Jews and Gentiles* (Philadelphia: Fortress, 1976), pp. 3–5. For an analysis that opposes the view of F. C. Baur, K.-G. Eckart, B. Pearson, H. Boers, H. Koester, G. Krodel, and the present writer that theological considerations as well as form-critical considerations make 1 Thess. 2:13–16 unacceptable even as a tangential excursus by Paul himself, see G. E. Okeke, "I Thess. ii. 13–16: The Fate of the Unbelieving Jews," *NTS* 27 (1981): 127–36. Okeke contends that Paul's view of the salvific purpose of God in Christ, as it affects the Jews, is different in 1 Thessalonians from what it was to be in Romans because of changes in the life situations of Paul and his companions during the interval between the times of the writing of the two documents. It is Okeke's opinion that when Paul wrote 1 Thessalonians his feeling was that the time was short and that since the Jews generally had chosen to be on the side of the foes of God, they were destined for the wrath of God, but that by the time that Paul wrote Romans he had developed the conviction that ultimately the Jews would accept the mercy of God in Jesus. Okeke considers it to be unacceptable exegesis to harmonize 1 Thessalonians with Romans by identifying 1 Thess. 2:13–16 as a redactional interpolation after Paul's death so that 1 Thessalonians will fit into the theological framework of Romans.

Okeke does not appear to be aware of Krister Stendahl's observation in *Paul Among Jews and Gentiles,* pp. 78–96 that the entire section of Rom. 10:18–11:36, including the great doxology in 11:33–36, was written without using the name of Jesus Christ.

19. Redactors and emulators of the literary style of Paul may also have welded into Paul's epistles statements disparaging to women and inconsonant with Paul's theological position as expressed in Gal. 3:27–28 and 1 Cor. 7:3–4.

20. Jules Isaac, *The Teaching of Contempt* (New York: Holt, Rinehart and Winston, 1964), p. 146.

21. For an account of the textual criticism work of Griesbach, see Bruce M. Metzger, *The Text of the New Testament; Its Transmission, Corruption, and Restoration,* 2d ed., (New York: Oxford, 1968), pp. 119–21.

22. See Ernst Käsemann, *Perspectives on Paul* (Philadelphia: Fortress, 1971), pp. 138–66. According the Käsemann, Paul "spurned neither scripture nor tradition, but recognized both as the 'speaking Word'—the documentation of the spirit. But at the same time he made the binding nature of scripture and tradition in the Christian church depend on their being interpreted in the light of the spirit and on their capacity for being so interpreted." P. 166.

23. Only two examples can be cited here. The writer of Acts 2:25–32 quoted Ps. 16:8–11, applied it to David, and considered David to have been a prophet who foresaw and spoke about the resurrection of Jesus. The psalmist's rejoicing that God had not given *him* up to *Sheol* became for the writer of Acts 2:25–32 a predic-

tion that *Jesus* would not be abandoned to *Hades,* nor would Jesus' flesh see corruption. The writer of Hebrews 2:5–9 used a portion of Psalm 8 which depicts mankind's glory and honor as created by God and placed in a vast and beautiful universe in which mankind was given dominion over the beasts, the birds, and the fish. This portion of the psalm was transformed into a proof that God will put everything into subjection to Jesus.

24. See Günther Bornkamm, *Jesus of Nazareth* (New York: Harper & Row, 1960), pp. 57–58, 96–100. In this case Jesus' freedom from a rigid adherence to the written code seems to have been expressed in a hardened attitude against divorce. It may be seen also as a firm affirmation of monogamy. It should be noted that Jewish scholars today doubt that the Pharisees in Judea and Galilee during Jesus' public ministry were as rigid regarding dietary regulations and the sabbath observance as the New Testament accounts would indicate.

25. An indication from the Fourth Gospel. See also D. R. A. Hare, *The Theme of Jewish Persecutions of Christians in the Gospel According to St. Matthew* (Cambridge: Cambridge University, 1967).

26. Harold H. Ditmanson, "Judaism and Christianity: A Theology of Co-existence," *Dialog* 16 (1977): 17–24. See also Kurt Hruby, "The Future of Christian-Jewish Dialogue: A Christian View," in *Christians and Jews,* ed. Hans Küng and Walter Kasper (New York: Seabury, 1974/5), p. 89, and John T. Pawlikowski, *What Are They Saying About Christian-Jewish Relations?* (New York: Paulist, 1980). Paul M. van Buren, *Discerning the Way: A Theology of the Jewish Christian Reality* (New York: Seabury, 1980), p. 48, has the courage and the insight to say that "If . . . we leave unchallenged and do not wipe out the tradition of anti-Judaism which we have inherited, we shall have failed those who will follow us. Whatever we say about the roots and rise of that tradition, we today—after 1945—can no longer continue it." Carl E. Braaten, "Jesus Among Jews and Gentiles," *Currents in Theology and Mission* 10 (1983): 197–209, suggests that the apostolicity and the catholicity of Christianity should now be expressed in Jewish-Christian dialogue on basic issues such as the messiah, the kingdom, atonement, and resurrection.

27. "The Church and the Jewish People," in *Speaking of God Today: Jews and Lutherans in Conversation,* ed. Paul D. Opsahl and Marc H. Tanenbaum (Philadelphia: Fortress, 1974), p. 168.

28. "Declaration of the Relationship of the Church to Non-Christian Religions," in *The Documents of Vatican II,* ed. Walter M. Abbott (New York: Guild, 1966), p. 666.

29. "Some Observations and Guidelines for Conversations between Lutherans and Jews," in *Speaking of God Today,* p. 165.

30. Arnold R. Mickelson, ed., *1974 Reports and Actions, Seventh General Convention of The American Lutheran Church* (Minneapolis, Minn.: Published by the Office of the General Secretary, The American Lutheran Church, 1974), pp. 645–46, 752–57, 917–22.

31. Ibid., pp. 917–22.

32. One unfortunate exception was the comment in the ALC-LCA Adult Augsburg Bible Studies 9, no. 4 (Sept., Oct., Nov. 1976): 48, that "In Romans 9, 10, and 11 Paul agonizes over the fact that the children of Israel were choosing no longer to be the chosen race." No Jew would accept the factuality of that statement! Writers such as Ellen G. White, "One Seventh of Our Time Belongs to God," *These Times 87,* no. 5 (May, 1978): 13–16, continue to offer for popular consumption statements such as "As the Jews departed from God, and failed to make the righteousness of Christ their own by faith, the Sabbath lost its significance for them." For an extensive study of the attitudes regarding Jews of persons in various Christian denominations, see Charles Y. Glock and Rodney Stark, *Christian Beliefs and Anti-Semitism*

(New York: Harper & Row, 1966). For an examination of Protestant Christian teaching materials nine years after the publication of Bernhard E. Olson, *Faith and Prejudice* (New Haven, Conn.: Yale University Press, 1963), had highlighted this problem, see Gerald S. Strober, *Portrait of the Elder Brother: Jews and Judaism in Protestant Teaching Materials* (New York: The American Jewish Committee, 1972). Eugene J. Fisher, *Faith Without Prejudice* (New York: Paulist, 1977), provides a similar study of Roman Catholic textbooks.

33. For two significant examples, see "The Church and the Jewish People, IV. On the Theology of the Church's Relation to Judaism," in *Speaking of God Today*, p. 171, and "The American Lutheran Church and the Jewish Community," in Mickelson, *1974 Reports and Actions*, p. 754.

34. This is seen most vividly in the controversy over the inclusion, revision, or elimination of the "Reproaches" in the Good Friday Service in Roman Catholic, Episcopal, and Lutheran liturgical circles. See Judith H. Banki, "AJC Hails Liturgical Development," *Interreligious Newsletter: A Review of Trends and Developments in Interreligious Affairs* 1, no. 3 (May 1977): 1–2.

35. Paul's caustic criticism of his opponents and of their tactics and their attacks upon him and upon his credentials were not constructive Christian self-criticism. Neither side appears to have been willing to modify its position to any extent.

36. See A. Salles, "La Diatribe anti-paulinienne dans le Roman Pseudo-Clémentin et l'origine des K II," *RB* 66 (1957): 526–51, and Hans Joachim Schoeps, *Paul: The Theology of the Apostle in the Light of Jewish Religious History*, trans. H. Knight (Philadelphia: Westminster, 1961), pp. 82–87.

37. The Church of Jesus the Messiah, which evolved and emerged at East Meadow, New York, on Long Island during the 1970s exhibits some, but not all, characteristics similar to those of the first- and second-century Judaizing Christians. Its members assert that they are a throwback to the original Jerusalem church rather than a blend of Judaism and Christianity. See the news article "Controversial Long Island Churches Merge," *The Lutheran Standard* 18 (March 7, 1978): 22–23.

38. Schoeps, *Paul*, pp. 74–87.

39. Walter E. Bauer, "Some Observations on History, Historicity, and the Historical-Critical Method," *The Cresset* 40 (Sept.–Oct. 1977): 24–29.

40. "Judaism" as "the Jewish way of belief and life" is used in 2 Macc. 2:21; 8:1; 14:38, 4 Macc. 4:26 and contrasted with Christianity in Ignatius to the Magnesians 10:3 and to the Philadelphians 6:1. In Ignatius to the Magnesians 8:1 there is a reference to living in accordance with Judaism. W. F. Arndt and F. W. Gingrich, *A Greek-English Lexicon of the New Testament and Other Early Christian Literature* (Chicago: University of Chicago Press, 1957), p. 380.

41. Krister Stendahl, *Paul Among Jews and Gentiles* (Philadelphia: Fortress, 1976), pp. 7–23. "Here is not that change of 'religion' that we commonly associate with the word *conversion*. Serving the one and the same God, Paul receives a new and special calling in God's service." P. 7. See also W. D. Davies, *Paul and Rabbinic Judaism*, 2d ed. (London: S.P.C.K., 1955) and Michael Grant, "Paul the Discontented Jew," *Midstream* (Aug.–Sept., 1976), pp. 32–40.

42. The greater part of this problem by far must be faced in the Gospel According to Matthew!

43. Jules Isaac, *The Teaching of Contempt: Christian Roots of Anti-Semitism* (New York: Holt, Rinehart and Winston, 1964).

44. Schoeps, *Paul*, p. 77.

45. Günther Bornkamm, *Paul*, trans. D. M. G. Stalker (New York: Harper & Row, 1971), pp. 71–77.

46. Hans Conzelmann, *I Corinthians*, trans. J. W. Leitch (Philadelphia: Fortress,

1975), p. 165, suggests that Paul wrote here as a Jew, but included his Gentile-Christian readers.

47. According to rabbinic tradition the rock from which Moses drew water (Num. 20:1–11) followed the Israelites during their wanderings so that they would always have water to drink. Paul interpreted this portable rock to be the Christ. Compare with this the Johannine tradition of Jesus as the source of the water of eternal life (John 4:7–15).

48. Bornkamm, *Paul*, pp. 241–42; Eduard Lohse, *Colossians and Philemon*, trans. W. R. Poehlmann and R. J. Karris (Philadelphia: Fortress, 1971), p. 188. The greeting from the saints who belong to Caesar's household (Phil. 4:22) remains a problem. However, Caesar's household, like the household staff of governments elsewhere, may have been represented in every major city of the realm. Also, if the theory of the composite nature of Philippians is valid, 4:21–22 may have had a separate, independent origin.

49. Bornkamm isolates three: A. 4:10–20; B. 1:1–3:1; and C. 3:2–4:9. The remaining three verses (4:21–23) would be a conclusion of uncertain origin. See his "Der Philipperbrief als Paulinische Briefsammlung," in *Neotestamentica et Patristica, Freundesgabe für O. Cullmann* (1962), pp. 192–202, and his *Paul*, pp. 246–47. For articles favoring the unity of Philippians, see Victor P. Furnish, "The Place and Purpose of Philippians iii," *NTS* 10 (1963): 80–85; T. E. Pollard, "The Integrity of Philippians," *NTS* 13 (1966): 57–66; and Robert Jewett, "The Epistolary Thanksgiving and the Integrity of Philippians," *NT* 12 (1970): 40–53.

50. Reference to Jesus as "Lord" and "Christ," particularly in the "Christ hymn" (2:5–11) in which Jesus is acclaimed as highly exalted by God, goes beyond what Jews who did not become disciples of Jesus would have said. Nevertheless, the great confessional hymns in Phil. 2:5–11, Col. 1:15–20, 1 Tim. 3:16, and even John 1:1–18 are not heavily anti-Jewish. Whatever polemic there may be in them is not vitriolic.

51. According to Lohse, *Colossians and Philemon*, p. 189, it is not the external circumstances but Christ Jesus alone who determines the way Paul has to go.

52. For examples of studies that advocate the unity of the epistle, see W. G. Kümmel, *Introduction to the New Testament*, rev. ed., trans. H. C. Kee (Nashville, Tenn.: Abingdon, 1975), pp. 287–93.

53. For an exegetical study which allows for authorship by Paul, see C. K. Barrett, *A Commentary on the Second Epistle to the Corinthians* (New York: Harper & Row, 1973), pp. 193–204. For parallels with Qumran material, see J. Knilka, "2 Cor. vi. 14–vii. 1 in the Light of the Qumran Texts and the Testaments of the Twelve Patriarchs," in *Paul and Qumran*, ed. J. Murphy-O'Connor (Chicago: Priory, 1968), pp. 48–68, and J. A. Fitzmyer, "Qumran and the Interpolated Paragraph in 2 Cor. vi. 14–vii. 1," in *Essays on the Semitic Background of the New Testament* (London: G. Chapman, 1971), pp. 205–17.

54. R. H. Strachan, *The Second Epistle of Paul to the Corinthians* (New York: Harper and Brothers, 1935), p. 84.

55. Perhaps we are entering a new phase of the Law-Gospel dialectic in terms of the ongoing and productive dialectic between the holy and just and good word of God from the past and the new and exciting and stimulating life given by the Spirit of God in the present, in accordance with what Paul was alluding to in Romans 7. In this new phase Jews and Christians can profitably participate together. For example, Gerard S. Sloyan, *Is Christ the End of the Law?* (Philadelphia: Westminster, 1978), pp. 95–106, writes that the correct contrast is not between the Law and the Gospel but between the Law of Sin and the Law of Grace, either of which can flourish under Mosaic Law or Christian Gospel.

56. James Barr, *Fundamentalism* (Philadelphia: Westminster, 1977).

57. See Bernardin Schneider, "The Meaning of St. Paul's Antithesis 'The Letter and the Spirit,'" *CBQ* 15 (1953): 163–207.

58. For an example, see Gerhard von Rad, *Biblical Interpretations in Preaching*, trans. J. E. Steely (Nashville, Tenn.: Abingdon, 1977). See also Bernhard Anderson, ed., *The Old Testament and Christian Faith* (New York: Harper & Row, 1963); Claus Westermann, ed., *Essays on Old Testament Hermeneutics* (Richmond, Va.: John Knox, 1963); Pierre Benoit, ed., *How Does the Christian Confront the Old Testament?* (New York: Paulist, 1968); Elizabeth Achtemeier, *The Old Testament and the Proclamation of the Gospel* (Philadelphia: Westminster, 1973), and Ronald M. Hals, *Grace and Faith in the Old Testament* (Minneapolis, Minn.: Augsburg, 1980).

59. As Samuel Sandmel, *Anti-Semitism in the New Testament?* (Philadelphia: Fortress, 1978), pp. 6–18, evaluates it, Paul aspersed historic Judaism, not individual Jews as such.

60. See the helpful collection of articles on this subject in Karl P. Donfried, ed., *The Romans Debate* (Minneapolis: Augsburg, 1977). An impressive number of major commentaries on Romans have appeared during the past decade. More are in progress.

61. Such a conjectural shorter form is presented in O'Neill, *Paul's Letter to the Romans*, pp. 264–71. See above, n. 1.

62. For the detailed exposition and support for these principles, see Donfried's article, "False Presuppositions in the Study of Romans," in *The Roman Debate*, pp. 120–48. Matthew Black, *Romans* (London: Marshall, Morgan and Scott, 1973), pp. 27–28, thinks that Romans did originally include chap. 16, but that the final chapter was eliminated from some manuscripts simply because it contained a tedious listing of names that were no longer of any interest when the epistle was more widely circulated. Harry Gamble, *The Textual History of the Letter to the Romans: A Study in Textual and Literary Criticism* (Grand Rapids, Mich.: Eerdmans, 1977), argues that Rom. 1:1–16:24 represents the original letter by Paul.

63. Paul Minear, *The Obedience of Faith* (London: SCM, 1971). This is consistent with Paul's concern for matters in the congregations to which he addressed his other epistles. Many other commentators, however, while agreeing that the epistle had a specific occasion, do not think that the occasion was a debate at Rome. For example, E. P. Sanders, *Paul and Palestinian Judaism* (Philadelphia: Fortress, 1977), pp. 488–89, thinks that the occasion was Paul's impending trip to Jerusalem and then to the west, and Paul's worry about the Jewish-Gentile problem because of his own recent difficulties.

64. Willi Marxsen, *Introduction to the New Testament* (Philadelphia: Fortress, 1968), pp. 92–109.

65. Wolfgang Wiefel, "The Jewish Community in Ancient Rome and the Origins of Roman Christianity," in *The Romans Debate*, pp. 100–119. I disagree, however, with Wiefel when he writes (pp. 114–15) that we must be surprised by what he calls Paul's change of thinking to a more positive attitude toward Israel. When 1 Thess. 2:13–16 is identified as an interpolation after Paul's death, Paul's attitude regarding Israel is not significantly different in Romans from his attitude elsewhere. For a further study of the early Christian house churches, see R. Banks, *Paul's Idea of Community: The Early House Churches in Their Historical Setting* (Leiden: E. J. Brill, 1979).

66. Ernst Käsemann, *Commentary on Romans*, trans. G. W. Bromiley (Grand Rapids, Mich.: Eerdmans, 1980).

67. However, the Jewish scholar Pinchas Lapide in "Is Jesus a Bond or a Barrier? A Jewish-Christian Dialogue," *JES* 14 (1977): 466–83, writes that he has discovered

germinal traces of Incarnation and self-abasement of God ideas among marginal groups in Judaism during the first century B.C.E. as well as during the first and second centuries C.E. For a discussion of this among the Jewish views of Christianity, see John T. Pawlikowski, *What Are They Saying About Christian-Jewish Relations?* (New York: Paulist, 1980), pp. 75–77, 100–101.

68. Within Judaism the Sinai revelation does not slip in on the side; it is front and center!

69. For an example of modern Jewish reaction to Paul's writings, see Sandmel, *Anti-Semitism in the New Testament?*, pp. 6–18.

70. Ever since the publication of Rudolf Bultmann's 1910 dissertation, *Der Stil der paulinischen Predigt und die kynisch-stoische Diatribe,* there has been interest in the possibility of an important connection between Paul's letters and the literary *Gattung* known as the diatribe.

71. See a presentation of evidence for this distinction in Paul Minear, *The Obedience of Faith* (London: SCM, 1971), and a refutation by Robert J. Karris, "Romans 14:1–15:13 and the Occasion of Romans," in *The Romans Debate,* pp. 75–99.

72. To this the church has added, for the most part not self-critically, the written code of its own "New Testament" as evidence of the alleged spiritual poverty of Jewish life and practice. For a particularly sensitive appraisal of this problem, see A. Roy Eckardt, *Elder and Younger Brothers* (New York: Charles Scribner's Sons, 1967), pp. 120–40. As Eckardt points out, the "lessons" of the New Testament have remained exempt from judgment, even though in some of them lies the guarantee of the continual denigration of "the Jews" by Christian people. Until the church recognizes the anti-Semitic allegations within the New Testament and repudiates them, it remains "caught in a fateful conflict between Christian morality and Christian dogma respecting Scripture" (pp. 125–26). The present study is a serious attempt to participate in the resolution of this conflict.

73. See the excursus "On Freedom from a Written Code for New Life in the Spirit" above, pp. 46–50.

74. For a view that within Rom. 9–11 there are three separate and independently conceived explanations for the rejection of Israel, see Robert M. Hawkins, "The Rejection of Israel: An Analysis of Romans IX–XI," *ATR* 23 (1941): 329–35. For Hawkins, the first explanation, which was the thought of Paul, is that Israel did not have faith in Jesus as *the* Christ. The second explanation, which Hawkins contends is not the view of Paul, is that God's purpose had always been confined to a small portion of Israel, and that at best only a remnant would be saved. The third explanation is that the failure of Israel is due to no fault of her own, "but solely to the sovereign and wholly irresistible purpose and power of God." According to Hawkins's analysis each of these three separate explanations was buttressed by quotations from the Old Testament. In addition, Rom. 9:9–17, and possibly also 9:18, were also a product of the later preaching mission of the church, with their own selected Old Testament quotations, and are not from Paul.

75. Rosemary R. Ruether, *Faith and Fratricide* (New York: Seabury, 1974), pp. 95–107, does not perceive this in Paul. She concludes that in Paul's opinion as expressed in Rom. 9–11 the Jews "must admit finally that it is not through Torah, but through faith in Jesus as the Christ, that they are intended to be saved" (p. 107).

76. Krister Stendahl, *Paul Among Jews and Gentiles* (Philadelphia: Fortress, 1976), pp. 3–5, 78–96. See also the application that Stendahl makes of Paul's panoramic view to the quest for world community by distinct, non-imperialist, witnessing communities in his article, "Towards World Community," in *Jewish-Christian Dialogue* (Geneva: World Council of Churches, 1975), pp. 59–63.

77. For an analysis of the struggle that Paul must have faced, the struggle be-

tween the claims of his strong sense of religious and nationalistic identity as a Jew and his newly established conviction that being "in Christ" was the basis for participation in the age to come, see W. D. Davies, *Paul and Rabbinic Judaism,* 2d ed. (London: S.P.C.K., 1955), pp. 58–85. Davies surveys three currents prevalent in the Judaism of Paul's time, namely, a yearning for the ingathering of the dispersed of Israel, the growth of the belief in the eternal relation of Israel and Yahweh, and the hope of a resurrection of Israel to share in the age to come.

78. Karl Barth, *The Epistle to the Romans,* trans. E. C. Hoskyns (London: Oxford, 1933), pp. 400–419, casts the net of those who are opposed to the Gospel much more widely so as to include "the 'other' man, the man of the world, the outsider, the Gentile." Barth's interpretation ignored the contrast within the verse between with respect to the Gospel "not loved" because of you and with respect to the election "beloved" because of the fathers. Matthew Black, *Romans* (London: Marshall, Morgan and Scott, 1973), p. 148, thinks that the interpretation could include also "enemies of the Church," although he is of the opinion that the interpretation of the versions that have "enemies of God" is justified in this context.

79. Here and in the next three examples the reader is subjected to not one but two interpretative additions. The result is an anti-Jewish statement that goes far beyond the Greek original. Fortunately, *Good News for Modern Man* continues later in the verse with, "But because of God's choice, they are his friends for the sake of the patriarchs." Goodspeed also pairs "enemies of God" with "God's choice," *The New English Bible* "God's enemies" with "his friends," William F. Beck "His enemies" with "He loves them," *The Amplified Bible* "they [the Jews, at present] are enemies [of God]," with "they are still the beloved [dear to Him]," *The Jerusalem Bible* "The Jews are enemies of God" with "they are still loved by God," and *The New American Bible* "the Jews are enemies of God" with "they are beloved by him," but neither Moffatt, *The Revised Standard Version,* nor J. B. Phillips mentions God with regard to the Jews being "beloved." In these translations they are simply "enemies of God."

80. The two usages of *Israel* in the Greek text of 11:25–26 were not counted in this listing. Neither were the additions of the *Jews* once in *The Living Bible* (in 11:28 cited above) and three times in *Good News for Modern Man* (in 11:12, 17, 24) in which the *Jews* was added in situations of a positive nature.

81. As indicated by Eldon J. Epp in "Jews and Judaism in The Living New Testament," *Biblical and Near Eastern Studies: Essays in Honor of William Sanford LaSor,* ed. Gary A. Tuttle (Grand Rapids: Eerdmans, 1978), p. 87, "anyone sensitive to Jewish-Christian dialogue readily will discern that . . . the LNT appears almost to take pleasure in castigating and chastening the Jews and Judaism—to punish them by tongue-lashing and to reprimand them for failing to accept 'their Messiah'— while all along wishing also, it would seem, to preach the gospel to any Jewish readers."

82. The early church traditions recorded in the Four Gospels and in Acts, in part at least, anachronistically express anti-Jewish polemic. The persons and communities that put these traditions into written form using a ministry-of-Jesus vehicle permitted their current animosities against various Jewish groups to influence their telling of the traditions, as we shall see in some detail in chapters 4–8 below.

83. See Ernst Käsemann, "Principles of the Interpretation of Romans 13," in his *New Testament Questions of Today* (Philadelphia: Fortress, 1969), pp. 196–216.

84. With 1 Thess. 2:13–16 excluded, on form-critical and on theological grounds, as an interpolation after the death of Paul, as indicated early in this chapter.

3

Anti-Jewish Polemic in Later Pauline Traditions

In terms of canon criticism the six documents to be given brief consideration in this chapter were incorporated by usage and then also by conciliar action into the New or "Second" Testament as writings of Paul. Differences from the basic seven epistles of Paul in literary style, distinctive terminology, theological perspective, and polemics, however, have led most of us in our time to look at these six more or less separately from the others. As indicated earlier, the line between the writings of Paul and those of his followers and admirers cannot be drawn with the degree of precision that we would desire in the Pauline corpus. Nevertheless, in this study of anti-Jewish polemic these six, with the Epistle to the Colossians, to the "Ephesians," and 2 Thessalonians considered here as "The Pauline Apocrypha" and the epistles 2 Timothy, Titus, and 1 Timothy as the Pastorals, require a separate evaluation for two reasons.

First, a degree of clarity in determining Paul's position on this issue is possible only when his views are distinguished as clearly as possible from those of his followers. Second, the polemic in the Pauline Apocrypha and in the Pastorals differs in significant ways from that in the basic seven, as has long been recognized.[1] Lacking in these six, for example, is the implication that Paul's personal credentials as an apostle were being questioned. Also, the polemic in these six is anti-Jewish only by implication and innuendo. Consequently, this examination of anti-Jewish polemic in these six writings will be relatively brief and undoubtedly inadequate in the eyes of experts in the study of these letters.

As I attempt to recognize, and to refute by a sensitive translation and use, the implied anti-Jewish material in these documents, the initial consideration involves the sequence in which I shall peruse them. Colossians, Ephesians, and 2 Thessalonians, here called the Pauline Apocrypha, are treated first, followed by the Pastorals, with no claim implied of special knowledge of their original chronological sequence.

A. The Pauline Apocrypha

Colossians and Ephesians obviously are related to each other in some way, while 2 Thessalonians stands apart in this grouping with its own separate attachments to and differences from 1 Thessalonians. The sequence of consideration chosen here is not entirely arbitrary; it is probable that Colossians has chronological priority over Ephesians. Colossians begins the sequence because in many ways among these six it has the closest relationship to the historical Paul.

1. Colossians

This epistle is composed of two primary elements: confession and polemic. Although its strongly confessional emphasis on the power that God has invested in Jesus as the Christ and Lord who is the image of the invisible God, the one in whom all things were created, is unacceptable to Jews, it is not likely that the polemic that stimulated these confessional masterpieces was directed against any conventional form of Judaism. According to Col. 2:8 it was directed instead against those in Hellenistic syncretism—incipient or developed Gnostic or otherwise[2]—who mythologized the elemental spirits (*stoicheia*), probably earth, fire, water, and air, as well as perhaps the stars, whose constellations were thought to control the order of the entire universe and with it the fate of each person here on the earth.[3]

Although there have been Jewish speculations that the stars are somehow related to the angels, and of course the Jewish calendar is based upon the lunar cycle, within Judaism the manifestation of God is not in the wind, or the earthquake, or the fire, but comes classically instead as a still, small voice (1 Kings 19:9–18). The elements testify to the glory of God, but worship and reverence are to be offered only to the one God who is the King of the Universe. Opposition to the mythologization of the elemental spirits of the universe is at least as strenuous within conventional Judaism as it is in conventional Christianity and in the epistle to the Colossians tradition. Also, the ethical teachings of Judaism are not significantly different from those emphasized in this letter.

The anti-Jewish polemic in Colossians, therefore, lies in the standard claim throughout most of the New Testament that the new religious community excels and supersedes its antecedents within Judaism and within the Hellenistic world of religion rather than in a polemic specifically directed against Jews and Judaism. It is our responsibility, in our exposition and repudiation of the anti-Jewish polemic of the New Testament, to make explicit in our translations and in our use of Colossians that Jews and Christians together have historically opposed what the Colossians tradition opposed, and together have advocated the ethical teachings expressed in that epistle. The differences that there are between Jews and Christians in regard to Colossians are in the area of the confession and in the claims of Christian superiority inherent in the document.

2. Ephesians

This is not the place for a prolonged discussion of the various theories regarding the authorship and intended destination of the epistle that in general use is labeled "Ephesians." Important as matters of authorship and destination are, our concern here is primarily with the content of the document.

Since the central theme of this epistle is the profound satisfaction of the writer over the insight gained that the great mystery of Christ is that, in Christ, Christians from Jewish backgrounds and Christians from non-Jewish backgrounds are now united as joint heirs, members of the same body, participants in the same promise, with one Lord, one faith, one baptism, it is not surprising that the anti-Jewish polemic that is present here is not in virulent anti-Jewish statements but in the claim, characteristic of the formative and normative writings of most militant religions, that the new religious community successfully and gloriously supersedes its antecedents.

The writer, who is apparently of Jewish background, presents the Jewish traditions of the past in a highly favorable manner. It is said that apart from Israel, politically as well as religiously, the Gentiles were strangers to the covenants of promise, without hope, and separated from divine manifestations in this world (2:12). Although it is recognized that all humans are sinners (2:3), no pejorative statements are made about Jews or about the Judaism that was prior to this new manifestation of the Spirit of God in Jesus as the Lord and the Christ. It is said that for those who had not been Jews an act of reconciliation to God was necessary, but it is not said that a similar act was required for Jews. Consequently, many commentators, most notably Markus Barth,[4] posit a progression in Paul from the hateful, vindictive utterance against the Jews in 1 Thess. 2:13–16 early in his letters, through the relatively balanced position taken in Romans in his maturity, to the mellow Paul who in Ephesians leaves all signs of bitterness and hostility far behind. A conclusion such as this, while logical if Paul wrote 1 Thess. 2:13–16 early and Ephesians late in his correspondence, is erroneous if 1 Thess. 2:13–16 is shown on form-critical and theological grounds to have been an interpolation and if Ephesians is among a Pauline Apocrypha.[5]

In summary, the anti-Jewish material in Ephesians, as in Colossians, is not in overtly anti-Jewish statements, but in the area of the object of faith and in the claims of Christian superiority inherent in this document.

3. 2 Thessalonians

The polemic of 2 Thessalonians is directed at two groups (1:8), at "those who have not and do not see and know God" and at "those who continually refuse to open their doors to the gospel of our Lord Jesus Christ." The reticence of the writer to identify these two groups any more specifically than this is surprising, and for this reticence we can be grateful. The people of influence in these two groups are said to be causing persecutions and afflictions to the people addressed. As a result, it is right in the sight of God (1:6) that God should pay back with affliction the ones who are afflicting those who will read this epistle. Even apart from the reasons generally given as to why it is unlikely that this letter, as we have it, was written by Paul,[6] the emphasis here upon the vengeance of God against these two groups is an indication that this epistle is allied more closely to those who would interpolate the vindictive 1 Thess. 2:13–16 into a letter of Paul than to Paul himself.[7] The emphasis upon persecutions and afflictions endured by the faithful and upon the apocalyptic expectation of the coming of the Lord Jesus from heaven with his mighty angels in the midst of flaming fire to punish with a vengeance those who have not and do not see and know God and those who continually refuse to open their doors to the Gospel of "our Lord Jesus Christ" (1:3–12) may be evidence for a post-90 C.E. date and for a milieu similar in various ways to that in which the Apocalypse was circulated for the development of this document. Regardless of whether 2 Thessalonians was written by Paul himself soon after he had written 1 Thessalonians, or whether, as evidence derived from a comparison of the two epistles would seem to indicate, most or all of 2 Thessalonians is pseudepigraphical, the anti-Jewish—and the anti-Gentile—polemic implied in 1:8 is not elaborated upon within this epistle. Separation from the Jewish community may have been substantially a *fait accompli* for the church in which this letter was formulated and the threat of imperial force may have been such that anything more than a veiled allusion to those who in the name of the Roman civil religion of that time were denying knowledge or faith in God as perceived by the Christians would have been foolhardy.

Apart from a vague allusion in 3:1–2 in which prayer is requested for deliverance from "out-of-place" and evil men who do not have faith, attention in this epistle is focused rather on an intra-Christian problem regarding tension between advocates of "futuristic" and of "realized" Christian eschatology. Whoever wrote 2:1–12 opposed the teaching that the Day of the Lord had already come. Instead, it was taught that the Day of the Lord was still a "futuristic" concept not yet "realized." The Christians of the first few centuries who through usage, and later also by conciliar action, included 2:1–12 and all of 2 Thessalonians in the Christian canon provided for the church an eschatology that is much more palatable to reason than the one rejected in this passage. Since evil obviously continues to be experienced by each of us, we can be grateful for the choice made here by the early church and that there has remained available to Christian theology the possibility of taking a paradigmatic and proleptic view of the messianic work of Jesus,[8] rather than one in which "all his work is ended." As a consequence, we have a continuing basis for theological dialogue with our Jewish and Islamic neighbors, and perhaps with others as well. Jews have the Torah given through Moses, we who are Christians have the Resurrection given through Jesus, and those who identify with Islam have the Koran given through Muhammad. Therefore each group has a model to share as we discuss the marvels of salvation history. If the position of "realized" eschatology that is refuted in 2 Thessalonians had prevailed within the church, we would have enclosed ourselves theologically in a citadel of our own making from which we would have excluded both reason and the common plight of all humanity in this world. We can therefore indeed be thankful for this definitive Pauline rebuttal in 2 Thess. 2:1–12 of a misrepresentation of Paul within the church late in the first century.

B. *The Pastoral Epistles*

The sequence in which the Pastorals are to be considered in this recognition and repudiation of the anti-Jewish polemic in the New Testament need detain us only briefly. The progression from 2 Timothy through Titus to 1 Timothy will be followed here in agreement with those who see in that sequence rather than in any other a logical three-fold trajectory of increasing development of church polity, an increase in intensity of opposition to "heresy," and a pronounced decrease in the personal element from document to document.[9]

1. 2 Timothy

As is typical in the greeting sections of the Pauline epistles, 1:1–2 is confessional. Jesus is "the Christ" and "our Lord." This immediately sets the document apart as Christian separate from Judaism, without making it overtly anti-Jewish.

If this epistle is considered to be an item of correspondence to Timothy, his younger fellow-minister in the church, by the historical Paul, as it is by large numbers of Christians still today, the mention of "being grateful to God, whom I serve as my ancestors did with a pure conscience" (1:3) may be taken as an expression of solidarity between Jewish and Christian modes of faith. This impression is strengthened in 1:5 with the parallel reference to the unhypocritical faith of Timothy, the faith that lived first in his grandmother, Lois, and in his mother, Eunice, and by 3:14–15, with its reference to the knowledge of the sacred writings that Timothy has had since his early childhood.

However, if 2 Timothy and the other Pastorals, with their well-developed concepts of Christian citizenship, were formulated for the most part pseudonymously a generation or two later than the time of Paul's activity, using Paul as a model of ministry and as the one who in spirit authenticates later ministries, the expression of solidarity between Jewish and Christian modes of faith is decreased significantly. The expression "as my ancestors did" *(apo progonōn)* was a common one in inscriptions during the Greco-Roman period and may simply reflect the style of the writer of this portion of the document.[10] That three generations of unhypocritical faith are represented within Timothy's family may convey a connotation of continuity that is positive toward Judaism, but may also be intended to indicate that unhypocritical faith begins when the Christian message is appropriated by a family. Moreover, the sacred writings in 3:14–15 are said to be able to make Timothy wise for salvation through faith that is based in Jesus as the Christ. The net result, therefore, of the thanksgiving portion of the letter (1:3–7), particularly when it is evaluated within its context in the letter, is that it is on balance neutral with regard to anti-Jewish material.

God saved us (1:8–9), but Jesus the Christ is also called "our Savior"[11] in 1:10, and the path that leads to the development of the doctrine of the Triune God is indicated with the reference to the "holy spirit which dwells in us" in 1:14.

The strongest polemic of this document, like that in 2 Thessalonians, is not against Jews and Judaism *per se*. Here it is directed against those such as Hymenaeus and Philetus within the Christian movement, "who have deviated with respect to the truth, saying that the resurrection has already occurred, and are upsetting the faith of some" (2:16–18). The brand of "realized" eschatology opposed in 2 Timothy is probably best attested in the tractate of the Christian Gnostics, "The Treatise on Resurrection," in which it was written (45:24–34) that

> indeed, as the Apostle said,
> "We suffered with him, and we arose with him, and we went to heaven with him."
> Now if we are manifest in this world wearing him, we are that one's beams, and we are embraced by him.[12]

and in 49:10–30,

> do not think in part, O Rheginos, nor live in conformity with this flesh for the sake of unanimity, but flee from the divisions and the fetters, and already you have the resurrection. For if he who will die knows about himself that he will die—even if he spends many years in this life he is

brought to this—why not consider yourself as risen and (already) brought to this? If you have the resurrection but continue as if you are to die—and yet that one knows that he has died—why, then, do I ignore your lack of exercise?[13]

In 2 Tim. 2:14–4:5 Timothy is instructed to avoid those who teach views such as these just quoted above. There is even within the setting of the illustrative example in 3:8 what is probably an identification of Moses with the truth.[14] Although within 2 Timothy references and allusions to specific passages from the Jewish Scriptures are relatively sparse and brief, there is the blanket endorsement in 3:14–16 of every (presumably Jewish— although also perhaps Christian) sacred writing as God-inspired and of value for teaching, for reproving, for improving, and for training in righteousness, in order that the man of God may be proficient, equipped for every good work. Second Timothy was accepted into the New Testament canon as a writing of Paul. With the implications that this document stemmed from Paul himself, the ties to the Jewish Scriptures, Jewish ancestors, Moses and the Torah, as well as to the God of Israel expressed in the document, were acceptable in the usage and canon-fixing practices of the early church.

We conclude, therefore, that in this document, perhaps in part because the writer was diverted from anti-Jewish polemic by a more immediate threat in the teachings of the Christian Gnostics, we have one of the New Testament writings with the least obvious anti-Jewish material. The writer, who was probably of Jewish background, wrote in Paul's name to warn *ex eventu* against a basic threat to mainline Christian teaching. Thus Paul's authority was pressed into service in this cause. Only in its confessional insistence that salvation is through faith that Jesus is the Christ is the document anti-Jewish.

2. Titus

Among the prescripts in the thirteen epistles attributed to Paul in the New Testament collection, Titus 1:1–4 is the one with the most emphasis upon God in comparison to emphasis on Jesus. Only here is Paul designated as "servant of God" rather than "servant of Jesus Christ" (Romans) or "servant of Christ Jesus" (Philippians). God is mentioned five times in this prescript; Jesus is named only twice. In the prescripts of only two other Pauline epistles is God mentioned more than Jesus (Galatians and 2 Corinthians, at the ratio of 3:2). In three they are mentioned an equal number of times (2 Thessalonians at a 1:1 ratio; Colossians and 2 Thessalonians, 2:2). In all others God or derivatives are named less often than Jesus or derivatives of Jesus (Romans 4:5; 1 Corinthians 3:4; Ephesians, 1 Timothy and 2 Timothy 2:3; Philemon 1:2; and Philippians 1:3). The result is, in Titus, a prescript with the lowest or least-expressed Christology within the Pauline corpus, and on that basis, the least anti-Jewish theologically.

However, when the complete texts of the Pastorals are compared, Titus is more openly anti-Jewish than is either 2 Timothy or 1 Timothy. In the epistle to Titus circumcision-party Christians and Christians influenced by "Jewish myths" are specifically denounced. Apparently the writer of the central portion of this epistle was attempting to isolate and to expel from the Christian communities on the island of Crete and perhaps elsewhere persons with certain characteristics identified as Cretan and as Jewish in origin and in nature. In spite of the multiplicity of specific nouns and adjectives with which these persons were rejected, gross generalities were used in the blanket condemnation of all things Cretan and Jewish in a way that is to be regretted in the canonical Scriptures of Christianity.

Of the two groups, the Cretans were treated much more harshly than were the Jews, so that it might be questioned how effective the Christian message can be to this day among Cretan nationals who are in 1:12–13 indiscriminately said to be "always liars, evil beasts, lazy gluttons." It is difficult to find any redeeming social value in this kind of condemnatory generality. From the standpoint of concern for people, the epistle to Titus would have been improved substantially if the theologians of the ecumenical councils that officially accepted Titus into the New Testament canon had deleted 1:10b ("most of all those who are from the circumcision party"), 1:12–13a ("One of them, a prophet from among them said 'Cretans are always liars, evil beasts, lazy gluttons.' This statement is true"), within 1:14 ("to Jewish myths and"), and in 3:9 ("and genealogies and discord and legality quarrels").

The combination "Jewish myths" and "genealogies and discord and legality quarrels" suggests that Christian Gnostic teachings using allegedly Jewish concepts were being opposed here.[15] With our present understanding of the word *myth* in history of religions and philosophy of religions study, it is apparent that this word can now be used in a positive manner, which makes it singularly inappropriate as a literal translation in Titus 1:14 and in 1 Tim. 1:4 and 4:7. Also, we know now that the "genealogies" spoken against in Titus 3:9 and in 1 Tim. 1:4 were not the Jewish genealogies of human descent such as those written in Gen. 5, Gen. 10, and in 1 Chron. 1–8,[16] but were Gnostic explanations of how the divine spark still evident among the "spiritual ones" among their own number had been transmitted by emanation from their all-inclusive source. For this reason, the literal translations "genealogies" in Titus 3:9 and 1 Tim. 1:4 are neither accurate nor adequate translations today. "Emanations" would more accurately and adequately represent the meaning today. The concept of the emanation of God into ever-decreasing quality of Deity in human form is quite foreign and reprehensible to Jewish thought. Within Judaism God does not come into mankind by emanation, incarnation, or any other form. Neither does mankind become Divine. Accurate and adequate translations of Titus and of 1 Timothy will take these matters into account.

In terms of canon studies, it is apparent that the ecumenical council theologians and church officials were willing to permit the blanket condemnations of the Cretans and of the Jews to remain in the text. This is not surprising, however, since much more extensive generalizing condemnation of the Jews had earlier been accepted in the Fourth Gospel and in Acts, and of Pharisees in all four Gospels, most blatantly in Matthew. It is ironic that the polemic in Titus was actually directed primarily against forms of Christian Gnosticism. But Christian Gnostics were never mentioned explicitly in the texts, so this is lost to most readers of the epistle. Instead, Cretan nationals and Jews are denigrated with generalizing condemnations, which most Christian readers have simply accepted uncritically because "The Bible says so."

In our own time, when Christianity has matured, it is hoped, to the point in which it is no longer necessary for it to slander either Cretans or Jews or to denounce the language of myth (language that is necessary in any attempt to describe divine-human encounter), the inclusion in 1:14 of "to Jewish myths" in a literal translation cannot be justified. Either the expression should be translated as "to ancient stories of encounter between God and mankind," or more accurately though less literally as "to Gnostic speculations of divine emanations," or it should simply be passed over silently when we translate. Since we have used euphemisms, circumlocutions, and omissions[17] for many centuries in our transmission and in our translations of biblical materials in order to communicate the Word of God with phraseology less expressive or direct but considered less offensive or distasteful to persons in an era different from that in which the language had been used earlier, the circumlocutions or omissions suggested above are by no means novel. If we seriously want the biblical accounts to retain, or in some cases to regain, their significant authority as Word of God for us, we cannot in our time passively and idolatrously let them have absolute authority over us.[18]

The epistle to Titus will have greater value for us in vernacular languages without rigidly literal translations of the generalizing condemnations of the Cretans and of the Jews in 1:10b, 12–13a, 14, and 3:9. When these portions are passed over silently, the value of the epistle is enhanced. It would have been much better if these unedifying portions had been excised or nullified in usage during the early centuries of the common era, but since early church practice and the early church leadership did not remove them, they become the responsibility of current church practice and current church leadership.

The proper arena for change in this respect now as in the past is not, however, in win-lose voting in church conventions or ecumenical councils nor in administrative decrees by ecclesiastical authority figures. The proper place for this kind of change is in the marketplace, that is, in the preparation, sale, and use of translations of the New Testament in which polemic that is harmful both to non-Christians and Christians alike is repudiated and nullified. Since there is neither textual nor form-critical support for removing the offensive and distasteful portions from the Greek text of the epistle to Titus, they would remain in our editions of the Greek New Testament where they would continue to be accessible to those who read the biblical language.

3. 1 Timothy

In this epistle, which externally is in the form of a letter from the older, more experienced apostle Paul to his genuine child in the faith, Timothy, internally are contained the most fully developed guidelines for church organization and practice within the New Testament canon, liberally interspersed with warnings against certain persons who are teaching differently. It is in these warnings that most of the polemic of the epistle is evident.

Although Jews as such are not identified as the opponents in 1 Timothy, references to the "law" in 1:7–11 in a not entirely successful imitation and emulation of the style of the historical Paul do implicate the Jews, or at least some kind of Gnosticism, which allegedly employed certain Jewish concepts syncretistically. Perhaps the discussion regarding use of the law is little more than a technique used by the writer in establishing the authority of Paul more firmly against various forms of Gnostic asceticism. What has been written above in relation to Titus regarding an adequate and appropriate translation of the words *mythois* and *genealogiais* applies also here in 1 Tim. 1:4, and of *mythous* in 4:7. What seems to be implied is that those opposed here were teaching that the divine element that was claimed to be still present within those who possessed "knowledge" could be traced by the elect through a complicated series of spiritual emanations. Such persons, such as Hymenaeus and Alexander, to whom reference had been made in 2 Tim. 2:17 and 4:14, are now said to have been handed over to Satan by Paul in order that they might be taught not to speak such weird things about God (1:19–20). The admonition that every creature of God is good and that nothing is to be rejected if it is received with thanksgiving (4:3–5) can be considered to have been a refutation of Jewish dietary laws and possibly of some Essene type of restrictions against marriage by Jewish mystical ascetics who survived the Jewish wars. However, within the context of the rest of this document, the polemic appears to be directed against Gnostics of some sort whose teachings were diverse and perhaps not well known to the writer of this epistle. To the misdeeds of the opponents was added the charge (6:3–10) that they were using their religious piety as a means of gaining wealth.

Finally, in any evaluation of anti-Jewish polemic in 1 Timothy, reference must be made to the beautiful liturgical doxologies in 1:17 and 6:15–16. Each is introduced with a remark about Jesus as the Christ. In 1:16 there is mention of belief in Jesus to gain eternal life, and in 6:14 to keeping what is commanded "spotless and above reproach until the appearing of our Lord Jesus Christ." The doxologies themselves utilize typical Jewish cultic formulas[19] in which all honor, glory, and dominion are ascribed to the one and only immortal, invisible, unapproachable Sovereign, the King over all time, space, and creatures. Therefore this epistle, along with the entire Pauline corpus and the rest of the New Testament documents except the Fourth Gospel and Acts, in spite of much emphasis upon the centrality of Jesus as Lord, Savior, the Christ, and a whole battery of other christological titles, carefully and consistently maintains that at the "end" Jesus will hand everything over to God so that God may be all in all. Apart from the Fourth Gospel and Acts, Jesus is the on-the-job "boss" for the Christian communities, but never more than the *Son* of God. God alone is *God* in the present, the past, and the future.

Excursus: Is There a Discernible Trajectory in the Pauline Epistles regarding Anti-Jewish Polemic?

Some writers find evidence for a strongly anti-Jewish stance in Paul from the time of his earliest extant epistle, 1 Thessalonians, and see a close correlation between the rise in Christology and the increase of anti-Jewish polemic in the early church.[20] As mentioned in the examination of anti-Jewish polemic in the Epistle to the Ephesians above, Markus Barth and others posit a downward trajectory in Paul from the hateful, vindictive utterance in 1 Thess. 2:13–16 early in his ministry of letter-writing through the relatively balanced position taken in Romans in his maturity to the mellow Paul who in Ephesians has overcome all bitterness and hostility.[21] Samuel Sandmel depicts Paul's views of Jews and Judaism as one of subjective partisanship. Sandmel censures Paul as a prime originator of the Christian sense of superiority over Judaism.[22]

It is possible also to argue that instead of a downward trajectory of anti-Jewish polemic an upward trajectory of increasing anti-Jewish polemic can be traced. For those of us who conjecture on form-critical and on theological grounds that the bitter invective of 1 Thess. 2:13–16 was not written by Paul but was interpolated after his death by someone who had an anti-Jewish attitude similar to that evident in the Fourth Gospel and Acts traditions, a trajectory of increasingly anti-Jewish polemic during the time in which the Pauline corpus took shape and was accepted as canonical might seem feasible.

The present study of anti-Jewish polemic in the Pauline corpus, however, has led to the conclusion that no discernible trajectory regarding anti-Jewish polemic can be traced in the Pauline epistles. Too little is known to us about the history of the development of the Pauline traditions. Many insertions, deletions, embellishments, new formations, and adjustments of the texts were made at times and places and under circumstances that we cannot recover with adequate precision. Some, perhaps much, of Paul's correspondence and all of his direct proclamation, teaching, and argumentation while on the scene in the various congregations are not available to us. We are not certain about the sequence in which many of these documents were written. Several of them, especially 2 Corinthians and probably Philippians, are composites pieced together from portions of correspondence prepared at various times during Paul's ministry. But most of all, we cannot trace a trajectory in the Pauline epistles on this issue because of the occasional nature of the epistles. No two epistles were concerned about precisely the same issue, and when comments were made on the same or on similar issues in more than one epistle, the writing was not done in the same volume or with the same intensity.

Within the overall theme of desirable life-style within the early Christian communities, attitudes regarding Jews who did not accept Jesus as *the* Christ was more often than not a peripheral issue. Only in Romans, and to a much lesser extent in 2 Corinthians, was the question of Israel, the Jews, and Judaism and their place in God's marvelous plan of salvation directly addressed, and no trajectory can be established between the two documents because of the composite nature of 2 Corinthians. The portions of these two epistles in which the question of Israel, the Jews, and Judaism was addressed probably were written at nearly the same time. Canon criticism might be helpful to some extent, but we lack the kind of detailed information about which communities were using which epistles and for what reasons that would assist us in establishing a trajectory.

There is a difference within the Pauline corpus that is related to this issue in that in the basic seven letters of Paul the polemic is directed for the most part against Judaizing Christians, while generally in the Pauline Apocrypha and in the Pastorals it is aimed against Gnostic or gnosticizing Christians. Nowhere in the Pauline corpus (apart from 1 Thess. 2:13–16) is the polemic aimed squarely at Israel, the Jews, and Judaism in the way that it is in much of Matthew, the Fourth Gospel, and Acts.

Nevertheless, there can be no doubt that every document within the Pauline corpus is partisan, even Ephesians with its theme of unity and Philemon with its brevity and specific personal concern. Every document is partisan in that it is implied consistently that the newer religious community supersedes and is superior to all others, including the claim of superiority over its principal parent, the Jewish community in its many forms. This is not surprising, of course, since canon criticism in the study of the history of religions indicates that the attitude of superiority is generally a major motivating factor in the development and acceptance of religious literature as sacred Scripture.

Notes

1. For a survey of trends in research since the time of the Reformation on the subject of Paul and his opponents, see E. Earle Ellis, "Paul and His Opponents," in *Christianity, Judaism and Other Greco-Roman Cults*, Part One, Studies in Judaism in Late Antiquity, ed. J. Neusner, vol. 12 (Leiden: E. J. Brill, 1975), pp. 264–98. Ellis assumes that Paul was the author of Colossians and, following the position of J. N. D. Kelly, *A Commentary on the Pastoral Epistles* (New York: Harper, 1963), that the non-Pauline emphases in the Pastorals were the result of the work in each case of an amanuensis who incorporated traditions of Paul's circle all under the watchful eye of Paul himself during the sixties. Ellis suggests that to a considerable extent the opponents of Paul were related to or influenced by the Qumran Essenes.

2. Joseph Burgess, "Colossians," in *Ephesians, Colossians, 2 Thessalonians, The Pastoral Epistles*, Proclamation Commentaries, ed. G. Krodel (Philadelphia: Fortress, 1978), pp. 41–47, is relatively certain that the opponents were "syncretistic Jews infected with the Gnostic Spirit." For a brief, helpful attempt to clarify terminology, see R. McL. Wilson, "Slippery Words: II. Gnostic, Gnosticism," *ET* 89 (1978): 296–301.

3. For a detailed exposition concerning the *stoicheia* of 2:8, see Eduard Lohse, *Colossians and Philemon*, trans. W. R. Poehlmann and R. J. Karris, Hermeneia (Philadelphia: Fortress, 1971), pp. 96–99. See, also R. McL. Wilson, *Gnosis and the New Testament* (Philadelphia: Fortress, 1968), pp. 31–59.

4. Markus Barth, *Israel and the Church* (Richmond, Va.: John Knox, 1969), pp. 43–78, and *Ephesians*, Anchor Bible, 2 vols. (Garden City, N.Y.: Doubleday, 1974).

5. For further elaboration on this issue, see the excursus: "Is There a Discernible Trajectory in the Pauline Epistles Regarding Anti-Jewish Polemic?" at the end of this chapter.

6. For a detailed argument against authorship by Paul, see Gerhard Krodel, "2 Thessalonians," in *Ephesians, Colossians, 2 Thessalonians, The Pastoral Epistles*, Proclamation Commentaries, ed. G. Krodel (Philadelphia: Fortress, 1978), pp. 74–96.

7. Krodel, in ibid., p. 87, suggests that the 2 Thess. 2:13–16 interpolation may be the work of those who taught that the Day of the Lord had already come. It is unlikely, however, that followers of Paul who, through usage and by design compiled the Pauline corpus, would knowingly have permitted an interpolation of four verses into 1 Thessalonians by a person or group opposed to the writer(s) of 2 Thessalonians, whose viewpoints they apparently shared.

8. See Rosemary R. Ruether, *Faith and Fratricide* (New York: Seabury, 1974), pp. 246–51.

9. The progression 2 Timothy–Titus–1 Timothy was proposed by B. S. Easton, *The Pastoral Epistles* (London: SCM, 1948). It is the view of a substantial number of commentators, including Reginald H. Fuller, "The Pastoral Epistles," in *Ephesians, Colossians, 2 Thessalonians, The Pastoral Epistles*, Proclamation Commentaries, ed. G. Krodel (Philadephia: Fortress, 1978), pp. 101–5.

10. Martin Dibelius and Hans Conzelmann, *The Pastoral Epistles*, trans. P. Buttolph and A. Yarbro, Hermeneia (Philadelphia: Fortress, 1972), p. 98.

11. For a study of the concept "Savior" in the Pauline Epistles and the back-

ground for the concept in Jewish, Hellenistic, and early Christian usage, see Dibelius and Conzelmann, *The Pastoral Epistles*, pp. 100–103.

12. *The Nag Hammadi Library*, trans. members of the Coptic Gnostic Library Project of the Institute for Antiquity and Christianity, James M. Robinson, Director (San Francisco: Harper & Row, 1977), p. 51.

13. *The Nag Hammadi Library*, p. 53. The polemic of the Nag Hammadi Library documents was directed primarily against "orthodox" Christianity rather than against "orthodox" Judaism. However, there are instances in which anti-Jewish feelings surfaced. The people who produced The Tripartite Tractate obviously considered themselves to be superior to the Jews (110–13) and although the allusions are veiled in 119–22, these Christian Gnostics probably considered the Jews to be primarily members of the psychic race determined for both good and evil. At the beginning of The Apocryphon of John, a Pharisee named Arimanius approached John to tell him that the Nazarene had deceived John and his group and closed them from their traditions. In The Gospel of Thomas 40, Jesus is represented as speaking sharply against the Pharisees and the scribes and the Jews. When his disciples asked (42) whether circumcision was beneficial or not, Jesus replied that if it were beneficial their father would beget them already circumcised from their mother. In The Gospel of Thomas 50, there is a saying of Jesus, "Woe to the Pharisees, for they are like a dog sleeping in a manger of oxen, for neither does he eat nor does he let the oxen eat." In The Gospel of Philip 75, there is a statement that we as a Christian people do not descend from the Jews. In The First Apocalypse of James 25 and 35, James is instructed to leave Jerusalem, which is said to be the one who always gives the cup of bitterness to the sons of light. The God who speaks in the Hebrew Scriptures is opposed, as in The Second Treatise of the Great Seth 64, where it is written that the Archon was a laughingstock for claiming that he alone is God. The Jewish view of the Torah and of God is ridiculed in The Testimony of Truth 29–30 and 47–49. However, in The Exegesis on the Soul 137, a position rather positive toward Israel is taken when it is said, "Certainly Israel would not have been visited in the first place, to be brought out of the land of Egypt, out of the house of bondage, if it had not sighed to God and wept for the oppression of its labors."

14. For citations of Jannes and Jambres as the names of magicians who argued against Moses in Pharaoh's presence, see Dibelius and Conzelmann, *The Pastoral Epistles*, pp. 116–17.

15. Compare 1 Tim. 1:3–4 and 4:7, where there are also warnings against myths and endless genealogies.

16. See the extended discussion in Dibelius and Conzelmann, *The Pastoral Epistles*, pp. 16–18.

17. Euphemisms and circumlocutions in translations are obvious to anyone who reads the biblical texts of Judaism and of Christianity in Hebrew and in Greek. Redaction studies, particularly of Deuteronomy, 1 and 2 Chronicles, Matthew, and Luke, have revealed the massive omissions of earlier biblical materials by later biblical writers whose purpose it was to produce documents suitable for their own religious communities. For the reader who may not be familiar with redaction studies, a comparison of 1 Chron. 20:1–3 with the earlier 2 Samuel 11–12 is suggested.

18. See further the excursus "On Freedom from a Written Code for New Life in the Spirit" above.

19. For documentation, see Dibelius and Conzelmann, *The Pastoral Epistles*, pp. 30–31, 89–90.

20. This is a basic theme in Ruether, *Faith and Fratricide.*

21. Markus Barth, *Israel and the Church* (Richmond, Va.: John Knox, 1969), pp. 70–76.

22. Samuel Sandmel, *Anti-Semitism in the New Testament?* (Philadelphia: Fortress, 1978), pp. 6–18.

4

Anti-Jewish Polemic in Mark

As we move from consideration of anti-Jewish polemic in the Pauline Apocrypha and the Pastorals to that of the Gospel According to Mark, we turn to a different literary genre and return to a period of development of a Christian community earlier than that represented in the Pauline Apocrypha and the Pastorals.

In recent years various Hellenistic models have been suggested as paradigms that the writer and the community that produced Mark may have used. Among the more important of these have been the aretalogy,[1] the Greek tragedy,[2] the Hellenistic romance,[3] the tragicomedy,[4] the martyrology,[5] and the chria.[6] In addition, the miracle story tradition within the eschatological literature of postexilic Judaism provides some useful analogies.[7] Nevertheless, when Mark is viewed as a literary unit, there are no prototypes from either Hellenistic or more specifically Jewish sources that are adequate. Sufficient evidence has been produced to show that the writer and the community that produced Mark might have been aware of some or all of these models, but the most satisfactory hypothesis remains that in expressing the meaning of Jesus as the Messiah in their particular situation a different literary genre, the Gospel, evolved.[8]

As an early written form of "the Gospel," Mark is not, of course, either "pure history" or "pure fiction," neither of which exists except in theory. Something had happened, something was happening, and something more was expected to happen for this community of believers. From what were probably several brief collections of sayings of Jesus and stories about Jesus that were previously circulating, and certainly from an abundance of oral tradition, this first Gospel was written. In this process the immediate needs and agenda of the writer and of the community had a significant effect. As had been done by other writers and communities in the Jewish tradition, particularly in sectarian communities such as the one at Qumran, Torah and prophecy materials were exegeted and reworked to meet the needs and agenda of this writer and community.

It is likely that the document that we call Mark underwent numerous additions and modifications during its formative period as well as later in the textual copying and transmission stage, so that it is impossible for us to attach a specific date to its composition. However, recent studies, particularly those which combine sociocultural with theological and literary factors,[9] make it feasible to conjecture the period during which the bulk of the composition of Mark occurred.

These same recent studies make it possible for us to understand the nature of the anti-Jewish polemic in Mark more clearly. Consequently, the analysis in this chapter will proceed in three parts: A. The Self-Consciousness of the Markan Eschatological Community as a Cause for Anti-Jewish Polemic in Mark; B. Anti-Jewish Polemic in Mark's Controversy Dialogues; and C. Anti-Jewish Polemic in Mark's Passion Account.

A. The Self-Consciousness of the Markan Eschatological Community as a Cause for Anti-Jewish Polemic in Mark

It is here that Howard C. Kee's *Community of the New Age: Studies in Mark's Gospel*[10] is most helpful. Kee utilizes Bryan R. Wilson's criteria[11] in classifying the Markan community as a sect.[12] Wilson has pointed out that whereas religious orthodoxy for the most part accepts the world and its value systems, sectarian movements reject the prevailing cultural values, goals, and norms, along with whatever facilities the dominant religious orthodoxy provides for salvation.[13] The people within the sectarian community are much more preoccupied with evil, as evil is seen to be manifested in human, demonic, and cosmic forces, than are members of the dominant religious orthodoxy. The sectarian community lives in hope of imminent vindication. Just as the community is thought to have been called together by a prophet sent from God, it is hoped that it will also be vindicated in the near future by God's agent.[14]

In defining itself and its role, the Markan eschatological community did not quote large blocks of the Jewish Scriptures. Neither did it attempt to explain what the Jewish Scriptures may have meant when they were first written, as we try to do in modern exegesis of biblical texts. Instead, they utilized smaller portions of the Jewish Scriptures, freely synthesizing them, merging and blending them so that the meaning derived from them frequently became something quite different from the meaning that they have in their context. The result was generally far more than a simple summation of the meanings of their components.[15] This can easily be seen already in the first two significant uses of the Jewish Scriptures in Mark 1:2–3 and 1:11. The person and work of John the Baptist were defined in 1:2–3 by combining materials from Mal. 3:1 and Isa. 40:3 and attributing them both as one quotation to "the prophet Isaiah." The impression is thereby given that the Baptist's work was specifically foretold by one prophet inspired by God hundreds of years before the Baptist appeared and that the primary function of the Hebrew prophet was to predict events that would not occur until the time of the Markan eschatological community. Similarly in 1:11 portions of Ps. 2:7 and of Isa. 42:1 became the "voice from heaven." In formulating this first Gospel the writer and the community showed little concern for the original importance of the texts.[16] This kind of interpretation of sacred Scripture is typical of the polemic of a new religious community against its principal parent.[17] It is therefore not surprising that, through a "creative" use of Jewish Scripture by the Markan eschatological community and by other early Christian writers, the life, suffering, death, and resurrection of Jesus were shown to be fully in accord with the divine plan.

The self-consciousness of the Markan community is further evident in the proportionately heavy use of Daniel in Mark. Only Daniel among the Jewish Scriptures is quoted from or has significant allusions in every chapter of Mark.[18]

> Not only in the synoptic apocalypse of Mark 13, but also in his portrayal of the career of Jesus, beginning—as Daniel does—with miracle stories, and moving through the issue of martyrdom (Mark 8.31ff.) to personal (Mark 9.2ff.; cf. Dan. 10) and cosmic revelations (Mark 13 = Dan. 7; 9), Mark has been influenced directly by Daniel in his representation of the career and intention of Jesus.[19]

The career and intention of Jesus provide the basis for the present life of the Markan community. The risen Jesus will soon meet the community in "Galilee" for the vindication. As in the vision of Dan. 10:6–11, those who hear the heavenly message (Mark 16:8) flee in fear, astonishment, and ecstasy. The present time in the Markan community (ostensibly as in Daniel) is not really its time, but the time of Jesus' public ministry. Mark opens with the witness of John the Baptist and the beginning of Jesus' ministry and closes with the women fleeing silently from the tomb, but salvation through the coming of the kingdom has been assured on every page. Mark's primary purpose is not to provide a historically accurate or a biographical account of Jesus nor to provide a detailed prediction of events at the end or after the end of time. It is the community's present that is the primary concern as "the Gospel of Jesus Christ" is related, reflected upon, and put into written form. The Markan community, just as the Daniel community two centuries earlier, was self-consciously apocalyptic. Only "the reader who understands" will perceive in this written Gospel the meaning of what it is said that Jesus has done and does and the significance of all of that for the community in its critical present and in its glorious future. The written account appropriately ends (16:8) without a conclusion, for the elect will understand esoterically.[20]

Since Mark lacks, even in its little apocalypse, specific detail about current events in the life of the writer and community such as are written in the latter chapters of Daniel, the time of the composition of this Gospel cannot be pinpointed with the precision possible for portions of Daniel. However, the lack of specifics in the description of the destruction of Jerusalem in Mark 13, coupled with the emphasis on the imminence of catastrophe, suggests the time of the first Jewish revolt, 66–69 C.E.[21]

Max Weber's analysis of the social dynamics involved in the development of "break-away" movements[22] is useful in our attempts to define more closely the nature of the Markan community. Weber has shown that such movements originate in situations in which social and political structures have reduced a segment of society to a state of near powerlessness. Persons who find themselves thus constricted conclude that evil seemingly prevails everywhere. Like-minded people band together in search for meaning in life and for their place in the divine purpose. An ethical prophet figure, regarded as the chosen instrument of the transcendent God, typically becomes the motivating force and catalyst for the movement, and his teachings become the expression of the divine will within the community. To this charismatic leader are attributed personal revelations and status with the Deity and special powers. The disciples of the ethical prophet, in their alienation from the mainstream of religious and political society, claim the world for God and await its ultimate social and political transformation.

K. O. L. Burridge[23] takes the analysis still farther. Because the teachings of the charismatic prophet provide solutions to some problems within the community, expectations arise that he will be able to solve also the ultimate problems or to transcend them. The status accorded the leader continues to rise. New rules to define the life-style of the community evolve. Obligations are imposed upon the people of the community both for the present time and for life in the age to come. These community guidelines are considered to have been lived and expressed initially within the life of the leader. Eventually it may become important to have a written record of that life in order that the life-style of the leader may be transmitted more effectively within the community.

Politically, the Markan community, alienated from the mainstream of Judaism, took a position different from the four principal options open to Jews in the 60s of the first century C.E. It refused to collaborate with the Roman forces and with their puppet leaders, although it continued to pay the required taxes, as Jesus' response to the taxation question in Mark 12:13–17 indicates. Its primary purpose was not to preserve the purity of the covenant people through intense study and continual reinterpretation and application of the Torah. It did not withdraw from society or cluster itself in a desolate area to avoid ceremonial pollution. Nor would it fight in a futile attempt to try to free the Jewish people from Roman rule. Claiming to be the heir to the prophetic promises associated with the new covenant (14:24), it was estranged from the Jewish groups that had earlier identified themselves in relation to that heritage and with that destiny. It is likely, therefore, that the Markan community and other groups similar to it were treated with suspicion and hostility by most Jews as well as by many Gentiles during the period of turmoil caused by the first Jewish revolt against Roman rule.[24]

Quite possibly the physical survival of the community was jeopardized as Roman troops systematically moved to wipe out Jewish resistance in the eastern Mediterranean area. The accounts compiled by Josephus and the known annihilation of the Qumran community testify to the thoroughness of the Roman response. Under these urgent circumstances a written symbol of the community's self-consciousness and a proof of its existence separate from Jewish leadership and committed to tax support of the Caesar would indeed have been appropriate.

Perhaps the conjecture of Kee that the geographical setting of this community was rural and small-town southern Syria rather than Rome[25] or Galilee[26] has the most to commend it.[27] The account of the exorcism performed at the request of the Syrophoenician woman (7:24–30) may have been given a setting in the region of Tyre and Sidon by the Markan community. For them also the high mountain on which the transfiguration occurred (9:2–8) may have been in the Mt. Hermon area of southern Syria. Most of all, the questions regarding various opinions about Jesus, the significant confession of Peter, and the first of the passion predictions are placed on the way to the villages of Caesarea Philippi at the edge of southern Syria.

In compiling a written account that would express the self-consciousness of the Markan community during a period of crisis, the writer and community would naturally evaluate the Jewish Torah traditions, assess the community's relationship to both the Jewish and the Roman authorities, and emphasize mutual responsibilities and support.[28] It is probable that much of the anti-Jewish polemic in Mark had its origin and development in this process. This polemic was later amplified and further developed in somewhat different situations in the Matthean and Lukan traditions, where it may have been supported by additional anti-Jewish polemic in the conjectured "Q" material. As we come to understand more fully the causes for the anti-Jewish polemic in Mark and in the other Gospel sources, we shall be better able to deal with it in our translations of the New Testament and in our teaching and proclamation today.

As in the writings of Paul, the Jewish Torah was used, reinterpreted, and in some instances rejected as necessary in order to meet the needs of the Christian communities. The amount of space given to controversy stories in Mark is an indication that the community was struggling with the issue of its attitude toward the Torah. The nature of the controversy stories and their resolutions in this Gospel indicate that the community had made its decision; it would not be limited to Jewish culture. Instead, it was open to other groups, although its basic origin was Jewish.

That the Markan community as it defined itself in this Gospel was a somewhat open society attempting to transcend social, ethnic, economic, and even sexual boundaries would have made its position unacceptable even to the Pharisees and the Essenes, who on other grounds might be considered the closest ideologically to the Markan community. It was the responsibility of the Jewish religious leaders and teachers to guard their monotheistic faith and their distinctive life-style. The attitude of the Markan community, to the extent that the Jewish leaders were aware of it at all, must have seemed repugnant to them. Since the time and the geographic location of the Markan community would have put it into contact with Pharisees but not necessarily with Essenes in any significant number, it is not surprising that the Pharisees were the primary opponents in the controversies, while there is no specific mention of the Essenes. Pharisees would have differed with many of the teachings of the Markan community and have sought to repress them. As opposition between the groups intensified, each side was likely to have described the other pejoratively. As we look at the situation with more detached objectivity, it is apparent that the Pharisees generally were certainly not so cold and lacking in compassion as they were depicted in the Markan account.[29]

Within the Markan community the eschatological fellowship probably included persons of both Jewish and non-Jewish backgrounds. The use of the symbolic numbers twelve and seven in Jesus' discussion with his disciples in Mark 8:14–21 and in other places is an indication of the composite nature of the community. Therefore, although Paul's language and terminology are not apparent in this Gospel, both Paul and Mark see in their new communities of faith the union of Jews and Gentiles.[30] Although in some respects the Markan community may have been similar to the Stoics with their vision of universal human brotherhood transcending national, socioeconomic, and ethnic barriers, this community differed greatly from the Stoics in its self-consciousness as a faithful eschatological remnant in which only those who saw in Jesus the unique agent of God could participate.[31]

The Markan community may be described, therefore, as a sect over against Judaism, an apocalyptic, eschatological sect that put into writing its self-conscious identity in the form of a series of connected stories about Jesus. The community prepared for itself and for its successors a manual in a basically new form, a Gospel, which to a considerable extent was intended to be understood only by those who had the ability to perceive it esoterically. The manual reveals a community that was evangelistic and demanding, requiring of its adherents the renunciation if necessary of home and family for the sake of the destiny of this divinely determined community waiting for the return of its leader.

As the community awaited the parousia of its leader, it recognized self-consciously that it was clothed with new unshrunken cloth (2:21) that could no longer be sewed into the older garment. It realized that it had new wine (2:22) that would burst the old wineskins. We cannot determine with certainty whether the historical Jesus had expressed these analogies. What we can see is that these analogies vividly expressed the manner in which the Markan community saw itself in relation to Judaism and to various Jewish groups contemporary with it. The verses fit rather loosely into their present context. That they follow 2:20, however, is an indication that they are applicable in the time when the bridegroom has been taken away from the wedding guests. The analogies are unmistakedly anti-Jewish, but not sharply so. The context suggests that the Pharisees and their disciples and the disciples of John are clothed in the old garment and have their wine in old wineskins. The concept of newness in Mark had a relevance for the Christian communities during the second half of the first century c.e. that it no longer has for Christians today. In our time the literature from communities of persons in spin-offs from Christianity such as Mormonism and Moonism claim the advantage of newness over against us. Our being aware of this will help us to keep the anti-Jewish polemic of Mark in perspective.

The concept of newness in Mark is seen also in Jesus' selection of the twelve disciples to constitute the new Israel (3:13–19). The selection was made on the mountain. If the "twelve" are a historical entity that goes back to the historical Jesus, the selection of that number and the location on a mountain may indicate a conscious attempt by Jesus to initiate a New Israel. In Mark, however, the call of the twelve is not connected specifically with the giving of a new Torah. The twelve are not the fathers of twelve Christian tribes. No attempts are made to establish genealogies based on them. If this document was developed within an apocalyptic eschatological community in rural and small-town southern Syria in the late 60s, the selection may have been located on a mountain with Mt. Hermon in mind. As has long been recognized, the twelve called and selected by Jesus to be with him and to be sent out to preach and to have authority to cast out demons are prototypes of the members of the evangelistic Markan community.

The demons, or the persons possessed, typically reacted to Jesus in the Markan accounts as they would have reacted to any other exorcist of that time by attempting to gain some control over the situation by naming their adversary. They were rebuked in the accounts and silenced by Jesus, who was depicted as having power much greater than theirs. They identified Jesus, however, as "the holy one of God" (1:24), "the son of God" (3:11), and "son of the most high God" (5:7), which represent close relationships with God. These designations themselves are not specifically anti-Jewish. The same can be said about the remark of the centurion in 15:39, "Truly this man was God's son!" These designations of Jesus do become anti-Jewish, however, within the context of Mark, where Jesus is presented as a new teacher with authority not like that of the scribes (1:21–28), the one about whom the voice from the clouds says, "This is my beloved Son. Listen to him!" (9:7). The designation of Jesus, the authority figure for the Markan community, as God's Son is anti-Jewish also in the manuscripts and editions of Mark 1:1 that include it, because in 1:2–3 Jesus is by implication "the Lord," whose way is prepared by John the Baptist.[32]

Finally, that the self-consciousness of the Markan eschatological community was a basic cause for anti-Jewish polemic in Mark is seen in the crucial Caesarea Philippi confession text and in the teachings regarding the experiences of "the Son of man" that follow it (8:27–38). The leader of this eschatological community is designated "*the* Christ" by the spokesman of the twelve, a designation of someone who is obviously intended to be regarded as greater than John the Baptist, Elijah, and any one of the prophets who have come in the past to the Israelites. The present generation is considered to be adulterous (faithless) and sinful, a value judgment typical of an apocalyptic community. The point is that all who will not accept Jesus and his teaching are deliberately excluding themselves from the people of God gathered around him, just as those who would not accept the word of the Lord at the time of Hosea and the other prophets excluded themselves from the Israelite community of faith of that time. Of such as these will the Son of man be ashamed when he comes in the glory of his Father. In this particular context in Mark the identification of Jesus as the Son of man is quite definite, for there is necessity that the Son of man suffer many things and be rejected by the elders, the chief priests, and the scribes, and be killed, and after three days be raised from the dead. Because of the nature of the situation, there is a "necessity" that the writings of this eschatological community be anti-Jewish ontologically.

B. Anti-Jewish Polemic in Mark's Controversy Dialogues

Given the nature of the Markan community, it was almost inevitable that much of its material about Jesus' ministry would be written as controversy dialogues, for it was largely through these controversy dialogues that the community established its own identity and self-consciousness. It is not possible for us to determine with certainty how many of these controversy dialogues or to what degree their intensity originated with the Jesus of history. If the Jesus of history was a prophet and reformer within the Palestinian Judaism of the first century, we may assume that he caused many people within the religious establishment of that place and time to take offense at what he did and said. We may assume also from the information available to us in the Gospel accounts that opposition and controversy between his followers and various Jewish groups grew and intensified during the decades after his death.

To the members of the Markan community their leader, like the nation Israel, had an experience in the wilderness. Cast out there by the Spirit, he was being tempted by Satan and was with the wild beasts, and the angels were ministering to him (1:12–13). The temptation was endured for forty days rather than Israel's forty years, but the process of telling stories about Jesus in such a way that the experiences of Jesus recapitulated those of the nation Israel, a process taken much farther in Matthew, was already underway.

A primary reason for controversy between Jesus and the religious leaders of the Jews in these accounts was the claim of the Markan eschatological community that Jesus acted and spoke with authority that was superior to that of the scribes. The scribes are depicted as merely following human tradition, as setting aside God's commandments wherever necessary by a carefully worked out casuistry (7:1–13). In 7:6 the Pharisees and the scribes are already labeled as "hypocrites," a designation to be multiplied three times in Luke and thirteen times in Matthew. The writer and the members of the community that produced Mark taught that Jesus' authority extended over demons and all causes of illness and deformity, over the elements of nature, and even over death. Again, these claims of authority were expanded in Matthew. Conflicting authority claims find expression in controversy dialogues not only in the Synoptics, but also at great length in the Fourth Gospel.

In the form in which we have them, the controversy dialogues in Mark are what Bultmann[33] called imaginative scenes that illustrate in some concrete occasion a principle that the Markan community ascribed to Jesus, its authority figure. Markan controversy dialogues follow more or less a set form, starting with an action or attitude that is seized upon by an opponent and used in an attack by accusation or question. The reply to the attack may be a counter-question or a metaphor, and it may include a quotation from a scriptural source. The matrix of these accounts was the Markan community in discussion with various Jewish groups, and within itself, in establishing its self-conscious identity. Rabbinic tradition carried on inquiry in a similar way, frequently in a much more complicated manner. If any portion of the controversy dialogues goes back to the historical Jesus, most likely it would be the decisive saying in each. Which of these and how many of these had been used also by Jesus is not possible for us to establish with certainty.[34]

Our task here is to recognize and to take steps to nullify the anti-Jewish polemic in our translation and use of these controversy dialogues in Mark. Rather than to follow Bultmann's detailed analysis of controversy dialogues occasioned by Jesus' healings, by the conduct of Jesus or the disciples, and the like, I shall proceed for the most part sequentially through these dialogues in the Markan account as it has come to us in the canon, considering in each instance the possible significance of the account for the Markan community and for our own. This methodology more readily takes into consideration redaction studies, literary studies, and canon studies of these texts, disciplines developed as we have them today since the time when Bultmann published his detailed form-critical analysis.

2:1–12: *The healing of the paralyzed man.* In the first of these Markan controversy dialogues a miracle story (2:1–5, 11–12) is interrupted by a controversy (2:6–10). The participation of the scribes is muted, since they question Jesus' pronouncement of forgiveness of the sins of the paralyzed man only within their hearts and within themselves. For the Markan community Jesus—here described as the Son of man—as God's representative has the power and authority to heal persons and to forgive their sins on the earth, one as easily as the other. The dialogue suggests that the scribes would not attribute to Jesus such authority. As significant and important as this difference was for the Markan community and, one may suppose, for the scribes, ultimately within theocentric religious systems such as we have in Judaism and in Christianity, it is God alone who forgives sins. Within both of these religious systems the forgiveness that God graciously provides is declared cultically, both privately and corporately. In practice, the primary difference is that Jesus is not named in one of these systems in connection with healing and the forgiveness of sins, but is in the other.

Since the controversy (2:6–10) interrupts the miracle story and since the miracle story is reintroduced rather awkwardly at the end of 2:10, the controversy appears to be secondary to the miracle story. A sensitive use of this text will include only the miracle story (2:1–5, 11–12) in lectionary readings, passing in silence over the controversy. Translations of the controversy should be at least neutral, not labeling the scribes religiously or ethnically as "the Jewish religious leaders" as they are in *The Living Bible* at this place and in similar texts.

2:13–17: *Eating with tax collectors and sinners.* The first in a series of controversy dialogues over life-style[35] pertains to table fellowship with tax collectors and sinners, the undesirables of the religious community. Analysis indicates in 2:15–17 an apophthegm, a saying of Jesus (2:17) placed in a brief context with which it has a somewhat loose connection. The presence of the scribes of the Pharisees as observers of the meal and the notation that the disciples of Jesus were questioned but Jesus answers are among reasons to suggest that the story was designed for the saying.[36] The account is not viciously anti-Jewish, although it bears an aura of superiority over the practices of the Jewish religious leadership. The point of the account has validity within Christian communities today in that our congregations are to be open even to those whom because of occupation or status some would consider to be undesirables. The emphasis upon the religious and ethnic identity of "the scribes of the Pharisees," who are said to have questioned Jesus' table-fellowship practices, is unnecessary in our translations and in our use of this text. The value of the text for Christian self-criticism would be enhanced if, instead of "the scribes of the Pharisees," which has little relevance within most Christian congregations today, a translation such as "some religious leaders of that time" would be utilized.

2:18–20: *Fasting.* Behind this account is the reminiscence that the Jesus of history had not emphasized the practice of fasting. Perhaps John the Baptist directly or through his disciples had queried Jesus about this and Jesus had replied with a question such as "Can the wedding guests fast during the wedding?"[37] After the crucifixion of Jesus his followers came to see Jesus as the bridegroom, as this text and its parallels, along with 2 Cor. 11:12, Matt. 25:1–3, Eph. 5:23–33, and Rev. 19:7–9 and 21:9 indicate. Since their bridegroom had been taken away, as expressed here in Mark 2:19–20 and in its parallels, many of them had adopted the practice of fasting,[38] probably on Fridays to commemorate Jesus' crucifixion. The unitary core of the account, therefore, may be said to have been based upon a remembered question and a remembered answer from the Jesus of history level.[39] "The Pharisees" and "the disciples of the Pharisees" were probably added at a later level, perhaps when this account was joined to the larger grouping of controversies with the Pharisees.

2:23–28: *The Sabbath walk through the grainfields at harvest time.* There are two controversy dialogues over life-style in relation to the attitude of the Markan community regarding observance of the Jewish Sabbath in 2:23–28 and 3:1–5, followed in 3:6 by the charge that the Pharisees left the synagogue to plot with the Herodians how they could destroy Jesus. The first of these two dialogues pertains to Jesus and his disciples going through the grainfields at harvest time. The harvest symbolism in other accounts suggests that here also there may be an eschatological motif. Perhaps, as Paul Achtemeier surmises,[40] the point of this account as we have it in Mark is not hunger (that in case of extreme necessity such as hunger the Torah may be disregarded), but Christology (Jesus as Lord of the Sabbath is the equal of and superior to David). Particularly because of the new introduction in 2:27, that verse is likely the core saying around which the account was developed. Jesus may have taught that "the Sabbath was instituted because of people *(anthrōpon),* and not people because of the Sabbath," and, for that matter, so also may have many of the Pharisees who were contemporary with the Jesus of history and with the Markan community. According to 1 Macc. 2:39–41, if the enemy attacks on the Sabbath, one must fight back rather than remain passive and be killed. In *Mekilta* 109b with reference to Exod. 31:14 Rabbi Simeon b. Menasya is quoted as having taught that "the Sabbath is delivered to you, and you are not delivered to the Sabbath." Twentieth-century Jewish writers such as Israel Abrahams,[41]

C. G. Montefiore,[42] and Samuel Sandmel[43] point to the acceptability in first-century Jewish thought of the saying about the Sabbath in 2:27.

Around the 2:27 core saying, an anti-Jewish controversy dialogue was developed into a story that to Eduard Schweizer[44] appears to be "fictitious." The most important purpose of the controversy dialogue apparently was to indicate what is stated in the "punch line" (2:28), that "the Son of man is Lord also over the Sabbath." The dialogue presents the Pharisees in a particularly bad light in that they are said to have objected to the rubbing out of a few heads of barley or wheat and not to the more serious matter of walking on the Sabbath. They are then refuted from their own Scriptures.

Since there is no mention in the Markan account that the disciples were hungry or that they ate the kernels, one may suspect that the symbolism of the account includes the idea of gathering people into the Markan eschatological fellowship and doing that even on the Sabbath to show that their Lord is indeed the Lord over the Sabbath and by implication over Jewish religious leaders. The account reveals much about the practices of the leadership within the Markan community, but little about which we can be certain with regard to Jesus. Since the accounts in Luke 6:1–5 and Matt. 12:1–8 do not include the core saying of Mark 2:27 and intensify the anti-Jewish polemic by stating that the disciples ate (Luke 6:1) and that they were hungry and ate (Matt. 12:1), a trajectory of increasing anti-Jewish polemic can be traced from Mark to Luke and Matthew in this piece of tradition.

It would be helpful in our time if "the Pharisees" of 2:24 were to be translated with something such as "some of the religious leaders," or "some people." This would be a small step toward counteracting what Bultmann found in the tradition, that is, an increasing tendency of the early church to clothe its dominical sayings, its views, and its fundamental beliefs in the form of controversy dialogues in which the scribes and the Pharisees are the sinister opponents.[45] This piece of the tradition (Mark 2:23–28 and parallels) is a good example of a tendency of the early church in its own particular *Sitz im Leben* to let its controversies with other groups obscure a dominical saying such as "the Sabbath was instituted because of people, and not people because of the Sabbath." We have a responsibility in our time to attempt to penetrate through the controversy dialogue in order to get back as much as possible to the dominical saying itself, which in this instance is not anti-Jewish.

3:1–6: *The Sabbath healing of the man with the withered hand.* The second controversy dialogue concerning observance of the Sabbath (3:1–6) may seem at first to reveal much about the thought patterns and emotions of the historical Jesus. Here Jesus is said to have looked around with anger at those who were so callous that they had lost concern for helping a poor man or for saving his life, deeply grieved at the hardness of their heart. The absence of these expressions of personality traits of Jesus in the Matthean and Lukan parallels seems to indicate that with the higher Christology in those accounts the humanity of Jesus was deliberately or subconsciously being repressed. The silence of Jesus' adversaries (3:4b seems to be confirmation of their callousness.

It is possible, of course, that the historical Jesus felt and displayed such emotions and that he felt them and displayed them in a situation such as that described in Mark 3:1-6. As we look more closely at the account, however, we see with much more certainty the thought patterns and emotions of the writer and members of the developing Markan eschatological community expressed in a life-of-Jesus vehicle as they and their traditions have constructed it than we see a documentary of the life of Jesus. The parallel accounts (Matt. 12:9-14; Luke 6:6-11; 14:1-6) are evidences of the same motif of healing on the Sabbath developed into somewhat different controversy dialogues. We see that the motivating factor in these accounts is neither the miraculous healings nor concern for reporting verbatim what Jesus had once said and done nor even concern for the person to be healed. What is central and basic in each of them is the controversy dialogue itself. The fundamental purpose of Mark 3:1-6 is to depict the dumbness, the silence, and the callousness of those who oppose the developing traditions of the followers of Jesus. The placing of this account at the end of a series of controversy dialogues that reach a crescendo here indicates the bitterness with which members of these communities regarded Pharisees who were contemporary with them. Because the Pharisees were not willing to join with these and with other followers of Jesus, they were to them in part at least what the Egyptians were to those who formulated the Exodus traditions centuries earlier. Just as the Egyptians had virtually no voice in the development of the Exodus traditions, so also the Pharisees were "silent," "callous," and "hard-hearted" in these contructions.

The statement in 3:6 that the Pharisees went out and immediately consulted with the Herodians against Jesus how they might destroy him is probably an anachronism that really applies to the situation remembered from 41-44 c.e. when Pharisees collaborated with Herod Agrippa.[46]

When it is recognized that is is likely that the situation of the Markan and pre-Markan communities was the matrix within which these controversy dialogues were developed, much of the sting of the anti-Jewish polemic in them is removed. The 3:1-6 text is an indication that there probably had been a time when it appeared to the members of these communities that contemporary Pharisees desired to destroy them and would collaborate with the Herodians, if necessary, to accomplish this objective.

Mark 3:1-5 and the concluding climax in 3:6 have redeeming social and religious value if the emphasis is upon the concern of Jesus and of his followers for human life and welfare. If "the Pharisees" and "the Herodians" were to be translated as "some of the religious leaders who opposed Jesus" and "some Roman government officials and others sympathetic to them," the anti-Jewish impact would be lessened. A rationale for Jesus' crucifixion as a significant prophet and reformer would be retained without so much damaging effect upon Jewish and upon Christian people today and in the future as there has been in the past. Beyond the translation by circumlocution would be the possibility of a major redaction of the controversy dialogue in our time, rewriting it to retain its theology without its anti-Jewish dress.

3:22–30: *The dispute about exorcism.* This dispute is particularly interesting because of the context in which it is placed in the Markan account. Instead of the exorcism that is presupposed in the controversy dialogue and included in the parallel accounts in Luke 11:14–23 and Matt. 12:22–32; 9:32–34, we read in Mark 3:20–21 the statement peculiar to Mark that "those from him," that is, his own family or his own relatives—probably defined more fully in 3:31–35 as his mother and his brothers and perhaps his sisters—having heard what he was doing, had gone out to seize him, for they were saying that he had lost his senses. In the Markan context, therefore, Jesus is engaged in a struggle on two fronts, one with the scribes who had come down from Jerusalem and the other with his own mother and closest relatives.

An analysis of the Synoptic interrelationships that would see no more than a simple progression of development from Mark and "Q" to Matthew and Luke would probably lead to the conclusion that Jesus' mother and siblings did not understand what Jesus was doing and tried to stop him. Later Synoptic traditions, with their greater interest in Jesus' parents, conception, birth, and childhood development, and with their higher Christology and diminishing emphasis on Jesus' humanity, suppressed the tradition of misunderstanding on the part of Jesus' family, retaining only Mark 3:31–35 in their own renditions and rejecting Mark 3:20–21 outright. Such an analysis may be a fairly accurate representation of what occurred, but it is possible that behind Mark 3:20–21 lies something more than, or other than, a historical reminiscence by Peter or by someone else within the tradition. If community self-consciousness was an important factor in the shaping of the Markan account, it is possible that the complete controversy dialogue here includes not only 3:22–30, but 3:20–35. If it includes all of 3:20–35, the community may have been polemicizing not only against the scribes from Jerusalem, its principal antagonists, but also against those from Jesus' background who did not understand what he was doing and as "mother and brothers" attempted to suppress him. According to 3:20–35 neither "those from Jesus' own family background" nor "the scribes from Jerusalem" are truly Jesus' mother and Jesus' brothers. Whoever does the will of God (the Markan community gathered around Jesus) is Jesus' brother and sister and mother (3:33–35).

In the Luke 11:15–22 parallel it is merely some of them from the multitudes who said that it was in the name of Beelzebul, the most prominent of the demons, that Jesus was casting out demons. Mark assigned to these objectors the identity of the scribes from Jerusalem and Matthew that of the Pharisees. Those who would try to separate Jesus from the ones who were sitting around Jesus in a circle (the Markan community) are not recognized (3:33) as Jesus' mother and brothers. Those who say that Jesus has an unclean spirit are speaking evil against the Holy Spirit and do not have forgiveness ever, but are guilty of an eternal sin (3:29–30).[47] The polemic is probably directed against both groups. It is gentle and subtle against the former from Galilee and intense and severe against the latter from Jerusalem. The warning and condemnation of 3:28–29 are separated by enough space in the account from the mention of the scribes from Jerusalem in 3:22 that most readers of Mark are probably not aware of how the complete controversy dialogue of 3:20–35 is constructed.[48] Consequently, they apply the warning against exclusion from fellowship with Jesus and against anyone who would speak evil of the Holy Spirit to themselves and to each other rather than to first-century or to contemporary Jewish groups. Therefore no suggestions for special care in translation or use of this pericope are needed.

5:21–43: *The restoration to life of Jairus's daughter.* This miracle story of the restoration to life of the daughter of Jairus, one of the rulers of the synagogue, is not a typical controversy dialogue. However, it is mentioned here as an example of an account that has subtle polemic in which the superiority of the wonder-working Lord of the Markan community over Jewish religious leadership is demonstrated. The "daughter" of one of "the rulers of the synagogue" is at the point of death. The ruler of the synagogue who is wise will come to Jesus with this problem, which presumably cannot be handled within the Jewish Synagogue. The inserted account of the healing of the woman with the flow of blood demonstrates the great healing potency of the Lord. The synagogue leader is told not to continue to be afraid, but to believe constantly. When the relatives and friends of the ruler of the synagogue are told that with Jesus death is merely a sleep, they laugh at him. But when Jesus takes her hand, she gets up and walks. Something is to be given to her to eat. This is the model that is presented of the "daughter" of "the ruler of the synagogue." If the elders of the synagogue would accept the superiority of Jesus and come to him for help, setting aside their fears and believing in him, their "daughter" would live again and be fed.

6:1–6a: *Unbelief in Jesus' hometown synagogue.* There are indications that the writer and the eschatological community that produced Mark were responsible for at least some of the anti-Jewish material in Mark 6:1–6a. Although parts of this pericope may have been circulated orally within the early Palestinian following of Jesus, the most plausible explanation is that the Markan writer combined into one narrative unit several traditions that previously had been independent. The saying that a prophet is not acceptable among his own people is attributed to Jesus without the Markan narrative context in the Coptic Gospel of Thomas, saying 31, and in the Oxyrhynchus Papyrus 1, lines 31–36, where it includes a parallel saying, "neither does a physician do works of healing for those who know him." In Mark 6:5 the second half of this saying is transformed into a narrative in which it is said that even the neighbors who had known Jesus and his family rejected him. This is consistent in Mark with the unbelief reported of those from Jesus' own family background in 3:21, 31–35, as discussed above.

The text under consideration here is introduced in typically Markan style (6:1–2a). Apart from "they were scandalized" in 6:3b and discounting the material that Mark attaches in 6:5–6a, the people of the synagogue react no more negatively than they do in the synagogue in Capernaum in 1:27–28.[49] It is probable that a tradition from the early Palestinian followers of Jesus in which amazement was expressed in Jesus' home area over his teaching was combined with the proverb regarding the ineffectiveness of a prophet and of a physician among kinfolk and acquaintances. This expression may have been affected also by the experiences of evangelists from or known to the Markan community who had worked in the area of Galilee around Nazareth. There is evidence in 6:7–13 that the missionary directives under which the Markan evangelists functioned were that if any place did not receive them and refused to hear them, they were to shake off the dust from their feet as a testimony against the people of that place. It is well documented in religious literature that when an active religious community attempts to proselytize members of another active religious community and is relatively unsuccessful, polemic will appear against the resistant objects of the proselytizing attempt within the literature of the proselytizing group, as is shown in the Introduction of this study. Centuries after the time of the writing of the polemic there remains little purpose or value in that polemic. Consequently, a text such as 6:1–6a is relatively unimportant for private or corporate devotional use in our time.

7:1–23: *The dispute over "clean" and "unclean."* This text, already mentioned above, is the longest controversy dialogue in Mark. As perceived by Bultmann,[50] this account has all the characteristics of pure polemic of the early church. The setting is that the Pharisees and some of the scribes, having come from Jerusalem, were gathering together over against Jesus. However, they observe not Jesus but some of his disciples—which may suggest an early church milieu—eating bread with hands not ceremonially washed. Jesus defends the practices of his disciples. The quotation from Isa. 29:13 has little or no connection with the content of the question raised by the Jewish religious leaders, nor does the use of Exod. 20:12, Deut. 5:16, and Exod. 21:7 in the additional saying in 7:9–13 attached to the basic segment 7:1–8. Teaching continues in 7:14–15 with the crowd and in 7:17–23 with Jesus' disciples. By this time the Pharisees and the scribes have long been forgotten and the original scene has no ending, much as in the extended teachings developed within the Johannine traditions.

The readership for this account obviously includes persons of non-Jewish backgrounds, since fundamental Jewish customs are explained in some detail (7:3–4). The response to the question of the Pharisees and scribes can best be described as overkill. The account is actually not a dialogue but a question followed by a series of monologues, which again is typical of this kind of polemic in religious literature. The opponent has no opportunity for even the slightest response, either in defense or in rebuttal.

What would be required in the translation and in the use of this account in order to direct the criticism of behavior away from the Pharisees and scribes of the first century and to apply it to ourselves within current Christianity where the account will be valid self-criticism? We see first of all that 7:14–23 is not offensive to others. The Markan community and the Christian Church can declare all foods to be acceptable for internal use without hurting other groups. The offensive portion is in 7:1–13. Actually the offensive portion is 7:6–13, which could be covered completely with little or no loss of sense in the account.[51] A redaction today that would repudiate and nullify 7:6–13—along with its parallel in Matt. 15:3–9 and the additional segment, Matt. 15:12–14—would be the most effective response to the problem caused by having this kind of material within our sacred Scriptures. The question, "Why do your disciples . . . eat with defiled hands?" would then be asked in 7:5 with the answer introduced immediately in 7:14 and given in 7:15ff. Without the intrusion of 7:6–13 there would be no necessity for the answer to be introduced so elaborately in 7:14. It is likely that at some stage of the oral or early written tradition, before the intrusion of the vitriolic anti-Jewish polemic of 7:6–13, the question that we have in 7:5 was followed directly by the answer that we now have as 7:15.

A redaction today of 7:1–23 might take various forms. A radical redaction could bracket verses 6–13 in our editions of the Greek New Testament, with the reason given in the critical apparatus, and move these verses from the text to a footnote in our translations into vernacular languages. A less radical redaction would leave the Greek editions untouched, but move the verses to a footnote in translations. Still less radical would be to leave the verses within brackets in the translation texts, with a footnote to explain the reason for the brackets. As a minimum response, 7:6–13 should be removed from our pericope series, which we read in public worship[52] and in preaching, and usage of these verses discouraged in educational and devotional materials. As long as this segment remains as it is in translation texts, anti-Semitism and religious bigotry will continue to be supported by texts that are sacred to Christian people.

8:11–12: *This generation seeks a sign.* In this brief text there is one of the many instances of what Bultmann labels an active tendency in the Synoptic traditions toward seeking to present the opponents of Jesus as scribes and Pharisees. It is probable that in the conjectured "Q" the demand for a sign was made by persons unnamed (Luke 11:16). These are replaced by scribes and Pharisees in Matt. 12:38. In Mark 8:11–12 the secondary nature of this identification is even more obvious, since Jesus is reputed to be in a different territory and the writer must bring the Pharisees out to him so that they may be able to challenge him. Already in Mark 2:6 the presence of the scribes of the Pharisees was inappropriate, but they were brought forth whenever needed as typical participants in the controversy dialogues.[53] If the specific references to scribes and Pharisees are secondary and indicate a tendency in the tradition, we now have the opportunity and the responsibility in our use of the tradition to reverse this tendency when we make new translations into vernacular languages and to move closer to the primary sources by stating merely that "some people" challenged Jesus.

8:15: *Beware of the leaven.* This warning to beware of the yeast of the Pharisees and the yeast of Herod is further evidence of the tendency toward establishing the Pharisees as the typical opponents of Jesus in the tradition. The original form and the original meaning of this 8:15 saying is obscure.[54] It occurs in Luke 12:1 in a quite different context. Without it, 8:16 makes much better sense. Chapter 8:14, 16–21 is then a story in which the disciples are concerned about their lack of bread and are reproved by Jesus for their lack of understanding.[55] Perhaps as the tradition was developing the point that was at one time the most prominent in the account was that the "one loaf" in the boat (8:14) was all that the disciples (the Markan community) needed, both for the Jewish-background Christians (the 5,000 referred to in 8:19 and earlier in 6:32–44) and for the Gentile-background Christians (the 4,000 mentioned in 8:19 and earlier in 8:1–10).[56] The feedings of the multitudes and this sequel here obviously have eucharistic implications. The disciples (the members of the Markan community) are to understand that one loaf is sufficient for all people.[57] Consequently, 8:15 not only is unnecessarily anti-Jewish, but also it obscures the sense of the pericope by diverting attention to a saying that is extraneous in this context. Its insertion here appears to have been made for anti-Jewish purposes. Our translations would be improved if we placed it in a footnote, noting that it is apparently an anti-Jewish saying that was inserted at some time into this account.

9:14c: *"And scribes contending against them."* Within the redactional connector that links this exorcism account to the Transfiguration pericope in Mark there is in 9:14c an expression of the typical Markan situation of the "disciples of Jesus" engaged in argumentation with the "scribes." Within the 9:14–29 exorcism account, the confrontation of the disciples of Jesus with the scribes is apparent only in 14c of the redactional connector. After 9:14 the scribes are not a factor; the cast includes only Jesus and his disciples, the dumb spirit, the boy, the father, and the crowd. It is probable that 9:14c is an indication of the *Sitz im Leben* of the Markan community. During the oral transmission of this exorcism account it is unlikely that "scribes" had any role to play.

10:1–12: *The Pharisees and divorce.* The teaching of the Markan community regarding marriage, divorce, and remarriage is also placed in the framework of a controversy, a dialogue between Jesus and Pharisees who have come to him "in order to try to cause him to fail." The Pharisees are the typical opponents of Jesus here, and their motives are labeled as sinister at the outset by the Markan community. As E. Schweizer observes,[58] real-life Pharisees would hardly have asked such a radical question as "Is it in accordance with the Torah for a man to divorce his wife?" since for the Pharisees divorce was regulated by Deut. 24:1–4, legislation designed to protect the wife and to guarantee for her a measure of freedom. The radical question is included here because the Markan community, in establishing its identity apart from Jewish groups, was impelled to raise the question and to provide an authoritative answer within its compilation of Jesus' teachings for its own use. As it established its identity self-consciously, it did it for the most part over against its Jewish antecedents. It is not surprising, therefore, that it tended to be comparatively strict, like the Qumran community in this respect. It rejected the Jewish Torah legislation (Deut. 24:1–4) in favor of the "two as one" descriptions in the creation accounts in Gen. 1:27 and 2:24. Probably perceiving the Genesis 1 and 2 accounts to have priority both in time (earlier than Moses) and in scope (for all people, not merely for the Israelites), it opted for these and accused the Pharisees of hardness of heart (10:5), because of which hardness Moses provided some possibility of a certificate of divorce.

In our translation and use of Mark 10:1–12, it is important that we recognize and stress that, in the theological opinion of the leadership of the Markan community, divorce was not permitted. They used the technique of controversy dialogue with the Pharisees as their opponents to clarify their own position and to show that it differed from that of the Pharisees. Since the controversy dialogue is of little value for us today, it should be treated as secondary in our proclamation and teaching. Our primary interest is in the position of the Markan community as we reflect on the issue of the possibility of divorce today. Accordingly, it would be advisable for us to translate "Pharisees" in 10:2 as "some religious leaders," and to express the text of 10:5b as "He wrote this commandment for our ancestors and for you because of human intransigence."

10:17–31: *The rich young man seeking eternal life.* Although this segment of Mark is usually included in listings of Mark's controversy dialogues, the polemic in this account is not overtly anti-Jewish. It is directed against the rich who will not relinquish their riches to follow Jesus as he leads them to the kingdom of God.

8:31; (9:12); 9:31; and 10:33–34: *The passion predictions.* As has been seen earlier during the consideration of 3:6, the controversy dialogues in Mark are closely associated with alleged motivations by various groups of Jesus' own people to reject him, to cause him to suffer, and to destroy him. The passion predictions of 8:31, (9:12), 9:31, and 10:33–34 recapitulate this theme, with the last mentioned adding the detail that they will deliver the "Son of man" over to the nations (Gentiles), who will actually be the ones to kill him.

These passion predictions lead the reader of Mark to the account of the entry into Jerusalem, the city in which the passion will be experienced. In 11:1–10 Jesus is described as "the Lord" who is in need of a colt on which, like Solomon and Jehu, he may ride into the city. The people sing the Hallel Psalms, and for the reader the distinction between the Lord Yahweh in whose name the pilgrims come and the Lord Jesus with whom the pilgrims come is blurred, probably intentionally, by the Markan community and by its traditions to produce a lasting *double entendre.*

11:12–25: *The fig tree and the temple.* Controversy dialogue with the chief priests and scribes, who merely are reported to have overheard Jesus' remarks regarding the purpose of the temple (11:15–19), is said to have motivated these religious leaders further to seek a way by which they might destroy him. In Mark the account of the cleansing of the temple is bracketed by a story of Jesus' cursing a fig tree (11:12–14, 20–25) in a way which indicates that the two accounts are to be interrelated.

Separately, the accounts are not primarily controversy dialogues, but when they are read together a controversy and a condemnation are enacted symbolically. Paul Achtemeier suggests[59] that for the Markan community, when they told the stories about Jesus attacking the temple money-changers and merchants and cursing the fig tree, Jesus was thought proleptically efficaciously to have ended Jewish cultic worship and Jewish ability to produce fruit. The slight delay between Jesus' cursing the fig tree and its withering (a delay eliminated in the Matthean account) signified the slight delay before Jewish cultic worship and ability to produce fruit would cease. By placing these two accounts in juxtaposition, the Markan writer and community were indicating that the fate of the fig tree would also become the fate of the temple. In place of Jewish cultic activity and fruit-fulness, which had been limited to a specific people in a specific location, the Markan community perceived its own developing cultic activity to be universal in scope and centered around Jesus as God's representative present in the eucharistic reactualizations.

Interpreted in this way, this composite account was clearly an attempt by the Markan community to use its ministry-of-Jesus vehicle to establish the "good news" of its superiority over the Jewish cult and to mark the imminent end of Jewish fruit-producing ability. How shall we as Christians late in the twentieth century utilize this account at a time when our own traditions are under attack and when they are said to have been superseded by the subsequent traditions of Islam, Mormonism, Moonism, and others?

If our desire is to emphasize the positive aspects of the composite account, we shall endeavor to apply its message vigorously self-critically. Therefore the mention of the chief priests' and scribes' hearing about this and seeking how they might destroy him (11:18), though important anti-Jewish polemic for the Markan community, will have little relevance for us today. Instead, our faithfulness to the Word of God in this account will be demonstrated when we place our emphasis upon insuring that Christian worship is accessible to all nations (11:17ab), that Christian people do not live as materialistic robbers who gather periodically as bands of hypocrites coming together in cultic ceremonies (11:17c), and that Christian life is fruitful in faith, prayer, and forgiveness (11:22–25).

11:27–33: *The question of authority.* In the Markan composition that introduces this account (11:27) "they went again into Jerusalem," the city which for Mark, as Kümmel shows,[60] was not only the place of Jesus' death but also the home base of Jewish obduracy toward Jesus (3:22, 7:1, 10:33, and 11:18). Consequently, with Jesus active in Jerusalem, controversy dialogues abound in this portion of the Markan record.

Regardless of whether 11:28–30 constitutes a genuine Palestinian apophthegm followed by composition by Mark or some other Hellenist,[61] or whether most of the account was already current in the earliest Christian community,[62] it is not likely that the religious leaders named in 11:27 would have admitted that they had no answer to Jesus' question.[63] Within religious systems such as ours, ultimately the origin of all authority is in God, but there is derived authority in traditions, in institutions, in communities, and in persons such as John, Jesus, the chief priests, scribes, and elders, and ourselves. For the Markan community and for us in the church there is in Jesus an extraordinary measure of derived authority. This account suggests that for the Markan community and its traditions, perhaps even for the historical Jesus, the claim was made that Jesus, like John, really was a prophet who spoke and acted as God's representative, and as such had significant derived authority. The baptism of John, as well as what Jesus was doing, was "from heaven," but it was also based on the authority that resided in those two individuals.

In summary, this account is one in which the questions, both of the religious leaders of Jewish groups and of Jesus and the early Christian traditions, are good, but the answers are not. The account would have much greater impact if our use of it terminated at 11:30 and the reader were left to struggle with the questions. This procedure takes us back, I think, to the historical ground and bedrock of the account. If we use the account in this way, we accomplish two desirable results. We shift the emphasis away from the anti-Jewish polemic, and we approach the founder of Christianity.

12:1–12: *The story about an owner of a vineyard collecting his rent.* This account, though introduced as a parable, is in Mark an allegory used as a controversy dialogue. It is probable that in this instance the most primitive form of the account available to us is not in the Synoptic Gospels, but in the Gospel of Thomas[64] of Gnostic Christians.[65] Within a thoroughly Jewish context the parable was likely an incisive call for repentance in view of the imminent coming of the kingdom of God when all would be held accountable. The rent must be paid. It must be paid now. If a threat was inherent in the parable—and we cannot assume that there was—it was perhaps that the poor would fare better comparatively than the wealthy in this process, since the poor were relatively less accountable. Unlike the Isaiah 5 love song, the issue in the most primitive strata of this account discernible to us was not the unproductivity of the vineyard but the unwillingness of the vineyard renters to pay their rent.

Many steps were involved in the process of adapting this story into a controversy dialogue in a thoroughly Christian context. If the poor were at one time favored in the story, as Jeremias surmised by analogy to related parables,[66] they were soon forgotten. The internal self-criticism of the love song of the Isaiah tradition became external polemic against the Jews as the story was being recast into the Isaiah mold by Greek-speaking Christians who used the Septuagint version of the love song. During this process the story developed into an extended allegory that utilized many but not all of the elements of the Isaiah love song. Experiences of the Markan community and of other early Christian groups informed the account.

The allegorical process was taken still farther in the Matt. 21:33–46 parallel where the son is no longer killed and thrown outside of the vineyard, but thrown outside the vineyard and killed, just as Jesus was said to have been killed outside the walls of Jerusalem. Ps. 118:22–23, used here as elsewhere in the New Testament and in other early Christian writings as a Messianic prophecy of the stone rejected by the builders but raised to preeminence by the Lord, was quoted from the Septuagint also as an obvious vindication of the founder of the Markan community. The context of the passage in Ps. 118 was disregarded when the segment was placed in its new context at the end of this story. The adaptation process was completed in Mark with the addition of the Markan composition 12:12, where the ones said to be seeking to destroy Jesus were presumably the chief priests and the scribes and the elders of 11:27b, related by intent with the chief priests and scribes seeking to arrest him and kill him in 11:18 and 14:1b.

How shall we as late twentieth-century Christians use this account? As a controversy dialogue on the surface of the Markan account, its value today is limited in our teaching and proclamation ministries. As an allegory as it is presented here, it arouses feelings of superiority for ourselves and contempt for the Jews, neither of which is necessary or desirable.[67] Whatever can be done to help us to go back into the pre-Markan period of the tradition when the account was in the form of a parable, perhaps a parable of the kingdom, or simply a story told to elicit immediate repentance, would be desirable. For this purpose our translations should now include in a footnote a translation of the Gospel of Thomas text. In lectionary series and in our preaching, Mark 12:1–12 and its Synoptic parallels should be separated in usage from the Isaiah 5 love song. Everything possible should be done to encourage use of the story to evoke self-examination leading to immediate repentance and positive response to God. We are the renters! The vineyard belongs to God! In this sense the point of the story is similar to that of the punch line of the one following it in 12:17: "Pay back to God the things which belong to God!"

12:13–17: *To pay or not to pay the Roman poll tax.* The saying in 12:17 is so memorable that for many readers it probably nearly completely overshadows the anti-Jewish polemic into which it is set in the Synoptic accounts. The introduction of the polemic with mention of the combination of Pharisees and Herodians in 12:13, as in 3:6, may be recollection of the situation of 41–44 C.E. when Pharisees collaborated with Herod Agrippa. The Pharisees and Herodians in complicity are depicted as totally unsuccessful in their efforts to trick Jesus with compliments into making a positional statement that would subsequently be used against him either among Jewish patriots or Roman officials. While the account, apart from portions of 12:13, may have come to the Markan community much as it is in 12:14–17,[68] the question regarding whether to pay or not to pay the Roman poll tax is one that followers of Jesus would have had to face in a new light as they separated themselves from the Jewish situation. The answer, "The things of Caesar pay back to Caesar and the things of God pay back to God," or rendered more freely, "The coin belongs to Caesar, but *you* belong to God!" is of such excellence that it needs no anti-Jewish foil for contrast. The Markan sectarian community apparently paid the poll tax but claimed a much higher loyalty than that which it paid to Caesar. Therefore the question may have been at least in part its own. The community may have considered this question, just as it must have considered many other questions as they arose, and written the answer as well into its Gospel of the eschatological prophet whom it claimed to be the Messianic Son of God. Today we need no more than that.

We can reduce emphasis on the anti-Jewish polemic of this text by describing Jesus' questioners in 12:13 as "some people who wanted to ask questions about the relationship between the religious community and the government," and in 12:15a as "But he, perceiving their intent, said to them." In our teaching and proclamation we can concentrate on the same religious community-government question within our own religious and political situation and on the significance of the answer given in this text, and disregard the anti-Jewish polemic of the setting.

12:18–27: *The Sadducees and the resurrection life.* In terms of anti-Jewish polemic this text is merely one more in a series in which Jesus, the community's champion, successfully takes on and soundly defeats another group of Jewish challengers. In the process two significant teachings are given, one related to a Torah text (Exod. 3:2–6) cited as proof that there is a resurrection and the other an indication of what the community taught that the resurrection would be like.[69] Today the Exodus text would more likely be cited as evidence of the process by which tribal "God of Our Fathers" traditions were incorporated into "Yahweh, the God of Israel" traditions than as a proof text for the resurrection of individuals.

Interest in this text should focus on what the Markan community was teaching about the nature of resurrection life rather than on the charge in 12:24, 27b that the Sadducees were in error.[70]

12:28–34: *The most important commandment.* If it were not for the connecting link in 12:28a, which attaches this account to the controversy dialogues that precede it, and for the way in which the animosity of the Pharisees, the Sadducees, and the Torah scholar from among them is expressed in the parallel account in Matt. 22:34–35, this pericope in Mark would receive no comment in this study of the anti-Jewish polemic in Mark.[71] This is the only instance in the Gospels in which a Torah scholar and Jesus are represented as being in substantial agreement. Jesus cites the great central Jewish confession of faith of Deut. 6:4–5 as the most important commandment. The Torah scholar responds in total agreement and comments further with the basic position of the Pharisees of the first century. Jesus' statement, "You are not far from the Kingdom of God," retains only the slightest distance between them. Perhaps the statement is to be regarded as an invitation to take the final step from "not far from" to "into" the kingdom of God, as Schweizer suggests.[72] The final step apparently is not taken, however, and abruptly Mark concludes this series of questions.

Perhaps in this pericope the Markan account has preserved a tradition that goes back to nearly the earliest followers of Jesus.[73] Jewish monotheism remains intact. Jesus is a respected teacher, and nothing beyond that. If there is an expression of superiority by the Markan community in 12:34b ("You are not far from the kingdom of God"), the expression is subtle and the degree of anti-Jewish polemic slight. Some people within the Markan community may have remained close to the basic position of the Pharisees of the first century, or there may have been recollection of a time when agreement between followers of Jesus and some of the Pharisees seemed possible. If this account goes back nearly to the earliest followers of Jesus, much farther than does the overwhelming majority of the Gospel accounts, perhaps the formative role of those who transmitted the Christian traditions during the initial decades may have been considerably greater—and the formative role of the Jesus of history correspondingly less—than most of us have realized.

12:35–37a: *How can the Messiah be the son of David when David has said that he is Lord?* It is by inference from the specified setting (Jesus teaching in the temple), position in Mark (between a series of controversy dialogues and a brief condemnation of the scribes), and further development in the Synoptic parallels that this account qualifies for consideration in a study of anti-Jewish polemic in Mark. The question raised in this text became a problem when early Christians, probably Greek-speaking Christians,[74] associated their "lord" (Jesus) with "my lord" (the king in the royal psalm). Disregarding the original *Sitz im Leben* and purpose of Psalm 110, their rather specious exegesis led them toward a position of denial that the Messiah would be a son of David[75] or of any other human father. Their "lord" must be God's son, a conclusion acceptable to Hellenistic Christians.

This account is probably as far from the earliest followers of Jesus as the preceding one is near to them. Chapter 12:35 does not follow well after the previous verse. It has just been stated in 12:34 that at this point no one would dare to ask him a question. This is followed in 12:35 by (literally) "and/having answered/Jesus/was saying/teaching." The problem of the early Christians was compounded because Ps. 110 had been attributed to David and the quotation is introduced in 12:36 as one that David himself said "in the Holy Spirit." When early Christians associated Jesus with "my lord" spoken about by "David," they had the problem stated baldly in 12:37a: "David himself says that he is Lord, and how then is he his son?" In the Markan account the situation that had been a problem for the early Christians is turned to their advantage when they put it into a ministry-of-Jesus vehicle and pit Jesus against the scribes.

The sophistry of the entire argument is probably lost to most modern readers. It is well that when Mark 12:28–34 is utilized as the Gospel reading for the Twenty-fourth Sunday after Pentecost, Series B, verses 35–37 are added only in parentheses in *Lutheran Book of Worship.* It would be appropriate to exclude 35–37 from the reading.

12:37b–40: *The scribes will be condemned.* One of the most significant aspects of the prophetic function is the criticism of one's own religious leaders who display outward signs of deep piety but take financial advantage of the poor. It is likely that John the Baptist, Jesus, and other Jews of the first century expressed openly this kind of criticism and condemnation of some persons within their own religious leadership. Internal criticism, however, becomes external criticism when a group separates itself from its parent community and continues to criticize and to condemn the parent community's leadership. It is particularly inappropriate when criticism of specific offenders becomes general criticism of entire groupings of people.

It is possible, as Kee suggests,[76] that in the Markan community there was already a tendency to prefer honor and rank to integrity and responsibility to one's neighbor. If this was the case, integrity and responsibility would indicate that the criticism that had become external should have been redirected into internal self-criticism. Therefore, within a maturing Christianity, we have the responsibility belatedly to translate "the scribes" of 12:38 and "the synagogues" of 12:39 as "our religious leaders" and as "our religious gatherings" respectively. In the *Sitz im Leben* of the Jesus of history they were "our religious leaders" and "our religious gatherings." Only after the separation of the followers of Jesus from a Jewish identity did they become "their religious leaders" and "their religious gatherings."

Among the functions of Mark 13[77] is its transitional role to take the reader from the public-controversy dialogues that constitute such a large portion of the Gospel to the more private teachings and activities that are recorded in the pre-arrest portions of the passion account.

The most pronounced anti-Jewish polemic in Mark 13 is in 13:2 (Jesus' prediction of the destruction of the temple) and in 13:9 (Jesus' prediction that they will deliver over his followers into courts and that they will be beaten in the synagogues). The historical Jesus may indeed have predicted, in view of the revolutionary activities of the Zealots and other nationalistic Jews, that a revolt culminating in the fall of Jerusalem and the destruction of the temple was likely to occur. If Mark was written during the Jewish revolt of 66–69, the likelihood of that catastrophe would have been even more obvious to the Markan community, many of whose members may have recently moved from Judea and from Galilee to avoid the tribulation. Jesus' prediction of destruction becomes anti-Jewish, not because he may have made it, but because of the context of that prediction in the Markan account and in its parallels. Since Jesus was the hero of the Markan eschatological community in its controversies with various Jewish groups, his prediction of the fall of the temple becomes polemical in 13:2.

The prediction of the suffering of followers of Jesus in Jewish courts and in synagogues may be *post eventu* in the Markan account. The followers were in those places "for a testimony to them," which may indicate that, in part at least, they were there because they chose to be there. In our translation and use of 13:9 today, it would be proper to represent *synagōgas* as "gathering places."

C. Anti-Jewish Polemic in Mark's Passion Account

As intensive study of Mark continues, it is becoming increasingly difficult to determine how much of the Gospel should be considered to be the passion narrative. If by passion narrative is meant the account of Jesus' activity in Jerusalem, 11:1 is the starting point and chapters 1–10 might be considered an extended introduction to the passion. Many commentators today find the beginning of the passion narrative at 14:1, with the announcement of the plans of the leading priests and the scribes to seize and kill Jesus secretly. A third possibility is to begin with 14:53, after all of Jesus' followers have fled and Jesus was led in bondage from Gethsemane to the high priest, and "all" the leading priests, the elders, and the scribes came together. After 14:53 Jesus speaks only rarely and very briefly, though with great dramatic effect, in Mark's account (14:62; 15:2b, 34, 37).

Analysis of the anti-Jewish polemic in Mark indicates no significant distinction between the nature of the polemic in the passion narratives and in the other portions of the Gospel, regardless of whether the passion narrative begins at 11:1, 14:1, or 14:53. Perhaps Kee is correct in concluding that the passion narrative in Mark, like the rest of the Gospel, is largely a literary product of the Markan community and that "there is no interpretative advantage in speaking of a pre-Markan passion narrative and no unambiguous evidence pointing to its existence."[78] Chapter 14:1 is considered the most recognizable point of transition to the passion in the present study primarily because beyond 14:1 there are no further controversy dialogues as such in which Jesus is pitted against Jewish religious leaders. In the remainder of the Markan account the polemic continues unabated but mainly in third-person narrative.

The often-repeated distinction between the Jewish people and their leaders in Mark's composition continues in 14:2. The impression is given that the people would protect Jesus or at least demonstrate against his public arrest and execution at the hands of their own authorities. It is interesting to note that in the *Divine Principle* of Moonism the same distinction is made; the "Lord of the Second Advent" will be opposed and persecuted by the leadership of the Christian Church, but Christian laypeople and those without any religious faith who are conscientious will accept the "Lord's" words.[79]

In 14:2 and throughout Mark 14–15 and parallels, it is difficult to determine the extent to which anti-Jewish prejudices among the early Christians who shaped the traditions and composed what was to be incorporated into the New Testament colored their composition of the accounts of Jesus' arrest, trial, and execution. Behind all of this, however, there may well be what Gerard Sloyan calls a "dependable historical tradition of antipathy" between Jesus and certain powerful priests in Jerusalem, an antipathy that contributed to Jesus' death.[80] At any rate, if antipathy between the historical Jesus and certain powerful priests in Jerusalem was a result of Jesus' activities as an eschatological prophet and outspoken religious reformer and a cause of Jesus' execution, there is every indication that animosities between many of his followers and large groups of priests, scribes, and Pharisees spread and intensified after his death.

Sufficient evidence remains in Mark's account that even at the time of the composition of Mark it was remembered and still proclaimed that certain leading Jewish officials, such as the scribe who asked about the most important commandment in 12:28–34 and Joseph of Arimathea who was said to have been a respected member of the council in 15:43, were "not far from the kingdom of God," or "waiting with anticipation for the kingdom of God." With the support of this evidence and with increasing awareness of the problems and prejudices of the Markan community, we may conclude that in our endeavor to achieve a sensitive and an accurate translation and usage of Mark's passion account we may be permitted and even encouraged to avoid generalizations and to speak only about "some of the leading priests and scribes" seeking a way that they might seize and kill Jesus secretly in 14:2. Similarly, we can say in 14:10–11 that Judas went to "the leading priests who were most opposed to Jesus." The chief priests and the scribes and the elders in 14:43 can be "some of the more powerful priests and scribes and elders" or simply "some of the religious leaders." The occurrence of *pantes,* "all" the chief priests and the elders and the scribes, in 14:53 and of *holon,* the "whole" council, in 14:55 is a problem of greater magnitude. Again, in view of the incidental references to the scribe in 12:28–34 and to Joseph of Arimathea in 15:43, the use of *pantes* and of *holon* in 14:53, 55 may be considered to be hyperbole.[81] We can therefore translate *pantes* as "many of" and *holon* as "powerful members of" in 14:53, 55.

The study of the extent of the anti-Jewish polemic in Mark and the recognition that hyperbole may have been used in Mark's passion account is congruent with the view of Solomon Zeitlin[82] that if there was a council assembled in the house of the high priest during the night it was not a religious Sanhedrin but a political one. There is little doubt that there was collusion between certain powerful sacerdotal leaders and Pilate. Such collusion, with or without an official hearing before a political Sanhedrin, could have occurred during the night and in the early morning hours, the times indicated in Mark 14:53–15:1.

Since the passion account in Luke lacks mention of a religious inquest during the night, it is possible that Mark inserted a nocturnal religious inquest (14:55–64) for theological reasons.[83] The account of the verbal exchange between the high priest and Jesus recorded in 14:61–64a provides much insight into the experiences and the Christology of the Markan community and writer.[84] For them Jesus was the Christ, the Son of the Blessed One. The way in which portions of Ps. 110:1 and Dan. 7:13 are combined in Mark 14:62 indicates that the members of the Markan community expected to see Jesus as the Son of man seated at the right hand of power and coming with the clouds of heaven. In the Markan account, except by prolepsis in the Transfiguration pericope, no one actually sees Jesus glorified.[85] But soon the faithful in the community will see his visible return in glory. In view of the intensifying hostility between the members of the Markan community and various Jewish groups, the community may have had reason to think that its expectations regarding Jesus' parousia would have been considered blasphemous by the Jerusalem "high priest." As in 14:53, 55 therefore, *hoi pantes* in 14:64c may be further hyperbole, an expression of what the leaders of the Markan community thought would have been a unanimous verdict. They claimed no eyewitness report, since their Gospel account, concluded at 16:8, relates no further verbal contact between Jesus and his followers after his arrest. Our interpretative translation of *hoi pantes* in 14:64c, consequently, can be "the associates of the high priest."

Also in consideration of 12:28–34 and 15:43 as above, the leadership of the opposition to Jesus and to his followers described in 15:1 may be translated as "some of the leading priests, with the support of certain elders and scribes and powerful members of the council." Sensitive translations in 15:3, 10, 11 would use "these leading priests." In 15:8, 11, 15 "the crowd" is inadequate in this setting as a translation of *ho ochlos*. The crowd that appears here was introduced anarthrously in 14:43 as a motley group that came to Gethsemane during the night armed with swords and clubs. Therefore "the group that had seized Jesus" would be an appropriate translation in 15:8, followed by "the group into a mob" in 15:11 and "the mob" in 15:15. This kind of attention to context in translation not only exonerates the multitude of Jews in Jerusalem from allegedly bloodthirsty complicity in demanding Jesus' crucifiixion, but also recognizes how unlikely it would have been for the identical crowd or multitude that listened approvingly and supportively to Jesus in Jerusalem in 11:18, 11:32, 12:12, and 12:37b to have appeared before Pilate and to have been persuaded so quickly and so thoroughly to cry out repeatedly, "Crucify him!"[86]

The heavy use of the psalms of the innocent sufferer, particularly Psalms 22 and 69, in Mark's crucifixion account and parallels has long been recognized. Because of the formative influence of Psalm 22 in this crucifixion account, we would probably come closer to what actually happened during the crucifixion if we translated *hoi paraporeuomenoi* in 15:29 as "some who were passing by" and the chief priests with the scribes in 15:31 as "some of the leading priests with some of the scribes," or "some of the religious leaders."

Finally, anti-Jewish polemic in Mark included the theological assertion in 15:38 that at the moment of Jesus' death the curtain of the temple was split from top to bottom and in 15:39 that the Roman official in charge of the execution (rather than any Jews, even Jewish disciples of Jesus) said, "Truly this man was God's Son." In our exposition of these verses their polemical nature should be acknowledged. Theologically they have value. We can say from them that through the sacrificial death of Jesus we have new access to the holiness of God. Jesus was obedient to God. Here is our archetype for our own divine-human encounter. The problem is that here as elsewhere in Mark a ministry-of-Jesus vehicle was used to express the theoelogical viewpoint of the Markan community. Repeated usage of the written accounts has imputed to them an impression that they are objective historiography.

Notes

1. Moses Hadas and Morton Smith, *Heroes and Gods: Spiritual Biographies in Antiquity* (New York: Harper & Row, 1965); Helmut Koester, "One Jesus and Four Gospels," *HTR* 61 (1968): 230–36; Morton Smith, "Prolegomena to a Discussion of Aretalogies, Divine Men, the Gospels and Jesus," *JBL* 90 (1971): 174–99; Theodore J. Weeden, *Mark—Traditions in Conflict* (Philadelphia: Fortress, 1971); David L. Tiede, *The Charismatic Figure as Miracle Worker* (Missoula, Mont.: Scholars, 1972); Jonathan Z. Smith, "Good News Is No News: Aretalogy and Gospel," in *Christianity, Judaism and Other Greco-Roman Cults*, Part One, Studies in Judaism in Late Antiquity, ed. J. Neusner, vol. 12 (Leiden: E. J. Brill, 1975), pp. 21–38.

2. H. B. Carre, *Studies of Early Christianity* (New York, 1928), pp. 105–26; E. W. Burch, "Tragic Action in the Second Gospel," *JR* 11 (1931): 346; Curtis Beach, *The Gospel of Mark* (New York: Harper, 1959); David L. Barr, "Toward a Definition of the Gospel Genre," Ph.D. diss., Florida State University, 1974.

3. Martin Braun, *History and Romance in Graeco-Roman Literature* (Oxford: Oxford, 1938), pp. 23–32.

4. Dan O. Via, Jr., *Kerygma and Comedy in the New Testament* (Philadelphia: Fortress, 1975).

5. H. A. Musurillo, ed., *The Acts of the Pagan Martyrs: Acta Alexandrinorum* (Oxford: Clarendon, 1954). Musurillo indicates that there are similarities rather than exact parallels.

6. Henry Fischel, "Studies in Cynicism and the Ancient Near East: The Transformation of a Chria," in *Religions in Antiquity*, ed. J. Neusner (Leiden: E. J. Brill, 1968), 372–411. Fischel shows that when the Cynic rhetorical form was utilized by sages within the Jewish tradition it was modified and adapted considerably.

7. For a survey and critique of the signifiance of Hellenistic and Jewish models for the literary form of Mark, see Howard C. Kee, *Community of the New Age: Studies in Mark's Gospel* (Philadelphia: Westminster, 1977), pp. 17–30.

8. See the earlier study by Amos N. Wilder, *The Language of the Gospel: Early Christian Rhetoric* (New York: Harper & Row, 1964).

9. Most notably, Kee, *Community of the New Age*. For the use of sociocultural factors, see also Martin Hengel, *Judaism and Hellenism*, 2 vols. (Philadelphia: Fortress, 1974), and Gerd Theissen, *Sociology of Early Palestinian Christianity*, trans. J. Bowden (Philadelphia: Fortress, 1978).

10. See above, n. 7.

11. Bryan R. Wilson, *Magic and Millennium: A Sociological Study of Religious Movements of Protest Among Tribal and Third-World Peoples* (London: Heinemann, 1973).

12. Kee, *Community of the New Age*, pp. 162–75.

13. Wilson, *Magic and Millennium*, p. 21.

14. Kee, *Community of the New Age*, pp. 106–107.

15. J. A. Fitzmyer, "The Use of Explicit Old Testament Quotation," *NTS* 7 (1960–61): 319–21; Kee, *Community of the New Age*, pp. 46–47.

16. E. E. Ellis, *Paul's Use of the Old Testament* (Grand Rapids, Mich.: Eerdmans, 1957), p. 141.

17. See "Introduction" above.

18. A. C. Sundberg, "On Testimonies," *NT* 3 (1959): 272.

19. Kee, *Community of the New Age*, p. 45.

20. Ibid., pp. 64–70.

21. Ibid., pp. 100–101. For an important alternative possibility, which assumes instead of a Christian vs. Jewish struggle during the first Jewish revolt an internal Christian situation in which Mark is representative of a north Palestinian Christianity in opposition to a south Palestinian Christianity some time after the fall of Jerusalem, see Werner H. Kelber, *The Kingdom in Mark* (Philadelphia: Fortress, 1974). Even though Kelber presents his position carefully, it may be that his thesis that Mark's Gospel mythologically reconstructs the critical moment in early Christian history that he suggests is overdrawn. See also the view of Theodore J. Weeden, "The Heresy that Necessitated Mark's Gospel," *ZNW* 59 (1968): 145–58; and *Mark—Traditions in Conflict* (Philadelphia: Fortress, 1971).

22. Max Weber, *Sociology of Religion*, trans. from the 4th German ed. (Boston: Beacon, 1963).

23. K. O. L. Burridge, *New Heaven, New Earth: A Study of Millenarian Activities* (New York: Schocken, 1969).

24. Kee, *Community of the New Age*, pp. 97–100.

25. As proposed by Vincent Taylor, *The Gospel According to St. Mark* (London: Macmillan, 1966), p. 32; William L. Lane, *The Gospel of Mark* (Grand Rapids, Mich.: Eerdmans, 1974), and many others.

26. Galilee is the choice of Lohmeyer, Lightfoot, and most of all, Willi Marxsen, *Mark the Evangelist* (Nashville, Tenn.: Abingdon, 1969), pp. 54–95.

27. For the evidence Kee presents, see *Community of the New Age*, pp. 100–105.

28. Ibid., p. 67.

29. See, for example, the reaction of Samuel Sandmel to the manner in which the Pharisees are depicted in Mark in his *Anti-Semitism in the New Testament?* (Philadelphia: Fortress, 1978), pp. 27–40.

30. Kee, *Community of the New Age*, pp. 93–97.

31. Ibid., pp. 104–105. See also Gerd Theissen, "Wanderradikalismus: Literatursoziologische Aspekte der Überlieferung von Worten Jesu im Urchristentum," *ZTK* 70 (1973): 245–71, ET in *Radical Religion* 2, nos. 2 and 3 (Berkeley, Calif., 1975): 84–93.

32. See "Study One: John the Baptist," in Willi Marxsen, *Mark the Evangelist* (Nashville, Tenn.: Abingdon, 1969), pp. 30–53.

33. Rudolf Bultmann, *The History of the Synoptic Tradition*, trans. J. Marsh, rev. ed. (New York: Harper & Row, 1963), pp. 39–41.

34. Ibid., pp. 41–50. See also the brief survey of this issue in T. Alec Burkill, "Anti-Semitism in St. Mark's Gospel," *NT* 3 (1959): 34–53, and the analysis of the formal structure of controversy dialogues in Arland J. Hultgren, *Jesus and His Adversaries* (Minneapolis, Minn.: Augsburg, 1979), pp. 52–59. Hultgren prefers the designation "conflict stories." Robert C. Tannehill, "Tension in Synoptic Sayings and Stories," *Interp* 34 (1980): 145–46, calls them "objection stories."

35. Bultmann's category is controversy dialogue occasioned by the conduct of Jesus or the disciples. *The History of the Synoptic Tradition*, pp. 16–21.

36. Ibid., p. 18.

37. As suggested by Joachim Jeremias, *The Parables of Jesus*, trans. S. H. Hooke, rev. ed. (New York: Charles Scribner's Sons, 1963), p. 52.

38. See also Matt. 6:16–18.

39. As shown by Hultgren, *Jesus and His Adversaries*, pp. 78–82.

40. Paul J. Achtemeier, *Mark*, Proclamation Commentaries, ed. G. Krodel (Philadelphia: Fortress, 1975), pp. 8–9.

41. Israel Abrahams, *Studies in Pharisaism and the Gospels*, I (Cambridge: Cambridge University, 1917), p. 129.

42. C. G. Montefiore, *The Synoptic Gospels*, 2d ed. (London: Macmillan, 1927), 1:63–65.

43. Sandmel, *Anti-Semitism in the New Testament?*, p. 28.

44. Eduard Schweizer, *The Good News According to Mark*, trans. D. H. Madvig (Atlanta, Ga.: John Knox, 1970), pp. 70–72.

45. Bultmann, *The History of the Synoptic Tradition*, p. 51. He has shown (pp. 52–54) that in most cases in the controversy dialogues, instances in which the scribes and the Pharisees are mentioned specifically are secondary ones. Pharisees and scribes, and to a lesser extent Sadducees and high priests, were conceived to be typical opponents of Jesus.

46. B. W. Bacon, "Pharisees and Herodians in Mark," *JBL* 39 (1920): 102–11. Hultgren, *Jesus and His Adversaries*, pp. 151–74, argues for the composition of 2:1b–2a, 3–12, 15–17, 18b–20, 23–28; 3:1–4, 5b–6 as a pre-Markan literary unit that interrupts the sequence of 1:45, 3:7–8. Hultgren places this composition in Galilee during the years ca. 40–44 C.E. as a response to criticism of followers of Jesus by Pharisees. It is unnecessary, however, to date this composition as early as ca. 40–44. Any date between 40 and the time of the writing of Mark would be possible.

47. See the discussion of the Beelzebul controversy on the level of the "Q" material in H. E. Tödt, *The Son of Man in the Synoptic Tradition* (London: SCM, 1965), p. 119, and on a level prior to "Q" in Hultgren, *Jesus and His Adversaries*, pp. 100–106.

48. For a carefully reasoned discussion of this question, see Raymond E. Brown, Karl P. Donfried, Joseph A. Fitzmyer, and John Reumann, *Mary in the New Testament* (Philadelphia: Fortress, and New York: Paulist, 1978), pp. 51–59.

49. Achtemeier, *Mark*, pp. 28–29.

50. Bultmann, *The History of the Synoptic Tradition*, pp. 17–18.

51. Because the argument in 7:6–8 is based on the Septuagint tradition of Isa. 29:13 and is in part a rephrasing of it rather than of the Hebrew Isa. 29:13 tradition, it is probable that this controversy dialogue was composed within a Hellenistic (Greek-speaking) environment. For a more detailed discussion of evidence for this development, see Hultgren, *Jesus and His Adversaries*, pp. 115–19.

52. The verses in Mark 7:6–8 are still being used in the reading of the Gospel recommended for the Fifteenth Sunday after Pentecost, Series B, which is Mark 7:1–8, 14–15, 21–23, in *Lutheran Book of Worship* (Minneapolis, Minn.: Augsburg, and Philadelphia: Board of Publication, Lutheran Church in America, 1978), p. 27. If we are serious about our Division of Theological Studies, Lutheran Council in the U.S.A., statement that

> Christians should make it clear that there is no biblical or theological basis for anti-Semitism. Supposed theological or biblical bases for anti-Semitism are to be examined and repudiated. (See p. 49 above.)

Mark 7:6–8 should be eliminated from this reading and 7:6–13 from the Daily Lectionary Year One, Week of 3 Epiphany, and Year Two, Week of 3 Lent in *Lutheran Book of Worship*, pp. 180, 188.

53. Bultmann, *The History of the Synoptic Tradition*, pp. 52–54.

54. Ibid., p. 131.

55. Schweizer, *The Good News According to Mark*, pp. 160–61.

56. Is it at all conceivable that the number of men within the extended Markan community in rural and small-town Syria and perhaps Galilee could have numbered 5,000 of Jewish background and 4,000 of Gentile background during the period 66–69 C.E.?

57. Since in 8:14, 16–21 there is concern among the disciples that they had forgotten to bring "loaves of bread" (*artous*), and except for "one loaf" (*hena arton*) they did not have any bread with them in the boat, is it possible that we can see in

this rather enigmatic pericope that at one time the members of the Markan community who were of Jewish background had been fed separately by Jesus from those among them who were of Gentile background, but that now Jesus was telling them that one loaf in the boat—"in the boat" meaning "in the Markan community," just as in Matthew "in the boat" has been shown to mean "in the Matthean church"—was all that was needed for all of them in table fellowship together? The words *artous ouk echousin* in 8:16 and *artous ouk echete* in 8:17 should not be translated as "they have no bread" and as "you have no bread," but as "they did not have several loaves of bread" and as "you do not have several loaves of bread." "No bread" in 8:16 and 8:17 fails to take into consideration the plural form of the noun in contrast to the singular form, "one loaf," in 8:14. Further, the translation "no bread" is nonsensical when it has just been stated that they had one loaf with them in the boat. Jesus tells his disciples in this account that when he is present with them in the boat one loaf of bread is sufficient. The important distinction between one loaf of bread and several loaves of bread is much more clearly seen when the extraneous anti-Jewish verse 15 is left out of consideration. See also Norman A. Beck, "Reclaiming a Biblical Text: The Mark 8:14–21 Discussion about Bread in the Boat," *CBQ* 43 (1981): 49–56.

58. Schweizer, *The Good News According to Mark*, p. 202.

59. Achtemeier, *Mark*, pp. 23–26.

60. Werner G. Kümmel, *Introduction to the New Testament*, trans. H. C. Kee, rev. ed. (Nashville, Tenn.: Abingdon, 1975), pp. 88–89.

61. This is the opinion of Bultmann, *The History of the Synoptic Tradition*, pp. 19–20.

62. Taylor, *The Gospel According to Mark*, pp. 468–69; Hultgren, *Jesus and His Adversaries*, pp. 68–75.

63. Schweizer, *The Good News According to Mark*, pp. 236–37. To have no answer is uncharacteristic of religious leadership anywhere that has an opportunity to respond. The leaders of first-century Jewish groups would certainly have been no exception in this respect. They simply were given no opportunity in this polemical account.

64. The Gospel of Thomas, saying 65, in *The Nag Hammadi Library* (San Francisco: Harper & Row, 1977), pp. 125–26.

65. See Jeremias, *The Parables of Jesus*, pp. 70–77.

66. Ibid., p. 76.

67. Predictably, *The Living Bible* provides anti-Jewish interpretative translation at its worst in 12:12a: "The Jewish leaders wanted to arrest him then and there for using this illustration, for they knew he was pointing at them—they were the wicked farmers in his story." *Good News for Modern Man* also unnecessarily identifies the unexpressed subject of the verbs in 12:12 as "The Jewish leaders."

68. Bultmann, *The History of the Synoptic Tradition*, p. 26, sees no reason for supposing that it is a product of the Christian community. In the Gospel of Thomas, logion 100, however, a parallel to Mark 12:13–17 and Matt. 22:15–22 occurs in what Hultgren, *Jesus and His Adversaries*, pp. 41–44, calls a "conflict-situation report, not a conflict story." Hultgren uses the Gospel of Thomas parallel as a control in his illustration of conflict story formation in the Synoptic tradition.

69. Schweizer, *The Good News According to Mark*, pp. 245–49.

70. Hultgren, *Jesus and His Adversaries*, pp. 123–31, suggests that the primary concerns of this pericope were the internal concerns of the Markan community (the remarriage of widows and the doctrine of the resurrection). In order to provide a framework for the teachings of the Markan Jesus, some question or challenge was needed. Since the disciples, the scribes, or the Pharisees would not be appropriate

candidates for this challenge, the Sadducees were selected as the most suitable opponents. Since the argument of Mark 12:26–27 is that the patriarchs are living immortals with God, it was probably written by a follower of Jesus whose thought was influenced by Hellenistic Jewish conceptions.

71. Bultmann, *The History of the Synoptic Tradition*, p. 51, calls it a pure scholastic dialogue *(Schulgespräch)* and notes that Matthew and Luke make a controversy dialogue *(Streitgespräch)* out of it. See also Hultgren, *Jesus and His Adversaries*, pp. 47–50, 186.

72. Schweizer, *The Good News According to Mark*, p. 253.

73. See the discussion of his pericope in Achtemeier, *Mark*, pp. 19–21.

74. The Hebrew text of Ps. 110:1 has *Yahweh* speaking to *Adoni* during the coronation ceremonies. *Yahweh* is the Lord, the God of Israel, for the psalmist; *Adoni* is the psalmist's political and cultic lord, the king and titular priest. The distinction in the Hebrew text between *Yahweh* and *Adoni* was lost in the Greek of the Septuagint and of Mark, where *Kyrios* was used for both.

75. This position reached a climax in the Epistle of Barnabas 12, in which the Davidic descent of the Messiah was denied.

76. Kee, *Community of the New Age*, p. 149.

77. For a summary of recent scholarly study of Mark 13, see Taylor, *The Gospel According to St. Mark*, pp. 498–500, 636–44, and Kee, *Community of the New Age*, pp. 43–45.

78. Kee, *Community of the New Age*, pp. 30–32. See also Achtemeier, *Mark*, p. 89, and the series of essays in Werner H. Kelber, ed., *The Passion in Mark; Studies on Mark 14–16* (Philadelphia: Fortress, 1976).

79. *Divine Principle* (Washington, D.C.: The Holy Spirit Association for the Unification of World Christianity, 1973), pp. 532–35. See also above, pp. 26–27.

80. Gerard S. Sloyan, *Jesus on Trial; The Development of the Passion Narratives and Their Historical and Ecumenical Implications* (Philadelphia: Fortress, 1973), pp. 63–64, 128. See also John Reumann, *Jesus in the Church's Gospels* (Philadelphia: Fortress, 1968), pp. 54–61.

81. A similar type of hyperbole may be present in certain accounts in the Hebrew Bible. For example, *kōl* "all" may be hyperbole in Exod. 8:17c, "all the dust of the earth became gnats throughout all the land of Egypt." The word *pantes* does not occur in the Matt. 26:57 parallel.

82. Solomon Zeitlin, *Who Crucified Jesus?* 5th ed. (New York: Bloch, 1964), pp. 76–83, 163–69.

83. For this, see Paul Winter, *On the Trial of Jesus*, Studia Judaica, vol. 1 (Berlin: de Gruyter, 1961), pp. 123–25, and "The Markan Account of Jesus' Trial by the Sanhedrin," *JTS*, n. s. 14 (1963): 94–102. Winter thinks also that *kai holon to synedrion* in 15:1 is probably Markan. *(On the Trial of Jesus, p. 25)*.

84. See Norman Perrin, "Mark 14:62: End Product of a Christian Pesher Tradition?" *NTS* 12 (1965–66): 150–55, and Sloyan, *Jesus on Trial*, pp. 48–62.

85. Assuming that the community and its writer ended the Gospel at 16:8.

86. Perhaps the text of verse 3 of Samuel Crossman's Lenten hymn, "My Song Is Love Unknown," should be reworded.

5

Anti-Jewish Polemic in "Q"

Before we begin our consideration of anti-Jewish polemic in Matthew and in Luke, it is necessary to examine such polemic in the conjectured written source thought to have been used together with early copies of Mark in the formation of Matthew and Luke. This examination of the hypothetical "Q"[1] is important for its own sake as well as to help us to see more clearly the nature of the anti-Jewish polemic in the redactional emendations of Mark and "Q" material and in new compositions by the writers of Matthew and of Luke.

Discussion will be limited to anti-Jewish polemic in texts that have close verbal agreement in Matthew and in Luke but are not present in Mark. Since studies of "Q" usually are based upon the sequence of texts in Luke, the Lukan sequence will be followed here with one exception.

Luke 3:7b–9; Matt. 3:7b–10: The *exhortation of John.* If "Q" material lies behind Luke 3:7a and Matt. 3:7a, it is probably retained more carefully in Luke rather than in Matthew, since Matt. 3:7a characteristically[2] specifies the Pharisees and Sadducees for condemnation. In Luke 3:7b–9 and in Matt. 3:7b–10 John exhorts in classic prophetic fashion. His censures become anti-Jewish only when they are used against Jews by non-Jews.

Luke 6:22–23; Matt. 5:11–12: *Thus they persecuted the prophets.* Verbal differences between these two accounts are considerable although the thoughts are similar. Most of the anti-Jewish polemic is centered in the references to persecutions of the prophets. Since we have seen earlier how much of the persecution of the prophets occurred while the Israelites were under the political domination of foreign powers, we can translate in Matt. 5:12 "for thus they persecuted others who were before you" and in Luke 6:23 "for thus others have done to religious zealots."

Luke 7:9; Matt. 8:10: *The faith of the centurion.* Nothing will be lost if we translate *en tō Israēl* as "among my own people," since this is clearly the intent if the setting of this saying is in the life of the historical Jesus. The point of the pericope is the strong approval given to the exemplary faith of the centurion, not the lack of faith of the Israelites. Matthew heightens the anti-Jewish effect by combining 8:10 with another "Q" saying (8:11–12; Luke 13:28–29) regarding who will recline at the table with Abraham, Isaac, and Jacob in the kingdom, texts to which we now turn.

Luke 13:28–29; Matt. 8:11–12: *Those who will recline at the table with the patriarchs in the kingdom.* If this saying was included in a hypothetical "Q" document, we cannot determine in what context. The Luke 13:28–30 arrangement suggests that it may have been part of a collection of sayings about the ones who are last now being first then and the ones who are first now being last then. The attachment to Luke 13:22–27 implies teaching and admonition of persons who have been eating and drinking with Jesus and traveling with him while continuing to be "workers of iniquity." The saying is typical of a Jewish eschatological prophet; unless you repent your places will be taken by others. In our usage we are much more likely to apply the prophetic message to ourselves if we utilize Luke 13:28–29 rather than Matt. 8:11–12, since in the latter, as noted above, this saying is combined with another in a way that heightens the anti-Jewish effect.

Luke 7:31–35; Matt. 11:16–19: *This generation is like children at play.* Apart from the infancy narratives and Mark 13 and its parallels, *genea* (generation) is always used pejoratively in the Synoptic traditions. The majority of these instances are in what is thought to be "Q" material (Luke 7:31; 11:29, 30, 31, 32, 50, 51; 17:25; Matt. 11:16; 12:39, 41, 42, 45; 23:36). Within a *Sitz im Leben* of the Jesus of history it would have been internal criticism to condemn "this generation" as petulant, evil, adulterous, and unrepentant. However, as Christian religious communities were formed, this criticism became external criticism of Jews. Apparently in the texts in question here, the "Q" community was castigating Jews who would not join into "play" with either their own group, which would "dance," or the followers of John the Baptist, who would "weep." Although the text may have been relevant during the time of the "Q" community, its value was probably already declining by the time it was incorporated into the Matthean and the Lukan accounts.

Luke 10:12–15; Matt. 11:20–24: *Judgment of Chorazin, Bethsaida, and Capernaum.* The people of these Jewish cities in Galilee are condemned while the non-Jews from Tyre and Sidon, cities which had been considered to have been notoriously dissolute in the prophetic traditions (Isa. 23; Ezek. 26–28; Joel 3:4–8), are said to be less susceptible to divine judgment, for if God's mighty works had been done among them they would have repented long ago. These geographical designations[3] could indicate that members of the "Q" community had fled from the Chorazin, Bethsaida, and Capernaum region to escape the anticipated wrath of God and were now living in the western portions of the Province of Syria near Tyre and Sidon. This might be construed as evidence that this text—or all of "Q"—was written or modified during the Jewish revolt of 66–69, perhaps contemporaneously with Mark but in the western rather than the southern portions of the Province of Syria.

Luke 10:21b; Matt. 11:25b–26: *Prayer of thanks to the Father for eschatological wisdom.* Luke 10:22; Matt. 11:27: *Esoteric knowledge of the Son and of the Father.* In the broad sense, both sayings have wisdom themes. Both sayings also express anti-Jewish polemic. The first saying addresses the Father directly in prayer form. Its polemic is against those who are usually considered to be wise and understanding; "these things" are hidden from them. The second saying speaks about the Father only in the third person. It exhibits many of the peculiarities of Fourth Gospel language and probably was developed separately from the first saying. In its polemic esoteric knowledge available only through the Son is acclaimed. The Son does not choose to reveal knowledge of the Father to everyone. Although the nature of this privileged knowledge is not expressed, we can infer[4] that it concerns God's eschatological purpose being achieved through Jesus, the prophet-Son of God. Since knowledge of God is accessible only through Jesus in this "Q" form of "proto-Gnostic"[5] one-wayism, Jews who reject Jesus as the one way are excluded. In Luke 10:23b and Matt. 13:16–17, behind which there may have been a "Q" saying, many prophets and leading men of the past wished to see and hear this eschatological knowledge but were denied it.

Luke 11:19–20, 23; Matt. 12:27–28, 30: *Exorcism by the power of God.* Since Jesus performed exorcisms by the power of God, the kingdom of God has arrived. Whoever is not with Jesus in the exercise of this power of God is against God. At the Jesus-of-history level, this discussion is an intramural matter; at the level of a "Q" community, which over against Jewish opponents claims possession of the one way to the Father, it becomes extramural and anti-Jewish. Because Mark 9:40 and Luke 9:50 present a quite different viewpoint, which is probably much closer to that of the Jesus of history, the opinion of the "Q" community as preserved in Luke 11:23 and Matt. 12:30 should not be emphasized in our usage of these texts.

Luke 11:31; Matt. 12:42: *The queen of the south as judge over the men of this generation.* If the queen of the south (1 Kings 10:1–13; 2 Chron. 9:1–12) came from the ends of the earth to hear the wisdom of Solomon, and if the men of this generation (Jews castigated because they will not "play" with the members of the "Q" community)[6] will not come even the short distance required to hear the wisdom of Jesus, the queen of the south will condemn them in the judgment. To put it more bluntly, a prudent non-Jewish woman will judge Jewish men! This interesting illustration is still appropriate today, but only if we can use it without defaming the Jews. "This generation" should be reapplied to each new generation. It should constantly be made contemporary. In our translations and usage it should be disengaged from the "generation" accused in the Gospel accounts of being the implacable enemy of Jesus. This could be accomplished by an interpretative translation such the "The queen of the south will rise up in the judgment and condemn all who do not repent now" in Luke 11:31; Matt. 12:42.

Luke 11:32; Matt 12:41: *The men of Nineveh condemning this generation.* The message that if they repent and change their actions and attitudes, even brutal aggressors such as the ancient men of Nineveh will at the judgment be in a more advantageous position than self-righteous people of the present generation is appropriate and timely if, as indicated in the paragraph above, condemnation is disengaged from the "generation" accused in the Gospel accounts of being the implacable enemy of Jesus. An interpretative translation "The men of Nineveh will rise up in the judgment and condemn all who do not repent now" in Luke 11:32 and Matt. 12:41 would serve the dual purpose of keeping the application of the message contemporary and reducing the anti-Jewish polemic.

(Luke 11:39–54; Matt. 23:1–36: *Blanket condemnation of Pharisees and Torah scholars in Luke and of scribes and Pharisees in Matthew.* Since the discussion in this chapter will be limited to anti-Jewish material in texts that have close verbal agreement in Matthew and Luke but are not present in Mark, these extensive blocks of anti-Jewish polemic will not be considered here. Because not only in sequence of arrangement but, more important, in vocabulary there are so many differences between these two texts, they will be discussed separately in the Matthew and Luke chapters that follow. If "Q" material lies behind these extensive blocks of material, perhaps it is nearest to the surface in Luke 11:49–51 in the references to the "Wisdom of God" making requirements of "this generation.")

Luke 12:54–56; Matt. 16:2–3: *You can predict the weather but not the signs of the times.* This text, which in its basic form is a wisdom saying appropriate in many circumstances, is not inherently anti-Jewish until it is given an anti-Pharisees and anti-Sadducees setting by Matt. 16:1 and given in addition the vocative epithet "Hypocrites!" in Luke 12:56 and late textual traditions in Matt. 16:3.

Luke 13:34–35; Matt. 23:37–39: *The lament over Jerusalem.* It is likely that the speaker here, as in Luke 11:49, was at one time the "Wisdom of God," a suprahistorical hypostasis. After the divine Wisdom calls in vain for men to follow her, she leaves and will not return until the Messiah comes.[7] The early church, and probably the "Q" community, gradually see in Jesus the same qualities that had earlier been attributed to the "Wisdom of God." The association was particularly appropriate to the "Q" community with its interest in motifs which Richard Edwards had identified as (a) eschatological hope, (b) wisdom teaching about the present, and (c) either a reference to the prophets as models and examples or the use of prophetic-messenger forms of speech.[8] In this text the "Q" community used these wisdom and prophetic forms and images in presenting its case against Jews who would not unite with it.[9] Once the association with Jesus had been made, Matthew placed the pericope in a Jerusalem setting after the entry of Jesus into the city and made 23:39 into a prophecy that the inhabitants of Jerusalem would not see Jesus again until they will say, "Blessed is the one who comes in the name of the Lord," presumably in acknowledgment of Jesus' sovereignty. Luke placed the text prior to the entry of Jesus into Jerusalem and made it into a prediction that Jesus would not perish until he entered Jerusalem, but that once there he would surely die at the hands of those whom he would have loved to have gathered together as a hen gathers her chicks under her wings to protect them. The inhabitants of the city would have to wait until he finally got there and then they would say, "Blessed is the one who comes in the name of the Lord." In any case, once the association of the Wisdom hypostasis with Jesus had been made, the lament became virulently anti-Jewish. Jerusalem was accused of continuously killing the prophets[10] and stoning the ones sent to her. The quotation based upon Jer. 22:5; 12:7 became external condemnation, and Ps. 118:26 was given a variety of new messianic possibilities.[11]

Because the text as it stands is viciously anti-Jewish, other pericopes should be used instead of this to demonstrate the love that the historical Jesus had for his fellow Jews. If the text is used,[12] a thorough redaction in which little more than the hen and chicks analogy is retained would make the text once more applicable to us in our time. This would take us back in the direction of what was probably the original significance of the saying.

(Luke 14:16–24; Matt. 22:1–10: *The parable of the great supper.* Although there is almost certainly anti-Jewish polemic in the anger of the host against those who had initially been invited to the great supper, and although the parable occurs in Luke and Matthew, and in the Gospel of Thomas, saying 64, but not in Mark, verbal differences between the accounts in Luke and in Matthew are so numerous that the texts will be discussed separately in the Matthew and Luke chapters rather than at this place.)

(Luke 16:16–17; Matt. 11:12–13; 5:18: *The Torah and the prophets before and after the time of John.* Anti-Jewish polemic in Luke 16:16 and Matt. 11:12–13 regarding violence accompanying the proclamation of the kingdom since the time of John is countered somewhat by the statement that as long as heaven and earth remain no portion of the Torah and the prophets will become void. Close verbal agreement and a unified pattern of presentation are lacking in these accounts. It is feasible that these and similarly disparate texts that have often been assigned to "Q" were derived instead from a variety of oral traditions or from more than one "Q" document.)[13]

Luke 22:30b; Matt. 19:28d: *Followers of Jesus judging the twelve tribes of Israel.* The anti-Jewish polemic is apparent in the brief portion of these sayings in which there is significant verbal agreement. Although it is unlikely that the historical Jesus assigned judgmental responsibility over the "twelve tribes" of Israel to his followers, the early Christians, possibly the "Q" community, obviously claimed dominical authority for this privilege.

We would almost without a doubt come closer to the earliest form of the expression if we rendered these verses as "and share with me in that kingdom" in Luke 22:30b and "you will sit with the Son of man in the kingdom" in Matt. 19:28d.

Conclusions regarding Anti-Jewish Polemic in "Q"

If there was a "Q" that was used by the writers of Matthew and of Luke along with early forms of Mark, there can be little doubt that considerable anti-Jewish polemic was present in it. Particularly conspicuous are the following: (a) the exclusive one-wayism evidenced in Luke 10:21b–22; Matt. 11:21–23a; and in Luke 11:23; Matt. 12:30; (b) the condemnation of Chorazin, Bethsaida, and Capernaum in Luke 10:13–15; Matt. 11:21–23a; and (c) various expressions of the rejection of the Jews and their displacement by others. We must conclude that, proportionately, "Q" was at least equally as anti-Jewish as is Mark.

Assuming that early forms of Mark and copies of "Q" material were accessible to those who wrote Matthew and Luke, anti-Jewish polemic in Mark's controversy dialogues and in the pronouncements and parables of "Q" material provided a considerably broad basis upon which additional expressions of anti-Jewish bias could be built.

Notes

1. For select bibliographies of the study of "Q" see Richard A. Edwards, *A Theology of Q: Eschatology, Prophecy, and Wisdom* (Philadelphia: Fortress, 1976), pp. 159–64, and Howard C. Kee, *Jesus in History: An Approach to the Study of the Gospels*, 2d ed. (New York: Harcourt Brace Jovanovich, 1977), pp. 119–20. For an example of a questioning whether there ever was a Q, see M. D. Goulder, "On Putting Q to the Test," and "Mark XVI. 1–8 and Parallels," *NTS* 24 (1977–78): 218–40.

2. Sjef van Tilborg, *The Jewish Leaders in Matthew* (Leiden: E. J. Brill, 1972), p. 29.

3. For geographical considerations see Edwards, *A Theology of Q*, p. 105. According to John 1:44 Peter, Andrew, and Philip were from Bethsaida. Mark 1:21–31 locates the home of Simon (Peter) and Andrew, and the parallel Luke 4:31–39 Simon alone, in Capernaum. In texts in which there is close verbal agreement between Matthew and Luke but which are not present in Mark, none of the disciples of Jesus is specified by name.

4. Kee, *Jesus in History*, pp. 105–6.

5. M. J. Suggs, *Wisdom, Christology and Law in Matthew* (Cambridge, Mass.: Harvard University Press, 1970), pp. 85–95. See the discussion of the possible "gnosticizing proclivity" of "Q" in James D. G. Dunn, *Unity and Diversity in the New Testament* (Philadelphia: Westminster, 1977), pp. 283–88.

6. See the discussion above of Luke 7:31–35 and Matt. 11:16–19.

7. Rudolf Bultmann, *The History of the Synoptic Tradition*, trans. J. Marsh, rev. ed. (New York: Harper & Row, 1963), pp. 114–15.

8. Edwards, *A Theology of Q*, p. 84.

9. Ibid., p. 133.

10. See above, pp. 67–68.

11. See Barnabas Lindars, *New Testament Apologetic* (London: SCM Press, 1961), pp. 171–73.

12. In the *Lutheran Book of Worship* (Minneapolis, Minn.: Augsburg, and Philadelphia: Board of Publication, Lutheran Church in America, 1978), pp. 18, 30–31, Luke 13:31–35 is the Gospel for the Second Sunday in Lent, Series C, and Matt. 23:34–39 for December 26 (St. Stephen, Deacon and Martyr). Among the denominations using this series, only the Lutheran lectionary uses Luke 13:31–35 for the Second Sunday in Lent, Series C. For December 26 the Lutheran and the Episcopal reading is Matt. 23:34–39; the Roman Catholic reading is Matt. 10:17–22.

13. For an example of an argument that what we call "Q" was not one but several documents, see W. F. Albright and C. S. Mann, *Matthew,* The Anchor Bible, vol. 26 (Garden City, N.Y.: Doubleday, 1971), pp. 49–53.

6

Anti-Jewish Polemic in Matthew

Having considered anti-Jewish polemic in Mark and in "Q" in some detail, we now move into a study of similar polemic in Matthew. We shall begin with the polemic in redactional emendations in Matthew's use of Markan material. Next I shall engage in the more difficult task of identifying such polemic in Matthew's use of "Q" material. This will be followed by an analysis of anti-Jewish polemic in Matthew's use of other written or oral sources and in Matthew's own compositions. Finally, in summary fashion I shall evaluate anti-Jewish polemic in the total Gospel According to Matthew. In the analysis of specific texts my task will continue to be not only to recognize anti-Jewish polemic and to try to determine how it developed but also to suggest ways by which we can repudiate it.[1]

A. In Matthew's Use of Markan Material

Mark 1:22c; Matt. 7:29b: *Not as their scribes.* Matthew increases the anti-Jewish polemic by adding the qualifying "their" ("of them") to Mark's "not as the scribes." In our translations and usage we can ignore the qualifying descriptive pronoun on the grounds that it reflects a Matthean bias. Actually, it would be preferable to pass quietly over Mark 1:22c and Matt. 7:29c in our translations and usage, since the negative-comparison phrase is not necessary to enhance the authority of Jesus.

Mark 1:32–34; Matt. 8:16–17: *An evening of healings and exorcisms.* Where Mark has the people bring *all* who are ill and demon possessed and he healed *many* and cast out *many* demons, Matthew heightens the supernatural power of Jesus by having the people bring *many* and he healed *all*. The anti-Jewish polemic surfaces in the somewhat forced quotation of Isa. 53:4 in Matt. 8:17, in which Jesus is identified as the suffering servant who took our infirmities and himself bore our diseases. Since in Isa. 49:3 the suffering servant had been identified, probably in a gloss, as Israel,[2] Jesus is now said to replace and to supersede Israel. This is one among many instances in which Matthew, in showing how activities associated with Jesus fulfilled the Jewish Scriptures, quotes from the Jewish Scriptures with little regard for the meaning that the passage quoted had in its former context.

Mark 1:39; Matt. 4:23: *Teaching and preaching in their synagogues.* Matthew adds descriptive details to Mark's summary, but the synagogues are already designated as "their" synagogues in Mark 1:39. It is possible that the word "their" ("of them") came into Mark 1:39 from Matt. 4:23 during the early textual transmission of Mark.

Mark 2:8; Matt. 9:4: *The controversy with the scribes over the healing of the paralyzed man.* The anti-Jewish polemic already present in Mark's controversy with the scribes is heightened in Matt. 9:4, where instead of having Jesus ask the scribes, as in Mark 2:8 followed by Luke 5:22, "Why do you *reason this way* in your hearts?" here Jesus is said to ask, "Why do you *think evil* in your hearts?" In sensitive translation and use of these texts we shall be aware of Matthew's increased anti-Jewish polemic in our translation of Matt. 9:4 and shall prefer the Markan and Lukan readings in our usage. If the Matt. 9:1–8 pericope is to be used, it would be desirable, as in Mark, to limit the reading to the miracle story itself (9:1–2, 6b–8), passing over the controversy, which here and in Luke 5:21–24a remains secondary to the miracle story.[3]

Mark 2:13–17; Matt. 9:9–13: *Eating with tax collectors and sinners.* "The scribes of the Pharisees" of Mark 2:16 become "the Pharisees" in Matt. 9:11. This brings the Pharisees as the principal opponents of the Matthean church directly rather than indirectly into dialogue with Jesus' disciples. The anti-Jewish polemic is increased still further in the Luke 5:30 parallel, in which the Pharisees and their scribes were murmuring against Jesus' disciples saying, "Why do *you* eat. . . ?"[4]

Mark 2:18–20; Matt. 9:14–15: *Fasting.* In a manner similar to that in the texts under consideration above, "the disciples of the Pharisees" of Mark 2:18 have become "the Pharisees" in Matt. 9:14. The insertion "and the Pharisees" earlier in Mark 2:18 does not occur in Matt. 9:14, possibly because this insertion was not present in the early form of Mark used during the composition of Matthew.

Mark 2:23–28; Matt. 12:1–8. *The Sabbath walk through the grainfields at harvest time.* As indicated in chapter 4 above,[5] the parallels of Mark 2:23–28 in Matt. 12:1–8 and Luke 6:1–5 intensify the anti-Jewish polemic by not including the Mark 2:27 core saying, which is not anti-Jewish, and by adding the supposition that the disciples were hungry and ate (Matt. 12:1) and that they ate (Luke 6:1–5). In addition, Matthew greatly increases the anti-Jewish polemic by adding the 12:5 reference to the Torah (Num. 28:9–10) as proof that the priests in the temple are not considered to be guilty of profaning the Sabbath when they officiate over burnt offerings on the Sabbath and by claiming in Matt. 12:6 that something greater than the temple is here. Matt. 12:7 piles insult upon injury by accusing the Pharisees (who were a particularly inappropriate Jewish group to accuse of this) of not knowing the meaning of Hos. 6:6, "I want mercy and not sacrifice of animals and of other agricultural products." As in many other instances in Matthew, the Jewish Scriptures are used as proof that Jesus and Jesus' interpretation of the Jewish Scriptures are superior to the Pharisees and their understanding of the Jewish texts. Thus much, perhaps most, of Matthew's increased interest in the Jewish Scriptures compared to Mark's is for polemical and apologetical purposes.[6]

It is appropriate for us to use the Markan text rather than its parallels, even though Mark 2:26 cites Abiathar as high priest rather than his father Ahimelech at the time when David ate the consecrated bread. Actually, the only portion of Mark 2:23–28 and its Matt. 12:1–8 and Luke 6:1–5 parallels that is particularly valuable for our understanding of the theology of the Jesus of history is Mark 2:27, which is not included in the Matthean and Lukan redactions.

Mark 3:1–6; Matt. 12:9–14: *The Sabbath healing of the man with the withered hand.* In Matthew's redaction "the synagogue" of Mark 3:1 has become "their synagogue" in Matt. 12:9. Where in Mark 3:2 they were watching him to see whether he would heal the man on the Sabbath, in Matt. 12:10 they questioned him whether it is lawful to heal on the Sabbath in order that they might accuse him. By putting the legality question into the mouths of the Pharisees, Matthew was able to depict the Pharisees in a more aggressive role and to introduce a non-Markan ("Q" type?) logion of Jesus into the account. Mark 3:5a is not included, perhaps because of a reluctance to depict Jesus as showing anger, and the Herodians' complicity with the Pharisees portrayed in Mark 3:6 does not occur in Matt. 12:14. The result is an account in Matthew that differs in its anti-Jewish polemic from that in Mark because Matthew's situation and Matthew's purposes are different from those of Mark.

Mark 6:7; 3:13–19a; 6:8–11; Matt. 10:1–16: *The calling and commissioning of the twelve.* If the Matthean account is following a form of Mark here, it has used a different form of Mark or has rearranged its source freely. At any rate, there are redactional emendations and new compositions that magnify whatever anti-Jewish polemic was already present in Mark regarding the twelve as founders of the "new Israel." That the twelve were given the responsibility of beginning the church only within Israel is clear from the additions to Mark's accounts in Matt. 10:5–8, 15–16. The twelve are sent to the "lost sheep of the house of Israel" (10:6). They are sent as sheep in the midst of "wolves" (10:16). It shall be more tolerable in the day of judgment for the land of Sodom and Gomorrah than for that city which rejects them (10:15). It is the opinion of the writer(s) of the Matthean account that all segments of Israel that reject the representatives of Jesus are doomed.

Mark 3:22–30; Matt. 9:32–34; 12:22–26: *The dispute about exorcism.*[7] In both Matthean accounts in which Jesus is accused of performing exorcisms in the name of the prince of demons (Matt. 9:34; 12:24) it is the Pharisees rather than Mark's "the scribes who came down from Jerusalem" who make the charges. The crowds were astonished, amazed, and pleased, but the Pharisees accused Jesus of being in league with Beelzebul. Here, as in many similar instances, in Matthew's accounts the anti-Jewish polemic is focused on the Pharisees.

Mark 4:10–12; Matt. 13:10–17: *A reason for parabolic speech.* Matthew elaborates on Mark's explanation by quoting a lengthier section of Isa. 6:9–10 and consequently adding greater judgment against the Jewish people.

Mark 5:21–43; Matt. 9:18–26: *The restoration of life to Jairus's daughter.* If Matt. 9:18–26 is a redaction of Mark 5:21–43—which seems likely since all three Synoptic accounts follow the same sequence through a complicated series of events[8]—Matthew's redaction has eliminated much Markan detail in shortening the account. It is possible, of course, that Markan detail was added later to Mark or was not present in the form of Mark that the writer(s) of Matthew used. Possibly a reason that Matthew did not add to the anti-Jewish polemic in this account is that it is not overtly a controversy dialogue, but a miracle story in which, however, the superiority of Jesus' power to that of the synagogue is demonstrated.[9] In Matt. 9:18, 23 the father of the little girl who had died is not identified by name. Since he is described merely as a certain ruler, not as one of the synagogue leaders, this Matthean redaction could be considered an instance in which a less overt form of anti-Jewish polemic was actually reduced from Mark to Matthew. We may conclude, therefore, that this reduction of polemic occurred or that numerous details present in the Markan manuscripts available to us were not present in the copies used in the Matthean redaction.

Mark 6:1–6a; Matt. 13:53–58: *Unbelief in Jesus' hometown synagogue.* In Matthew's redaction "he began to teach in *the* synagogue" became "he began to teach (inceptive use of the Greek imperfect) *them* in *their* synagogue," an indication of the separation of Matthew's community from identity with the Jewish synagogue as an institution. Mark's limitation that "*many* (but presumably not all) as they listened were astonished" was dropped and "*they* (presumably every one of them) were astonished." Later, in Matt. 13:57, Mark's "and among his own relatives" was deleted in this Gospel, which has incorporated a virgin birth narrative. Finally, the Markan limitation that "he *was not able to do* any mighty act there except that by placing his hands upon a few sick people he healed them, and that he marvelled because of their unbelief," was removed in favor of what may have been intended to be the more magisterial "he *did not do* many mighty acts there because of their unbelief." The cumulative result is a moderate increase in anti-Jewish polemic.

Mark 6:6b; Matt. 9:35: *Teaching in their synagogues.* If Matthew is dependent upon Mark here, the teaching of Jesus is placed by Matthew in "their" synagogues. Since Matthew's bias against Jewish religious expressions is apparent in numerous instances of Matthean use of Markan material, in our translation and usage of Matt. 9:35 we can simply say "teaching in *the* synagogues."

Mark 7:1–23; Matt. 15:1–11, 15–20: *The dispute about "clean" and "unclean."*[10] The Mark 7:2–4 explanations regarding ritual cleanliness traditions of the Pharisees and of all the Jews were not included in Matt. 15:1 either because it was felt that Matthew's audience was already well acquainted with these Jewish practices or because these explanatory details were not present in the form of Mark used in the Matthean redaction. They could have been added to Mark manuscripts in the decades following the major composition. The sequence of material is somewhat different in Matthew's account, but the most significant evidence of increased anti-Jewish polemic in Matthew's account lies not in the redactional emendations but in the addition of Matt. 15:12–14. In this addition 15:14b is probably based on a "Q" saying (compare with Luke 6:39) and 15:12–14a is probably Matthean composition similar to 23:13, 15–36.

In our use of this account today, the 15:3–9, 12–14 portions, which elaborate most bitterly the late first-century conflict between the Matthean church and the Pharisees, are of little value for edification unless they are redacted or explained in such a way that they become valid self-criticism for us. The portions that have the most enduring value (15:10–11, 15–20a) should receive the greatest emphasis. If antagonisms between Christian communities and groups of Pharisees contributed significantly to the formation of the polemic in 15:3–9, 12–14, it is likely that the 15:10–11, 15–20a portions of this account most clearly reflect the thought of the Jesus of history.

Mark 7:24–30; Matt. 15:21–28: *The persistence of the Syrophoenician woman.* In the Matthean redaction Jesus is addressed as "son of David," a christological title not included in Mark 7:24–30. In Jesus' response to his disciples, Jesus appears to agree with them that the woman should be sent away since he is quoted as having said, "I was not sent except to the lost sheep of the house of Israel." This saying may be considered to be both positive and negative with regard to the Jews. It is positive in that Jesus is identified closely with Israel, but negative in that Israel is composed of "lost sheep." When these factors are balanced, the Matthean redaction appears to exhibit an anti-Jewish tendency. The placement in Mark of this account within a series of texts in 6:30–8:21 in which teachings regarding the "breaking of bread" are the dominant theological interest indicates that during the Markan stage of the tradition of the persistence of the Syrophoenician woman the purpose of the account was to demonstrate who was to be permitted to share in the "breaking of bread" rather than to preserve a documentary record of Jesus' cultural and religious bias against Syrophoenician women.

Mark 8:11–12; Matt. 12:38–39; 16:1, 4: *This generation seeks a sign.* The sign-seeking texts provide a fascinating case study of the interrelationships among Mark as it developed, "Q" material, usage of Mark and of "Q" material in Matthew and in Luke, and the quite different line of development in the Johannine traditions. We may assume that early oral tradition carried the reminiscence that during Jesus' public appearances he was asked somewhat as we have it in John 6:30, "What sign do you do that we may see and believe you?" The Johannine traditions developed a positive response to that question, possibly in an early written "signs source," certainly later in an extensive Gospel of "signs." The traditions that were to produce "Q" and Mark, and later following them, Matthew and Luke, developed instead a negative response to the same question, so that the Synoptics became Gospels of "no signs."

It is probable that in the conjectured "Q" the request for a sign was made by persons unnamed, as in Luke 11:16.[11] Mark 8:11 and Matt. 12:38 indicate the tendency in Mark and Matthew to designate the adversaries of Jesus as scribes and Pharisees. In Matt. 16:1 it is said that the Pharisees and Sadducees came. Among the four similar accounts (Mark 8:11; Matt. 12:38; 16:1; Luke 11:16) the one with the least anti-Jewish polemic is Matt. 12:38, for it alone lacks the circumstantial participle *peirazontes*, "testing," (in a bad sense), and only in it is Jesus addressed respectfully. The pejorative testing of Jesus may have come into the tradition in "Q" material. In early forms of Mark it may have been lacking until someone introduced it at the end of the Mark 8:11 sentence in the early process of making minor additions to Mark to harmonize it with Matthew and Luke.

The designation "this generation" of Mark 8:12 becomes "this generation is an evil generation" in Luke 11:29 and "an evil and adulterous generation" in Matt. 12:39 and 16:4. The exception to the "no signs" Synoptic tradition that no sign shall be given to this generation "except the sign of Jonah" may have come from "Q" material, or may have developed in oral tradition after Mark had been written. From oral tradition it would have been taken into both Matthew and Luke or into one of them and then in the later harmonizing process been added to the other.

The utility of the sign-seeking texts for us today in worship and proclamation situations is limited because of the opposite directions in which the traditions in the Synoptics over against the Fourth Gospel developed and because of the anti-Jewish polemic in nearly every segment of these texts. Matt. 12:38–39, with the least amount of anti-Jewish polemic, is the text with comparatively the most utility in the church of our time. All of the sign-seeking texts are valuable, however, for academic purposes as we attempt to trace the history of the development of these traditions.

Mark 8:14–21; Matt. 16:5–12: *Beware of the leaven.* In the Matthean redaction the point in the Markan text that one loaf in the boat was all that was needed both for the followers of Jesus who were from Jewish backgrounds and for the followers of Jesus who were from Gentile backgrounds[12] was lost, as Matthew's omission of the Mark 8:14 words "and except for one loaf they did not have any bread with them in the boat" indicates. Consequently, the early insertion of the Mark 8:15 logion into Mark 8:14–21 because there seemed to someone to be a logical connection between yeast and bread resulted in a Matt. 16:5–12 parallel account in which the saying "Beware of the yeast of the Pharisees and Sadducees" became the principal point. The end result is that a Mark 8:14, 16–21 text which emphasizes table fellowship with Jesus in the "breaking of bread" of one loaf for both Jewish-background and non-Jewish-background followers became a Matt. 16:5–12 text in which anti-Jewish polemic is predominant.

Our translations of Matt. 16:5–12 would be improved if we placed 16:6, 11–12 in a footnote, noting that apparently like Mark 8:15 these verses were inserted at some time into this account. Mark 8:14, 16–21 then becomes clearly the earlier and the preferred reading of the two, with its emphasis upon "one loaf" breaking of bread for followers of Jesus from both Jewish and Gentile backgrounds.

Mark 9:14–29; Matt. 17:14–20: *The exorcism after the transfiguration.* Among the details deleted in the Matthean redaction of the Markan account—or not included in the form of Mark used in the Matthean and Lukan redactions—was the note in Mark 9:14 that they saw scribes contending against the disciples. In Matt. 17:17 and in Luke 9:41 the epithet "perverted" is added to "O faithless generation," but in the context of the saying and especially because of Matt. 17:19–20 it is apparent that the disciples of Jesus rather than other Jewish groups are being chided. All things considered, Matt. 17:14–20 is no more anti-Jewish than is Mark 9:14–29.

Mark 10:1–12; Matt. 19:1–12: *The Pharisees and divorce.* Apart from rearrangement of materials there is little difference between these two accounts. Perhaps with the rearrangement the Pharisees are presented even less favorably in Matt. 19:1–12 than in Mark 10:1–12. Since "testing him," or "trying to cause him to fail," is written at the end of the sentence in Mark 10:2 as in Mark 8:11, it is conceivable that this clause also was part of an early process of minor additions to Mark to harmonize it with Matthew, and in some other cases with Luke as well.

As in Mark 10:1–12,[13] here also in Matt. 19:1–12 the controversy dialogue should be treated as secondary in our proclamation and teaching. We can here also translate "Pharisees" in 19:3 as "some religious leaders" and express the text of 19:8 as "Because of human intransigence Moses allowed our ancestors and permits you to divorce, but from the beginning it was not this way."

Mark 10:17–31; Matt. 19:16–28a, 29–30:[14] *The rich young man seeking eternal life.* The changes in the Matthean redaction result in an account that lacks the warmth of Mark 10:17–31, but the anti-Jewish polemic is not notably increased. Mark 10:17b, "Good teacher, what shall I do to inherit eternal life?" becomes in Matt. 19:17a, "Teacher, what good thing shall I do in order that I may have eternal life?" More significantly, in Matthew's redaction of Mark 10:21a "and Jesus, having looked at him closely, loved him" is eliminated. The same tendency toward detachment in the Matthean redaction is apparent in Jesus' relationship with his disciples later in the account, where the vocative "children" is dropped from Jesus' words of Mark 10:24b.

Mark 8:31; (9:12); 9:31; 10:33–34; Matt. 16:21; 17:22b–23; 20:18–19: *The passion predictions.* None of the minor changes in the three passion predictions results in a heightening of anti-Jewish polemic from Mark to Matthew. The nonuse of the words "and how it is written about the Son of man that he should suffer many things and be treated contemptuously" of Mark 9:12—either as emendation deletion or because these words were not present in the form of Mark used by Matthew—gives us actually less anti-Jewish polemic in Matthew than in Mark as far as the passion predictions are concerned.

Mark 11:12–25; Matt. 21:12–22: *The fig tree and the temple.* There are two significant differences between Mark and Matthew regarding these two accounts. The first is that Mark's "sandwich" method of bracketing the account of the cleansing of the temple by the story of Jesus' cursing the fig tree to show an interrelationship between these two accounts is not followed in Matthew. Instead, Matthew has separate but adjoining accounts of the cleansing of the temple and the cursing of the fig tree. Any loss of anti-Jewish polemic as a result of the separation of the two incidents is probably balanced by Matthew's judgment from a post-70 C.E. point of view that the fig tree that Jesus cursed was withered immediately.

The other difference is that Matt. 21:14–16 has replaced Mark 11:18. In Mark 11:18 the chief priests and the scribes heard Jesus' teachings and were seeking how they might destroy him, for they were afraid of him because all of the people were astonished at his teaching. In Matt. 21:14–16 the chief priests and the scribes were indignant when they saw Jesus performing miracles in the temple and not rebuking the children who were crying out and saying, "Hosanna to the son of David!" The change also makes it convenient to have Jesus add a quotation from the Septuagint version of Ps. 8:2 (8:3 in the Septuagint). When indignation over miracles performed in the temple and over children's acclamations (Matthew) is weighed against murder plots by the religious leaders who were said to have been afraid of Jesus because of his popularity (Mark), Matthew's text here appears to be somewhat less anti-Jewish than Mark's.

Mark 11:27–33; Matt. 21:23–27: *The question of authority.*[15] Except for stylistic changes and the absence of "and the scribes" in Matt. 21:23 where it is present in Mark 11:27, there are no substantive differences between these two accounts. Anti-Jewish polemic is not increased.

Mark 12:1–12; Matt. 21:33–46: *The story about an owner of a vineyard collecting his rent.* In this redaction the anti-Jewish polemic is increased.[16] The chief priests and the Pharisees are specified as the ones who were seeking to arrest Jesus (Matt. 21:45). It is added that "the kingdom of God will be taken away from *you* and given to a nation producing the fruits of it" (Matt. 21:43). Jesus' hearers, particularly the chief priests and the Pharisees, are induced to label themselves as "such evil men" whom the owner of the vineyard "will destroy in a terrible way" (Matt. 21:41), a *post eventu* 70 C.E. addition. The allegory of Jesus as the vineyard owner's son who was killed by the defiant renters is strengthened by changing "they killed him and threw him out of the vineyard" of Mark 12:8 to "they threw him out of the vineyard and killed him" in Matt. 21:39.

As with Mark 12:1–12 we have the responsibility whenever we use Matt. 21:33–46 to ensure that it evokes self-examination leading to repentance and a positive response to God rather than a negative reaction against Jews. This can be done, in part at least, if we include in our vernacular editions of this story in the Synoptics a translation of the Gospel of Thomas account in a footnote and if in our lectionaries and in our preaching we separate Matt. 21:33–46 and its Synoptic parallels from the Isaiah 5 love song. Finally, the Mark 12:1–12 text should be given preference in usage over Matt. 21:33–46.

Mark 12:13–17; Matt. 22:15–22: *To pay or not to pay the Roman poll tax.* Among the various rearrangements of words and phrases and other stylistic changes there are two notable differences between these two accounts in terms of anti-Jewish polemic. The limitation of involvement in Mark 12:13 to "some of" the Pharisees and the Herodians is eliminated in Matt. 22:15. The change from "but seeing through their hypocrisy he said to them" in Mark 12:15 to "but Jesus having been aware of their maliciousness said" seems to balance evenly until we see that Matthew also characteristically has Jesus address the whole group of Pharisees collectively with the vocative "Hypocrites!" These differences cause the anti-Jewish polemic already present in Mark 12:13–17 to stand out more starkly in Matthew's account. In addition to the suggestions for sensitive translation and use of the Markan account described above,[17] the vocative "Hypocrites!" should be reduced to footnote status or passed over in silence in our translations of Matt. 22:18, with the explanation where deemed necessary that the use of this vocative appears to be a characteristic of the writer(s) of the Matthean tradition rather than of Jesus.

Mark 12:18–27; Matt. 22:23–33: *The Sadducees and the resurrection life.* In Matthew's redaction the polemic against the Sadducees is reduced in that the nonuse in Matthew of Mark 12:27b, "You err greatly," more than counterbalances the change from the somewhat respectful Mark 12:24, "Do you not err because of this?" to the more direct Matt. 22:29, "You err."

As stated earlier,[18] our interest in these accounts should focus on what the Markan and the Matthean communities were teaching about the nature of the resurrection life rather than on the accusations that the Sadducees were in error.

Mark 12:28–34; Matt. 22:34–40: *The most important commandment.* The Matthean redaction greatly increases the anti-Jewish polemic, which was only slight and subtle[19] in the Mark 12:28–34 account. The "one of the scribes" of the Markan account becomes one of the Pharisees. It is added that when the Pharisees had heard that Jesus had silenced the Sadducees they were (all) gathered together in the same place (or for the same purpose), and one of them, a Torah scholar, asked him a question "testing him," (to try to draw from Jesus something that could be used to discredit him). The elements of the Markan account that retained fraternity and warmth between Jesus and the scribe (Torah scholar) in Mark—the quotation of the "Shema" (Deut. 6:4) and the congenial scholastic conversation of Mark 12:32–34—are not included in Matt. 22:34–40.

In our translations "the Pharisees" of Matt. 22:34 should be rendered as "other religious leaders," and in our usage the Mark 12:28–34 account should always be given preference. In this connection, the time has come for us to reverse the sequence of Matthew and Mark in our New Testament editions so that Mark will be read more frequently and so that the chronological and theological development from Mark to Matthew will be more clearly seen. Luke-Acts can be placed together next, followed by the Fourth Gospel, the Johannine epistles, and the Apocalypse. 2 Peter should be the concluding document of the New Testament collection, as it is in this study.

Mark 12:35–37a; Matt. 22:41–46: *How can the Messiah be the son of David when David has said that he is Lord?* Matt. 22:41 is almost entirely Matthean composition. In the verses that follow in Matthew the somewhat rhetorical questions of Jesus in Mark 12:35–37a are adapted into a dialogue between Jesus and the Pharisees, a dialogue that concludes a series of dialogues that end with Jesus in complete control.[20] The anti-Jewish polemic is increased from Mark to Matthew, and the pattern is established for subsequent one-sided dialogues such as Justin Martyr's *Dialogue with Trypho,* in which Christians handle both sides of all arguments in Christian-Jewish "debates" in Christian sermons and in Christian literature.

The Mark 12:35–37a (or the Luke 20:41–44) account is to be preferred rather than Matt. 22:41–46 whenever it is felt that this pericope should be used.

Mark 12:37b–40; Matt. 23:1–12(14): *The scribes (and the Pharisees) will be condemned.* Matthean redaction here includes extensive composition that becomes the base for the series of vicious "Woe to you, scribes and Pharisees, hypocrites!" condemnations in Matt. 23:13, 15–36.[21] As indicated earlier,[22] for our own integrity we have the responsibility to redirect what in these texts has become external criticism into internal self-criticism.

The least we should do with Matt. 23:1–12[23] is to translate "the scribes and the Pharisees" of 23:2 as "our religious leaders" and "the synagogues" of 23:6 as "our religious gatherings." Beyond that, "their phylacteries" and "their tassels" should be rendered as "their devotional aids" and as "their religious garments" in 23:5 and "rabbi" in 23:7–8 should be translated as "my lord," in order that we may use these verses properly for internal self-criticism. If they are used even subconsciously in defamation of the Jews, it would be better not to have used them at all.[24]

Mark 13:1–37; Matt. 24:1–51; 10:17–22a; 25:13–15: *The eschatological discourse.* The prediction of the destruction of the temple is reproduced in Matt. 24:2 with only stylistic changes and the addition of the solemn introduction "Truly I say to you" to Mark 13:2. Anti-Jewish polemic is intensified somewhat in the Matt. 10:17 parallel to the Mark 13:9 prediction of the suffering of followers of Jesus in Jewish courts and synagogues by the use of *mastigōsousin hymas* ("they will flog you") instead of *darēsesthe* ("you will be beaten"), and "synagogues" becomes "their synagogues." Here, as in Mark 13:9,[25] it is proper for us to translate "synagogues" as "gathering places."

Mark 14:1–2; Matt. 26:1–5: *The religious leaders plan to arrest and kill Jesus.* Matt. 26:2 adds a brief prediction that the Son of man will be delivered up to be crucified at the time of the Passover. The plotting of "the chief priests and the elders of the people" (Matt. 26:3) rather than "the chief priests and the scribes" (Mark 14:2) is given with more detail than in Mark. The Markan distinction between plot against Jesus by the religious leaders and objection by the people is maintained.

Mark 14:10–11; Matt. 26:14–16: *The betrayal contract.* Since the rejoicing of the chief priests over the prospect of the betrayal of Jesus by one of his twelve disciples and their promise to give money to Judas (Mark 14:11) is not expressed in Matt. 26:14–16, anti-Jewish polemic is lessened. Nevertheless, the chief priests set out for (offered to) him thirty pieces of silver (Matt. 26:15).

Mark 14:43–52; Matt. 26:47–56: *The arrest of Jesus.* Judas and the mob (the "sinners" of Mark 14:41; Matt. 26:45), which came during the night to arrest Jesus, were from the chief priests and elders of the people (Matt. 26:47), the scribes of Mark 14:43 having been deleted.

Mark 14:53–65; Matt. 26:57–68: *The nocturnal religious inquest.*[26] Stylistic and minor differences between these two accounts cause no change in the level of anti-Jewish polemic, unless the absence of the word *all*, which had occurred in Mark 14:53 and 14:64c, is interpreted as a lessening of polemic.

Mark 15:1; Matt. 27:1–2: *Jesus delivered over to Pilate.* Anti-Jewish polemic is greater here in Matthew than in Mark. Instead of "the chief priests, with the elders and scribes, and the whole council reached a decision," (or "held a consultation") (Mark 15:1), Matt. 27:1 has "all the chief priests and the elders of the people formed a plan" against Jesus so that they might put him to death.

Mark 15:2–15; Matt. 27:11–23, 26: *The trial before Pilate.* Apart from the addition of "the elders" in Matt. 27:12, 20 to those who were against Jesus, there is no significant difference in the amount of anti-Jewish polemic in the two accounts until Matt. 27:24–26, where in a composition for which there are no parallels in the Four Gospels Pilate is said to have declared his innocence and "all the people" are said to have answered, "Let his blood be upon us and upon our children!" Consideration of the vicious anti-Jewish polemic of Matt. 27:24–26 must be postponed, however, until we come to the analysis of Matthew's other compositions from written or oral sources, since Matt. 27:24–26 is not a redaction of Markan material.

Mark 15:22–41; Matt. 27:33–42, 44–56: *The crucifixion.* The "elders" are added to those who mocked Jesus on the cross (Matt. 27:41), cataclysmic events are said to have accompanied the death of Jesus, and the centurion's confessional comment is said to have been shared by those who were with him guarding Jesus. Even aside from Matt. 27:43, which is not a redaction of Markan material,[27] the changes that Matthew introduced into the Markan crucifixion account increase the anti-Jewish polemic already there by rephrasing and adding to Mark 15:30 in Matt. 27:40 "If you are the Son of God," (the terminology of the tempter in Matt. 4:3, 6).

B. In Matthew's Use of "Q" Material

Luke 3:7b–9; Matt. 3:7b–10: *The exhortation of John.* Since the content of John's message is almost identical in these two accounts, no increase in anti-Jewish polemic is apparent in Matthew's use of "Q" material in the message itself. There is an increase in the polemic in Matt. 3:7a, however, where Matthew characteristically specifically designated Pharisees and Sadducees for condemnation.

Luke 6:22–23; Matt. 5:11–12: *Thus they persecuted the prophets.* Compared to the Lukan account, the anti-Jewish polemic is less in Matt. 5:12, since there is no mention of "their" fathers in Matthew.

Luke 7:9; Matt. 8:10: *The faith of the centurion.* As indicated earlier,[28] Matthew heightens the anti-Jewish effect of this saying by combining it with another "Q" saying (8:11–12; Luke 13:28–29) that is more blatantly anti-Jewish.

Luke 13:28–29; Matt. 8:11–12: *Those who will recline at the table with the patriarchs in the kingdom.* Matthew placed this saying in a context in which the sons of the kingdom who will be thrown into outer darkness are associated with the Israelites who were contemporary with the Jesus of history, of whom the faith of not one is found by Jesus to be equal to the faith of the Gentile centurion. Also, because the Luke 13:28-29 account is the more direct and personal of the two, the manner in which the saying is employed in Matt. 8:11–12 may be secondary. There is probably, therefore, some increase in anti-Jewish polemic in Matthew because of the way in which the saying is used.

Luke 6:39; Matt. 15:14b: *A blind man cannot lead a blind man.* In its Lukan context, and perhaps also in "Q" material, this saying is instruction for followers of Jesus. In Matthew it is developed into a renunciation of the Pharisees, who are called "blind guides." In the Matthean context, therefore, this saying becomes distinctively anti-Jewish polemic.[29]

Luke 7:31–35; Matt. 11:16–19: *This generation is like children at play.* In this text with its three typical wisdom-teaching forms—parable, comparison sentence, and concluding sentence[30]—Matthew increased the anti-Jewish polemic over against the form used in Luke by generalizing about this generation in the parable, where Luke particularized with "the men of this generation" and by speaking of the adversaries in the third person in the comparison sentence, where Luke addressed them in the second person.

Luke 10:12–15; Matt. 11:20–24: *Judgment of Chorazin, Bethsaida, and Capernaum.* Analysis indicates the probability that Luke reduced anti-Jewish polemic in the "Q" material here or Matthew increased it, or that there was some of each. Since the introductory words of judgment in Matt. 11:20 appear to be Matthew's own composition, and since there is emphasis upon judgment both internally (Matt. 11:22, 23b, 24) and externally (Matt. 11:16–19, 25–27) compared to Luke, where the saying is used in a context of encouragement to dejected disciples, it seems likely that much of the difference between the two uses of the account is because Matthew has increased the anti-Jewish polemic here as in many instances of Matthean use of Markan material. The manner in which Matthew has combined in 11:23a, 24 what we see in Luke 10:12, 15 and added 10:23b may be evidence that at the time Matthew was written there was little or no following of Jesus in Capernaum.

Luke 10:21b; Matt. 11:25b–26: *Prayer of thanks to the Father for eschatological wisdom.* Luke 10:22; Matt. 11:27: *Esoteric knowledge of the Son and of the Father.* Differences between the Lukan and the Matthean renditions of these two sayings are not sufficient to enable us to discern any development of anti-Jewish polemic between "Q" material and Matthew.

Luke 11:19–20, 23; Matt. 12:27–28, 30: *Exorcism by the power of God.* Differences between the two accounts are slight. The anthropomorphism of Luke 11:20 "finger of God" is reduced in Matt. 12:28 to "Spirit of God." As A. H. McNeile suggested,[31] "finger" is almost certainly the earlier reading, since Luke would not likely have avoided "Spirit," which occurs so frequently in the Lukan material. Matthew seems to have used "Spirit" in preparation for the account that follows in 12:31–32 regarding blasphemy against the Spirit. In the intervening segment (Luke 11:21–22; Matt. 12:29) Matthew follows Mark, while Luke has a different but similar saying. The exclusivism and anti-Jewish polemic is nearly identical in the Matthean and the Lukan use of this particular "Q" material.

Luke 11:31; Matt. 12:42: *The queen of the south as judge over the men of this generation.* Matthew has increased anti-Jewish polemic compared to Luke by generalizing condemnation to include all of "this generation and condemn it," where Luke limits it to "the men of this generation and condemn them." Because of the tendency clearly seen in Matthew to polemicize against entire categories of Jews, it is more likely that Matthew increased the anti-Jewish tenor of this account than that Luke decreased it.

Luke 11:32; Matt. 12:41: *The men of Nineveh condemning this generation.* These verses are verbally identical.

Luke 12:54–56; Matt. 16:2–3: *You can predict the weather but not the signs of the times.* In Matthew this saying of reproof is directed against the Pharisees and Sadducees (16:1). In Luke it is addressed to the crowds. The weather indicators differ considerably. In this instance the vocative "Hypocrites!" occurs in Luke but is included in Matthew only in relatively late textual traditions. When this vocative is absent from the Matt. 16:2–3 reading, the Matthean text is less anti-Jewish than the Lukan.

Luke 13:34–35; Matt. 23:37–39: *The lament over Jerusalem.* Anti-Jewish indications are evident in the addition of *erēmos* ("desolate") in the textual transmission of Matt. 23:38 (an application of Jer. 22:5 to produce the reading, "Behold, your house is left desolate," the judgment of the post-70 C.E. Matthean church) and in the deletion[32] of *hēxei hote* ("he—the Lord—shall come when" or "it—the time—shall come when") in the textual transmission of Luke 13:35.

Luke 16:16–17; Matt. 11:12–13; 5:18: *The Torah and the prophets before and after the time of John.* The textual evidence suggests that these sayings that are difficult for us may have been incorporated into Matt. 11:12–13 and 5:18 relatively unchanged from "Q" materials or from oral traditions, but that in Luke 16:16–17 they are given somewhat more coherence.[33]

Luke 22:30b; Matt. 19:28d: *Followers of Jesus judging the twelve tribes of Israel.* The emphatic "you" and the double use of "twelve" in the Matthean reading can be considered anti-Jewish emphases in Matthew's use of this "Q" fragment.[34]

C. In Matthew's Use of Other Written and Oral Sources and in Matthew's Own Compositions

The purpose here is to recognize anti-Jewish polemic in the portions of Matthew in which there appears to be no direct dependence upon Markan or "Q" material. It is assumed throughout this section that in addition to forms of Markan and of "Q" material the writer(s) of Matthew utilized other written and oral sources during the composition of this Gospel. As much as possible I shall attempt to determine stages in the development of the tradition, particularly as we are informed by the preceding study of anti-Jewish polemic in Matthew's use of Markan and of "Q" material. Because of the multitude of unknown factors that remain in our understanding of the history of the development of the traditions, it shall be difficult in many instances to distinguish Matthean composition from Matthean redaction in this material.

It is my purpose also to suggest ways by which in our translations and in our usage of these portions of Matthew we may repudiate anti-Jewish polemic in them in accordance with my stated objectives.[35] As this study progresses, the necessity for corporate responsibility both in the recognition and in the repudiation of the anti-Jewish polemic of the New Testament becomes ever more apparent. In areas where church polity is significantly democratic, persuasion and appeal to conscience are appropriate; in areas of the church where authoritarian polity remains, authoritarian methods can be employed. In any case, change that occurs in the "marketplace" of usage rather than in legislative councils of debate and "win-lose" voting is highly desirable.[36]

Among the variety of ways in which I might proceed in this portion of the study, analysis of anti-Jewish polemic within successive blocks of material has been chosen as probably the most productive.[37] With this method, Matthew's use of and interpretation of the Jewish Scriptures, relationships between anti-Jewish polemic in the various portions of the Gospel, and what the polemic reveals about the extended community by which and for which this Gospel was prepared will be examined as they occur. I begin, therefore, with the genealogy and with the birth narrative.

1:1–17: *The book of the origin of Jesus the Christ.* Already in 1:1, the superscription of the genealogies and perhaps of the entire Gospel, Jesus is tied politically (as son of David) and culturally (as son of Abraham) with the Jewish people and identified as Messiah. The genealogies themselves[38] focus attention symmetrically upon Abraham, David, and the deportation to Babylon, key points in Israel's story. To designate Jesus as Messiah is to depict him as the culmination of the old and the beginning of the new.

1:18–25: *The birth narrative.* Probably for most of us who have been reared in Christian traditions the anti-Jewish polemic in this birth narrative is so subtle that it is almost nonexistent. However, the Jewish emphasis here becomes anti-Jewish within the context of the entire Gospel. It becomes anti-Jewish as the Jesus figure of this Gospel requires a righteousness greater than the righteousness of the Jewish scribes and Pharisees. It becomes anti-Jewish as the Jesus of whom conception, development, and birth accounts are depicted here opposes and is opposed by Jewish leadership, repeatedly described in this Gospel with the use of third-person pronouns. When Jewish leadership is castigated as severely as it is in this Gospel, and when the Jewish people are made to cry out ever more emphatically, "Let him be crucified!" and all together as if in unison, "May his blood be upon us and upon our children!" just when Pilate and his wife were trying to release Jesus as an innocent man, this account of extraordinary circumstances associated with Jesus' birth is made anti-Jewish by its context in this document. If the origin of Jesus is from the Holy Spirit of God, his adversaries are obviously not of the Spirit of God. If the angel of the Lord announced that Jesus would save his people from their sins, and most of his people reject him as the Savior-Messiah, their sin is greatly magnified. When a symbolic illustration of the certainty and the immediacy of God's action in the time of Ahaz (Isa. 7:1–25) is employed as proof that Mary was still a virgin in spite of her pregnancy and that in her son God would be with us, it becomes polemic against Jews who do not think that God would ever become a human being or that a human being would ever become God.

Persons in a new religious community can of course think as they wish about God and can freely interpret the religious traditions of their parent religious groups and of others. It would be appropriate, however, for us today to translate *parthenos* in Matt. 1:23 as "young woman" or as "maiden" in recognition that the use of *almah* in Isa. 7:14 claims nothing extraordinary about the conception *per se* of the son to be born. Beyond that, no special care is required in repudiation of anti-Jewish polemic in Matthew's birth narrative. The special care is called for in other Matthean texts in which the anti-Jewish polemic is virulent and damaging both to Jews and to Christians.

2:1–23: *The infancy narrative.* Anti-Jewish polemic is apparent in the designation of Jesus as having been already by birth "king of the Jews," a title not used for Jesus elsewhere in the Synoptic traditions except in the trial and crucifixion accounts.[39] In this narrative Jesus is the one born king of the Jews, but ironically, his kingship is accorded homage only by non-Jewish magi from the East. Matt. 2:1–12, therefore, can be seen as an exceptionally subtle polemic on three separate fronts. The wise Zoroastrian will come from the East to worship Jesus, those who rely on Roman civil religion will continue to be troubled by Jesus, and the chief priests and scribes of the Jewish people unwittingly proleptically acclaim him as their own leader and guide. Later in the account Pilate will question him about the designation "king of the Jews" (27:11), and the soldiers of Pilate will use it to mock him and to taunt him (27:29). He will be charged with this identity as he is crucified (27:37). Adding further insult to injury, the chief priests, together with the scribes and elders, will mock him to come down from the cross to be king of Israel (27:41–43). Because of the derisive way in which the title is used in Matthew, our translation in 2:4 would be better expressed as "Where is the one who has been born among you as king?" "Among you" would express the Jewish identity contained in the words of the text "of the Jews" and would have the added advantage of placing that birth in the broader context of all of humanity in every age, as well as reducing the sting of the expression, "king of the Jews."

The chief priests and scribes of the people are assembled for the first time in this document at the request of Herod, and in the service of the tradition in this Matthean "testimony"[40] they readily report that according to the prophet (Mic. 5:2) Bethlehem will produce the Messiah who will lead and guide God's people Israel. The Jewish hope of political messianism is thus employed in the service of this infancy account of the one who in our Christian traditions rejects political messianism. In the "testimony" that follows in 2:15b Jesus is identified with Israel, the loved "son of God" in Hos. 11:1.

3:1–6, 11–12: *John the Baptist prepares for the kingdom.* The anti-Jewish polemic here, as in the interrelated traditions in Mark, Luke, and John, is most of all in the assumed identification of Jesus as "the Lord" (whose way is prepared by John) with Yahweh as "the Lord" (whose way was prepared in the Isa. 40:3 tradition). It is not inherently anti-Jewish for Jesus to baptize with the Holy Spirit and perhaps not even metaphorically to gather his wheat and to burn the chaff, but these become anti-Jewish within the broader context of Matthew's Gospel. It is, of course, entirely appropriate for us as Christians to identify Jesus with Yahweh if we wish—even though in Jewish theology Yahweh would not assume the form of a human being— as long as we do not defame Jews in the process.

3:13–17: *The baptism of Jesus.* As in the Markan, Lukan, and Johannine parallels, this account is anti-Jewish when it is perceived that Jesus is represented as superseding Israel. Again, this is not inappropriate for us if we do this without defaming the Jews.

5:20–22, 27–28, 31–32a, 33–39, 43–44a, (48): *The superior righteousness.* In what is possibly a redaction of "Q" material, it is stated in Matt. 5:17–19 that Jesus has not come to invalidate the Torah but to fulfill it. As long as heaven and earth remain, not a single minor marking will disappear from the Torah. The Torah remains untouched, it is claimed, but the interpretation of the Torah in the life-style of the followers of Jesus must be superior to the interpretation of the Torah in the life-style of the scribes and Pharisees. Hence Matthew's Gospel is characterized, particularly in the verses of this section, as the Gospel of the "better righteousness."[41]

One of the ironies of Christian relationships with Jews throughout the nearly twenty centuries of the Common Era is that the radical statement of Matt. 5:20 has fostered within Christians a sense of self-righteous superiority over Jews and all "scribes and Pharisees," without which according to this verse we will "never enter into the kingdom of heaven," a sense of self-righteous superiority that must be as great as that of any Jew, or scribe, or Pharisee. We as Christians have often expressed self-righteous concern for Jews without recognizing the same self-righteousness in ourselves that we have been conditioned in our traditions to attribute to Jews, scribes, and "Pharisees" of all kinds.

Among the most effective ways we can counteract a supercilious attitude of Christians toward Jews is by our own study and teaching of the Hebrew concept of *ts^{e}daka* ("righteousness").[42] Where there is greater understanding among Christians of the importance placed in Jewish theology and ethics upon right relationships with God, with people, and with the environment within the minimum keepable demands of the Decalogue there will be measurably less "contempt for the Jews." In addition, if we would translate and teach that the meaning of Matt. 5:20 is something like: "Unless you change your life-style, your attitudes, and your relationships with God, with each other, and with the environment in which you live, you will never be ready to enter into the kingdom of heaven," we would come closer to the Jesus of history in whom Jews and Christians today can find common ground as reformation and renewal occurs both in synagogue and in church.

6:1–8, 16–18: On giving alms, praying, and fasting privately. The basic instruction regarding the manner in which a Christian should engage in the practices of giving alms, praying, and fasting is always timely and appropriate. It is the set of associations in the illustrative examples: "as the hypocrites do in the synagogues" (6:2), "as the hypocrites, because they love to pray standing prominently in the synagogues and on the street corners" (6:5), and "as the hypocrites with a gloomy face" (6:16) which is offensive.[43] The "Gentiles," that is, other persons in addition to the Jews who are not participants in the Christian communions, are also cited in 6:7 and in "Q" type material in 6:32 as examples not to be followed, but without the bitter invective heaped[44] upon the Jewish leaders.

In our translations and use of 6:2, 5, 16, for Christians who are sensitive to the problems caused by this type of anti-Jewish polemic the most clear-cut way to proceed would be to excise the illustrative examples in these verses so that they would read in our translations: "Therefore, whenever you perform an act of kindness, do not blow your own horn so that you will be praised by other people" (6:2); "And when you pray, enter into your room and close your door and pray to your Father privately" (6:5–6); and "When you fast, do not look gloomy, but clean your hair and wash your face" (6:16–17). The reason for these omissions from the text in the translations can be explained briefly in footnotes. For people who prefer circumlocution and interpretative translations to more drastic surgery, 6:2 and 6:5 can be translated "as hypocrites do in public places" and 6:16 "like hypocrites who disfigure their faces." This less drastic expedient may suffice if the other associations of hypocrites with scribes, Pharisees, and other Jewish groups are eliminated from the Synoptic material. In either case, it would take several generations for Christians to eliminate associations of "scribes and Pharisees" with "hypocrites" from their conscious and subconscious thinking.

10:23: *On being persecuted in the towns of Israel.* It is probable that this verse reflects conditions encountered during Christian evangelistic endeavors in Israelite cities in Galilee while these early Christians were anticipating Jesus' return as the Son of man during the period before and after 70 c.e.[45] We can reduce the intensity of the polemic against the Jews here and in similar contexts if we translate forms of *diōkō* as "drive out," "drive away," "expel," or "reject," rather than "persecute." The translation "Whenever they reject you in any city, hasten on to the next" may more accurately report conditions during the earliest sharing of Jesus' message by his followers in the cities of Galilee than the familiar "Whenever they persecute you in one city, flee to the next."

12:17–21: *Identification of the Servant of the Lord.* Here, as in other New Testament references in which Jesus is identified as the Servant of the Lord of the Isaiah traditions, there is a subtle form of anti-Jewish polemic in that the Isa. 49:3 identification of the Servant as Israel is replaced with the identification as Jesus. These identifications of the Servant as Jesus, as Israel, as a segment within Israel, as a composite figure of the prophets of Israel, as an ideal prophet, and as a particularly respected and admired prophet—possibly in the earliest strata the Isaiah of history himself—can be made by Jewish and Christian interpreters as they separately or in cooperation study the history of the development of the Servant Songs and of other complex Isaiah traditions. No single identification will do justice to the profound religious poetry of these Servant Songs.

12:34a: *You sons of snakes!* This bitter invective, followed by "How can you possibly speak good things when you are evil!" injects a strong dosage of anti-Jewish venom into logia that elsewhere do not refer to the Pharisees. Perhaps Tilborg is correct in concluding that for Matthew the Pharisees are not really so much a historical group as they are types of evil, representations of the wrong choice.[46]

In our translations and use of Matt. 12:34 and 23:33 it would be appropriate for us to pass in silence over the epithet *gennēmata echidnōn.* Although the words of this bitter invective, "You sons of snakes!" probably stem from the writer(s) of the Gospel According to Matthew rather than from the Jesus of history,[47] they are presented in these texts as words of Jesus. Since the words and actions of Jesus continue to provide a model for us even today, since most of us prohibit our children from calling people disparaging names, and since we discourage such name-calling in adults, it is not appropriate to have the founder of the Christian religion and the most important model for our behavior addressing entire categories of people in that manner in broad generalities, especially when it is probably the writer(s) of Matthew rather than the Jesus of history who is really talking in these texts.

12:45c: *Thus it shall be also for this evil generation.* This comment, which Matthew appends to the "Q" material of Matt. 12:43–45b, causes the entire pericope to have an anti-Jewish flavor. It also tends to limit the significance of the account to the mid-first century, thereby lessening its value for us today. Matthew made an application of the pericope that appeared to be appropriate to the Matthean writer(s), but it is an application inappropriate for our time. Therefore 12:45c can be reduced to a footnote status in our translations[48] and in our usage much as we have reduced texts that do not appear in early manuscripts of the textual tradition even when these latter, as in the case of the doxology to the Lord's Prayer in Matt. 6:13, are obviously edifying.

15:12–14a: *Let the Pharisees be offended!* Matthew's use of Markan material in Matt. 15:1–11, 15–20 has been considered above.[49] Matt. 15:14b is "Q" material that has its counterpart in Luke 6:39.[50] There remains 15:12–14a to be considered here. The portions 15:12, 14a appear to be Matthean composition in which the Pharisees (the epitome for Matthew of all those who do not accept the Matthean community's expression of Jesus' teachings) are summarily dismissed as "blind guides." The "Q" material 15:14b and another traditional saying 15:13 ("Every plant which my heavenly Father has not planted shall be rooted out") were incorporated into the Matthean composition and the total product placed in the Markan material Matt. 15:1–11, 15–20.

In order to counteract Matthew's biased polemic against the Pharisees, which we have no reason to maintain today, in our translation and use of Matt. 15:12 we can by periphrasis render "the Pharisees" as "some people," and read "Are you aware that some people were offended when they heard what you have said?"

16:17–19; 18:18: *You are Peter.* The claim that the identity of Jesus as the Christ, the Son the living God, was revealed to Peter by Jesus' Father who is in heaven, the proclamation of the plan of Jesus to build his church, and the promise of the power to bind and loose on earth can be considered to be anti-Jewish in this Matthean composition, but anti-Jewish polemic would not appear to be the primary purpose of this account.

21:4–5: *Your king comes riding on a donkey.* By this addition of prophetic traditions Matthew has made explicit Mark's reference to "The Lord has need of it" and has emphasized the literal fulfillment of elements of Isa. 62:11 and Zech. 9:9.[51] Jesus has entered Jerusalem in order to be crowned as its king.

21:9–11: *All the city is shaken by the arrival of this son of David.* Matthew adds "to the son of David" to Mark's "Hosanna." As in Matt. 2:3 all the city of Jerusalem was shaken by the prospect of Jesus as its king.

21:31b–32: *The addition to the parable of the two sons.* The parable itself (21:28–31a) has come to us in some of the early manuscripts with mention first of the son who refused initially and later obeyed and in other early manuscripts with mention first of the son who agreed initially and yet did not work in the vineyard. Obviously, the parable could be expressed in either sequence. The sequence in which the son who had been sent first agreed but did not go could be utilized allegorically against the Jews who had agreed to the will of the Father and yet allegedly, according to their Christian antagonists, did not go to work in the vineyard. The parable itself, particularly in the sequence in which the son instructed first eventually does the will of the father, is appropriate and timely for any audience. The addition to the parable (21:31b–32) puts the parable into the context of the Markan series of controversy dialogues. The somewhat similar reference in Luke 7:29–30 to responses of various groups to the activities of John the Baptist may have been available in some way to the one who formulated Matt. 21:31b–32, or the lack of the parable of the two sons in Luke 20 or anywhere else suggests that Luke followed the Markan series of controversy dialogues at that point and did not have available or did not choose to use the parable of the two sons. It is possible also that Luke 7:29–30 was composed as an appendage to 7:24–28 in recognition of persons who had been baptized with the baptism of John and later had become Christians.

22:1–10: *The allegorized parable of the king who arranged a marriage feast for his son.* Because of the substantial differences between this pericope and the account in Luke 14:16–24 and in the Gospel of Thomas, logion 64, about the man who invited busy guests, the Matthean text is considered here rather than with the study of Matthew's use of "Q" material.

This allegorized parable is placed within a context of allegorized parables and controversy dialogues both by position and by the redactional connector in 22:21. The servants of 22:3 are probably intended to represent Jewish prophets. The other servants of 22:4–6 would be Christian evangelists. Chapter 22:7 depicts the fall of Jerusalem of 70 C.E., and 22:8–10 describes the situation among Christians after the fall of Jerusalem. Chapter 22:11–14 is a separate and loosely related parable.

In this account, therefore, the chief priests and the Pharisees are depicted as murderers who insult the king (God), who retaliates by sending his armies, destroying them and burning their city. Even though Jews are not specifically cited in the account, by implication they are condemned. Since there is a somewhat similar pericope in Luke 14:16–23, which emphasizes the inclusion of the poor, the crippled, the blind, and the lame rather than the destruction of the Jews, we should use Luke 14:16–23 rather than Matt. 22:1–10 in our devotions, proclamation, and teaching.[52]

23:13, 15–33: *Woe to you, scribes and Pharisees, hypocrites!* The stage for this vicious series of denunciations is set in the Matt. 23:1–12 redaction of Mark 12:37b–40 material.[53] If "Q" material lies behind Matt. 23:13, 15–33 and Luke 11:37–48, 52, Luke has placed it in a context in which Jesus is a dinner guest in the home of a Pharisee. Matthew, however, placed it in 23:1 in a situation in which Jesus addressed the crowds and his disciples and talked about the scribes and the Pharisees in the third-person plural. The direct address to the scribes and Pharisees, "Woe to you, hypocrites!", utilized six times[54] in Matt. 23:13, 15, 23, 25, 27, 29, appears almost certainly to have been the work of an editor.[55] The bombastic repetition of "Woes" in this context and in the broader context of the Matthean document, where they contrast with the series of beatitudes in 5:3–12, is reminiscent of the contrast between the series of blessings and curses in Deut. 28:2–35 and gives these "Woes" a character similar to that of the Shechemite Dodecalogue curses of Deut. 27:15–26. Luke also has a series of beatitudes in 6:20–22 and 11:27–28 and of contrasted "Woes" in 6:24–26 and 11:42–44, 46–47, 52, but these are much less developed editorially than those in Matthew.

The development of the Matthean traditions must have been a complex process. For example, although Matt. 5:34–37 forbids swearing an oath at all, Matt. 23:16–22 assumes an ascending order of seriousness of oaths sworn by the gift, the altar, the temple, the Presence of God in the temple, heaven, the throne of God, and God, which leads some commentators to postulate that, although both portions are peculiar to Matthew, they could hardly have been penned by the same person or by persons of like minds. The Jesus of history, as a courageous prophet and religious reformer, probably denounced publicly and privately the practices of certain scribes, Pharisees, priests, and other religious leaders of his own people. In direct confrontation with individuals and small groups he may have used some exceedingly uncomplimentary epithets. There is little doubt that his activity as a prophet and religious reformer was a significant cause of his arrest, trial, and crucifixion. However, neither Jesus nor any other historical figure of the first century would have addressed all Jewish scribes, Pharisees, priests, and other religious leaders throughout Palestine and the extensive Diaspora at one time and the same time. Most of the Jewish religious leadership in the Diaspora and much of it in Palestine itself probably had no acquaintance with or knowledge about the Jesus of history. Generalized condemnation of scribes and Pharisees and other Jewish religious groups would have occurred only in the process in which Jesus' words and actions and a variety of versions and interpretations of his words and actions were disseminated over an extend period of time over large areas of the Roman Empire and put into written form. Comparisons among Synoptic accounts—such as a comparison of address by Jesus to a small group of Pharisees in the home of one of them in which he was a guest in Luke 11:37–52 with the generalized and much more severe condemnation of presumably all scribes and Pharisees in Matt. 23—indicate that even in the small intervals of time and development to which we have direct access in the Synoptic parallel comparison, important changes in the tradition can be traced.

The "tree" or "vine" (John 15:2) of the Christian traditions grew. As it grew, some branches developed that did not "bear fruit." To use the John 15:2 analogy, every branch that does not bear fruit is cut away and every branch that does bear fruit is pruned in order that it may bear more fruit. On the January weekend in which I was writing comments on the anti-Jewish polemic in Matt. 23:13, 15–33, I pruned the young trees and shrubs around our home and heard the John 15:2 text read and commented upon in the Men's Bible Class of my local congregation. It occurred to me that if our Christian traditions and our biblical traditions as a part of those Christian traditions are living traditions—and I would claim that they are—we may still be involved in the careful pruning and shaping of these traditions in order that now and in the future the "tree" or the "vine" may bear more fruit.

The Matt. 23:13, 15–33 branch of the "tree" or "vine" of our traditions would bear much more and better fruit if the generalizing condemnation of the Jews in them would be pruned, at least in our translations of these texts and in our usage of them. Source, form, redaction, and literary studies indicate the high degree of probability that these generalizing condemnations were developed within the historical context of conflict between the emerging church and certain Jewish groups later during the first century and were not present in the words and activities of the Jesus of history. Therefore it appears appropriate for our common good, and indeed in accordance with the spirit of John 15:2, that in our translation and use of Matt. 23:13, 15–33 we "prune away" into a footnote "scribes and Pharisees, hypocrites!" in 23:13, 15, 23, 25, 27, 29, and in the latter formulation in 23:14 as well. The result would be:

> Woe to you who lock the door to the kingdom of heaven while people are waiting to enter it. (23:13)
> Woe to you who travel over the sea and throughout the land to try to make one convert. (23:15)
> Woe to you who tithe mint and dill and cummin and have neglected the more important matters of justice and mercy and faith. (23:23)
> Woe to you who clean the outside of the cup and of the plate while inside they are full of stolen goods and evil self-indulgences. (23:25)
> Woe to you who are like whitewashed tombs that appear on the outside to be beautiful but inside are full of the bones of dead people and of decaying bodies. (23:27)
> Woe to you who build the tombs of the prophets. (23:29)

The result more likely retains the essence of Jesus' message in a form that is applicable in our time and in any time and that offers much less likelihood of being avoided through scapegoating. In addition, and extremely important, Jews would be much less likely to be defamed and injured with Jesus' message in this form.

For consistency, and for the same reasons, "You blind Pharisee!" in

23:26a and "You serpents, you sons of snakes!" in 23:33a should also be relegated to footnotes.

Finally, since "the prophets" and "the righteous" appear to be synonymous in 23:29, "the righteous" can be an interpretative translation of "the prophets" in 23:30–31, particularly since, as indicated earlier,[56] the charge that the Jews murdered their own prophets is largely unfair.

23:34–36: *You will be blamed for the death of all the righteous.* What is predicted in these few verses has been fulfilled. As a result of these verses and others such as Matt. 27:24–25, the Jews have been blamed in our Christian traditions for the death of their own best people, for the death of Jesus, and for the death of Christian martyrs. Since in most instances this blame has been placed unfairly, we have a moral responsibility at this late date to do something about Matt. 23:34–36 and about its parallel in Luke 11:49–51.

To respond adequately we should place these verses in footnotes in our translations and usage and admit that basically what is predicted in these verses has been done; the scribes and Pharisees of the first century of the common era, their fathers, and their children have been blamed for the death of "all the righteous." A less satisfactory partial response would be to use interpretative translations, rendering "synagogues" in 23:34 as "your meeting places," "whom you murdered"[57] in 23:35 as "who was murdered," and "this generation" in 23:36 as "you."

27:24–25: *May his blood be upon us and upon our children!* Since washing one's hands after completion of a particularly dirty or messy task is a common practice, and since various ritual handwashings to indicate innocence of responsibility are known to us from both Jewish and Greek sources, it is, as Schweizer proposes,[58] not inherently impossible that Pilate may have washed his hands to signify his own nonculpability after he had given the order to have Jesus crucified, but it is hardly conceivable that Pilate would have made a *public* spectacle of his own illegal decision and the impotence of Roman justice when pressured by demands by a mob from within a subject population. It would have been physically impossible for the entire Jewish nation *(pas ho laos)* to have spoken with one voice as if in unison. Even if it could have spoken in unison, it is not likely that it would have accepted for itself in perpetuity the full responsibility for the death sentence imposed by an oppressive occupation force upon a popular leader from among its own people. It is apparent that Matt. 27:24–25 is not a documentary of events but a literary composition that had as its purpose the removal of blame for Jesus' death from Pilate and Roman power and the transferral of guilt to all of the Jewish people forever. The bitterness of the invective here is approached in the New Testament only in some other portions of Matthew that are not redactions of Markan or of "Q" materials,[59] in the interpolation of 1 Thess. 2:13–16 into Paul's writing,[60] and in the Fourth Gospel[61] and the Acts of the Apostles.[62]

For nearly nineteen centuries most of us who as Christians heard or read

Matt. 27:24–25 have considered these verses to be a record of events as they actually happened, and we have responded with what we thought were appropriate anti-Jewish attitudes and actions. During the twentieth century, however, and particularly since 1945 many of us have called Matt. 27:24–25 into question. Christians within the Roman Catholic tradition have been notably sensitive to this issue, especially during the time when Vatican II was considering important changes in the Roman Catholic position regarding relationships with Judaism. For example, Dominic M. Crossan, in a brief study of the "crowds" in Luke, the Jews in John, the mob in the passion accounts, and the confrontation of Diaspora Judaism and Paul, took the position that the often-repeated statement that the Jews rejected Jesus and caused him to be crucified is historically untenable and must be removed completely from Roman Catholic Christian thinking, writing, teaching, preaching, and liturgy.[63] Continuing discussion of the issue, Joseph A. Fitzmyer recognized that there was no possibility that Vatican II would delete Matt. 27:25 from the Roman Catholic editions of the New Testament, or even tamper with its wording, since it is the inspired Word of God. In Fitzmyer's opinion, therefore, Christian exegetes will have to endeavor to bring the proper focus to the understanding of this crucial text. Fitzmyer attempted this with perhaps a measure of success by interpreting Matt. 27:25 within the context of Fitzmyer's postulated secondary theme in Matthew, namely, that Matthew was trying to explain to Jewish-background Christians why the "nations" were taking over the kingdom of heaven.[64]

If our attitudes and our actions are to be changed significantly, however, more drastic measures are necessary. The content of Matt. 27:24–25 will not be "removed completely" from our "thinking, writing, teaching, preaching, and liturgy" so long as it remains in the New Testament translations that we as Christians use. With equal respect for the New Testament documents as inspired, dynamic, living Word of God we can "prune away" Matt. 27:24–25 into a footnote in our translations and usage in order that the "vine" or "tree" of the Word of God may bear more and better fruit. Only if the "vine" were dead would it be diminished by this careful and conscientious pruning.

As stated elsewhere in this study, the pruning is to take place not in debate and "win-lose" voting in church conventions and ecumenical councils—not even in a truly ecumenical council—but in the marketplace of ideas, in the books we read, in the usage of the people. Only after hundreds of years of change in the marketplace of ideas will conventions and councils ratify that which by then has already occurred. None of us who are here during these latter decades of the twentieth century will live to see all of this happen to Matt. 27:24–25. This does not excuse us from the responsibility now to take courageously what to many of our fellow Christians will seem to be the overly drastic measure of relegating Matt. 27:24–25 to a footnote in our translations and usage.

27:43: *He trusts in God; let God rescue him now if God wants him!* At this point the Matthean tradition uses Ps. 22:8 and Wisdom of Solomon 2:13–20 to compose an additional expression of spite and attribute it to the chief priests, scribes, and elders mocking Jesus as he hung suspended on the cross. The verse coheres with Matt. 12:34a, 45c; 15:12–14a; 23:13–33, 34–36; and 27:24–25 in its anti-Jewish intensity. For us as Christians, our teaching about the resurrection of Jesus within history is adequate vindication of the Jesus of history. We do not need in this instance—nor perhaps in others that are similar—the "left hand" of anti-Jewish polemic inherent in this verse in order for us to have the "right hand" of Christology central in Christianity.[65] We would do well, therefore, to acknowledge that Matt. 27:43 is another piece of anti-Jewish invective in Matthean composition and relegate it to footnote status in our translations and usage.

27:62–66; 28:4, 11–15: *The guard at the tomb, their embarrassment, and the cover-up arrangements.* From what may have been an oral tradition that attempted to present the resurrection of Jesus as an objective, provable fact, the Matthean redactor apparently fashioned and wove into the Markan sequence in three different places an account designed one more time to show the utter depravity of the chief priests, Pharisees, and elders. Rather than to list the many improbabilities in these accounts as many others have done,[66] my purpose here will be to consider ways in which we today may repudiate the anti-Jewish polemic that appears to be the main reason for these verses in the Matthean account.

The most desirable response on our part would be for us to drop Matt. 27:62–66; 28:4, 11–15 to footnote status in our translations and usage. For those who are not willing to do this and for those who wish to continue to try to prove the resurrection of Jesus to those who do not believe, interpretative translations and circumlocutions can be employed in which the chief priests, Pharisees, and elders in 27:62, 28:11–12 are rendered as "certain religious leaders," and "among the Jews" in 28:15 becomes "among many who do not believe in Jesus' resurrection."

D. In the Total Gospel according to Matthew

The preceding analysis indicates the following:

1. The anti-Jewish polemic already present in Matthew's sources (Markan and "Q" materials, as well as most likely in other written and oral sources utilized in Matthew) was heightened considerably in Matthean redactions.

2. The most bitter anti-Jewish invective in Matthew (12:34a, 45c; 15:12–14a; 23:13–33, 34–36; 27:24–25, 43, 62–66; 28:4, 11–15) is written in Mat-

thew's use of non-Markan or "Q" materials or in Matthew's own compositions.

3. The "Torah and the prophets" were of interest in the formulation of the Matthean Gospel not for their own sake or for their inherent value, but almost entirely in the service of Matthean proclamation and parenesis and to "prove" its points in theological polemic. More specifically, the Jewish Scriptures were used in Matthew as proof that Jesus and Jesus' interpretation of the Jewish Scriptures are superior to the Pharisees and their understanding of the Jewish texts.

4. The principal editor-writers who formulated the Matthean Gospel were for the most part probably not of Jewish background, or if they were, they had disassociated themselves almost completely from their Jewish background.[67]

5. The most vicious anti-Jewish material in Matthew can be repudiated by interpretative translations and by pruning to footnote status without damage to the basic Christology of Matthew's Gospel.

Notes

1. In order that the reader may visualize how the relationships and interrelationships between the Synoptic Gospels and the Fourth Gospel are perceived in the present study, an illustrated diagram which attempts to trace the history of the traditions and the relationships and interrelationships of the Synoptic and Johannine Gospels is included as Appendix A.

2. At earlier stages of the development of the suffering servant passages the servant was probably seen as a single great prophet from the past and then as a composite of all of Israel's great self-sacrificing prophets who had passed away but hopefully would some day return in a new form to speak for God to the people.

3. The awkwardness with which the miracle story is reintroduced in Mark 2:10b is retained in Matt. 9:6a and in Luke 5:24a. See above, p. 104.

4. See below, p. 169.

5. Pp. 105–106.

6. See Barnabas Lindars, *New Testament Apologetic* (London: SCM Press, 1961), and M. D. Goulder, *Midrash and Lection in Matthew* (London: S.P.C.K., 1974).

7. See above, pp. 108–109.

8. This series of events includes a healing miracle story sandwiched (a Markan characteristic) between portions of a restoration-to-life miracle story.

9. See above, p. 109.

10. See above, pp. 110–11.

11. See above, p. 112, as well as Arland J. Hultgren, *Jesus and His Adversaries* (Minneapolis, Minn.: Augsburg, 1979), pp. 46–47, and D. Lamar Cope, *Matthew: A Scribe Trained for the Kingdom of Heaven*, CBQ Monograph Series 5 (Washington: Catholic Biblical Association, 1976), pp. 40–44, 49–52.

12. See above, p. 112.

13. See above, p. 113.

14. Since Matt. 19:28b appears to be "Q" material, it is not included here.

15. See above, pp. 115–16.

16. See the detailed analysis of the Markan text above, pp. 116–17.

17. See above, pp. 117–18.

18. See above, p. 118.

19. See above, p. 118, and Arland J. Hultgren, "The Double Commandment of Love in Mt 22:34–40: Its Sources and Composition," *CBQ* 36 (1974): 373–78.

20. Hultgren, *Jesus and His Adversaries*, pp. 45–46, compares these texts to demonstrate how early Christians deliberately formed materials into controversy dialogues.

21. The problem of these "woes" will be addressed below, pp. 156–59.

22. See above, pp. 119–20.

23. Matt. 23:14 is apparently a late formulation of a "woe" saying in which the material of Mark 12:40 was utilized.

24. Matt. 23:1–12 is used on the Twenty-sixth Sunday after Pentecost, Series A, in the lectionary included in *Lutheran Book of Worship* (Minneapolis, Minn.: Augsburg, and Philadelphia: Board of Publication, Lutheran Church in America, 1978), p. 29. Among the denominations using this series only the Lutheran lectionary has the Matt. 23:1–12 reading.

25. See above, p. 120.

26. See above, pp. 121–22.

27. Since Matt. 27:43 has no parallels elsewhere in the Four Gospels, it is considered along with 27:24–26 below in the analysis of Matthew's other compositions from written or oral sources.

28. See above, pp. 129–30.

29. This saying is not discussed in the section on anti-Jewish polemic in "Q" material on pp. 129–34 above because it is not likely that as "Q" material it was polemic against the Pharisees or against other Jews as Jews.

30. See Richard A. Edwards, *A Theology of Q; Eschatology, Prophecy, and Wisdom* (Philadelphia: Fortress, 1976), pp. 96–99.

31. A. H. McNeile, *The Gospel According to St. Matthew* (London: Macmillan, 1915), p. 176.

32. An evaluation in agreement with Lindars, *New Testament Apologetic*, p. 172.

33. See above, p. 133, and below, p. 183.

34. See above, pp. 133–34.

35. See above, pp. 31–35.

36. See above, pp. 46–50.

37. This method is chosen for present purposes in preference to more "systematic" methods such as that employed by G. D. Kilpatrick, *The Origins of the Gospel According to St. Matthew* (Oxford: Clarendon, 1946), pp. 37–58.

38. See Marshall D. Johnson, *The Purpose of the Biblical Genealogies* (Cambridge: University Press, 1969).

39. Mark 15:2, 9, 12, 18, 26; Matt. 27:11, 29, 37; Luke 23:3, 37, 38. "King of Israel" occurs in Mark 15:32; Matt. 27:42.

40. See the study of the "testimonies" in Matthew in Lindars, *New Testament Apologetic*, pp. 13–31.

41. See Günther Bornkamm, Gerhard Barth, and Heinz Joachim Held, *Tradition and Interpretation in Matthew*, trans. P. Scott (Philadelphia: Westminster, 1963), pp. 24–32, 62–105, 159–64. Polemic against alleged antinomians in Matthew's account is an important related matter, but one that cannot be considered in detail here. See also W. D. Davies, *The Setting of the Sermon on the Mount* (Cambridge: University Press, 1964).

42. See Gerhard von Rad, *Old Testament Theology*, trans. D. M. G. Stalker (New York: Harper & Row, 1962), 1:370–84.

43. See the analysis of hypocrites in Matthew in Tilborg, *The Jewish Leaders in Matthew* (Leiden: E. J. Brill, 1972), pp. 8–26.

44. For studies of the Pharisees and other first-century Jews that demonstrate the injustice inherent in generalizing condemnations, see Israel Abrahams, *Studies in Pharisaism and the Gospels*, 2 vols. (Cambridge: Cambridge University, 1917, 1924).

45. See D. R. A. Hare, *The Theme of Jewish Persecution of Christians in the Gospel According to St. Matthew* (Cambridge: Cambridge University, 1967).

46. Tilborg, *The Jewish Leaders in Matthew*, pp. 26, 28–29.

47. The expression, which translated into idiomatic English would be "You sons of bitches!" occurs as words of Jesus solely in Matthew's own material in Matt. 12:34 and 23:33. The only other New Testament occurrence is in the words of John the Baptist in Matt. 3:7b and Luke 3:7b. Although Matt. 3:7b–10 and Luke 3:7b–9 are "Q" material, the expression may have been prefaced to the words of John the Baptist at the time Matt. 3:7b was being formulated and from there have been carried over in early harmonizing activity into Luke 3:7b. In our voluminous literature on the Synoptic Problem we have not taken this early harmonizing activity adequately into consideration. Yet it is this early harmonizing activity that more than any other factor weakens the evidence that we otherwise can marshall in support of the Two Document Hypothesis. It is this same early harmonizing activity that provides sufficient evidence to keep the Griesbach Hypothesis alive.

48. Matt. 12:45c should be retained in our Greek editions to preserve the integrity of the restoration of the textual tradition process.

49. P. 140.

50. See above, p. 148.

51. Eduard Schweizer, *The Good News According to Matthew*, trans. D. E. Green (Atlanta, Ga.: John Knox, 1975), pp. 404–5.

52. It is regrettable that Matt. 22:1–10 (11–14) is the Gospel reading for the Twenty-first Sunday after Pentecost in Series A while Luke 14:16–23 is not included within the lectionary printed in our *Lutheran Book of Worship*, pp. 13–41. The other denominations using this series also have Matt. 22:1–14 as the reading for the Twenty-first Sunday after Pentecost, Series A.

53. See above, pp. 145–46.

54. Plus an additional time in Matt. 23:14 where it is probably a later formulation in which the material of Mark 12:40 was utilized.

55. In a saying distantly related to Matt. 23:13 the Luke 11:52 reading is "Woe to you who are Torah scholars." Matt. 23:15 has no parallel in the Gospel accounts. Fairly similar to Matt. 23:23 is Luke 11:42, "Woe to you who are Pharisees." Compared to Matt. 23:25 in Luke 11:39 is written "You Pharisees clean the outside of the cup." In shorter forms of what is written in Matt. 23:27, 29 in Luke 11:44, 47 we read simply "Woe to you." See also Ernst Haenchen, "Matthäus 23," *ZTK* 48 (1959): 38–63; and Tilborg, *The Jewish Leaders in Matthew*, pp. 18–24, 104–6.

56. See above, pp. 67–68, 129.

57. The Matthean tradition apparently mistakenly added "son of Barachiah" instead of "son of Jehoiada" (2 Chron. 24:21) to Zechariah in 23:35.

58. Schweizer, *The Good News According to Matthew*, pp. 508–9.

59. Matt. 12:34a, 45c; 15:12–14a; 23:13–33, 34–36; 27:43.

60. See above, pp. 40–46.

61. See below, chap. 9.

62. See below, chap. 8.

63. Dominic M. Crossan, "Anti-Semitism and the Gospel," *TS* 26 (1965): 189–214.

64. Joseph A. Fitzmyer, "Anti-Semitism and the Cry of 'All the People' (Mt 27, 25)," *TS* 26 (1965): 667–71.

65. For further discussion of this important issue, see below, chap. 11, and Rosemary R. Ruether, *Faith and Fratricide: The Theological Roots of Anti-Semitism* (New York: Seabury, 1974); John M. Oesterreicher, *Anatomy of Contempt: A Critique of R. R.*

Ruether's "Faith and Fratricide" (South Orange, N.J.: The Institute of Judaeo-Christian Studies, Seton Hall University, Institute paper no. 4 1975); and Thomas A. Idinopulos and Roy Bowen Ward, "Is Christology Inherently Anti-Semitic: A Critical Review of Rosemary Ruether's *Faith and Fratricide*," *JAAR* 45 (1977): 193–214.

66. See, for example, Schweizer, *The Good News According to Matthew*, pp. 518–21, 524–27; and Tilborg, *The Jewish Leaders in Matthew*, pp. 106–8. For those who are interested in seeing how the account continued to develop, in the Gospel of Peter a name is given to the officer in charge of the guard at the tomb, and teachers of the Torah, Pharisees, and elders assist the soldiers in rolling the huge stone over the entrance to the tomb. These religious leaders then secure the stone with seven seals and join the military detachment in keeping watch while all the people from the greater Jerusalem area observe the entire scene.

67. See the argumentation of B. T. Viviano, "Where Was the Gospel According to St. Matthew Written?" *CBQ* 41 (1979): 533–46, that Caesarea Maritima is the most plausible localization for the final redaction of Matthew.

7

Anti-Jewish Polemic in Luke

The starting point of this analysis will be anti-Jewish polemic in redactional emendations in Luke's extensive use of Markan material.[1] This will be followed by a study of similar polemic in Luke's use of "Q" material.[2] Then anti-Jewish polemic in Luke's use of other written or oral sources and in Luke's own compositions will be examined.[3] Finally, in summary form, there will be an evaluation of anti-Jewish polemic in the total Gospel According to Luke. Analysis of specific texts will continue to include recognition of the polemic, attempts to try to determine how it developed, and suggestions of ways in which we can repudiate it in our own translations and usage.

A. In Luke's Use of Markan Material

Mark 1:14–15; 6:1–6a; Luke 4:14–30: *Glorified and rejected.* The objective stated in the Lukan preface, to write an account that will rearrange the oral traditions and written word into a new, more logical pattern,[4] is amply illustrated in this account, which in Luke introduces Jesus' Galilean ministry. The impression is given that the Lukan writer knew Mark 1:14–15 and 6:1–6a, but here as frequently elsewhere freely "pruned and adorned"[5] Mark's Gospel to juxtapose Israel's contrasting responses by which it first glorified and then rejected Jesus and his ministry. The resultant narrative is a program of many of the main themes of Luke and Acts *in nuce,*[6] even though the reader is hardly prepared at this point in the reading of Luke for the "cold front" that in the middle of Luke 4:22 marks the transition from glorification to rejection.

In Luke's thorough redaction of Mark 1:14–15 the power and glory of Jesus are greatly magnified. The separation of Jesus from any possible dependence upon John the Baptist, accomplished in Luke 3:20–21, is maintained.[7] Where Mark had Jesus merely coming into Galilee, Luke has him returning to Galilee in the power of the Spirit of God. Luke adds that

Jesus' fame spread throughout the area[8] and that he taught in "their" synagogues where he was glorified by everyone. The keynote of Mark, Mark's use of the word *gospel,* and Jesus' incisive call to repentance in view of the imminent coming of the kingdom of God are all passed over here in favor of Luke's emphasis upon the initial and desirable glorification of Jesus by all people from his own area and background. Although neither Jewish groups, the Jews collectively, nor Israel corporately is specifically mentioned in Luke 4:14–15, this expression of the power and glory of Jesus in "their" synagogues is clearly more anti-Jewish than is the Markan basis for this account.

Even though, as John Drury has seen,[9] Luke avoids some Markan and Matthean anachronisms, it is probable that some new ones are formed in the Luke 4:16–30 account of Jesus' experiences in his hometown. The townspeople who in their intense anger were intent on throwing Jesus from a high cliff to his death on the rocks below were probably not friends and relatives of the Jesus of history; they were instead those who several decades later bitterly opposed the followers of Jesus who entered Jewish synagogues to claim for Jesus more than Jewish monotheism would permit. The vicious wrath of all the men of the synagogue (4:28) is simply not accounted for in what Jesus is reported to have said in 4:23–27, or by anything else in Luke's account up to this point.[10]

Luke apparently brought the Mark 6:1–6a account forward to this place and thoroughly refurbished it with the Septuagint as the most extensive source. The disciples who followed Jesus in Mark 6:1b were dropped, since Luke had not as yet introduced them at this point in the account. The reading of Isa. 61:1–2a (58:6) and Jesus' announcement that on that day this Scripture of good news for the poor had been fulfilled were said to have been received as words of grace. Luke replaced Mark 6:2b–3 with its references to Jesus as a man, a carpenter, and one who had brothers and sisters with the single question of those who would not know or accept Jesus' theological paternity, "Is this not Joseph's son?" Also omitted was Mark 6:5, the observation that Jesus was not able to do any mighty act there except, having placed his hands on a few who were ill, he healed them. To Mark's proverb "A prophet is not lacking in honor . . ." Luke added another, "Physician, heal yourself!" with the interpretation, "You who would heal, do what you have just read from Isaiah." The offense that is in the hands of the people in the Nazareth synagogue in Mark 6:3b is taken over by Jesus in Luke with his remarks about the activities of Elijah and Elisha with non-Israelites in 4:25–27.[11] Nevertheless, the violent reaction of the men of the synagogue in Jesus' hometown is almost certainly an exaggeration and an anachronism. (Nazareth during Jesus' public ministry was hardly a *polis* (city), and it was not built upon an edge of a steep hill.) Luke's attitude against the Jews turns much harsher in Acts, but the harshness is already evident here in Luke 4:16–30.[12]

In Luke 4:25–27 the Elijah and Elisha stories are interpreted in such a way that preservation of life and healing of body are offered to non-Israelite persons rather than to Israelites. Actually, in the Elijah story the prophet was sent outside of Israel, one may surmise, not to preserve the life of the woman of Zarephath but primarily because Ahab was trying to kill him. Since there is no reason to suppose that Elisha could not have cleansed or did not cleanse men from leprosy also within Israel, Luke 4:27 uses an argument from silence in making its principal point. While there is little evidence that the offering of salvation to non-Israelites was high on the agenda of the Jesus of history, there can be no doubt that according to Luke-Acts it was of prime importance for the Lukan writer.

As for the present use of Luke 4:14–30, the 4:14–22a portion is obviously the most significant, although it is important that we recognize from 4:22b–27 that the good things that God may accomplish—such as the preservation of life and the healing of dreaded diseases—are not nor should they be limited to persons within one's own particular religious persuasion. Luke 4:28–30, the segment of the pericope that exhibits the most concentrated anti-Jewish polemic, should not be included in our lectionary readings. This story about the vicious wrath of all the men of the synagogue and their abortive attempt to lynch Jesus (and on the Sabbath!) is much more likely a Lukan composition late in the first century than it is the reporting of a historical occurrence from the time of the Jesus of history. Not only is 4:28–30 relatively lacking in value for edification, but also Jesus' superhuman ability to slip through the hands of an angry mob appears to run counter to his reported refusal to use such power in the Luke 4:1–13 temptation account earlier in the same chapter.

In summary, we see that with the Mark 1:14–15 and 6:1–6a *Vorlage* as the base, Luke used a midrashic type of application of the Jews' own Scriptures in constructing an account in which anti-Jewish polemic was greatly expanded. This new construction, with its sharp contrast[13] between the glorification and the rejection of Jesus, was then placed at the beginning of Jesus' ministry in Luke's "more orderly" account.[14]

Mark 2:1–12; Luke 5:17–26: *The healing of the paralyzed man.* Both Luke 5:17–26 and Matt. 9:1–8 follow the Markan account closely, retaining the sequence in which Mark sandwiched the controversy within the miracle story.[15] Where Matthew increased the anti-Jewish polemic by changing Jesus' question addressed to the scribes to "Why do you *think evil* in your hearts?"[16] Luke increased it by adding the Pharisees to those who questioned Jesus' pronouncement of forgiveness (Luke 5:21) and by integrating the controversy more fully into the miracle account by introducing Pharisees and Torah teachers from every village of Galilee and Judea and Jerusalem into the setting for the miracle story (Luke 5:17b). Luke also added in 5:17c that the "power of the Lord was present so that he was able to heal." The Pharisees and Torah teachers were added in Luke but not in Matthew. When the Luke 5:17–26 pericope is used today, it would be advisable, as in Mark and Matthew, to limit the reading to the miracle story (Luke 5:17–20, 24b–26), passing over the controversy which interrupts the powerful flow of the miracle account.

Mark 2:13–17; Luke 5:27–32: *Eating with tax collectors and sinners.* As indicated above,[17] the anti-Jewish polemic is increased in Luke 5:30 by having the Pharisees and their scribes murmur against Jesus' disciples, saying, "Why do you eat and drink with these tax collectors and sinners?" As in the Markan account the value of this text for Christian self-criticism would be enhanced if "the Pharisees and their scribes" were translated as "some religious leaders of that time."

Mark 2:18–20; Luke 5:33–35: *Fasting.* Redactional changes in this account[18] are merely stylistic and not substantive as far as anti-Jewish polemic is concerned. However, in the sayings about patching garments and putting new wine into old wineskins, which are attached to this account about fasting in Mark and retained in Matthew and in Luke, there is the interesting addition of Luke 5:39. Apparently somewhere along the line of the transmission of these sayings the Lukan writer or some later connoisseur of fine wines added the observation[19] that "No one who is able to drink the older wine wishes to have the new, for he says, 'The older is *chrēstos* (delightful)' "[20] The connoisseur and most of the Lukan tradition apparently were not aware of or concerned for the Markan eschatological community's identification of itself as the new wine that could not be contained in the old Jewish wineskins.[21] Unwittingly the connoisseur and most of the Lukan tradition thereby incorporated into the normative Scripture of Christianity a most subtle endorsement of the older wine, Judaism!

Mark 2:23–28; Luke 6:1–5: *The Sabbath walk through the grainfields at harvest time.*[22]

Mark 3:1–6; Luke 6:6–11: *The Sabbath healing of the man with the withered hand.* Anti-Jewish polemic is increased in the Lukan account by the identification as "the scribes and the Pharisees" of those who were watching Jesus maliciously to see whether he would heal on the Sabbath in order that they might find something with which to accuse him in a trial, and by the report in 6:11 that they were filled with fury because Jesus had restored the man's hand on the Sabbath. Not incorporated into the Lukan account are the references to Jesus' anger, to his grief over the hardness of their heart, to the Pharisees' complicity with the Herodians, and to their intent specifically to destroy Jesus. The anger of Jesus in Mark is translated into the fury of the scribes and the Pharisees in Luke. As Frederick Danker suggests,[23] "what they might do to Jesus" in 6:11 is a dramatic understatement; Luke seems to prefer to emphasize Jesus' own initiative as he proceeds inexorably to his death in Jerusalem.

In the interpretation and use of Luke 6:6–11 and its parallels, the emphasis should be upon concern for life and health. If "the scribes and the Pharisees" were translated as "some of the religious leaders who opposed Jesus," the anti-Jewish impact of the account, which distracts from a Christian self-criticism, would be reduced. In its present state in all three Synoptic accounts the controversy dialogue is so predominant that the miracle itself is almost incidental.

Mark 3:22–30; Luke 11:14–23: *The dispute about exorcism.* The literary interrelationships are particularly complex in this section. It is probable that Luke drew more heavily here from "Q" material than from Markan. Since "Q" material likely contained an exorcism that the Markan account lacked, Luke began this segment with "Q" material and continued from "Q" material "some of them" said rather than from Mark "the scribes who had come down from Jerusalem." Anti-Jewish polemic is increased in Luke over that in Mark, Matthew, and probably in "Q" material in this pericope by Luke's insertion of "and others, testing him, were seeking a sign from heaven from him" (Luke 11:16).[24]

Mark 5:21–43; Luke 8:40–56: *The restoration to life of Jairus's daughter.*[25] Compared to the Markan account available to us, Luke's is shortened and rearranged. The power of Jesus and his superiority over the religion of the synagogue are enhanced somewhat in that in Luke's concise report the healing of the woman's hemorrhage and the restoration to life of Jairus's daughter seem to occur more quickly and with less effort on Jesus' part.

(Mark 7:1–23); Luke 11:37–41: *The dispute about "clean" and "unclean."* Although direct dependence upon any substantial portions of Mark 6:45–8:26 is not apparent in Luke,[26] and although Luke 11:37–41 may have preserved a "Q" materials setting[27] for the "Woe to you!" sayings of Luke 11:42–52 and Matt. 23:13, 15–33, there is sufficient similarity between Mark 7:1–23 and Luke 11:37–41 on the issue of ritual purity to warrant consideration here.

The lack of verbal dependence in Luke upon Mark 6:45–8:26 and the resultant omission of the extensive dispute in Mark 7:1–23 between Jesus and the Pharisees about what is "clean" and what is "unclean" is sometimes thought to be evidence for a deliberate reduction of anti-Jewish polemic in Luke. As Robert Brawley has seen,[28] Luke's attitude regarding the Pharisees is indeed complex and perhaps in some respects ambivalent. Only Luke has three occasions in which Jesus is a guest of a Pharisee (the text under consideration here, plus 7:36–50 and 14:1–24). Some Pharisees advise Jesus to "go out and go away from here" because Herod wants to kill him (Luke 13:31). Luke presents the Pharisees in a fairly positive, or at least neutral, position also in Acts 5:34–39; 23:6–10; and 26:5. Both Brawley and J. A. Ziesler[29] are of the opinion that in Luke-Acts, compared to the other New Testament documents, the Pharisees stand relatively close to

Christianity as political if not always as theological friends of the followers of Jesus. A reason Luke presented the Pharisees in a relatively favorable light, according to Brawley, was that Luke expected readers who were of Jewish origin to identify with the Pharisees in these accounts. Therefore Luke used the Pharisees as a point of contact with such readers.[30]

With regard to Luke 11:37–41, however, Jesus is presented as responding to the hospitality extended by the Pharisee, and to the Pharisee's amazement that Jesus did not participate in the Jewish ritual washing prior to the meal, with direct, abusive condemnation. Luke's use of the epithet *aphrones* in direct address ("you foolish people") here in 11:40 and less frontally in a parable in 12:20 is unique in the Gospels, as Frederick Danker has observed.[31] Jesus, as the Lord,[32] is made to tell his host in 11:39 that his host and others like him are full of *harpagē* (stolen plunder) and *ponēria* (evil). This affront, particularly in the face of Oriental hospitality, results in anti-Jewish polemic at least equal to, if not greater than, that expressed in Mark 7:1–23 and its Matt. 15:1–20 parallel, where Jesus is not presented as a houseguest of a Pharisee.

As we attempt to traverse the steps that may have occurred in the development of this account from a possible *Sitz im Leben* in the life of the Jesus of history to the canonical Luke 11:37–41, we can assume that Jesus may have been a guest on various occasions in the home of a Pharisee. He may have considered the ritual washings to be unnecessary or at least relatively unimportant, and he may have expressed his opinions about the practice. If he accepted an invitation to a home where the ritual washings were important for the host, however, it seems probable that as a guest he would have followed the practices of the host family. Since there probably were occasions in which Jesus bluntly condemned rapacity and other evil in the lives of his own people, it is likely that in the reminiscences of his followers several of these factors were combined into an account that verified the practices of the followers of Jesus and at the same time condemned the Pharisees.

For those Christians today who have some understanding of the processes by which the Gospel texts attained their canonical form, the anti-Jewish polemic in a text such as Luke 11:37–41 can probably be neutralized for the most part merely because there is an awareness of the process of development. But only a small though increasing minority of Christians have an awareness of the process of development of the Gospel accounts. For those who do not have an awareness of this process of development, or who reject opportunities to become familiar with the process, the anti-Jewish elements in a text such as this will remain blatant, unless we can and are willing to blunt them somewhat in our vernacular translations. In the case of this text, such a translation could retain and emphasize the teaching portion but reduce to footnote status the name-calling and the situation in the Pharisee's house with no loss of Christology. The result, in sequence after the related body-imagery teaching material in Luke 11:34–36, would be as follows:

> 11:34 "The lamp of your body is your eye. When your eye is clear, your whole body is radiant. But when it is evil, your whole body is darkened. 35 Watch out, therefore; you do not want the light that is in you to be extinguished. 36 If your body is fully radiant, not having any part darkened, it will be as brilliant in every part as a lamp is when it shines on you with its light.* Did not the one who made the outside of you also make the inside? 41 Give charitably the things that are within you, and every part of you is going to be clear."

This type of translation recognizes the probability that animosity between followers of Jesus and Pharisees during the decades after the ministry of Jesus was so bitter that followers of Jesus were willing to present Jesus as a most ungracious guest in order to make their point against the Pharisees. The translation is an attempt to move back behind the Lukan text, and perhaps behind Mark and "Q" material also, in the direction of the Jesus of history. It provides a more edifying account, it deemphasizes the presentation of Jesus as an ungracious guest, and it reduces the anti-Jewish polemic.

Mark 8:15; Luke 12:1: *Beware of the leaven.* It is possible that this caveat, inserted at some point into the Markan story about the lack of more than one loaf in the boat,[33] was inserted into Luke 12:1 from an anti-Pharisaic oral tradition that was circulating among the followers of Jesus. It might also have been one of a few fragments of Markan material utilized from Mark 6:45–8:26. Regardless of its origin, the form of the caveat in Luke 12:1 is more pejorative of the Jews and of the most significant Jewish group after 70 C.E. than is either the Markan or the Matthean parallel. Since the identification of the Pharisees as hypocritical is otherwise more characteristic of Matthew than of Luke, this identification may have come into the Luke 12:1 text as a gloss. A sensitive translation of Luke into vernacular language will reduce 12:1c to footnote status, so that 12:1b–2 will read, "And he began to say to his disciples, 'Nothing is covered which will not be uncovered. . . .'" The words *prōton* (first) and *de* (but) in 12:1b and 2a are probably indications of the insertion of the gloss.

Mark 10:1–12: Luke 16:18: *The Pharisees and divorce.* At first glance the nonuse in Luke of Mark 10:1–10 (Matt. 19:3–8) appears to constitute a

---

*37 "And while he was speaking, a religious leader invited him to eat with him, and he went into the man's house and reclined where the food was served. 38 The religious leader, having seen this, was surprised that Jesus did not participate in the customary ritual washing before the meal. 39 And the Lord said to him, 'You religious leaders clean the outside of the cup and the platter but the inside of you is full of stolen plunder and of evil. 40 You foolish people!'"

substantial reduction of anti-Jewish polemic in Luke, since the references to the Pharisees having come to Jesus testing him and Jesus' mention of the Pharisees' hardness of heart are consequently omitted. However, a closer look at the Lukan context of 16:18 indicates that this verse is set in a thoroughly polemical framework.

It is said in 16:14–15 that the Pharisees, being lovers of money, scoffed at Jesus when they heard him teaching that it is not possible to serve God and money at the same time. Also it is said that the Pharisees justify themselves before men and that their actions are abominable to God. In 16:16–17, the fulcrum for Conzelmann's interpretation of time in Luke-Acts,[34] the Torah and the prophetic traditions are validated as they are, and as a religious reformer Jesus is represented as calling his own people back to conformity to their own purest traditions. The story about the rich man and the poor man Lazarus that follows 16:18 is further indication of the claim that Jesus is acting in full accord with Abraham, Moses, and the authoritative prophetic traditions. The Torah and the prophets developed up to the time of John the Baptist. John marked the time of the proclamation of the kingdom of God and everyone who enters it goes into it under threat of violence from those enemies of Jesus and of the Gospel who would try to keep them out. In this setting over against the Pharisees, 16:18 claims that Jesus and his followers adhere to the original deontological intent of the Torah. As Danker puts it,[35] the standards of the kingdom are here presented as being as high or even possibly higher than are those of the Torah, and the Pharisees rather than Jesus are accused of undermining the Torah. Here also Luke is demonstrating that this new presentation of the things that have been accomplished is more logical and convincing than were the accounts previously available.

Mark 8:31; (9:12); 9:31; 10:33–34; Luke 9:22; 9:44; 18:31b–33: *The passion predictions.* In Luke's more concise account there is some reduction of anti-Jewish polemic in the passion predictions, most notably in Luke 18:31b–33, where Luke does not reproduce Mark's "prediction" that the Son of man "will be delivered over to the chief priests and to the scribes and they will condemn him to death." In its place Luke has the statement that "all things written about the Son of man by the prophets will be fulfilled." It is probable that this substitution is not because Luke wished to reduce anti-Jewish polemic but because Luke wanted here as elsewhere to show that Jesus' life, death, and resurrection were "according to the Scriptures."

Mark 11:12–25; Luke 13:6–9; 19:45–48; 21:37–38: *The fig tree and the temple.* In this instance it is likely that a parable that may go back to the Jesus of history is recorded in Luke 13:6–9.[36] With regard to spiritual value and edification, as well as level of anti-Jewish polemic, it is preferable in each instance to the account about Jesus' cursing the fig tree in Mark 11:12–14, 20–25.[37] It is probable that Luke included this account rather than the cursing the fig tree incident not so much to reduce anti-Jewish polemic, however, since elsewhere Luke increases it, but because Luke recognized how much greater spiritual value the parable contained.[38]

There is little difference in the degree of anti-Jewish polemic between the Markan and the Lukan temple-cleansing accounts. Luke's report is characteristically more concise. The other difference is that Luke included "And he was teaching every day in the temple" at 19:47a, prior to the mention of the desire of the religious and political leaders to destroy Jesus, so that Luke separates their animosity somewhat from the temple cleansing and attaches it more closely to Jesus' teaching. Luke also added *hoi prōtoi tou laou* (the most prominent men among the people) to the listing of those who, according to Mark, were seeking how they might destroy him.

Mark 11:27–33; Luke 20:1–8: *The question of authority.*[39] Luke's account follows Mark closely, even verbally in places. There is some shortening of the controversy conversation and a few editorial adjustments in the introduction to the pericope, by which Luke emphasized that Jesus was teaching the people in the temple daily (as in Luke 19:47a, noted above), and that Jesus was proclaiming the good news about the kingdom of God. Overall, there is no significant change in the amount of anti-Jewish polemic from Mark to Luke in this instance.

Mark 12:1–12; Luke 20:9–19: *The story about an owner of a vineyard collecting his rent.* Unlike Mark or Matthew, Luke makes a distinction between the people and the religious leaders.[40] In Luke the allegorized parable used as a controversy dialogue is told to the people rather than to the chief priests, the scribes, and the elders, and since there is only a single parable at this place Luke corrects Mark's "in parables" to "this parable." Only Luke has "having heard this, they (presumably the people) said, 'May this never happen!'" Consistently then, Luke changed Mark's "they were seeking to seize him but they feared the crowd" (Mark 12:12a) to "the scribes and the chief priests sought to get their hands on him at that time but they feared the people" (Luke 20:19a). These changes, along with the nonuse of Mark's wine-production-preparation detail drawn from Isaiah 5, can be interpreted as a reduction of anti-Jewish polemic compared to the Markan account. On the other hand, Luke allegorized the parable more than Mark had at two key places. In Luke 20:13 the son (the only emissary to be killed in the Lukan account) has become the "beloved" son ("What should I do? I will send my beloved son"), and as in Matt. 21:39, the renters, having thrown him out of the vineyard, killed him on the outside just as Jesus had been killed outside the walls of Jerusalem. Also, Luke did not reproduce with Mark and Matthew from Ps. 118:23 ("This is the Lord's doing; it is marvellous in our eyes"), but added "Everyone who has fallen upon that stone will be dashed into pieces; upon whomever it may fall, it shall crush him,"[41] an addition that entered into many manuscripts of Matthew also at 21:44.

Mark 12:13–17; Luke 20:20–26: *To pay or not to pay the Roman poll tax.*

Luke's redaction of this account heightens the anti-Jewish polemic by adding to the detail of the plotting against Jesus at the beginning of the account that they (the scribes and the chief priests from 20:19), "having watched him closely, sent spies who pretended to be righteous in order that they might catch him in something which he might say, so that they could deliver him over to the rule and the authority of the governor," and at the end that "they were not clever enough to catch him in anything that he said in the presence of the people and they became silent." As in our use of the Markan and Matthean parallels,[42] our attention should be focused on the question addressed to Jesus and on his answer (in Luke 20:21–22, 23b–25), not on the controversy-dialogue setting provided for the question and for his answer.

Mark 12:18–27; Luke 20:27–40: *The Sadducees and the resurrection life.* Most of Luke's changes here are merely stylistic. However, polemic against the Sadducees is reduced in Luke in that the Mark 12:24b, 27b statements by Jesus that the Sadducees err much, not having either the Scriptures nor the power of God, are not reproduced from Mark. In their place Luke has additional teachings regarding the condition of people "in this age" and "in that age," and from a comment in Mark that occurs in the conversation between Jesus and the Torah scholar (Mark 12:34a), the words "Teacher, you have spoken well." Except for the editorial conclusion (Luke 20:40), moved up from Mark 12:34c, the Lukan account is not a *Streitgespräch* (controversy dialogue) at all, but a *Schulgespräch* (scholastic dialogue). For this reason we should give preferential usage to Luke 20:27–39 (but not 20:40) rather than Mark 12:18–27 and Matt. 22:23–33.[43]

Mark 12:28–34; Luke 10:25–28: *The most important commandment.* Luke moved the Markan pericope to a different sequence of accounts and altered it considerably, reducing it in volume and making it the introduction to the parable of the Good Samaritan.[44] As the introduction to the parable, the question asked of Jesus was changed to "Teacher, having done what thing shall I inherit eternal life?" Luke's redaction, nearly as much as Matthew's,[45] drastically increased the anti-Jewish polemic, which is slight and subtle in the Mark 12:28–34 account. In Luke the Torah expert *(nomikos)* stood up, not as in Mark because he was favorably impressed with Jesus' answers,[46] but in order that he might test him. In the Lukan arrangement of this pericope there is no place for the Jewish confessional "Shema" (Deut. 6:4), and the only portion of the Mark 12:32–34 section—in which the fraternity and warmth between Jesus and the Torah scholar is most noteworthy—that Luke utilized was what in 10:28 comes across much more coldly as Jesus' statement, "You have answered correctly. Do this and you will live." In the parable that follows, as will be noted below,[47] Jewish religious leaders pass by on the other side when they see their own countryman in dire need, while a non-Jew risks his life to show compassion.

Mark 12:35–37a; Luke 20:41–44: *How can the Messiah be the son of David when David has said that he is the Lord?* The changes from Mark are primarily stylistic, with little effect upon the level of anti-Jewish polemic.[48]

Mark 12:37b–40; Luke 20:45–47: *The scribes will be condemned.* Here also the changes are mostly stylistic from Mark to Luke. As in the Markan account we have the responsibility to translate "the scribes" and "the synagogues" of Luke 20:46 as "our religious leaders" and as "our religious gatherings" respectively.[49]

Mark 13:1–37; Luke 21:5–36; 12:11–12; 12:40; 17:23; 19:12–13: *The eschatological discourse.* In the Lukan redaction there is an increase in the use of the second-person plural, but the more significant changes involve the elimination of Mark 13:10 ("And it is necessary first that the gospel be proclaimed to all the nations") and the replacement of some uncertainties regarding events that will occur in the apocalyptic future (such as Mark 13:8c, "These will be the beginning of the birth-pains"; 13:18, "Pray that it may not happen during the winter"; and 13:22, "False Messiahs and false prophets will be raised up. . . .") with some certainties regarding the fall of Jerusalem *post eventu.* Most notable of these latter include Luke 21:20, "When you see Jerusalem surrounded by armies, then you will know that the time of its desolation has come near"; 21:21b, "Let those who are in the midst of Jerusalem get out, and let those who are in the rural areas not enter Jerusalem"; 21:22, "These are days of vengeance in order to fulfill all the things which have been written"; and 21:23b–24, "and wrath upon this people; they shall fall by the edge of the sword and be led away as captives into all the nations, and Jerusalem shall be trampled upon by the nations until the times of the nations are fulfilled." The anti-Jewish material of Mark 13:9 is further magnified in Luke 21:12 by the addition of "they will put their hands upon you and persecute you." The result is that in Luke 21:5–36; 12:11–12; 17:23; and 19:12–13 the discourse is less apocalyptic and more anti-Jewish than is Mark 13:1–37.

In our translation and use of Luke 21:12 and 12:11 today, it would be appropriate to represent *synagōgas* in each instance as "gathering places" or "assemblies."

Mark 14:1–2; Luke 22:1–2: *The religious leaders plan to arrest and kill Jesus.* Changes from Mark to Luke are principally stylistic, resulting in a more concise account. As suggested above,[50] because there is evidence in the Gospel accounts that certain of the leading Jewish officials were friends of Jesus, in Luke 22:2 as in Mark 14:1b a sensitive and accurate translation will avoid generalizations and report that "some of the leading priests and scribes" were seeking how they might destroy him.

Mark 14:3–9; Luke 7:36–50: *Jesus anointed by a woman.* Although many commentators[51] think that these two narratives record separate incidents, it is also conceivable in view of the stated purpose in 1:1–4 that, as John Drury suggests, Luke took a story from Mark, lifted it from the end of Jesus' ministry to the middle, and changed and amplified it so brilliantly that Luke's version is the one that people remember.[52] For this reason the pericope will be considered here rather than later.

Compared to the Markan account, which is relatively innocuous in terms of anti-Jewish polemic, Luke's account is disparaging to the Pharisee. It should be placed alongside Luke 11:37–41, where Luke even more thoroughly redacted Markan material and produced direct, abusive condemnation.[53] In Luke 7:36–50 the Pharisee is treated less harshly, but nevertheless he is embarrassed in the presence of his friends. Although the anti-Jewish polemic in this text is probably of tertiary significance compared to the important emphasis placed upon the forgiveness of sins and the woman's love and upon the role and identity of Jesus, it is a factor in the account. In our translation and use of this pericope we can counter the anti-Jewish polemic somewhat by translating "Pharisees" and "Pharisee" in 7:36, 37, and 39 as "religious leaders" and "religious leader."

Mark 14:10–11; Luke 22:3–6: *The betrayal contract.* As in Mark 14:10–11 we can show by an interpretative translation that we realize that not all of the Jewish religious and political leaders opposed Jesus. Luke 22:4 can be rendered as "And having left the group Judas discussed with some of the leading priests and officials who were most opposed to Jesus how he might deliver him over to them."

Mark 14:43–52; Luke 22:47–53: *The arrest of Jesus.* Initially, it appears that Luke has lessened the anti-Jewish emphasis here by omitting portions of Mark's Gethsemane account, which include the reference in Mark 14:41c that the Son of man is about to be betrayed into the hands of sinners, and by simplifying the arrest narrative by deleting the description of the crowd, that is, that it was from "some of the more powerful priests and scribes and elders,"[54] and that the crowd was armed with swords and clubs. However, the anti-Jewish impact of the account is actually heightened when in Luke 22:52–53 it is said that the crowd is not merely "from" the religious leaders but is composed of the chief priests and officers of the temple and elders who had come out against Jesus with swords and clubs to seize him. Moreover, "the hour" of Mark 14:41 has now become "your hour," the hour of the chief priests and officers and elders, and "your authority" has become the authority of darkness and of Satan.[55] As a result, the chief priests and officers and elders seized Jesus (Luke 22:54), a more direct confrontation than in Mark and Matthew, in which the crowd from the religious leaders arrested him.

Mark 14:53, 55–65; Luke 22:54a, 63–65, (66–71): *The nocturnal religious inquest.* Luke lacks the formality of the nocturnal religious inquest presented by Mark and Matthew.[56] Luke's "inquest" is informal and crude; its components are mocking, physical abuse, taunting, and blaspheming against a man who had not even had the benefit of a formal hearing. In addition, the men who are afflicting Jesus are supposedly not inferior rabble as Mark and Matthew suggest but the chief priests and officers of the temple and elders. Thus the abuse that in Mark and Matthew is a sequel to the nocturnal religious inquest becomes the "inquest" itself in Luke, with no lessening of anti-Jewish impact.

Other elements of Mark's nocturnal religious inquest (Mark 14:61b–64) are utilized in Luke's description of an assembly of the elders of the people, both chief priests and scribes, after day breaks (Luke 22:66–71). In place of Jesus' affirmative response to the christological question in Mark 14:62a, Luke 22:67b has Jesus' more polemical reply, "If I were to say that I am, you would never believe, and if I were to ask you anything, you would not even answer."

Mark 15:1; Luke 23:1: *Jesus delivered over to Pilate.* Luke's account is characteristically more compact, with the anti-Jewish polemic of Mark correspondingly compacted.

Mark 15:2–15; Luke 23:2–5, 13–25: *The trial before Pilate.* It is difficult in this section to separate Luke's redaction of Mark and possibly of other written sources from Luke's own composition. To provide some consistency, all elements of the trial before Pilate in Luke will be considered here, with Luke's trial-before-Herod account (23:6–12) reserved until later, when anti-Jewish polemic in Luke's use of written or oral sources other than Mark or "Q" material and in Luke's own more extensive compositions will be considered.[57]

The specific accusations of the whole multitude of elders of the people, chief priests, and scribes added by Luke to the Markan account of this trial (Luke 23:2) are strikingly anti-Jewish because they are presented in Luke as obviously false and pernicious charges. According to Luke, Jesus' purpose had always been not to pervert the Jewish nation but to bring Jerusalem and the nations of the world to peace. Jesus had advocated the paying of tribute to Caesar and had not called himself Christ a king. Yet only Luke presents these accusations. In Luke 23:4, 14–16 Pilate declared Jesus to be innocent of the charges, but the religious leaders nevertheless urgently and shrewdly charged again perversely that "he agitates the people."[58] Only Luke specified that the voices of the Jewish religious leaders prevailed and that Pilate accordingly delivered Jesus over to their will (23:23–25). The impression is thereby given in Luke that the chief priests and the rulers and the Jewish people took Jesus away and crucified him. Since no new subject is introduced in 23:26, the antecedent of the unexpressed subject of the verb in 23:26 and elsewhere in this section appears to be the Jewish authorities and the Jewish people listed in 23:13. By omitting all of the Markan and Matthean references to Jesus' being mocked by the Roman military personnel (Mark 15:16–20a; Matt. 27:27–31a), grammatically the antecedent of the unexpressed subject of the verb in Luke 23:26 and others that follow is not the soldiers, whom Luke does not introduce until 23:36, but the Jews. In this manner Luke achieved a consistency with the charges made in Acts 2:22–23 and even more with Acts 7:52–58 that the Jews betrayed and murdered Jesus, the Righteous One. The impression is given that for Luke anti-Jewish invective was more important than was historical clarity, since the administration of death by crucifixion was a Roman prerogative in the occupied provinces during this period.

In the interests of historical accuracy and, belatedly, of justice, our careful and sensitive translation of this account will render "the chief priests and the rulers and the people" of Luke 23:13 and by implication all unexpressed subjects of verbs dependent upon them in 23:14–25 as "the enemies of Jesus," which is an accurate representation of what those who would bring such false charges so vehemently against Jesus would be. Second, we should specify the subject in 23:26 as "the Roman soldiers," from Mark 15:16 and Matt. 27:27 and from what is known from other sources about execution practices in the Roman provinces, so that the subsequent unexpressed subject of verbs in the crucifixion proceedings in Luke will refer back to Roman military officials rather than to Jews.[59] This kind of careful attention to context in translation will partially counteract the popular supposition among Christians even in our own time that "the Jews" killed Jesus.[60]

This kind of sensitive translation is essential rather than optional in our time. Having identified these serious instances of anti-Jewish bias in Luke (as well as in Acts), it becomes our responsibility as spiritual descendants of the Lukan writer to counter them. The extent to which we as Christians shall be willing to do this will be determined during the coming decades and centuries in the marketplace of ideas as, led by the Spirit of God, we interact with the living, dynamic Word of God and pass it on to our children and to their children.[61]

Mark 15:22–41; Luke 23:33–49: *The crucifixion.* Compared to Matthew, which followed the sequence and the content of the Markan account of the crucifixion closely, adding only a few comments and making relatively minor adjustments,[62] Luke freely transposed the Markan account, replacing the cry of despair from Ps. 22:1 with three expressions of forgiveness, assurance, and trust peculiar to Luke.[63] Dependence upon or relationship with Matthew's account apart from Mark's is slight, being limited to the comment in Luke 23:49b (Matt. 27:55b) that women had followed Jesus from Galilee.

In terms of anti-Jewish polemic, at the inception the polemic is intensified, since, as noted above, the impression is given in Luke that Pilate had delivered Jesus over to the Jewish leaders and the Jewish people, and that they rather than the Romans had crucified him. Luke's addition (in certain textual traditions), "Father, forgive them, for they do not know what they are doing," maintains the impression that the Jews were doing the crucifying, particularly because in Acts 3:17 Peter is made to express similar magnanimity toward the Jews with the words, "And now, brothers, I realize that you acted in ignorance, as also your rulers did."[64]

Farther into the account Luke assigned culpability for Jesus' crucifixion more particularly to the Jewish rulers than had Mark and Matthew, stationing the people in 23:35 as merely standing watching, compared to the rulers who were mocking Jesus, where in Mark and Matthew those who were passing by were blaspheming Jesus along with the religious authorities, so that no one in the immediate vicinity of the cross was supportive of Jesus. In 23:35c the rulers' mocking includes a conditional sentence, "If this man is the anointed one of God, the chosen one, let him save himself," similar to the conditional sentences assigned to the devil in Luke 4:1–13.[65] Consistent with this, in Luke 23:48, after the crowds had seen the things that had happened, they returned beating their breasts. The reaction of the centurion to all of this was to glorify God and say, "Certainly this was a righteous man!" All of these factors heighten the contrast with the Jewish rulers, although the rulers are not, in Luke's crucifixion account, specified as chief priests and scribes as they are in Mark 15:31, nor is their mocking given with Mark's detail.

In summary, superficially in Luke's crucifixion account it appears that the anti-Jewish polemic is lessened compared to Mark, primarily because of the Lukan condensations of portions of the Mark 15:29–32 mocking account. However, careful analysis indicates that this lessening of polemic is more than counterbalanced by Luke's rather subtle transferal of blame for Jesus' death from Roman to Jewish authority.

B. In Luke's Use of "Q" Material

Luke 3:7b–9; Matt. 3:7b–10: *The exhortation of John.* As noted above,[66] the content of John's message is almost identical in these two accounts, and John's prophetic censures become anti-Jewish only when they are used against Jews by non-Jews, as they are in the context of both Matthew and Luke. In Matthew the polemic is more overt, with many of the Pharisees and Sadducees specifically cited for vilification (Matt. 3:7a). In Luke the polemic is more convert but hardly less. In the Lukan context this "Q" material follows a more extensive quotation of Isaiah 40 than that included in Mark 1:3, so that in Luke the work of John anticipates salvation not merely for Israel but for "all flesh."[67] Only Luke labels John's exhortations as the proclamation of good news to the people (3:18). For Luke it is those who are repentant in Israel who form the nucleus of the people of God,[68] but tragically, according to Luke, "Jerusalem" (in the Third Gospel) and "the Jews" (in Acts) will not repent and permit this message to become "good news" for all people.

Luke 6:22-23; Matt. 5:11-12: *Thus they persecuted the prophets.* The anti-Jewish polemic is greater in Luke than in Matthew.[69] Only Luke has "their" fathers excluding and reviling and casting out the prophets, and only Luke has the proleptic "in that day" when they will cast out your name—presumably the name "Christian" identified in Acts 11:26—because of the Son of man. The anti-Jewish polemic can be blunted somewhat by using a translation in Luke 6:23c such as "for thus others have done to religious zealots."[70]

Luke 6:26: *Thus they spoke well of the false prophets.* This antithesis of Luke 6:23 and Matt. 5:12, which occurs only in Luke, may have been "Q" material or it may have been, along with 6:24-25, a Lukan composition of a series of "woes" set over against the "blessings" of 6:20b-23. For consistency, our translation of 6:26b should be "for thus others have done to false prophets."

Luke 7:9; Matt. 8:10: *The faith of the centurion.* As suggested above,[71] *en tō Israēl* should be translated as "among my own people," since this is the sense of the expression within the setting of the Jesus of history. In the principal Lukan additions to this account (7:3-5), in which the centurion is described as one who loves the Jewish people and built the Capernaum synagogue, and in the description of Cornelius in Acts 10:2 as "a devout man and one who fears God with all his household, giving alms for all the people, and prays to God through everything," Eric Franklin[72] finds an attitude in which there is something that seems to come close to a self-portrait of the writer of Luke-Acts. In Franklin's opinion, the Lukan writer was greatly influenced by the Jewish faith, was led to see in Jesus a fulfillment of Jewish hopes and the climax of God's saving actions, and consequently could hardly have turned his back on the people and nation whose hopes were recorded in the Jewish Scriptures.[73] In 7:3-5, however, and throughout the 7:1-10 account, the emphasis is on the faith of the centurion, a faith that does not request a sign, or even a personal contact, but relies entirely on Jesus' word. The elders of the Jews are merely of tertiary importance; they are made to beseech Jesus in behalf of their Gentile benefactor, who ends up with his request granted, his slave healed, and his faith lavishly praised at the expense of Israel, which suffers in comparison.

Luke 13:28-29; Matt. 8:11-12: *Those who will recline at the table with the patriarchs in the kingdom.*[74]

Luke 7:31-35; Matt. 11:16-19: *This generation is like children at play.* Although the Matthean text is the more anti-Jewish of the two because of Matthew's more inclusive generalization "this generation" in the parable and because of the increased distance at which the adversaries of Jesus are placed in Matthew's third-person usage in the comparison sentence,[75] Luke provided the more anti-Jewish context by suggesting that "the men of this generation" were the Pharisees and the Torah scholars who rejected the purpose of God for themselves by not having been baptized by John (7:30).

Luke 10:12–15; Matt. 11:20–24: *Judgment of Chorazin, Bethsaida, and Capernaum.* The amount of anti-Jewish polemic appears to be greater in this instance in the Matthean account than in the Lukan.[76] It is probable that Luke merely reproduced "Q" material here, whereas Matthew expanded it in 11:20, 23b–24 with a redactional introduction, with other "Q" material evidenced in Matt. 10:15 and Luke 10:12, and on the basis of the prevailing judgments of the Matthean communities. Comparison of the Matthean and Lukan texts indicates fhat it is more likely that both were dependent upon "Q" material here rather than that Luke was dependent upon Matthew, since Luke would probably have retained Matt. 11:23b, "because if the mighty acts which have occurred in you had occurred in Sodom, the city of Sodom (or 'the results of these actions') would have remained until today."[77]

Luke 10:21b; Matt. 11:25b–26: *Prayer of thanks to the Father for eschatological wisdom.* Luke 10:22; Matt. 11:27: *Esoteric knowledge of the Son and of the Father.*[78]

Luke 11:19–20, 23; Matt. 12:27–28, 30: *Exorcism by the power of God.* As noted earlier,[79] Luke's text appears to have reproduced the earlier reading, but the level of anti-Jewish polemic is similar in the two accounts.

Luke 11:31; Matt. 12:42: *The queen of the south as judge over the men of this generation.* Anti-Jewish polemic in "Q" material was probably retained unchanged by Luke here but increased by Matthew's generalizing condemnation of all of "this generation."[80]

Luke 11:32; Matt. 12:41: *The men of Nineveh condemning this generation.*[81]

Luke 11:49–51; Matt. 23:34–36: *The judgment of the Wisdom of God upon this generation.*[82]

Luke 12:54–56; Matt. 16:2–3: *You can predict the weather but not the signs of the times.* Cloud and wind indicators provide vivid images for wisdom sayings, as the various meteorological examples in the Lukan and Matthean accounts testify. The vocative epithet "Hypocrites!" in Luke 12:56a and late textual traditions in Matt. 16:3 is an unfortunate and unnecessary intrusion that makes the Lukan account particularly anti-Jewish. It is unlikely that the vocative stems from the Jesus of history, at least in the generalizing manner in which it is addressed to the crowds in Luke 12:54–56. In our translations of Luke 12:56 the vocative should be relegated to a footnote and labeled as a Lukan or post-Lukan intrusion.

Luke 13:34–35; Matt. 23:37–39: *The lament over Jerusalem.* As indicated earlier,[83] since these texts as they have developed in the early church are viciously anti-Jewish with their unfair condemnation of Jerusalem for killing its prophets and stoning its apostles and in their glorying in the forsaken and desolate condition of the Jewish capital after 70 c.e., other accounts should be used instead of these to demonstrate the love and concern that the Jesus of history had for his fellow Jews. If these texts are used, they should be redacted and addressed to the church self-critically as follows: "O my people! O my people! How you have turned from me! How many times have I wanted to gather together your children as a hen gathers her chicks under her wings, but you have not wanted me to do this." It is apparent that a thorough redaction of these texts, which would reverse the process of development within the early church, would put them back once more into a series of sayings of Jesus such as they must have circulated in "Q" type of material.

Luke 16:16–17; Matt. 11:12–13; 5:18: *The Torah, the prophets, and the proclamation of the kingdom of God.* If I may venture briefly into an interpretation of this most difficult saying,[84] I might paraphrase it in its context as follows: The Torah and the prophets remain unchanged, but it is through the words and works of John and most of all of Jesus that to them have been added the good news about the kingdom of God. Those who have responded to this good news have suffered because of their commitment. While the Jewish Scriptures have been upheld by John the Baptist, by Jesus, and by Jesus' followers, first-century Jewish interpreters have acted violently toward his followers and have done violence also to their own Scriptures, so that they are losing possession of them.

Hence, within this obscure saying in its Lukan setting, there is certainly a substantial measure of anti-Jewish sentiment, but it is all couched in language (probably as it already had been in one or more "Q" sayings) so enigmatic that most people would have no more than a vague presentiment that it is anti-Jewish. Therefore, in our translations intended for popular usage, it would be advisable to translate these verses quite literally, rather than to paraphrase them as has been done above.

Luke 22:30b; Matt. 19:28d: *Followers of Jesus judging the twelve tribes of Israel.*[85]

C. In Luke's Use of Other Written and Oral Sources and in Luke's Own Compositions

There is scholarly consensus about only a single source used in the composition of Luke's Gospel: the Septuagint version of the Hebrew Scriptures.[86] Direct quotations from the Septuagint are relatively rare in Luke and in Acts, however, since the Septuagint is obviously neither an account of the sayings of Jesus as such, nor of the ministry of Jesus during the first century C.E., nor of the development of early Christianity. Luke apparently chose to use the extensive earlier literature mainly in allusions and as a stylistic model for many portions of the Luke-Acts corpus. It would be difficult, therefore, to do a thorough redaction study of Luke's use of the Septuagint, but what has been done in this regard shows that Luke as well as Mark and Matthew fostered anti-Jewish polemic in this process by using

Jewish internal self-criticism externally against Jews and Jewish religious groups.

It is a widely held hypothesis that Luke used a copy of the Markan tradition[87] in constructing a more "orderly" account than had previously been available for the instruction and edification of "Theophilus." We have seen to some extent earlier in this chapter the manner in which, as Luke "pruned and adorned" Markan material, anti-Jewish polemic was magnified, generally subtly rather than blatantly as in Matthew, but effectively nonetheless.

If there was written "Q" material that Luke as well as Matthew used as a literary source, we have seen that in many instances here also Luke increased the anti-Jewish tenor of this material more covertly than did Matthew, but no less effectively.

Because of the skill and artistry with which Luke utilized resources and painted new literary portraits, it is more difficult than in redaction study of Matthew to trace the history of the development of individual texts and to discern how redaction and composition progressed. Nevertheless, analysis of anti-Jewish polemic in Luke's use of written sources other than Mark and "Q" and in Luke's own compositions is possible, and to that we now turn.

In considering anti-Jewish polemic in the so-called infancy narrative[88] in Luke 1:5–2:52, we face the methodological question of whether to consider it at the beginning or at the end of this section, or even after the chapter on anti-Jewish material in Acts, since the evidence suggests that Luke may have written and prefixed the infancy narrative after the Gospel and the Acts had been completed, though not necessarily as an afterthought.[89] For our purposes of recognizing and repudiating anti-Jewish polemic in Luke's written and oral sources other than Mark and "Q" and in Luke's own compositions, it will be most advantageous to consider the infancy narrative first, being aware that it may have been prepared and placed between the prologue and 3:1 after the remainder of Luke had been compiled.

Luke 1:5–23: *The annunciation to Zechariah.* With the fine sense of time characteristic of Luke—what Drury has called "the historian's nose"[90]—the annunciation to Zechariah is written in lines most of which could clearly be a continuation of the Septuagint. What is most noteworthy here in terms of anti-Jewish polemic is the third strophe (1:17) of the message of the angel. In 1:32 Jesus is to be called "the Son of the Most High," and "the Son of God" in 1:35. Mary is called the handmaid of the "Lord" in 1:38 and addressed by Elizabeth as "the mother of my Lord" in 1:43. In 2:11 the new-born Jesus is "Christ the Lord." These identifications make it possible for the Elijah role to be assigned to John the Baptist here, an association not clarified in Luke's account of Jesus' public ministry but made specifically in this annunciation to Zechariah.[91]

John the Baptist is to lead the way as a herald in front of the Lord, the God of the sons of Israel. The parallelism with 1:15 makes it obvious that the antecedent of the word *him* of 1:17 is at first glance to be the Lord God, not Jesus whose coming birth has not yet been introduced at this point in the narration. However, the broader context of Luke's Gospel suggests that the reader is to see that John is also the herald more specifically for Jesus as the Lord.[92]

John's task is further elaborated as being "to turn the hearts of the fathers to the children and the disobedient unto the wisdom of the just, to arrange for the Lord a people prepared." At this crucial point Luke has altered the sense of Mal. 3:23–24 (4:5–6) from a reciprocal turning of the heart of the fathers toward the children and the heart of the children toward the fathers[93] so that the second part reads "to turn the disobedient unto the wisdom of the just." Only by interpreting Luke's parallelism chiastically is it possible to restore the reciprocal turning and to consider the fathers to be just so that the children can become disobedient and in need of being turned to the wisdom of their just fathers. A chiastic interpretation of Luke's parallelism, however, seems to undo what Luke has done in modification of the Malachi text. Synonymous parallelism seems to have been Luke's intent, so that the fathers are disobedient and the children are just. This is consistent with Luke's view of salvation history, in which the great majority of first-century Jews rejected Jesus and the message proclaimed by his followers while on the contrary the largely Gentile "children" attained the wisdom of the just.[94] John's task, therefore, which came to an early end, was to turn the hearts of the disobedient fathers, and herein lies Luke's subtle anti-Jewish polemic. Much of the Luke 1:17 terminology occurs also in other Lukan accounts in which the Jewish crowds are castigated by the Baptist and by Jesus. We see, for example, in Luke 3:8 that "God is fully capable of raising up children for Abraham from these stones," and 7:35 indicates that "Wisdom is justified by all of her children." The message of the Baptist, of Jesus, and of Jesus' followers is to result in a new generation of children who maintain the wisdom of the just minority of Jews, such as the devout Elizabeth and Zechariah, Mary, Simeon, and Anna, while the preponderant majority of Jews who claim the patriarchs as their fathers are disobedient to the message of Jesus and consequently are not justified.[95] Not these, but the followers of Jesus, are said to be the people prepared. Thus Luke 1:17 in the context of the theology of Luke-Acts is subtle but effective anti-Jewish polemic, typical of Luke in the Third Gospel. In Acts the polemic becomes blatant, similar to that in Matthew, the Fourth Gospel, and 1 Thess. 2:13–16.

Luke 1:26–38: *The annunciation to Mary.* Subtle anti-Jewish polemic in the annunciation-to-Mary account comes at 1:32–33, the place that architecture analysis of the two annunciation stories pairs with 1:14–17.[96] In isolation, and even when the interpretative context extends no farther than the infancy narrative, the words of 1:32–33, like those of 1:14–17, are merely reason for "joy and gladness." They are predictions that Jewish expectations of a truly great political messiah will soon be realized. The Davidic line will be reestablished and endure forever. Closer analysis, however, shows that not a succession of rulers but this one "Son of the Most High" will receive David's throne and reign over the house of Jacob forever.[97] When the context of Luke-Acts is considered, Luke 1:32–33 is seen as a prediction that the kingdom of Jesus, the Lord raised from the dead and ascended into heaven, will rule over the Jews and over Israel for all ages, so that Jewish messianic hopes are completely preempted by Christian claims. The triumphantism of the annunciation-to-Mary message in which Christians rejoice is achieved at the expense of Jewish spirituality.

Luke 1:39–45, 56: *The visitation.* The use of "Lord" in narrative to refer to Jesus is a distinguishing characteristic of Luke.[98] Here in response to Mary's greeting Elizabeth uses "Lord" with reference to Jesus to be born the child of Mary (1:43) and the same word in the sense of the Jewish Scriptures for the Lord who had spoken through the angel. The expression "Jesus is Lord" became standard in Christian usage largely because of the popular use of the Third Gospel and Acts. This identification is as inherently impossible in Jewish theology as it is normative in confessional Christian thought. As such, its usage in Luke's Gospel should be recognized but not repudiated. It is a difference—the basic difference—between Judaism and Christianity. The difference is, and should be, respected and honored by the persons in both religious communities. At the same time, in a mature and dynamic Christianity, along with the classical expressions of Christology that were developed during the early Christian centuries there will be new ways in which persons led by the Spirit of God will depict the significance of the person and work of Jesus as Messiah and Lord. Just as there is variety in the manner in which Christology is understood and expressed within the New Testament documents, so also there will be variations in the interpretation of the confessional statement, "Jesus is Lord," within mature Christianity.[99]

Luke 1:68–79: *The Benedictus.* As a mosaic of phrases and ideas from the Old Testament and interestamental literature,[100] the Benedictus is in terms of its parts primarily Jewish, but as a sum of these parts, because of biblical context and liturgical usage, it has become Christian tradition.[101] The Christianizing of the hymn was accomplished above all by the *double entendre* of the word *Lord* in 1:76. In its Jewish background in Isa. 40:3 and Mal. 3:1 the "Lord" is the Lord God of Israel; in Christian usage John the Baptist is the forerunner of Jesus the "Lord." Theologically, therefore, as noted in the preceding paragraph, this *double entendre* of the word *Lord* makes a distinction between Judaism and Christianity.[102]

Luke 2:8–15: *The annunciation to the shepherds.* The distinction between Judaism and Christianity continues with the double use of the word *Lord* in the annunciation-to-the-shepherds account. In a revelation of the "Lord" (2:15) by means of an angel of the "Lord" (2:9a) amidst the glory of the "Lord" (2:9b) is announced the birth of Christ the "Lord" (2:11). Again, it is important that we as Christians recognize this double usage and this *double entendre* and celebrate our kinship with our Jewish relatives as well as the separate identity of each group as a valid expression of spirituality.

Luke 2:34–35: *Simeon's comments to Mary.* The comments are couched in the form of an ominous prophetic woe on Israel.[103] Jesus is to become a divisive factor for Jews. According to the theological and political posture of Luke-Acts, most Jews did not accept Jesus as the "Lord" and, consequently, they fell. For those who did accept Jesus as the "Lord," Jesus was to be the cause of their rising. As generally in classical prophecy, here also the judgment precedes the word of hope. The pangs of the passion and crucifixion of Jesus are prefigured in the mention of the child as "a sign spoken against" and of the sword as piercing through the psyche of Mary.

In all fairness, in our translations and usage of this account this judgment said to have been occasioned by Jesus should not be limited to Israel, even though that may have been Luke's intent. Since we claim that the Gospel is to be offered to people throughout the world, in our translations and usage "in Israel" in Luke 2:34b should be relegated to a footnote as a Lukan limitation. In this way we can remove a limitation from the Gospel while at the same time partially nullifying the most overt expression of anti-Jewish polemic within the Lukan infancy narrative.

Luke 2:38: *Anna's testimony.* Anna's testimony about the child to all who were anticipating the redemption of Jerusalem is more positive than were Simeon's comments to Mary. Nevertheless, they are directed against the Jews, since in Luke-Acts Jerusalem is not redeemed.[104]

Luke 2:46–47: *The boy Jesus' understanding and answers in the temple.* Within Jewish circles interest in the Torah and understanding of it are highly admirable qualities. The text is cited here only because in the context of Luke (as well as of the other three Gospels) Jesus' superiority over the Jewish Torah scholars is amply illustrated in the controversy dialogues.

Luke 7:29–30: *Contrasting responses to Jesus' words concerning John.* The addition of these verses to the "Q" material that precedes them serves as a transition to 7:31–35 and underscores Luke's "rejection" theme.[105] They also provide another example of the characteristic of sharp contrast in Lukan compositions.[106] Possibly the verses were composed as an appendage to 7:24–28 in recognition of persons who had been baptized with the baptism of John and later became Christians.[107] At any rate, the endorsement of John results in the development of an opinionative anti-Jewish judgment that, because there were Pharisees and Torah scholars who had not been baptized by John, such persons had nullified the purpose of God, even though Luke 3:7–9 implies that Pharisees and Torah scholars had been among those who came to be baptized by John and that they had been castigated severely. Apparently for Luke this was a situation in which the Pharisees and Torah scholars were damned if they had and damned if they had not.

Both 7:29 and 7:30, therefore, appear to be contrasting comments or value judgments added to the tradition at some time by an observer or editor. Chapter 7:29 has a positive and edifying thrust, but 7:30 is a negative general condemnation of people among whom were numbered many who sincerely sought to know and to do the will of God. It would be desirable for us to assign 7:30 to a footnote as a Lukan opinion, or to use a circumlocution such as "But there were others who had nullified the purpose of God for themselves because they had refused to be baptized by John."

Luke 10:29–37: *The parable of the Good Samaritan.* In this memorable parable in which Luke redefines the term *neighbor,* Jewish religious leaders pass by on the other side though they see their own countryman in dire need, while a non-Jew risks his life and shares his resources to show compassion.[108] In a Jesus of history *Sitz im Leben* this parable would be internal self-criticism and hence not anti-Jewish polemic. In its Luke-Acts setting and within the New Testament canon, however, it contains external anti-Jewish criticism. Fortunately, in this case, for many Christians the word *priest,* which describes the function of persons in many different religions, calls to mind a Christian religious leader as much as or more than it does a Jewish one, and a "Levite" is merely assumed to be an associated religious type of person. Also in teaching and in preaching situations Christians frequently apply the message of this parable self-critically, even substituting another ethnic group for the Samaritans, so that relatively little anti-Jewish polemic remains. We should recognize that at the time of the composition of Luke the anti-Jewish polemic in this account was much more pointed than it is today.

Luke 10:38–42: *With Martha and Mary.* Luke presents Martha and Mary as contrasts of two types, similar to the priest and the Levite vs. the Good Samaritan in 10:29–37, the elder vs. the younger son in 15:11–32, the rich man vs. the poor man Lazarus in 16:19–31, the nine lepers who did not return vs. the one leper who did in 17:11–19, the Pharisee vs. the tax collector praying in 18:9–14, and the scoffing criminal on the cross vs. the believing criminal in 23:39–43. In every one of these series of contrasts— each peculiar to Luke—the one mentioned first is discredited in some way and the one mentioned last is given approval. Several of those mentioned first in each sequence are clearly observant Jews; none mentioned last are of this category. Not one of those mentioned first typifies followers of Jesus in Luke-Acts; every one of those mentioned last is in some way a type of the followers of Jesus. The probability exists, therefore, that in each of these instances Luke with skillful artistic subtlety expressed a degree of anti-Jewish polemic, and that one of Luke's purposes in this account of

Jesus' visit with Martha and Mary was to present Martha as a type representing the Jewish religion and Mary a type representing the Christian.[109] Although the anti-Jewish emphasis in this account is not expressed openly, subconsciously it is an element in Christian usage of this pericope, and frequently Martha and "her house" have been equated with Judaism in Christian teaching and parenesis.

Luke 11:27–28: *The greater blessedness.* Subtle anti-Jewish polemic continues in this brief saying, which Bultmann[110] considered to have been conceived as a unity, with its point in its opposition to the Jewish outlook expressed in 11:27. The thought here is similar to that written in Mark 3:20–35, although there is probably no literary connection between the two accounts. The blessedness of Jesus' followers in hearing the word of God and keeping it is said to be greater—as in the Martha and Mary account above—than is the blessedness of Jesus' ancestry (his mother) in bearing and nursing him.

Luke 11:42–48, 52: *Woe to you, Pharisees! Woe to you, Torah scholars!* If anti-Jewish polemic is subtle in many of Luke's literary artistries, it is not subtle in this composition! Perhaps the blatancy here is due to Markan and "Q" material lying deeply beneath this and portions of the Matt. 23:1–36 account. However, because of extensive differences in sequence of arrangement and, more important, in vocabulary, the Matt. 23:1–36 segments and the Luke 11:42–48, 52 material here are treated as separate compositions.

Compared to the Matt. 23:13, 15–33 series of woes to scribes and Pharisees, Luke's series of woes to Pharisees and to Torah scholars appears less bombastic. The series is shorter and the characteristic Matthean epithet "Hypocrites!" is lacking. However, in the Lukan setting, unlike the Matthean, Jesus is presented as delivering this direct, abusive, blanket condemnation of Pharisees and of Torah scholars during the time that he was a house guest of a Pharisee and being served a meal at which there was personal interaction and conversation (11:45–46).

As suggested in connection with Matt. 23:13, 15–33 above,[111] it would be appropriate in our translation and usage of Luke 11:42–43 to "prune away" to a footnote the generalizing word *Pharisees,* so that the result would be, "Woe to you who tithe mint. . . ." and "Woe to you who love the best seat. . . ." As in similar contexts, "synagogues" in 11:43 should be represented as "worship centers" or "gathering places." The word *nomikoi* in our contexts such as Luke 11:45, 46, 52 should not be translated as "lawyers," which in our time certainly has a connotation and significance different from that intended by *nomikoi* in the New Testament texts. In Luke 11:45 it should be rendered as "those present," so that the reading will be: "One of those present responded to him, saying, 'Teacher, by saying these things you are reproaching us also.'" In 11:46, 52 "Torah scholars" should be placed in footnotes. As a result of such steps to arrive at a more sensitive translation, these verses will take on new value as self-critical admonitions for us as Christians. No longer will Jews and attorneys be cited as scapegoats for the responsibilities that belong to all of us.

Luke 11:49–51: *The judgment of the Wisdom of God upon this generation.* Although these verses probably represent a Lukan adaptation of "Q" material, the manner in which they, as well as Matt. 23:34–36, are incorporated into the redactors' compositions indicates that they are illustrations of the thought of the redactors perhaps as much or more than they are of that of the "Q" material communities. Therefore they are considered here.

As noted above,[112] these verses should be placed in a footnote in our translations and usage. Theologically, they (particularly 11:50, 51b) are incongruent with the Gospel, as well as with most other portions of the biblical account. They should be retained in our Greek editions for scholarly purposes,[113] but should not remain within the texts of translations intended for private and public devotional use. In addition by their oblique reference to the siege and destruction of Jerusalem in 70 c.e., they have been damaging to the human decency and sense of justice of Christians and to the well-being and the survival of Jews.

Luke 11:53–54: *Plotting against Jesus by the scribes and the Pharisees.* These verses, with their significant textual variants,[114] occur only in Luke, where they function as a transition between the "woe sayings" of 11:42–48, 52 and the warning against the yeast of the Pharisees in 12:1. In order to reduce the anti-Jewish emphasis of these verses, "the scribes and the Pharisees" should be interpreted as "those whom he had offended" in our translations and usage.

Luke 13:10–17: *Controversy with the ruler of a synagogue over Jesus' healing a crippled woman on the Sabbath.* This account and Luke 14:1–6—both peculiar to Luke—are similar in that both are more concerned about polemic against members of the Jewish religious leadership than they are about the miracles themselves.[115] Both accounts are vehicles for delivery of Jesus' teachings as presented by Luke in a section of the Third Gospel devoted almost entirely to Jesus' teachings. Both accounts declare Jesus to be victorious in controversies with Jewish leaders about the meaning of the Sabbath and the application of the Sabbath regulations in the Torah.[116] Both accounts are related entirely from the Christian vantage point, in which Jesus' healings are acts of mercy needed as much on the Sabbath as on any other day. That which is presented as the official Jewish view is one in which the healings are merely work that could have waited and should have waited until after the Sabbath. Jesus' answer to the objection placed by the synagogue ruler is the answer of "the Lord" (13:15), who begins by addressing the Jewish synagogue leaders as "Hypocrites!" Jesus is successful in this account in putting his adversaries to shame and in silencing them, and the brief parables about the phenomenal success of the kingdom of God (13:18–21) that follow the 13:10–17 controversy account provide assurance that Jesus' teachings as presented are the correct ones, pleasing to God, and a cause for rejoicing for all the people. Jewish leadership and its teachings, on the other hand, are discredited. They are depicted as callous and unfeeling toward those who are suffering, even when a Jewish daughter of Abraham has been bound by Satan for eighteen years.

Obviously Luke added to the Markan collection of controversy stories here. As in the similar account in Mark 3:1–6 and parallels,[117] our concern should be for life and health, that is, our emphasis should be upon the miracle and upon the meaning of the miracle. Since 13:10–13, 17b are interrupted and reduced in significance by the controversy element in 13:14–17a—an element that with its confessional "the Lord" and the epithet "Hypocrites!" may have developed during the transmission of the account—a sensitive selection of lectionary readings will limit the reading to 13:10–13, 17b. In our translations, at least the word *Hypocrites!* if not all of 13:14–17a, should be relegated to footnote status as a relatively late development pejorative to Jewish spirituality. Perhaps this type of sensitivity in translation and usage will also help us as Christians to gain an increased appreciation of the value of setting apart one day each week and remembering it, to keep it holy.

Luke 13:31–33: *Some Pharisees warn Jesus that Herod wants to kill him.* Although this text, along with Luke 7:36–50; 11:37; 14:1; Acts 5:34–39; 23:6–10; and 26:5, is frequently cited as evidence that, when compared with other writers of New Testament documents, for the author of Luke-Acts the Pharisees stand relatively close to the followers of Jesus and are capable of acting rather benevolently toward Jesus and his followers,[118] the Pharisees are also castigated severely in Luke 11:39–44 and are frequently reported on unfavorably elsewhere in Luke.

According to Luke 13:31–33 "some" Pharisees warned Jesus that he should leave the area because his life was in danger. It is probable that some Pharisees were sympathetic to the Jesus of history and were concerned about him. Nevertheless, even in this text these Pharisees are presented as being in communication with Herod, and Jesus, as in 7:36; 11:37; and 14:1, accepts their favors but develops no relationship of trust with them. Perhaps Luke is suggesting that Jesus' followers later during the first century should also accept any favors offered by the Pharisees of their time but should develop no relationships of trust with them and should always be critical of them and of their teachings. The text that functions here as an introduction to the "Q" material lament over Jerusalem is probably the result of a combination of factors: (a) something that occurred during the ministry of the Jesus of history; (b) sayings of Jesus shared in the reminiscences of his followers; and (c) the experiences of the Lukan writer.

Luke 14:1–6: *Controversy with the Torah scholars and the Pharisees over Jesus' healing a man who had been suffering with dropsy.* Since this account has already been given some consideration together with the similar controversy text 13:10–17 above,[119] mention will be brief at this point. The

Torah scholars and the Pharisees are silent throughout this pericope; they are dominated and defeated by Jesus.

The teaching expressed in this pericope is consistent with that of the logion in Mark 2:27, that people are more important than institutions, a point upon which there would probably be general agreement among Jewish and Christian interpreters today. This should be emphasized in our use of the text.[120]

Luke 14:7-24: *Parables and other teachings to instruct the Torah scholars and the Pharisees at the table with Jesus.* These teachings, all of which are given a setting at the table in the house of the ruler who belonged to the Pharisees (14:1), will be examined in three segments: 14:7-11; 14:12-14; and 14:15-24.

The "parable" of 14:7-11 is directed against those who had been invited to the table. Apart from this and apart from its seeming rather presumptuous for one of the guests to be instructing the group in this manner, the teaching is not specifically anti-Jewish. The same can be said about 14:12-14, the apparently unsolicited advice given to the host regarding who should be invited when the host wishes to show hospitality in the future.

The segment 14:15-16a is a Lukan introduction to the parable about the guests invited to replace those who chose to excuse themselves from a great banquet (Luke 14:16b-24), which occurs in a somewhat different form as a parable of the kingdom in Matt. 22:1-10. In Luke—much more directly than in Matthew—the parable is used as polemic against the Torah scholars and the Pharisees. The minor theme in Luke's Gospel of a degree of friendliness shown toward Jesus on the part of some among the Pharisees is repeated here, and again that friendliness is rebuffed, in this case by means of a parable that has as its point that none of those who had originally been invited will taste the banquet in the kingdom of God. Their places will be taken by the poor, the maimed, the blind, and the lame, and by those way out on the highways and among the hedges who are compelled to come in, that the house may be filled. Although the anti-Jewish polemic is not crude or blatant here, it is nevertheless effective. Any hearer or reader who is at all aware of Luke's designations will realize that Luke is saying here that no Jews (those invited guests who made excuses) shall taste the banquet in the kingdom (14:24). As Marshall has noted,[121] at this point in the account the host has become "the Lord" with an obvious allegorical indication, "For I say to you,[122] 'Not one of those men who had been called earlier shall taste my banquet.' "

Actually, although the Matt. 22:1-10 text has been developed more extensively into an allegory of the plan of salvation,[123] Luke 14:22-23 is also an expansion when compared to the account in Matt. 22:1-10 and the Gospel of Thomas (64), in that the second summons for additional guests probably indicates a call beyond the tax collectors and sinners in Israel to Gentiles on the highways and among the hedges of the known world. As the Lukan text reads at its fullest extent (14:15–24), outcasts from Jewish religious society and many Gentiles will taste Jesus' banquet in the kingdom, but none from among Jewish religious society will be present. Luke 14:16b–21 and the Gospel of Thomas (64) without its final sentence ("The buyers and the merchants will not enter the places of my father") are likely to be the closest to the Jesus-of-history *Sitz im Leben*. Because of this, Luke 14:16b–21 (or expanded to 14:16b–23) should be used in our devotions, proclamation, and teaching.

Luke 15:1–32: *The parables of the finding of the lost sheep, the lost coin, and the lost son.* Without the Lukan editorial introduction in 15:1–3a these parables would not be specifically anti-Jewish, although as has been noted in consideration of the Luke 10:38–42 account above,[124] in many Lukan series of contrasts of two types, the ones mentioned first representing observant Jews are discredited while the ones mentioned last and composed of types of followers of Jesus are given approval. But with the Lukan editorial introduction these three parables are directed against the Pharisees and the scribes.[125] Conceivably the wasteful but repentant son may be a personification of "nonreligious Jews"[126] rather than of followers of Jesus.

In our translation and usage of 15:1–32 we should render "the Pharisees and the scribes" by the interpretative circumlocution "many of the religious leaders." In our lectionary readings we could start the readings at 15:3 or 15:3b.

Luke 16:14–15: *Reproof of the Pharisees.* This segment is peculiar to Luke.[127] Linguistic evidence and Luke's propensity to compose editorial connections between logia suggest that 16:14–15a is Lukan or Lukan-tradition composition.[128] Without the Lukan editorial connection the saying in 16:15b would be addressed to anyone who would attempt to practice self-justification or, from the other indications in 16:1a, to the disciples of Jesus. Therefore, the Lukan composition directly condemns the Pharisees collectively as "money-lovers," scoffers at Jesus, ones who attempt to justify themselves in the sight of other people, and as exalting something that is an abomination in the sight of God.

In our translations and usage it would be appropriate to relegate 16:14–15a to a footnote as Lukan comment and to begin our translation of 16:15b as "You try to justify yourselves in the sight of other people. . . ." In this way the saying is applied to those who read or hear the Gospel in each new generation and it becomes pertinent in their lives.

The strongly worded indictment against the Pharisees in this segment, along with the condemnation of the Pharisees that occurs elsewhere in Luke, suggests that the Lukan readings such as Luke 7:36; 11:37; 13:31; 14:1; Acts 5:34–39; 23:6; and 26:5, in which some Pharisees are described as at least initially favorably disposed toward Jesus and his followers, may reflect actual conditions as they had been, whereas the animosity against the Pharisees generally within the Markan community, by the Lukan writer and tradition, and most of all within the Matthean tradition, in most in-stances completely obscured the reporting of this earlier favorable disposi-tion.[129] If this is what actually occurred, our relegating Luke 16:14–15a to footnote status takes us back more closely to the situation of the Jesus of history and of the earliest followers of Jesus.

Luke 16:19–31: *The parable about the rich man and Lazarus.* This graphic Lukan parable, which is probably related to the Egyptian folk tale of the journey of Si-Osiris to the underworld and to the Jewish story about the condition after death of the poor scholar and of the rich publican Bar Ma'jan,[130] has anti-Jewish overtones, although anti-Jewish polemic may not be its only or its most important function. The rich man, mentioned first, along with his five brothers who remain in his father's house, seem to represent the Jewish religious establishment.[131] As such, he is buried, and in the Lukan viewpoint consigned to Hades, where he would soon be joined by his five brothers. He calls across the chasm to Abraham, whom he claims as his father. Abraham answers, but will offer to him no special favors at this point. The brothers are to be referred to their own Scriptures, but there is little likelihood that they will repent, either on the basis of their own Scriptures or if someone raised from the dead (Jesus) were to come to them. Lazarus, mentioned second (frequently the "Christian" position in Lukan parings of contrasts),[132] had been poor but now enjoys the favored position in Abraham's bosom. Furthermore, the Lukan context for this parable suggests that it was directed against the Pharisees. There are other indications as well that, among the parables of Jesus peculiar to the Third Gospel, this is one of those most likely to have been largely a Lukan composition, a skillful expression of Luke's evaluation of the fate of the Jews who would not repent and join the associates of Lazarus who, though they may be "poor" in this life, would be secure with Abraham after their death.

Having emphasized the importance of faith, of hearing the Scriptures, and of how one's position in this present life determines one's destiny, the parable ends on a note that is almost completely pessimistic regarding the fate of the Jews who do not wish to associate with the Lazarus type of people during this life. As such, it (Luke) takes a position much different from that of Paul in Romans, particularly in Romans 11. Here again Luke has achieved with considerable artistic skill what Matthew had done crudely in condemnation of a continuing Jewish spirituality.[133]

Luke 17:11–19: *The ten men cleansed from leprosy.* The extent to which this incident can be traced back to the Jesus of history cannot be clearly deter-mined. It is possible, as Hans-Dieter Betz has suggested,[134] that the identity as a Samaritan of the one who returned to Jesus to praise God was added at some point during the transmission of the account and that the resulting anti-Jewish polemic is a theological additive. As G. B. Caird notes, for Luke the most attractive portion of the story was that the appreciative Samaritan showed up his Jewish fellow-sufferers.[135]

Luke 17:20–21: *The Pharisees ask Jesus when the kingdom of God is coming; Jesus tells them how it will come and where it is.* Because of the difficulty of the account, it is not likely that it is entirely a Lukan composition. Perhaps 17:21a was added by Luke to link 17:20, 21b to 17:22–37.[136]

The attitude of the Pharisees is not presented as disrespectful. They are answered only indirectly, however, being told—as the caption above indicates—not *when* the kingdom is coming but *how* it will not come and *where* it already is. The radical portion of the response comes at its conclusion when the Pharisees are told that the kingdom of God is even then "among you."[137] Possibly the Jesus of history, but certainly the Luke of the Third Gospel, was stating rather categorically that where Jesus is present and active, there the kingdom of God is present and God's will is being done. The implication is that if the Pharisees will neither recognize nor accept the kingdom as it is manifested in Jesus (and later among Jesus' followers), they thereby exclude themselves from that kingdom. Again, as is typical of Luke many places in the Third Gospel, the anti-Jewish polemic here is implied. Displays of anger and tirades of name-calling are not necessary in Lukan compositions. For Luke, the point can be made more effectively with literary subtlety.

Luke 17:25: *Before the coming of the Son of man it is necessary for him to suffer many things and to be rejected by this generation.* Markan and "Q" material both are utilized to some extent in 17:22b–24 and again in 17:26–37. But the introduction in 17:22a appears to be Lukan redaction to switch Jesus' address from the Pharisees to his disciples. The remainder of 17:22 possibly reflects the longing of some of Jesus' followers after 70 c.e. for the coming of the Son of man. Chapter 17:25 is peculiar to Luke at this point, though derived from Markan passion predictions and "Q"-material terminology. Its use of "generation" is polemical against the Palestinian Jewish religious establishment of the middle and latter decades of the first century.

Luke 18:9–14: *The parable of a Pharisee and a tax collector praying in the temple.* This well-known parable is critical of an attitude that a Pharisee from the time of Jesus' ministry could certainly have adopted, for it is an attitude to which those who are devout in any theistic religious system are susceptible, and there are examples of prayers of thanks similar in many respects to this in Jewish literature of the period 200 b.c.e.–200 c.e.[138] The language of the parable—with Semitizing asyndeta in 18:11–13 in greater profusion than in any other Lukan parable,[139] evidence in 18:11 of an Aramaic reflexive behind the words *pros heauton* ("with intensity" rather than "with himself"), and other features cited by Jeremias[140]—indicates that the parable is from an early Palestinian tradition. In a Jesus-of-history *Sitz im*

Leben the surprising judgment within the parable in which the tax collector who could claim nothing except reliance upon the mercy of God was declared to have been justified more than the thankful Pharisee would have been an intramural, almost self-critical, censure of one Jew by another. It coheres also with the supposition from Synoptic Gospels evidence that the Jesus of history practiced table fellowship with tax collectors and sinners and spoke out against certain types of external religiosity. Parables such as this would have aroused opposition to Jesus among some of the prominent religious functionaries of Jesus' time.

On the other hand, the absence of this parable in Mark and in Matthew, where there is an abundance of material critical of the Pharisees, and the manner in which it exhibits certain characteristics of Lukan parables as a group, characteristics such as the contrast in which the person or group mentioned first is a representative of the Jewish religious establishment and the latter is a representative of the mélange within the followers of Jesus, suggests the possibility of development within the tradition. The lack of obvious marks of later development within the parable, however, is an indication that the parable is probably not the result of a long period of development. Luke may have incorporated it into the Third Gospel because it was available in the traditions accessible to Luke and because Luke was in close agreement with its message.

Commentators are divided in their opinions as to whether the "some people who trusted in themselves that they were righteous and despised the rest" to whom the parable is directed in 18:9 were intended by Luke to be Pharisees within Judaism or self-righteous followers of Jesus. For Jeremias[141] and Marshall[142] that the parable was addressed to the Pharisees is confirmed by its content. On the other hand, Danker, for example, thinks that since a Pharisee appears as one of the two principal characters in the parable itself, it is doubtful that the remarks were addressed specifically to Pharisees, [143] and Karris holds that Luke updated the target of the parable to address it to "those paragons of virtue in his community who think they have a corner on sanctity."[144]

Difficult as it will be to gain acceptance of terminology that differs from that which through a long period of usage has become familiar to many people, the word *Pharisee* in 18:10–11 should be replaced in our translations and usage by a circumlocution such as "devout, religious person." At first, people who already know the parable will still within their minds replace this with *Pharisee*, but after several generations have passed the transition to terminology more conducive to self-critical analysis will have been accomplished, and in the meantime more Christians will begin to realize that Pharisees were devout, religious persons who were similar in many respects to a large number of Christian people in every age.

Luke 19:39–40: *Jesus refuses to rebuke his disciples as some of the Pharisees request.* The motif of an objection by Jewish religious leaders to any type of acclamation of Jesus—whether it would be by children in the temple (Matt. 21:15–16), by disciples of Jesus during the entry into Greater Jerusalem (Luke 19:39–40), or by the Jerusalem crowd that went out to meet Jesus (John 12:19)—and of the overriding of their objection in each instance, along with the terminology used in the saying of Jesus in 19:40, suggests that 19:39–40 is a tradition modified by Luke to suit the purposes intended in the Third Gospel. No specific reason is given in this account as to why the Pharisees objected. The incident is anti-Jewish in that the Pharisees are represented as wishing to silence pilgrims who speak a blessing and express their deep longing for peace in heaven (and then on earth) and glorify God. The anti-Jewish emphasis would be lessened somewhat if in our translations and usage we were to render "some of the Pharisees" as "some people."

Luke 19:41–44: *Jesus weeps over Jerusalem.* Although the disciples of Jesus had just in Luke 19:38b expressed their longing for peace in heaven—the prelude to peace on the earth—the city of Jerusalem is here represented as not willing to accept Jesus' message and receive that peace. Consequently, this action of Jesus (similar in some respects to the symbolic acts of the Hebrew prophets)[145] prefigured tragic results for this nerve center and heart of Jewish spirituality. In our use of the account its value will be enhanced if instead of Jerusalem we think in terms of our own culture.

Luke 23:6–12: *The religious leaders accuse Jesus during his ordeal in Herod's court.* Regardless of the extent to which the account may be a Lukan composition, it serves three principal purposes in which anti-Jewish polemic is significant. The polemic is most apparent in 23:10–11, where it is reported that also in Herod's court the chief priests and the scribes had assumed the role of the prosecution and its witnesses, vehemently charging that Jesus was guilty of serious offenses. This gives the impression that the attitude of the Jewish religious authorities encouraged Herod and the soldiers to treat Jesus with contempt and to mock him. Second, the emphasis upon Jesus' nonculpability deepens the guilt imputed to the Jewish religious leaders. Third, the account claims that the Jewish religious leaders were not merely a partner but the motivating force in the coalition of evil powers arrayed against Jesus.

This account, like many others in Luke's Gospel, is carefully constructed.[146] At the beginning (23:6) and at the end (23:12) Pilate figures prominently. As we move into the pericope from both its beginning and its ending, we see Jesus in the custody of the soldiers of Pilate and of Herod, subject to their cruelty. Next the Herod figure is introduced and shown to be curious to see what Jesus would do, and then later depicted as frustrated and treating Jesus with scorn and contempt. At the center of the account (23:10) the chief priests and the scribes vehemently accuse Jesus, who in his innocence will answer to no one.

Since the anti-Jewish polemic lies at the heart and center of the account, any serious repudiation of its anti-Jewish polemic will of necessity strike at the nucleus of the structure. A token step at reduction of the polemic would be to translate "the chief priests and the scribes" as "some of the religious leaders" or "some of Jesus' enemies." A more radical move would be to drop 23:10 to footnote status. Another possibility would be to translate the pericope literally but reduce usage of it in lectionary readings, as a sermon text, and in teaching situations. Reduced usage in favor of more edifying texts would cause little loss of theology, of Christology, or of Gospel essential to us as Christians.

Luke 23:27–31: *Prophecy against the daughters of Jerusalem.* The great multitude of the people and of women who beat their breasts in mourning and lamentation while Jesus was being led to his crucifixion appear to be presented by Luke as sympathizers with Jesus rather than as his mockers.[147] Nevertheless, Luke has Jesus utter an oracle of prophetic judgment against them in words similar to those in the "Q"-material saying of Luke 13:34–35 and the weeping-over-Jerusalem account of 19:41–44.

According to this account the death of Jesus is not a tragedy for Jesus but for Jerusalem.[148] All the inhabitants of Jerusalem, particularly the women who are alive at the time of Jesus' crucifixion and their children, are condemned to a fate worse than death. Therefore, with devastating effectiveness, the siege and fall of Jerusalem—within forty years by Luke's reckoning—is directly tied to Jesus' crucifixion in skillfully portrayed anti-Jewish polemic.

Luke 23:50b–51a: *Joseph of Arimathea is contrasted with the majority of the council members who are said to have condemned Jesus to death.* Luke alone, by describing Joseph as a good and righteous man who had not agreed with the decision of the council and their implementation of the death sentence against Jesus, implies that the majority of the Jews on the council were neither good nor righteous and that their will was accomplished when Jesus died on the cross. Along with other Lukan texts this suggests that there were a few "good and righteous" Jews, but that the Jewish people generally and especially the inhabitants of Jerusalem were doomed.

Luke 24:6–8: *The passion and resurrection prediction recalled.* The identification of Jesus, crucified and resurrected, as the Son of man is unmistakable in this text. Luke's recollection of the passion and resurrection prediction, said to have been given by Jesus while he was in Galilee, stands in the Lukan text in the place in which Markan and Matthean parallels have the risen Jesus said to be preceding his followers into Galilee where they would see him. This change makes it possible one more time for Luke to describe the religious and political leaders as sinners.

Luke 24:20: *Our chief priests and rulers handed him over for the death sentence and they crucified him.* Within the account of the appearance of Jesus to two disciples on the road to Emmaus is the final instance in the Third Gospel in which, as in the speeches of Peter and of Stephen in Acts, it is emphasized that the Jewish leadership was directly responsible for Jesus' death. The frequent repetition of this charge in Luke-Acts has contributed heavily to instilling the idea of Jewish guilt into the consciousness of Christians during the past nineteen centuries.

D. In the Total Gospel according to Luke

The analysis of Lukan redaction and of Lukan composition just completed results in the following conclusions:

1. In most instances Luke increased the anti-Jewish polemic that already was present in Luke's Markan source. In Luke's passion account, compared to that in Mark, much of the blame for Jesus' death is subtly transferred from Roman to Jewish authority.

2. Compared to Matthew's use of the hypothetical "Q" source material, Luke's anti-Jewish polemic in these portions is in some places more covert but hardly less in content than Matthew's. Luke's sense of history may have caused the elimination of some anachronisms that contained anti-Jewish material, but this is frequently counterbalanced by Luke's placing "Q" material in settings in which Jewish leaders and Jewish people are depicted pejoratively.

3. In Luke's use of other written and oral sources and in Luke's own compositions Jewish messianic hopes and many manifestations of the Lord God of Israel are preempted by Christian claims. The aged Simeon and Jesus himself are said to have pronounced prophetic woes of judgment against Israel and Jerusalem. In many Lukan parables and stories observant Jews are with skillful literary artistry contrasted to nonobservant Jews and followers of Jesus, always to the discredit of the observant Jews. In controversy stories peculiar to Luke the Jewish leadership is presented as callous and unfeeling, while by contrast Jesus' teachings are shown to be pleasing to God and a cause of rejoicing for all the people.

4. Analysis of the anti-Jewish polemic of the Third Gospel indicates that this document appears to have been written primarily for Christian use, and only secondarily as an appeal to "good," "righteous," and "intelligent" Jews who would reject their Jewish religious leadership and maintain the wisdom of the "just," of whom Elizabeth and Zechariah, Mary, Simeon and Anna, and Joseph of Arimathea are prototypes.

5. Although representatives of the Pharisees are on certain occasions in Luke (and in Acts) presented as trying to be hospitable or at least open to Jesus, they are generally rebuffed with abusive language by Luke's Jesus, embarrassed in front of their friends and supporters, and used in Jesus' teachings as poor examples of spirituality who nullified the purposes of God.

6. Much of the anti-Jewish polemic in Luke can be diminished by sensitive interpretative translations, by reducing a few scattered words and

sentences to footnote status, and by selecting alternative accounts as lectionary readings. This can be accomplished without derogative effect on the Christology of the Third Gospel. However, because of the greater literary artistry of Luke compared to Mark and to Matthew, these measures are taken with more difficulty in Luke's Gospel.

7. The confession within the Third Gospel (and Acts) that Jesus is "Lord," a confession and assumption that is not possible in Jewish theology but is normative in Christian thought, should be recognized when it occurs but not repudiated.

Notes

1. For discussions of the difficulty of this task, see among others, Joseph B. Tyson, "Source Criticism of the Gospel of Luke," in *Perspectives on Luke-Acts,* ed. C. H. Talbert (Danville, Va.: Association of Baptist Professors of Religion, 1978), pp. 24–39, and Charles H. Talbert, "Shifting Sands: The Recent Study of the Gospel of Luke," *Interp* 30 (1976): 382–95. In our analysis of Luke's theology it is essential that we do not disregard the material in which Luke reproduces traditions with little or no change, since as Talbert warns (p. 393), "If we confine our attention to what can clearly be identified as redactional, we stand in danger of producing an eccentric picture of Lukan theology."

2. The "Q" hypothesis is retained as useful in this study of Luke even though some commentators, such as Austin M. Farrer, "On Dispensing with Q," in *Studies in the Gospels,* ed. D. E. Nineham (Oxford: Oxford, 1955), pp. 55–88, and John Drury, *Tradition and Design in Luke's Gospel; A Study in Early Christian Historiography* (Atlanta, Ga.: John Knox, 1977), prefer the hypothesis that Luke drew heavily upon Matthew. In the majority of the instances in which hypothetical "Q" material was utilized, Luke rather than Matthew appears to have maintained the more primitive form. See above, pp. 129–34.

3. Although the Septuagint version of the Hebrew Scriptures was also used extensively as a source by Luke, not merely of quotations but as an exercise in a type of *midrash,* it seems preferable in this study to treat Luke's use of the Septuagint as it occurs within the categories outlined above rather than separately.

4. See the description of Luke's preface provided by Gerhard Krodel in the editor's foreword to Frederick W. Danker, *Luke,* Proclamation Commentaries (Philadelphia: Fortress, 1976), pp. v–vii. See also Schuyler Brown, "The Role of the Prologues in Determining the Purpose of Luke-Acts," in *Perspectives on Luke-Acts,* ed. C. H. Talbert (Danville, Va.: Association of Baptist Professors of Religion, 1978), pp. 99–111.

5. The expression is taken from Drury, *Tradition and Design,* p. 10.

6. I. Howard Marshall, *The Gospel of Luke* (Grand Rapids: Eerdmans, 1978), pp. 177–78.

7. A major consideration in Hans Conzelmann, *The Theology of St. Luke,* trans. G. Buswell (New York: Harper & Row, 1960).

8. Compare John 4:45.

9. Drury, *Tradition and Design,* pp. 12–13.

10. Except possibly 2:34–35.

11. Marshall, *The Gospel of Luke,* pp. 188–89, thinks that these verses may have been added to this story from an originally independent saying of Jesus.

12. James A. Sanders, "From Isaiah 61 to Luke 4," in *Christianity, Judaism and Other Greco-Roman Cults*, ed. J. Neusner, Part One: New Testament (Leiden: E. J. Brill, 1975), pp. 75–106, places the Luke 4:16–30 account more firmly in the stratum of the Jesus of history and sees the Lukan writer as portraying that it was Jesus' exegesis of Isa. 61:1–2a by a midrashic application of the Elijah and Elisha stories, which applied the hermeneutic axiom of prophetic critique even to the end time, that deeply offended the men of his hometown synagogue. However, in the Lukan account Jesus' ministry is not the end time. The Markan emphasis on the end time (Mark 1:15) is passed over in silence in Luke in favor of concern for the present. The midrashic application of the Elijah and Elisha stories is demonstrably typical of Luke; it is not demonstrably typical of the Jesus of history.

13. For other examples of this characteristic of sharp contrast in Lukan compositions in Luke 11:1–13; 11:21–26; and 19:38–42, see Danker, *Luke*, pp. 9–10.

14. Architecture analysis of Lukan literary patterns in the genre of Luke-Acts by Charles H. Talbert, *Literary Patterns, Theological Themes, and the Genre of Luke-Acts* (Missoula, Montana: Society of Biblical Literature and Scholars Press, 1975), pp. 16–19, 40–41, indicates additional editorial activity in the correspondence between Luke 4:16–30 and Acts 2:14–40 and between Luke 4:16–30 and 7:18–30, with each of the latter used to introduce a major section (4:16–7:17 and 7:18–8:56).

15. See above, p. 104.

16. See above, p. 137.

17. Pp. 104–105, 137.

18. See the discussion of the Markan text above, p. 105.

19. For Jewish and Hellenistic parallels to this proverbial expression, see H. Seesemann, *TDNT* 5:163. Compare with this the advice regarding the use of wine in 1 Tim. 5:23.

20. Many later manuscripts have *chrēstoteros* (more delightful). Codex D, all or a greater number of the Old Latin witnesses, Marcion, Irenaeus, and Eusebius do not include 5:39.

21. See the discussion about the Markan community's use of this illustration on p. 101 above.

22. See above, pp. 105–106, 137–38.

23. Frederick W. Danker, *Jesus and the New Age According to St. Luke* (St. Louis: Clayton, 1972), p. 78.

24. See the detailed reconstruction in Arland J. Hultgren, *Jesus and His Adversaries* (Minneapolis, Minn.: Augsburg, 1979), pp. 100–106.

25. See above, pp. 109, 139.

26. For discussion of Luke's extremely limited use of Mark 6:45–8:26 material (the "great omission"), see Drury, *Tradition and Design*, pp. 96–102, and Marshall, *The Gospel of Luke*, p. 364.

27. As suggested, for example, by Marshall, *The Gospel of Luke*, p. 491. See also above, pp. 156–57.

28. Robert Brawley, "The Pharisees in Luke–Acts: Luke's Address to the Jews and His Irenic Purpose," Ph.D. dissertation, Princeton Theological Seminary, 1978 (Ann Arbor: University Microfilms, 1978), pp. 8–9.

29. J. A. Ziesler, "Luke and the Pharisees," *NTS* 25 (1979): 146–57.

30. Brawley, "The Pharisees in Luke–Acts," pp. 14–15. From his appraisal of Acts 13:46; 18:6; and 28:28, Brawley concludes that Luke did not reject Jewish Christianity. It is part of Brawley's thesis that, according to Luke, Jews who believed in Jesus were "true Jews" rather than proponents of a new religion. See pp. 16, 41–42, 189–98.

31. Danker, *Jesus and the New Age*, p. 143. See also G. Bertram, *TDNT* 9:220–35.

32. The use of "the Lord" for Jesus is probably an indication of the distance in

time between this account and the Jesus of history. It is characteristic of Luke. See Marshall, *The Gospel of Luke*, p. 81.

33. See above, pp. 112, 141–42.

34. Conzelmann, *The Theology of St. Luke.*

35. Danker, *Jesus and the New Age*, p. 175.

36. See Jeremias, *The Parables of Jesus*, pp. 170–71. In Jeremias's opinion, Jesus used the folk-tale of Ahiqar which was probably current in various versions as the basis for this parable, but gave it a different ending.

37. See above, pp. 114–15, 143.

38. It is difficult to see why Marshall, *The Gospel of Luke*, pp. 552–53, writes that "there is no reason to believe that the parable and the story are variants of one basic motif" when he recognized that the parable has certain affinities with the story of the cursing, which Luke omits.

39. See above, pp. 115–16.

40. See above, pp. 116–17, 144.

41. An allusion from Isa. 8:14 and Dan. 2:34–35, 44–45.

42. See above, pp. 117–18, 144.

43. Such is the practice in the lectionary printed in the *Lutheran Book of Worship*, pp. 13–41, where Luke 20:27–38 is to be read in Series C on the Twenty-fifth Sunday after Pentecost and Mark 12:18–27 and Matt. 22:23–33 are not listed.

44. Talbert, *Literary Patterns, Theological Themes, and the Genre of Luke–Acts*, pp. 51–53, provides an analysis of a Lukan chiastic pattern, in which 10:25–37 is paired with 18:18–30 within the larger sections 10:21–13:30 and 14:1–18:30.

45. See above, pp. 118–19, 145.

46. This omission in Luke is surprising in view of Luke's account about the favorable impression caused by the youthful Jesus in the Temple in 2:41–50.

47. P. 188.

48. For consideration of this pericope in Mark and Matthew, see above, pp. 119, 145.

49. See above, pp. 119–20.

50. Pp. 121–22.

51. For example, Marshall, *The Gospel of Luke*, pp. 304–14.

52. John Drury, *The Gospel of Luke* (New York: Macmillan, 1973), pp. 87–88. In the opinion of E. Earle Ellis, *The Gospel of Luke* (London: Nelson, 1966), p. 121, "Nowhere in Luke is the art of a descriptive writer more evident." Talbert, *Literary Patterns, Theological Themes, and the Genre of Luke–Acts*, pp. 16, 20, depicts an artistic parallel between Luke 7:36–50 and Acts 11:1–18 in that in the former the Pharisees criticize Jesus and in the latter the circumcision party people criticize Peter, and in that in both instances the cause for their criticism is association with the "wrong" kind of people.

53. See above, pp. 170–72. See also Hultgren, *Jesus and His Adversaries*, pp. 84–87.

54. See above, pp. 121–22.

55. See Drury, *Tradition and Design*, p. 111.

56. See above, pp. 122–23, 146.

57. Pp. 197–98. Talbert, *Literary Patterns*, pp. 17, 22, notes that the Luke 23:6–12 account of Pilate's sending Jesus to Herod for questioning (an account peculiar to Luke) has a literary-pattern parallel in Acts 25:13–26:32 when a Herod hears Paul with the permission of Festus.

58. But see the interesting presentation of Richard J. Cassidy, *Jesus, Politics, and Society* (Maryknoll, N.Y.: Orbis, 1979).

59. Even though we may agree with Marshall, *The Gospel of Luke*, p. 862, that

Luke's earliest readers would have known that crucifixion was a Roman prerogative, many Christians who read Luke nearly 2,000 years later are not aware of this.

60. I shall have to deal with the problem in Acts 2:22–23 and 7:52–58 in chap. 8
below.

61. See the excursus "On Freedom from a Written Code for New Life in the
Spirit" above, pp. 46–50.

62. See above, p. 147.

63. See the analysis of Luke's editorializing of the Markan account in Drury,
Tradition and Design, pp. 113–17.

64. See also Acts 2:22–23; 7:52–58.

65. As noted also, for example, in Danker, *Luke*, pp. 38, 80. See also Arland J.
Hultgren, "Interpreting the Gospel of Luke," *Interp* 30 (1976): 354–55.

66. Pp. 129, 147.

67. Hultgren, "Interpreting the Gospel of Luke," p. 357.

68. Jacob Jervell, *Luke and the People of God: A New Look at Luke–Acts*, trans.
D. Juel, et al. (Minneapolis, Minn.: Augsburg, 1972).

69. See above, p. 147.

70. See above, p. 129.

71. Pp. 129–30.

72. Eric Franklin, *Christ the Lord: A Study in the Purpose and Theology of Luke–Acts*
(Philadelphia: Westminster, 1975), pp. 178–79.

73. Ibid., pp. 77–79.

74. See above, pp. 130, 147–48. As above, the Matthean sequence is followed
here.

75. See above, p. 148.

76. See above, pp. 130–31, 148.

77. As intimated by Richard A. Edwards, *A Theology of Q; Eschatology, Prophecy,
and Wisdom* (Philadelphia: Fortress, 1976), pp. 104–5, Luke 10:13–14 and Matt.
11:21–22 may be evidence that during the mid-first-century decades the followers
of Jesus were more successful in the Tyre and Sidon region than they were in
eastern Galilee.

78. See above, pp. 131, 148.

79. See above, pp. 131, 148–49.

80. See above, pp. 131–32, 149.

81. See above, pp. 132, 149.

82. See above, p. 190.

83. See above, pp. 132–33, 149.

84. The crux for the interpretation of Luke's view of the periods in salvation
history by Conzelmann, *The Theology of St. Luke*. Many critics of Conzelmann's
analysis think that Conzelmann put too much weight on Luke 16:16.

85. See above, pp. 133–34, 149.

86. Perhaps it is no exaggeration to say with Drury, *Tradition and Design*, p. xi,
that the Old Testament "could well be as important a source for Luke's work as his
Christian documents."

87. The proponents of the "Two-Document Hypothesis" and of the "Farrer
Hypothesis" consider the priority of Mark to be the more likely. Those who hold to
some form of the "Griesbach Hypothesis" or of the "Lindsey Hypothesis" place
Luke earlier than Mark. See the description of options in the source criticism of
Luke in Tyson, "Source Criticism of the Gospel of Luke," pp. 24–38.

88. As Raymond E. Brown, *The Birth of the Messiah: A Commentary of the Infancy
Narratives in Matthew and Luke* (Garden City, N.Y.: Doubleday, 1979), p. 25, points
out, the terminology "infancy narrative" is both inaccurate and inadequate, since

this account is not limited to Jesus' (or to Jesus' and John's) infancy and since it is not all narrative.

89. Brown, *The Birth of the Messiah*, pp. 239–41. Others, such as Danker, *Luke*, pp. 105–6, consider the infancy narrative to be the first main part of Luke's introduction, followed by the other, the credentials of John and of Jesus in 3:1–38. Franklin, *Christ the Lord*, pp. 80–87, thinks that Luke's infancy narrative functions as the theological introduction to Luke's two volumes and that there is no inconsistency between them and the rest of Luke–Acts. For Franklin, the basic purpose of Luke 1:5–2:52 is to set forth Jesus as God's final action for Israel, as the one in whom God has confirmed his earlier promises, met Israel's longings, and brought her history to a triumphant climax. In Franklin's opinion, the remainder of Luke's Gospel progressively unfolds the themes that the infancy narrative proclaims.

90. Drury, *Tradition and Design*, p. 13.

91. See Brown, *The Birth of the Messiah*, pp. 275–79.

92. For a brief description of Luke's use of *double entendre*, see Danker, *Luke*, pp. 102–3.

93. Sirach 48:10 has "to turn the heart of the fathers toward the children and to restore the tribes of Jacob."

94. See particularly Acts 28:17–29, as well as Acts 13:14–48 and 18:5–7.

95. See Brown, *The Birth of the Messiah*, pp. 278–79.

96. See Talbert, *Literary Patterns*, pp. 43–45, and Brown, *The Birth of the Messiah*, pp. 156, 292–98.

97. Luke's annunciation-to-Mary message reflects the christological language and formulas of the postresurrection church. See Raymond E. Brown, Karl P. Donfried, Joseph A. Fitzmyer, and John Reumann, eds., *Mary in the New Testament* (Philadelphia: Fortress, and New York: Paulist, 1978), pp. 117–19.

98. Marshall, *The Gospel of Luke*, p. 81. Marshall cites also Luke 1:76; 2:11; 7:13, 19; 10:1, 39, 41; 11:39; 12:42; 13:15; 17:5–6; 18:6; 19:8, 31, 34; 20:42, 44; 22:61; and 24:3, 34. To this list should be added 10:17.

99. See further below, pp. 283–84.

100. With striking parallels in the Qumran scrolls.

101. See the exposition in Brown, *The Birth of the Messiah*, pp. 377–92. It is Brown's opinion that the Benedictus was composed by early Jewish Christians of an Anawim mentality, then adapted and employed by Luke.

102. Although each of the remaining instances in Luke in which Jesus is identified as "the Lord" separates Christianity from Judaism, their occurrences will not be noted specifically during the remainder of this chapter unless more virulent anti-Jewish polemic accompanies their usage. For the list of pertinent texts, see n. 98 above.

103. Brown, *The Birth of the Messiah*, p. 460.

104. According to Franklin, *Christ the Lord*, pp. 81–82, this episode, along with the one with Simeon that precedes it, shows Luke's belief that those who were true to the old covenant should be led to Jesus in whom they would find fulfillment. However, Luke shows that there were divisions in Israel because of Jesus and that the majority of the Jews did not acknowledge Jesus as the climax of God's saving actions.

105. Ellis, *The Gospel of Luke*, p. 119.

106. See above, pp. 166–68, for the discussion of sharp contrast in Luke 4:14–30.

107. For a consideration of the somewhat similar material in Matt. 21:31b–32, see above, pp. 155–56.

108. See above, p. 175.

109. Even though, as indicated by Drury, *Tradition and Design*, p. 149, Deut. 8:3

emphasizes the perils of being so occupied with material things (living by bread alone) that it is forgotten that life is to be lived by everything that proceeds from the mouth of the Lord.

110. Rudolf Bultmann, *The History of the Synoptic Tradition*, trans. J. Marsh, rev. ed. (New York: Harper & Row, 1963), pp. 30–31.

111. Pp. 156–58.

112. P. 159.

113. Danker, *Jesus and the New Age*, pp. 145–46, thinks that instead of drawing upon "Q" material at this point, Luke used a variant form of "Q" from Hellenistic Jewish-Christian circles, a source that included reflection based on a combination of viewpoints expressed in Wisdom 19:3–4 and 2 Chron. 24:19–22. Zechariah, however, may be Zechariah the son of Barischiah who, according to Josephus, *The Jewish Wars* 4:334–44, was murdered in the temple courts during 67–68 c.e.

114. See G. D. Kilpatrick, "Western Text and Original Text in the Gospels and Acts," *JTS* 44 (1943): 24–36.

115. See also Paul J. Achtemeier, "The Lukan Perspective on the Miracles of Jesus: A Preliminary Sketch," in *Perspectives on Luke–Acts*, ed. C. H. Talbert (Danville, Va.: Association of Baptist Professors of Religion, 1978), p. 154.

116. Robert J. Karris, *Invitation to Luke* (Garden City, N.Y.: Doubleday, 1977), p. 166.

117. Matt. 12:9–14; Luke 6:6–11. See above, pp. 106–108, 138, 169–70.

118. As in Brawley, "The Pharisees in Luke–Acts."

119. Pp. 190–91.

120. In the *Lutheran Book of Worship*, p. 27, in the Gospel selection for the Fifteenth Sunday after Pentecost, Series C, the miracle and the silence of the Torah scholars and of the Pharisees are passed over in the 14:1, 7–14 reading, which is also the reading for the other denominations using this series.

121. Marshall, *The Gospel of Luke*, p. 591.

122. "You" is plural here although the parable had been directed to a single individual in Luke 14:15–16a.

123. See Jeremias, *The Parables of Jews*, pp. 63–66, 67–69, 176–80. See also above, p. 156.

124. Pp. 188–89.

125. It is unnecessary to say with Danker, *Jesus and the New Age*, p. 168, that "With superb gentleness Jesus tries to bring the Pharisees to God's point of view."

126. Ellis, *The Gospel of Luke*, p. 196.

127. The position of Drury, *Tradition and Design*, p. 160, that Matthew is the source of these sayings against the Pharisees is unconvincing.

128. Bultmann, *The History of the Synoptic Tradition*, pp. 334–35; Marshall, *The Gospel of Luke*, pp. 624–25.

129. Conditions as they actually had been may likewise be indicated in the lack of mention of the Pharisees as enemies of Jesus in Luke's temple and passion accounts.

130. Jeremias, *The Parables of Jesus*, pp. 182–87.

131. Danker, *Jesus and the New Age*, p. 176, calls him "a pious Israelite."

132. See above, pp. 188–89, 193.

133. Other interpreters of the parable postulate a different Lukan *Sitz im Leben*. For example, Robert J. Karris, "Poor and Rich: The Lukan *Sitz im Leben*," in *Perspectives on Luke–Acts*, ed. C. H. Talbert (Danville, Va.: Association of Baptist Professors of Religion, 1978), pp. 121–23, thinks that the parable was directed against rich followers of Jesus within Luke's community of faith. Such an interpretation is possible only by labeling such rich Christians as "Pharisees," as Karris does. But

this use of "Pharisees" to represent rich Christians cannot be maintained with any consistency throughout Luke–Acts.

134. Hans-Dieter Betz, "The Cleansing of the Ten Lepers (Luke 17:11–19)," *JBL* 90 (1971): 314–28.

135. G. B. Caird, *The Gospel of St Luke* (Baltimore, Md.: Penguin, 1963), p. 195.

136. Marshall, *The Gospel of Luke*, p. 653.

137. "Among you," that is, when Jesus is among you the kingdom of God is present, is to be preferred as a translation of *entos hymōn* to "within you," since elsewhere Jesus is quoted as speaking about people entering into the kingdom, not the kingdom entering into people.

138. Jeremias, *The Parables of Jesus*, pp. 142–43.

139. Matthew Black, *An Aramaic Approach to the Gospels and Acts*, 2d ed. (Oxford, 1954), pp. 41, 43.

140. Jeremias, *The Parables of Jesus*, p. 140.

141. Ibid., p. 139.

142. Marshall, *The Gospel of Luke*, p. 678.

143. Danker, *Jesus and the New Age*, pp. 184–85.

144. Karris, *Invitation to Luke*, p. 205.

145. Norman A. Beck, "Efficacious Symbolic Acts of Jesus Christ during His Public Ministry," Ph.D. dissertation, Princeton Theological Seminary, 1967 (Ann Arbor, Mich.: University Microfilms, 1967), pp. 115–22. For descriptions of the way in which certain actions of the Hebrew prophets were thought to have initiated divine activity, see the following: H. Wheeler Robinson, "Prophetic Symbolism," in *Old Testament Essays*, ed. D. C. Simpson (London: Charles Griffin, 1927), pp. 1–17; "The Hebrew Conception of Corporate Personality," in *Werden und Wesen des Alten Testaments*, ed. P. Volz, F. Stummer, and J. Hempel (Berlin: A. Töpelmann, 1936), pp. 49–62; "Hebrew Sacrifice and Prophetic Symbolism," *JTS* 43 (1942): 129–39; Adrianus van den Born, *De symbolische Handelingen der Oud-Testamentische Profeten* (Utrecht: Dekker en Van de Vegt, 1935); *Profetie metterdaad; Een Studie over de symbolische Handelingen der Profeten* (Roermond: J. J. Romen en Zonen, 1947); and Georg Fohrer, "Die Gattung der Berichte über symbolische Handlungen der Propheten," *ZAW* 64 (1952): 101–20; *Die symbolischen Handlungen der Propheten* (Zürich: Zwingli-Verlag, 1953).

146. For an outline and description of Lukan parallels between details in Jesus' trials in the Third Gospel and Paul's trials in Acts, see Talbert, *Literary Patterns*, pp. 17–18, 22.

147. Marshall, *The Gospel of Luke*, pp. 863–64.

148. Danker, *Jesus and the New Age*, p. 236. Compare Zech. 12:10, which may have been instrumental in the formation of Luke 23:27–31.

8

Anti-Jewish Polemic in Acts

The following presuppositions are operative in the present study of anti-Jewish polemic in Acts:

1. The Third Gospel and Acts were written by the same person, whom tradition has called "Luke."

2. "Luke" may or may not have been Luke, the physician companion of Paul, but it is somewhat more likely that these writings were ascribed to Luke the physician than that they were written by him.[1]

3. It is probable that the writer of Acts utilized some written sources, such as possibly an Antioch tradition and more likely a travelogue of portions of Paul's journeys, but "style criticism"[2] rather than source criticism or form criticism has been the more effective methodology in our analysis of how Acts was composed.

4. The writer of Acts presented a theological perspective from a period several decades after the death of Peter and the death of Paul.

5. The theological position of the writer was expressed in numerous extensive speeches of Peter, Stephen, and Paul[3] and in various notable scenes into which events that must have occurred over long periods of time were condensed.[4]

6. In these speeches and scenes it was of primary importance to the writer to demonstrate that thousands of the most devout Jews became followers of Jesus during the first few decades after Jesus' crucifixion,[5] but that contrasted to these were many other Jews who rejected the message about Jesus and vehemently opposed its spread.

7. For the writer of Acts it was the Jews who became followers of Jesus who were truly Israel, the people of God, whereas those Jews who refused to follow Jesus thereby forfeited their membership in the people of God.[6] Herein lies the essence of the anti-Jewish polemic in Acts, which is the most devastating and the most destructive of Judaism in all of the New Testament documents. In the opinion of the writer of Acts, the Jews who repented of the sin that allegedly they had committed in crucifying Jesus

and turned to become disciples of Jesus became Christians, and the Jews who would not repent and follow Jesus lost their right to be called the people of God. Therefore they were lost to Judaism if they were baptized as Christians, and Judaism itself was lost if they were not. Either way, there was nothing left for Judaism. It was an empty shell to be discarded. The followers of Jesus were now the people of God.

In accordance with these presuppositions it will be more advantageous in our study to proceed through Acts sequentially scene by scene rather than by analysis of hypothetical sources and of Luke's redaction of them, or by consideration of the speeches apart from the scenes in which they are placed.

This present study of Acts, from the standpoint of the various scenes depicted and of the formal speeches of the key figures Peter, Stephen, and Paul, has raised the possibility that the Lukan writer may have functioned in producing this document in many ways as a playwright who wrote a theological drama and entitled it *Acts of Apostles*. The actions of the drama unfold in numerous scenes that could be produced on a stage for an audience, but more likely were designed instead to appeal to the imaginations of their readers and hearers.

The drama genre is of course well known in Greek literature. The Lukan writer is not to be credited, therefore, with the development of an entirely new literary form. Certainly Luke's Acts of Apostles differs considerably in form, language, and content from the great classical Greek tragedies, which were written expressly for stage performances. Acts of Apostles follows instead the tradition of what may be called the literary drama, written primarily for the reader, in an appeal to the reader's imagination. Dramas of this type became frequent as early as the fourth century B.C.E. Philosophers, rhetoricians, and historians of this period used drama forms in their efforts to influence their readers, with no expectation of having their work performed upon any stage other than their readers' imaginations. Included in this group were Timon the Skeptic (beginning of the third century B.C.E.), the elder Philostratus (a rhetorician at Athens during the reign of Domitian), and Oenomaus the Cynic (active during the time of Hadrian's rule). Nicolaus of Damascus, a famous historian and friend of Herod the Great, also wrote dramas, including one on the subject of Daniel and Susanna.[7] Luke's Acts may be classified as largely theological and political drama, a creative adaptation of Greek literary drama to the purposes of a skillful writer in the late first-century church.

More than any other early Christian writer whose work has been preserved for us, the Lukan writer was an innovator in using the literary drama genre as a vehicle with which to express early Christian thought. That the Lukan writer was not the only early Christian writer to use this type of genre is copiously attested by the Fourth Gospel traditions, in which a number of miracle stories were developed into extensive and interesting drama dialogues.

It is to be understood that when Acts is described as a literary drama in the present study there is an awareness that there will be a mixture of genre types in any literature. This is merely an attempt to provide evidence that the primary genre of the document is that of a literary drama rather than that of an objective history of the beginnings of the Christian church.

Analysis of Acts as a literary drama indicates that the drama was developed in three major parts or what I shall call "action areas."[8] I am calling them three "action areas" rather than three "acts" because of the nature of the material. In addition, I have no desire to modernize the Lukan writer's literary drama into a three-act play such as those written later, nor do I wish to see it cast into a different form to be staged for audiences today, although obviously this could be done. If it were done, it would have to be written and produced with great sensitivity. If it were not, a modern stage production of Acts as a three-act drama would almost certainly foster Christian anti-Semitism, as a sequel to the tradition of the Oberammergau passion play. I would prefer to maintain Acts in the form of literary drama, in which it can continue to make its appeal to the imagination of its readers, not as objective history but as literary drama.

In action area one of this literary drama (Acts 1:1–5:42) the full contingent of twelve apostles is reestablished with the selection of Matthias to replace Judas. The twelve are listed as the *dramatis personae* of action area one, and potentially there could be many scenes depicting the role of each of the twelve in spreading the message of Jesus and about Jesus. However, only the first two on the list, Peter and John, are singled out for consideration, and Peter is clearly the dominant character in action area one. After several scenes in which, in spite of great opposition, the church under the power of the Spirit grew rapidly in the Jewish setting in Jerusalem, action one closes with Peter and the other apostles said to be teaching and preaching Jesus as the Christ each day in the temple and in their homes.

Action area two (6:1–12:24) opens with the introduction and commissioning of an additional list of seven workers of Hellenistic background to complement the number and work of the twelve. Although seven are listed, characterizations are developed for only the first two on the list, as in action area one. The Stephen scene ends with the stoning of Stephen, whose role here is that of the first and the ideal Christian martyr, and whose words as he is dying echo those of Jesus himself in the Third Gospel passion account. At the end of the martyrdom-of-Stephen scene Saul is introduced. His violent persecution of the church, his experience on the road to Damascus, and gradual acceptance of him by the church are interspersed with scenes in which Philip and Peter have major responsibilities.

Barnabas is eased into the drama with little fanfare as the principal sponsor and companion of Saul. During action area two the mission to the Gentiles is validated through the baptism of the Ethiopian eunuch by Philip, the vision to Ananias that Saul will be a message-bearer to Gentiles, and the scene involving Peter and Cornelius. Action area two ends dramatically not with the death of Peter as might have been expected, but in a quick twist with the horrible death of the evil villain Herod who, having been acclaimed as a deity, accepted this honor and consequently was eaten by worms. The writer closes action area two with the announcement that the word of the Lord caused growth and multiplication of the number of those who followed the apostles' teachings.

Action area three (12:25–28:31) opens with a third list, naming the prophets and teachers in the church at Antioch. Again from this list, which numbers five, so that the five at the beginning of action area three added to the seven at the beginning of action area two equal the number of the twelve at the beginning of action area one, only two are given prominence. In this list Barnabas is first and Saul, the late arrival, last. But Barnabas and Saul are listed together in the first verse of action area three (12:25) and again in 13:2, and Saul (also called Paul in 13:9 and Paul thereafter) soon eclipses Barnabas in importance. After many scenes staged in a variety of religious and political settings, the writer of this literary drama concludes action area three, just as the writer concluded action area one and action area two, on a note of success. Paul, though under house arrest, is said to be preaching the kingdom of God and teaching the things about Jesus in Rome with all openness and unhindered.

The scope and the magnitude of the action expands drastically from "Jerusalem" (action area one) to "all of Judea and Samaria" and beyond them to Galilee, Damascus, Antioch, Phoenicia, and Cyprus (action area two), and across Asia Minor, Greece, Crete, and Malta to Rome, from which power and influence extend to the "end of the earth" (action area three), just as foretold in the final words of Jesus to his disciples in the Ascension scene in Acts 1:8.[9]

Already in the Third Gospel, in the portions in which the Lukan writer was not dependent upon Markan and other written materials, the writer frequently used extensive dramatic scenes such as the annunciation to Zechariah, the annunciation to Mary, the visit of Mary to Elizabeth, the circumcision of John, the birth of Jesus, the purification scene, the twelve-year-old Jesus in the temple scene, and the Emmaus account to present the theological messages desired. In many of these scenes there are lengthy speeches from which the theological position of the writer can be discerned. In a few instances, most notably in the Luke 4:16–30 account, even when Markan material was utilized, there was extensive Lukan composition into an interesting dramatic scene. This technique was used for all portions of Acts, with the single exception of the "we" section travelogues.

Although the Third Gospel is not in the form of a literary drama in three action areas to the same extent that Acts appears to be, in the Third Gospel the ministry of Jesus is portrayed in three segments: (1) in Galilee; (2) on the road to Jerusalem; and (3) in Jerusalem itself. Since Mark and perhaps others had already written accounts using a ministry-of-Jesus framework, the Lukan writer's creativity in reshaping the Gospel accounts is less pronounced than it is in the Acts literary drama.

It has been customary to express as a gross generalization that certain writings in the Jewish Scriptures, particularly the Pentateuch, and certain writings in the specifically Christian Scriptures, particularly the Four Gospels and Acts, are "historical" writings. Such a generalization is unfortunate and misleading, especially for those who have not had the leisure or the desire to study them extensively. Behind these writings there obviously had been events that had occurred. The structure of Acts, with its introductions of *dramatis personae* and its elaborate scenes, suggests, however, that its writer was interested not merely in what had occurred, but also in the theological and the political significance of what had occurred for the lives of people within a community or communities of believers.

The drama genre is well suited as a message-bearing vehicle. In the development of drama, events that have occurred are important as resource material. But drama gathers resource material from many times and many places and combines it creatively with the interpretations and the experiences of various people into scenes by which an audience, or in the case of literary drama a reader, is informed, influenced, or simply entertained. It is not suggested here that early Christian communities presented the Acts drama publicly for large audiences, but it is possible that scenes from Acts were acted out within local Christian communities, particularly within house church settings. Portions of the New Testament, especially within the Third and Fourth Gospels, and most of Acts, would be better understood, or at least less misunderstood, if they were seen to be expressed in literary drama form. Our liturgies, especially in "Western" Christianity, have not maintained much awareness of drama and usage of drama as a valuable form of religious expression. Even though our church buildings are "theaters" and those who lead in worship are obviously "actors" playing certain roles, large numbers of Christians read their Bibles and listen to biblical readings during worship services as if they were merely verbatim recitals of events recorded exactly as they had occurred, without any comment or interpretation.

In the background of the Acts literary drama certain things had happened. Various resources, both written and oral, were available to the Lukan writer. With consummate literary skill the writer fashioned them into an interesting theological and political literary drama, in three action areas and in many scenes, with a specific message for Theophilus and for all who "love God" to ponder.

The original script of a drama in the language in which it was written should be recovered as carefully as possible and maintained as the basis for all who would produce and develop that drama for presentation in their own time. Whenever producers and directors prepare a drama for presentation, however, they have a measure of freedom to make changes and modifications in the script and in the way in which the drama is presented. If we see that the genre of most of Acts—as well as of some other portions of the New Testament writings—is literary drama, we also have a measure of freedom in our translation and usage of these materials to be sensitive to changes and modifications by selection and by production in order that the message may come across to the audience in ways that are appropriate for our times.

This proposed outline of a drama in three action areas, therefore, will be utilized in this present study of anti-Jewish polemic in Acts. Analysis will begin with anti-Jewish polemic in the speeches of Peter and in the scenes in action area one in which Peter and in some instances Peter and John are the main characters. This will be followed by a similar analysis of the Stephen scene and Stephen speech and of other scenes and speeches in action area two in which anti-Jewish polemic is involved. Finally will come consideration of anti-Jewish polemic in the scenes and speeches of action area three where Paul is the principal character. In each instance we shall be concerned not only about recognition of the polemic in the context in which it occurs, but also about ways in which we can deal with this problem in our translations and usage of Acts texts.

A. In the Speeches of Peter and in Peter and John Scenes in Action Area One (1:1–5:42)

Acts 2:1–47: *Peter's speech within the context of the Pentecost scene.* The *dramatis personae* of the Pentecost scene are all Jews (including some proselytes to Judaism). They are devout, observant Jews from every nation, settling once more in Jerusalem or visiting there from as far away as Rome. Apparently, therefore, they are the people to whom the message of Jesus' life, death, and resurrection will be given.[10] By introducing all of these characters, the writer set the stage in the reader's imagination for a drama with the potential for many more scenes than actually were developed.[11] Jewish settlements in the Parthian Empire, among people formerly known as the Medes and Elamites, and with other residents of Mesopotamia, along with those in Egypt, parts of Libya, and Arabia, receive little other attention in Acts. The spotlight is placed instead upon certain geographical areas on the road to the Gentile capital, Rome itself. There are two obvious reasons for this extensive listing of the more substantial and significant Jewish settlements during the first half of the first century C.E. One is that these are the people (representatives of all of the Jews) to whom the message of the life, death, and resurrection of Jesus is to be offered first. The other—of greater concern in the present study—is that all Jews, both Palestinian and in the Diaspora, are hereby declared guilty of crucifying and killing Jesus.[12] In Luke's opinion, even visitors from Rome, both Jews and proselytes, are guilty of nailing Jesus to the cross, because they are Jews!

Between the two direct accusations of guilt for all Jews there are two instances in which the original sense of portions of Ps. 16 and 110 are disregarded in favor of an interpretation of them intended to "prove" to Jewish hearers that David was the writer of these psalms, that David was a prophet, and that David foresaw and spoke about the resurrection of the Messiah. Actually, the writer or speaker in Ps. 16:8–11 was rejoicing that God had kept him alive and had not yet given him over to death and the grave. He was talking about himself, not about Jesus who would live hundreds of years later. But with some assistance from the Septuagint translation in which "in safety" of Ps. 16:9 became "in hope," Luke was able to interpret the psalmist's references to the path of his present life (16:11) as references to the life of Jesus, the "Holy One" who would never see corruption but would know and experience the ways of the resurrected life. So also the words of the enthronement Ps. 110 spoke by the Israelites, "The Lord says to my lord (the king being crowned), 'Sit at my right hand (to rule on the earth) . . .'" became for Luke a proof that David had said, "The Lord said to my Lord (Jesus), 'Sit at my right hand (to rule in heaven). . . .'"

The result is that Peter's speech within the context of the Pentecost scene twice makes the direct accusation that all Jews are guilty of deliberately nailing Jesus to the cross, and twice does violence to the original intent of portions of the Jewish Scriptures. From the time of Luke's writing until the present, Jews have justifiably rejected these accusations and these interpretations of their own Scriptures. When we as Christians look objectively at these accusations and at these interpretations, we also should be mature enough to reject these accusations and to repudiate these interpretations. After nineteen centuries we no longer need to make these accusations and we no longer need to try to "prove" the resurrection of Jesus by using these forced interpretations of the psalmists.

Here as elsewhere in Acts, however, it is difficult to reduce or nullify the unproductive and damaging anti-Jewish material because it is such a significant portion of the account. A fairly thorough approach to the problem—an editorial redaction actually—would proceed somewhat as follows:

1. In 2:5 the word *Jews* simply would not be reproduced in the translation, or would be relegated to a footnote. In this instance, there is textual support in Codex Sinaiticus, which does not include the word. The result would be: "There were residing in Jerusalem at that time devout people from every nation under heaven."

2. In 2:14 Peter's address would be directed more generally to all who

read the text, as follows: "Listen, all of you! Let this be known to you, and pay attention to my words." (People in a Christian congregation, hearing the address in this way, would more likely feel that the words were being directed to themselves and would pay more attention to them than with the literal rendition, "Jews and you who live in Jerusalem! Let this be known to you, and pay attention to my words." The literal translation permits the hearer in a Christian congregation today largely to disregard the message, since it was obviously directed to people within a different religious grouping in a far away city many centuries ago.)

3. In 2:22 the vocative "Israelites" would not be reproduced in the translation, or would be relegated to a footnote for the reasons given in the previous paragraph.

4. In 2:23b the words "you nailed him to the cross and killed him, using non-Jews as your instruments of execution" would simply not be reproduced in the translation, or they could be relegated to a footnote in which "non-Jews" would be printed as "lawless people," or they could be retained in the text (with the word *anomōn* rendered as "lawless people"), since with the revisions of 2:14, 22 above, the message would be addressed more generally and not specifically to Jews.

5. The two examples of Lukan exegesis of the psalm passages in 2:25–31, 34–35 could be placed in a footnote as Lukan exegesis that completely disregards the original intention of these psalm passages, or it could be retained without upper case letters for "holy one" in 2:27 and for the second use of "lord" in 2:34. The second example (2:34–35) in particular has little meaning for most hearers or readers today, and as in certain situations of similar use of Ps. 110:1 in the Synoptics,[13] if we are sensitive to the issue of anti-Jewish polemic we shall select texts other than these for our lectionary readings.[14]

6. Consistent with the editorial redactions suggested for 2:14, 22, 23b, in 2:36 the translation should be merely: "Therefore, know beyond a doubt that God has made him Lord and Messiah." The words "all the house of Israel" and "this Jesus whom you crucified" could be printed in footnotes as Lukan judgments.

7. Acts 2:40 is what Dibelius[15] called an artistic device widely used in "great" literature to indicate that the speaker said more than has actually been imparted. The exhortation "Be saved from this unscrupulous generation!" is an echo of polemic against "this generation" of Jews in the Synoptic Gospels, particularly in Luke 11:51.[16] The words "from this unscrupulous generation" should be relegated to a footnote as a Lukan judgment. Without these words in the text, the exhortation "Be saved!" is an interesting and compelling passive imperative. It should not be translated as "Save yourselves!"

With these editorial redactions, Peter's speech within the context of the Pentecost scene becomes more edifying, more appropriate, more conducive to Christian self-critical examination, and less damaging to Jewish people who have no independent voice in the account.

Acts 3:1–26: *Peter's speech in the scene of the lame man healed in Jesus' name.* This speech of Peter functions in the Acts account as a transition from the great day of Pentecost to the arrest of Peter and John. Apparently an account circulating in early Christian tradition about a crippled man healed by Peter was used to emphasize that this miracle was accomplished in Jesus' name, not by Peter's power, and to elaborate further on a theme from the Pentecost sermon, namely, that the Israelites were guilty of rejecting and killing the servant of the "God of Our Fathers," Jesus the Christ.[17] Even this sin would be covered, however, for those Israelites who would repent and turn to Jesus, the prophet whom Moses had foretold (3:19–22). But the Israelites who would not listen to the prophet Jesus would be rooted out from the people of Israel (3:23). Here again the destruction of Judaism is envisaged as complete. The adherents of Judaism are to repent and turn to Jesus or they will be torn up and cast away from the people of God, where they will wither and die.

It is difficult but possible here also to separate the anti-Jewish polemic in this speech of Peter from the basic kerygma of salvation and to repudiate it without damage to the kerygma. Indeed, with the repudiation of the polemic, the kerygma is given room to grow and to bear more fruit, even in our time. There are five places in this speech of Peter in which editorial redaction is necessary in order to accomplish this.

1. In the address of Peter to the people in 3:12b the explicit "Israelites!" can be relegated to a footnote as an unnecessary Lukan limitation to the audience addressed.

2. The words

whom you delivered over and denied in the presence of Pilate even when Pilate had decided to release him. But you denied the holy and righteous one, and you requested that a murderer be set free among you. And you killed

in 3:13b–15a are not essential to the basic kerygma of salvation. They interrupt it and distract from it.[18] With these words in a footnote as bitter Lukan anti-Jewish polemic, the portions that precede and follow them in 3:13–15 read smoothly to express the fundamental Christian proclamation: "The God of Abraham and of Isaac and of Jacob, the 'God of Our Fathers,' glorified this dearly loved son Jesus as the pioneer of eternal life, whom God raised from the dead, of whom we are witnesses."[19]

3. The rather condescending "I know that you acted in ignorance, as did also your rulers" in 3:17, and the postpositive *de* ("but") in 3:18 give evidence of the skill of Luke the speech writer, but they are not really consistent with Luke's judgment of the Jews as Luke depicts them else-

where, where their "ignorance" of what allegedly they have done does not excuse them from condemnation. With the words cited above placed in a footnote, 3:17–18 would read as follows: "And now, my friends, God has fulfilled what God had announced earlier through the mouth of all the prophets, that is, that God's Messiah would suffer."

4. The message of that which the followers of Jesus believe that God has provided through Jesus is adequately argued and offered to Jewish people in this speech of Peter without the threat of destruction expressed in 3:23. The threat weakens the argumentation and tarnishes the offering of salvation. When we publish this drama in vernacular languages for use in our time, this threat should be relegated to footnote status.

5. The words at the end of the speech in 3:26b, "in order to turn each of you from your wicked actions," change what would otherwise be a beautiful ending, "When God had raised up from the dead God's dear son, God sent him to you first, in order that God might bless you," to one in which a sweeping generalization brands all Jews as guilty of lives filled with evil actions. These words at the end of the speech in 3:26b should also be placed in a footnote as evidence of Luke's sectarian attitude.

Once these editorial redactions have been made, Peter's speech emphasizes the basic Christian proclamation of salvation and the power of healing accessible in Jesus' name, as a reading of the speech with these redactions will indicate. Without these redactions the proclamation of salvation and the power of healing accessible in Jesus' name remain overshadowed by the anti-Jewish polemic.[20]

Acts 4:1–31: *Peter's speech in the scene of the arrest and release of Peter and John.* This text continues the scene presented in 3:1–26, with its anti-Jewish polemic unabated. Here also we have the choice between an attitude of *laissez-faire* with regard to the text or taking steps to reduce and repudiate the anti-Jewish polemic through sensitive translation and editorial redaction. When the leaders of our community theater and of our college theater prepare a dramatic production, certain modifications of the script are made to suit the sensitivities of the intended audience. Within a mature Christianity similar modifications of the script of the canonical Acts are appropriate to suit it to our time and place. The alternatives to these modifications are (1) to continue to fan the flames of anti-Semitism within Christians who read or hear these Acts texts, or (2) to put most of Acts away into ecclesiastical mothballs.

If our choice is to do something other than to maintain the *laissez-faire* attitude toward the Acts texts, which has become traditional during the past centuries, appropriate modifications of the Acts 4:1–31 script might include the following:

1. In 4:2 the words "the priests and the chief administrator of the temple and the Sadducees" could by interpretative translation become "some of the religious leaders." Although this modification is less essential than are many others, it would be helpful to audiences in our time to add, as an

interpretative gloss after "the resurrection from the dead" at the end of 4:3, the words "which they did not profess," to clarify that some Jews, including most notably the Sadducees, did not accept innovations by the Pharisees and other Jews that included the concept of a resurrection hope.

2. In 4:10–11 the proclamation of the Gospel and of the healing power of Jesus' name would be enhanced and much more adequately appropriated by Christian audiences today if the limitation of the address of Peter's words to all the people of Israel were relegated to footnote status. The words affected would be "to all of you, and to all of the people of Israel" and "whom you crucified" in 4:10 and the words "by you" added to the Ps. 118:22 quotation in Acts 4:11. The modified text of 4:10–11 would read, "Let it be known that in the name of Jesus Christ of Nazareth, whom God raised from the dead, this man is standing in front of you in good health for the first time in his life. This is the stone that was rejected by the builders. It is the one that has now become the most important stone of the structure."

3. Because Acts 4:12 is among the key confessional statements of the New Testament, modification of the anti-Jewish polemic inherent in its exclusivistic claim of "salvation" only in the name of Jesus Christ of Nazareth is an extremely delicate matter. Along with John 14:6 it stands as a prime example of religious "advertising" in the New Testament canon, and it is not surprising that these two examples occur in the two New Testament documents that have the most sustained anti-Jewish polemic. This type of religious-advertising claim is to be expected in a situation such as that which occurred during the latter decades of the first century of the common era, when competition for people's allegiance was apparently intense and when various groups of followers of Jesus struggled to obtain a larger portion of the religious market.

A solution to this delicate issue lies first of all in the recognition that 4:12 is intensely confessional, and second in the making of that confessional element even more explicit. Since it is a perfectly understandable confessional-advertising-claim scene, the intent of the author of 4:12 can be shown even more clearly by a translation that permits the one playing the role of Peter to make the stirring confession, "I believe that salvation is not attainable in any other way, and I believe that there is no name given under heaven different from this in which salvation is designated for us." Salvation for the Christian is in the name of Jesus. This is a matter of confession that any Christian, indeed every Christian, is entitled to make. When it is clearly presented as a statement of faith rather than as a general statement of fact (which presumably could be verified by empirical means!), the anti-Jewish polemic is lessened at the same time that the Christian confession is highlighted.

4. In 4:23 "the chief priests and the elders" can be rendered as "these religious leaders."

5. In 4:24–28 the words of Ps. 2:1–2 are reapplied against the chief

priests and the rulers of Israel by associating the rulers of Israel, Herod, and Pilate with the kings of the earth and rulers who oppose Yahweh and Yahweh's appointed king in the psalm. Much of the blame that the Lukan writer was transferring here from Roman authority to Jewish responsibility can be returned to Rome if in 4:27b we interpret the words "with the Gentiles and the people of Israel" as "with the power of the Roman empire and the support of some of our own religious and political leaders." Since we are no longer in danger of reprisal from the Roman Empire, we can express more fully what the Lukan writer might have written if an open acknowledgment of which authorities had decreed Jesus' death had been prudent and desired.

Acts 5:17–42: *The speech of Peter and the apostles and of Gamaliel in the scene of the hearing before the council.* After an interlude (4:32–5:16) in which a Levite from Cyrpus,[21] who was a follower of Jesus, is contrasted to Ananias and Sapphira—for unlike Ananias and Sapphira he had brought the entire proceeds from the sale of his field to the apostolic "ayatollahs" and had not lied to them—another scene of major triumph of the followers of Jesus over all parties of the Israelites is staged.

There are two noteworthy Lukan themes in this scene. First, it is shown here (as in Acts 23:6–10) that the Jews, with their diverse views on concepts such as the resurrection from the dead at the end of this age, could during the latter decades of the first century be pitted against each other in such a way that they could not move decisively against the followers of Jesus. Second, the Jewish council and, by association, all Jews are portrayed as acting in opposition to the God they claim to serve, even though the Pharisees at least are depicted as cautious in this regard. This second theme in particular is used effectively by Luke as a vehicle for virulent anti-Jewish polemic. Here, as in so many other Lukan scenes, the Jews have no opportunity for an independent voice; their lines are all written by a Christian playwright and their characters are all portrayed by Christian actors, even when the speaker is a well-known figure such as Gamaliel.

Acts 5:17–42 is a Thespian's delight. There are the villains and the heroes, a role for an angel to express the power of God and a directive from God, and a degree of suspense in the test of time proposed by Gamaliel. The audience is privy to the situations in which the villains are taken by surprise and dismayed, and the members of the audience, clearly partisan themselves, know that, in spite of great odds and difficulties, God is on the side of the heroes and that their success is assured.

The following redactional modifications are suggested as appropriate in adapting this scene for use in our time:

1. In 5:17–18 it is adequate to state that certain religious leaders, jealous of the success of the apostles, laid their hands upon them and put them into the public prison. There appears to be some exaggeration in the Lukan text in the mention of all who were with the high priest as the party of the

Sadducees. The purposes of the playwright were accomplished in gathering all of the party of the Sadducees into this scene, but the critic will realize that, in the many events that lie somewhere behind this scene, not all of the Sadducees would ever have been present at one time and not all of them would have agreed on such a course of action.

2. Again in 5:21b it is sufficient to state that the religious leaders who opposed the activities of the apostles held a hearing and summoned the apostles from the prison. The textual reference to "all the Senate of the sons of Israel" suggests that the Lukan writer was not familiar with the institutional structure of the Jews in Jerusalem during the period depicted[22] and that an analogy to the Roman Senate may have been in mind.

3. In 5:24 specific reference to "the captain of the temple and the chief priests" is an unnecessary anti-Jewish specification, a designation important to the Lukan writer but not essential today. For consistency with 5:17–18 and 21b, it would be advisable simply to state that when the religious leaders heard these words they were greatly perplexed about what might be happening.

4. "The official in charge and his assistants" is adequate in 5:26. There is no reason to reproduce a connotation that this official was in charge of the Jewish temple. We no longer are under compulsion to take every opportunity afforded to stress Jewish opposition to the social ministries performed by Chrtistians.

5. The proclamation of obedience to God and the witness to the belief that God had raised Jesus from the dead come across more clearly when the vicious anti-Jewish polemic of 5:30b, 31b is relegated to a footnote. The following is an example of the kind of translation of 5:29b–31 that can result from this type of sensitivity.

It begins with what in a drama presentation would be delegated to a chorus, "We must obey God rather than obey people." From within that chorus Peter would continue alone with the sterling confession, "We believe that the 'God of Our Fathers' raised Jesus from the dead and has exalted him as our Leader and Savior at the right hand of God to provide for our repentance and the forgiveness of our sins." In this sensitive translation the onus is taken from "Israel" and from the "villains" of this scene. Instead, the confessional nature of Peter's speech is highlighted. The necessity of "our" repentance and the need for the forgiveness of "our" sins is acknowledged in a manner that theologically is far more attractive than if repentance is demanded of others while it is assumed that "we" have no need for it. The apostolic witness expressed in the verse that follows immediately (5:32) is enhanced by this kind of translation, which emphasizes our confession of faith. This witness is robbed of much of its power when the emphasis is upon the alleged guilt of other people and upon "their" need for repentance. The Lukan playwright's zeal to incorporate anti-Jewish polemic so frequently in these scenes detracted from the witness, from the confession of faith that presumably should have been the more important consideration. That was the Lukan playwright's privilege, and the early church in its usage of this material and in its incorporation of it into its canon obviously gave its approval. But within a mature Christianity we are no longer bound to that particular emphasis, especially when it has been shown to have been damaging to Jews for nineteen centuries and when it detracts from an otherwise clear confession of the Christian faith.

6. If we were to print Acts in the form of a drama, 5:33 would be one of many verses that would not be a part of the dialogue, but would be printed in italics as directions for the supporting cast of actors. Most of the next verse (5:34) would probably today become the self-introduction of the actor who would play the role of Gamaliel: "I am Gamaliel, a respected Torah teacher, held in honor by all of the people. Put these men outside so that we can discuss this case." As in several of the Peter speeches discussed above, *andres Israēlitai* need not be rendered literally as "Israelite men." Something such as "My esteemed colleagues," or "My friends" would be a good idiomatic translation, accurately reproducing the sense of the Greek vocative. The right to use the respected name of Gamaliel in this manner might be questioned, but perhaps that license may be given to the playwright.[23]

Thus ends action area one with its sequence of Jerusalem scenes and its limitations to specifically Jewish situations.

B. In the Speeches of Stephen and of Peter and in the Summaries Provided in the Various Scenes in Action Area Two (6:1–12:24)

Acts 6:8–8:3: *Stephen's speech within the context of the martyrdom of Stephen scene.* The initial opposition to the person and work of Stephen in this scene does not come from the Sadducees in Jerusalem but from Hellenistic Jews (6:9–14). To them are attributed many of the same tactics that were said in Mark and Matthew to have been employed by the enemies of Jesus. The logion from the Gospel tradition regarding the role of Jesus in destroying the temple is also introduced here. In this way Luke was able to demonstrate that Hellenistic Jews, along with their Palestinian counterparts, were guilty of continuing opposition to Jesus and to his followers. The impression is given that although there may have been a man named Stephen who was the first martyr (or the ideal martyr) for the Christian faith, this scene is contrived to show beyond any doubt that it was Jews—Hellenistic Jews as well as Palestinian Jews, elders, scribes, the people, and the council—who opposed the Spirit of God and betrayed and murdered Jesus of Nazareth, the Righteous One who now "stands at the right hand of God." Since it was widely known that Jesus' death had been by crucifixion, an execution reserved as a Roman government prerogative, it was impossible for the Lukan writer to have Jesus stoned by Jews. Since it was also apparently not possible to portray the death of well-known early Christian leaders such as Peter, or Paul, or even James the brother of John as executed by Jews, an otherwise rather obscure figure, Stephen, is depicted as stoned by an angry mob of Jews. This can be said from the evidence of Luke-Acts; whether or not behind this dramatic scene a follower of Jesus named Stephen was actually stoned by a Jewish mob can no longer be either proved or disproved as historically verifiable.

The beautiful witness of the martyr Stephen in this scene is spoiled to a great extent by the speech attributed to Stephen. If 7:2–53 and the cue for the actors in 7:54 were covered, the character Stephen would belie the accusations of his detractors by his silence and by his vision of heaven, the glory of God, and of Jesus in 6:15, 7:55–60.

Most of Stephen's lengthy speech[24] is a recital of the patriarchal and Mosaic traditions in which Stephen identifies himself with his hearers in speaking about "our fathers," their strengths and their weaknesses in the best self-critical prophetic tradition. However, 7:51–53, the vitriolic, name-calling denunciations—the portion most consistent with the agenda of the Lukan writer as author—are in tone and content so foreign to the verses that they follow that they constitute, in effect, a separate, different speech. Nevertheless, it must be admitted that in this scene they serve their purpose; they constitute the provocation for the angry mob. Therefore repudiation of the anti-Jewish polemic in the Stephen speech is especially difficult.

The first and most obvious step that this repudiation should take is to revise our lectionary-readings usage of the Stephen scene. It must be said to be unconscionable to read Acts 6:1–9; 7:2a, 51–60 and Acts 6:8–7:2a, 51–60 on the Fourth Sunday of Easter, Series A, and on the lesser festival of St. Stephen, Deacon and Martyr, respectively, as we now do.[25] Certainly better selections are possible that remove the emphasis from the violence and from the generalizing accusations of Jewish guilt, from the denial of any continuing validity in Jewish spirituality, and place it instead upon the beautiful witness of this archetypal Christian martyr.

In our translation for popular usage it would be appropriate to relegate 7:51–54 to footnote status as Lukan bias. That which precedes and that which follows these verses fit together well with the heaven motif in the Acts 7:49–50 quotation of Isa. 66:1–2a, followed immediately by 7:55 in which Stephen, full of the Holy Spirit, having looked intently into heaven, saw the glory of God and Jesus standing at the right hand of God. It is neither accurate nor just to accuse the Jewish people generally of always opposing the Spirit of God, much less of being stiff-necked and uncircumcised in their hearts and in their ears, and of betraying and murdering Jesus, as Luke does in Acts 7:51–53.

Acts 8:1b–3: *Persecution and dispersion, the burial of Stephen and the damage done to the church by Saul.* This brief section is not a developed scene. Its nature is that of transitional remarks by a "stage manager" while actors and the stage crew prepare for the next scene. The audience is told that devout men, presumably Jews or followers of Jesus, buried Stephen. The contrast is sharp between them and Saul, who is said to be inflicting great damage to men and women among the followers of Jesus. There is anti-Jewish polemic present, therefore, in this transition, but it is not given dramatic substance.

Acts 9:1–31: *The enlistment of Saul scene.*[26] The possibilities for developing a dramatic scene to portray the enlistment of Saul, the zealous persecutor of the followers of Jesus, to the Christian cause as a chosen carrier of Jesus' name to "nations and kings and sons of Israel" were not lost to the Lukan playwright. The raw materials for this great scene were probably readily available within Paul's letters, most notably in Gal. 1:13–17; 1 Cor. 1:1; 9:1; 15:8; and 2 Cor. 12:1–12, and perhaps also in reminiscences by admirers of Paul who were still alive. The result was a memorable scene with visions, a light and a voice from heaven, and dialogue produced by the playwright to delight the appreciative partisan audience. The scene was so successful that it was modified and given further development twice more in the same drama. The impression given is sufficiently vivid that the Christian "playgoer" soon becomes certain that it all must have occurred precisely as shown here.

It is readily seen that anti-Jewish polemic is basic to this account, in this dramatic enlistment of the superstar of the opposition in the Christian cause. Nevertheless, by sensitive translation and usage, emphasis can be permitted to fall instead upon the more positive aspects of the scene.

1. In 9:1–2 "chief priest" and "synagogues" can be rendered as "chief religious administrator" and "religious assemblies," so that Christians in our time will not associate this introduction to the scene so closely with Jewish synagogues and Jews whom they may know within their own communities. The resultant reading will be something such as, "But Saul . . . having gone to the chief religious administrator, requested from him written authorizations to take to the religious assemblies in Damascus. . . ."

2. It should merely be noted that Acts 9:5, 22:7, and 26:14 are indications that to the Lukan playwright for anyone to persecute the followers of Jesus is to persecute Jesus himself, the one crucified but raised by God from the dead and exalted to the right hand of God in heaven.

3. In Ananias's initial response to the voice of the Lord in a vision (Acts 9:13–14), *kaka* can be translated as "destructive things" rather than as "evil," and *tōn archiereōn* as "the top political and religious officials" rather than as "the chief priests." This shift in emphasis may appear to be inconsequential, but it is a way of stressing that opposition to Jesus and to followers of Jesus was political as well as religious in nature.

4. Also in 9:20–21 *synagōgais* and *tous archiereis* can be translated as "reli-

gious assemblies" and as "the top political and religious officials" respectively, rather than as "synagogues" and as "the chief priests."

5. More important than the above is the problem caused by Luke's use of *Ioudaious*[27] in 9:22 and of *hoi Ioudaioi* in 9:23. Luke apparently chose to ignore that even after Paul became a leader in carrying the name of Jesus to "nations and kings and sons of Israel," Paul continued in his writings to call himself a Jew, a Hebrew, and an Israelite, and to claim his Jewish heritage.[28] We are confronted, therefore, with dozens of instances from 9:23 until the end of the Acts drama, as well as with dozens of other similar instances in the Fourth Gospel,[29] in which the words *the Jews* are used in a general sense pejoratively for all who oppose the teachings and the actions of Paul in Acts and of Jesus in John and often seek to kill them, even though the historical Paul continued to claim to be a Jew in his own writings and although the historical Jesus obviously was numbered among "the Jews" himself. These numerous pejorative generalizations, which rather anachronistically reflect conditions at a later date, account for much of the anti-Jewish emphasis in the New Testament. While each instance must be assessed separately, particularly since in some places *hoi Ioudaioi* is probably a geographical designation for "the Judeans," it can be stated here that in most instances the generalization *hoi Ioudaioi* should not be translated literally as "the Jews," but more accurately according to the sense from the context as "some Jews," "some of his fellow-countrymen," "his opponents," or "his enemies." Most translators rather insensitively have not bothered to make this distinction, and simply along with the Lukan playwright and with those who formulated the vivid anti-Jewish drama scenes in the Fourth Gospel have continued to portray "the Jews" generally as the villains. As a result, for nineteen centuries the avid Christian reader of these documents, or even the casual one, consciously or subconsciously has envisioned the Jews in that role, and those Christians who have read the New Testament the most extensively have often become the most thoroughly bigoted against the Jews.

In Acts 9:22, therefore, *Ioudaious* should be translated as "many of his countrymen" ("Saul . . . confounded many of his countrymen who lived in Damascus by demonstrating to them that this Jesus was indeed the Messiah"), and 9:23 should be rendered as "And when some time had passed, his enemies made plans to assassinate him." This kind of sensitivity in translation has as a by-product the further advantage incidentally of removing the inconsistency with 2 Cor. 11:32–33 that the Lukan playwright introduced in 9:23–25. The tension between whether it was the governor under King Aretas who guarded the city of Damascus in order to seize Paul, as Paul himself wrote, or whether it was "the Jews" who were watching the gates day and night in order to kill him, as suggested by the Lukan playwright much later, is resolved if we permit Paul in describing his own experience to be explicit about this, and let the playwright describe those who were out to get Paul as what they obviously were, his enemies.

6. In 9:29 Saul is presented as speaking and disputing against the Hellenists, so that these Greek-speaking Jews in Jerusalem are also specifically cited as attempting to kill him. In this case, for us to identify the Hellenists further in our translations and usage of 9:29 would only make Luke's anti-Jewish polemic more explicit.

Acts 10:1–11:18: *Peter's speech in the Cornelius scene.* In this, the most important scene in the Acts drama depicting how the followers of Jesus were led by God to share fully in community with non-Jews, there is an inherent criticism of Jewish spirituality in the claim of new, special revelation from God that annuls Jewish dietary regulations and Jewish exclusivism. The new emerging community of the followers of Jesus had the right, of course, to define itself and its life-style as a new religious entity as it wished, and the primary purpose of this Cornelius scene is not to engage in virulent anti-Jewish polemic. Even in the formal speech of Peter, in this instance the emphasis is upon the proclamation of the "good news" rather than on defamation of Jewish people. In the one place in the speech where anti-Jewish material is near the surface (10:39), we can safeguard the emphasis on the proclamation of the Gospel by translating the geographical designations as "in the rural and small-town areas of the Jewish nation and in Jerusalem," and by specifying the unexpressed subject of the verb in "They killed him by hanging him upon a cross of wood" as "The political authorities."[30]

Acts 12:1–24: *The final dramatic scene of action area two with Herod, the Jews, and the idolaters from Tyre and Sidon pitted against James, Peter, the church, and the angel of the Lord.* This carefully constructed, complex scene, which begins with the horrendously violent act of the despotic Herod executing James, the brother of John, and ends with the horrible death of Herod, struck by an angel of the Lord and eaten alive by worms because Herod had accepted the acclamation of deity by the emissaries from Tyre and Sidon, includes what is perhaps the most blatant and vicious anti-Jewish polemic in all of the New Testament. Here the Jews collectively are allied with the worst kind of ruler imaginable, one who capriciously executes his subjects who are doing no harm. Furthermore, Herod's execution of James is depicted as pleasing to the Jews and the motive for the rapacious Herod to seize Peter as well and to plan to dispatch him also at the first opportune time to please the Jews still more. The evil league of Herod and the Jews is joined later in the scene by the wicked emissaries from Tyre and Sidon, areas notorious already in the Jewish Scriptures for their dangerous idolatry. In order to counter this evil league that the Lukan playwright has arrayed against Peter and the church, an angel of the Lord is summoned twice to play a miraculous role, the first time to rescue Peter from the heavily armed prison and then again to destroy Herod. The result is a dramatic scene prepared by a heavily partisan playwright to delight an equally partisan audience just before the "curtain" comes down on action area two.

It is our responsibility in the translation and usage of this scene to recognize first of all that this is not an incident that occurred precisely in this way in the year 44 C.E., but that this is a scene in a literary drama composed much later.[31] James died, and Herod died, and followers of Jesus were frequently persecuted by political authorities during the first century, but the Lukan playwright went far beyond these raw materials of history in preparing this elaborate scene. Mature Christianity will be able to recognize and appreciate this, and will be able to accept some modification of the scene in order to retain the substance of it to pass on to future generations. Actually, the modifications needed, though incisive, are limited in scope. There is no necessity of any adjustments within the miracle portions that contribute so much to the enjoyment of the scene. Only in two places is there need for circumlocution in translation or, if more radical measures are desired, for relegating two clauses to footnote status. These two places are as follows:

1. In 12:3a "when he saw that it was pleasing to the Jews" should be dropped to footnote status, or by circumlocution "the Jews" should be rendered as "those who opposed the church." In this instance circumlocution is preferable because it retains the meaning of the text without deletion. If pruning to footnote status is employed, it should be combined with a circumlocution translation in the footnote. Otherwise the footnote may even draw to the attention of many readers the alleged guilt of "the Jews" in this matter. The clause could simply be deleted, of course, in our translations and usage. If we are truly concerned about the "dynamic Word of God," we shall be willing to entertain this possibility.

2. At the end of 12:11 the possibilities cited in the previous paragraph are appropriate also for the words "and from all the expectations[32] of the Jewish people." The suggested circumlocution would be "and from all the expectations of our enemies." These words could be dropped completely in our translations if we dare to redact as we translate. If we dropped them completely in our translations, we would no longer be suggesting in this biblical text that "the Jews" are "our enemies."

C. In the Speeches of Paul and of Others in the Scenes in Action Area Three (12:25–28:31)

Acts 13:6–12: *The controversy with the Jewish false prophet Bar-Jesus.* The religious arena for the scene depicted here and for this section of the drama has already clearly been defined as Jewish. It is hardly necessary, therefore, for the Lukan playwright or for us to indicate specifically the religious and cultural identity of the magician, the false prophet on whom Saul (henceforth to be called Paul) inflicted temporary blindness. The name Bar-Jesus in itself provides sufficient identity. Paul's vilification of him in 13:10 should be restricted to him as an individual and not be extended by association to all Jews. This interesting and dramatic scene, with its victory of "our" side over the forces of our opposition so typical of the Lukan playwright, will be improved, therefore, if we pass in silence over the word "Jewish" in our translation and usage of Acts 13:6.

Acts 13:14–52: *The speeches of Paul and the comments of the Lukan writer as "stage manager" in the scene at Antioch of Pisidia.* The speech that the Lukan playwright prepared for Paul for this scene is relatively polite and restrained. Paul is made to identify himself with the Israelites and those who fear God along with them. They share their descent from the patriarchs and address each other as brothers. It is those who live in Jerusalem and their rulers (13:27–28) who, through lack of understanding, are said to have condemned Jesus and requested that Pilate have him executed. Paul stresses the good news of the fulfillment of God's promises to the fathers (13:32), and this type of emphasis is effective (13:43).

The anti-Jewish polemic in this scene comes in the comments in 13:45, 50–51, which inform the audience that when "the Jews" saw the crowds, they were filled with envy and blasphemed, speaking against the words of Paul, and that "the Jews" stirred up the prominent devout women and the most important men of the city and they incited persecution of Paul and Barnabas and drove them out of their area. It should be apparent at once that the use of "the Jews" in this context is a gross generalization that should not be perpetuated. Since it has just been stated in 13:43 that "many of the Jews and of the devout proselytes[33] had followed Paul and Barnabas," it is strange and biased play-writing to say next that "the Jews" were filled with envy and acted persistently against Paul and his co-worker. It would be comparable for us to say that "many Americans supported and voted for the president," and then in the next breath to state that "the Americans" despised and tried to despose the president from office. Obviously what is meant is that "the Americans" in this latter usage are those people who are the political opponents of the president and want to get rid of the incumbent. If that is what is meant, that is what should be stated. So also in Acts 13:45, 50 in our translations and usage we should state that when "those who opposed Paul and Barnabas" saw the crowds, "the opponents of Paul and Barnabas" stirred up the prominent devout women and the most important men of the city.

Acts 14:1–7: *Comments by the "stage manager" regarding activities at Iconium.* The views of the playwright are given free rein[34] in these comments by the "stage manager" while the next scene is being prepared. It is of interest to note that even though Paul and Barnabas had been said to have turned to the Gentiles (13:46), in 14:1 they are made to follow their previous practice of entering into the synagogue of the Jews.[35] The pattern is repeated: success, opposition, flight. Here in 14:1–2, however, Luke makes a distinction between Jews who believed what Paul and Barnabas were proclaiming and Jews who did not, though in 14:4 the generalization "the Jews" returns. At the end of 14:1 a sensitive and careful translation would produce "a great multitude of people both of Jewish and of Greek background believed." Likewise it would be preferable in a sensitive and careful translation of 14:2 to say that "those who were of the same religious and cultural background as Paul and Barnabas, but who did not believe and follow what they were proclaiming, stirred up trouble and turned away many of the people of that city against Paul and Barnabas" rather than to say that the unbelieving Jews stirred up and poisoned the minds of the Gentiles against the brethren. Within mature Christianity biased and prejudicial playwriting, even when it is incorporated within one's sacred Scriptures, can be countered somewhat when it is recognized that the playwright gave the opposition no opportunity to express its own point of view and when Jewish people have been harmed for so many centuries in part because of this kind of writing.

In 14:4–5 the sense of the comments is that some of the people of the city took their position with the opponents of Paul and Barnabas and some with those apostles. When the religious and political coalition against them made an attempt to mistreat them and to stone them, the apostles moved quickly to another area. There is no necessity of stressing repeatedly that "the Jews" were against them, or that Jews among others were attempting to "molest" them, as some of our popular translations interpret the Greek text. Sexual connotations are not inherent in the word *hybrisai;* the sense is rather that of "to treat arrogantly or spitefully, mistreat, scoff at, or insult."[36]

Acts 14:19–20: *Comments regarding the stoning of Paul.* Among the experiences cited in 2 Cor. 11:23–33, there is the mention that "once I was stoned." With or without any detailed traditional source the Lukan playwright placed a stoning incident at Lystra in the "stage manager's" lines. The account is not developed into a major scene, and whether or not Paul's recovery is intended to be miraculous is uncertain. *Ioudaioi* in 14:19 will be rendered by circumlocution as "enemies of Paul" in a sensitive translation and usage of the account.

Acts 15:1–35: *The council at Jerusalem scene necessitated by the objections of believers who belonged to the party of the Pharisees.* Since this council at Jerusalem scene involved an intra-Christian matter in which the validation of Gentile Christianity appears to have been the primary purpose, anti-Jewish polemic is not the primary consideration. However, since those who opposed Paul and Barnabas and advocated the requirement of circumcision according to the custom of Moses were said to have been some believers who were from the *haireseōs* of the Pharisees, anti-Jewish polemic is involved. In Luke's opinion (Acts 26:5) the Pharisees were at that time considered *tēn akribestatēn hairesin* ("the most strict group") among what had formerly been for Paul "our religion." Since in Acts 15:5 the Lukan writer stipulates that there had been other Pharisees, in addition to Paul who is said to have been a Pharisee, who had become "believers," and since in Acts 5:34–39 and 23:6–9 even the Pharisees who do not "believe" in Jesus as the Christ and Lord are presented as friendly or at least neutral toward the followers of Jesus, apparently for the Lukan writer during the early development of the church the Pharisees stood relatively close to the early Christians both theologically and politically—at least prior to 66 C.E.[37]

The anti-Jewish polemic in the scene under consideration here is not vicious. Its polemic is subtle. It is present in the assertion that, as the council at Jerusalem ruled, it is not necessary to be circumcised according to the practice of Moses in order to be saved, and in the underlying assumption of the superiority of the religion of those who followed Jesus over that of the Jews and of others who did not. To put it another way, the Lukan playwright was showing in this scene that the best members of the best group within the Jewish religion, that is, the Pharisees who believed that Jesus was the Christ and Lord, were out of favor with God and with the church. They were depicted as trying to test God in Peter's speech (15:10). They were given minimal support in the compromise suggested in James's speech (15:13–21). Finally, they were voted down by the Christian council in Jerusalem so decisively that in the apostolic degree that resulted they were said to have troubled the community in Antioch with their words, upsetting them, with no authorization from the Christian leaders in Jerusalem (15:23–29).

Acts 17:1–9: *The scene in Thessalonica.* Again, although in 13:46 it had been stated that Paul and Barnabas were now turning to the Gentiles, when Paul and Silas entered Thessalonica, Paul is reported to have entered a synagogue of the Jews and on three Sabbaths to have demonstrated to them from the Scriptures that Jesus is the Christ who should suffer and be raised from the dead. Here in 17:2 and in 17:17; 18:4, 19 are four more instances in which our popular translations are more anti-Jewish than is the Greek original.[38] The Greek verb that expresses in each instance what Paul did with the Jews is a form of *dialegomai*, for which the English counterparts "I discuss, conduct a discussion, converse with" are common.[39] There is nothing in the immediate context of these verses to require the selection of the more polemical translation "argue," which the RSV, for example, employs. Also, as in the 13:45, 50–51 portions, it is a gross generalization to state that "the Jews" were jealous when some of the Jews had been persuaded and joined themselves to Paul and Silas. In our translations and usage we should, therefore, translate *hoi Ioudaioi* in 17:5 as "the enemies of Paul."

Acts 17:10–14: *The scene in Beroea.* "The synagogue of the Jews," though a literal translation in 17:10, is a tautology today. "The synagogue" or "the place where the Jews gathered for study and worship" would be preferable. "The people there" or "these people" would represent *houtoi* at the beginning of 17:11 more accurately than does "these Jews." Careful consideration of the context, as well as sensitivity in translation, suggests again that *hoi apo tēs Thessalonikēs Ioudaioi* in 17:13 are "the enemies of Paul from Thessalonica."

Acts 17:16–17: *Paul in the synagogue at Athens.* Paul's activity in the synagogue at Athens is greatly overshadowed by the scene and speech at the Areopagus that follow. Particularly in the Athens location, the translation[40] "he was holding discussions in the synagogue" rather than "he argued in the synagogue" is appropriate.

Acts 18:4–6: *Paul in the synagogue at Corinth.* For the third time (17:2, 17; 18:4) a form of *dialegomai* occurs in the Greek text, and again here it should be translated as "he was holding discussions" in the synagogue rather than as "he argued" in the synagogue.

As the drama continues, there is a noticeable decrease in the degree of success in persuading Jews that Jesus should be considered to be the Christ, even though the attempt continues to the final scene in Rome. For popular Christianity after nineteen centuries and perhaps as early as the final decade of the first century, the identity of Jesus as the Christ is hardly to be questioned, but for Jews, as more time passed after the crucifixion of Jesus, that identification became more difficult. The messianic age of peace and security had obviously not come to the Jews, nor, from what they could observe, to the world at large. As the process of apotheosis of Jesus continued and intensified within Hellenistic Christianity, it must have become increasingly difficult and rare for devout Jews—for whom God would never become human nor a human become God—to make the drastic adjustments to their thinking necessary for them to do as they are urged to do in 18:5, to join with the followers of Jesus. Personal experiences of the Lukan playwright are most likely reflected in references such as in 18:6 to the opposition that most of the Jews in the Diaspora expressed to Paul and to others like Paul.

Jacob Jervell[41] concludes that Luke attached such great importance to showing how Jews in various cities responded to the message of the followers of Jesus not in order to portray that the promises made to the people of God were transferred from the Jews to the Gentiles, but to show that these promises have come to the Gentiles through repentant Israel. For Jervell, Luke wanted to demonstrate that the division of the Jews was necessary so that the promises of God could be fulfilled. The unbelieving portion of the Jews was to be shown as having been rejected. Further mission to Jews was precluded. Those "genuine" repentant Jews who had been willing to accept the message of Peter, Paul, and the others both in Jerusalem and in the Diaspora were the cornerstone of the true Israel into which the Gentiles were incorporated.

Although it is certainly possible to read Acts as Jervell reads it, his interpretation of the three accounts of turning to the Gentiles (Acts 13:46; 18:6; 28:28) is not entirely convincing. The Lukan playwright may have been as sophisticated as Jervell supposes, but the same level of sophistication can hardly be attributed to the audience of the literary drama.[42] It may be instead that the explicit expression of turning from the Jews to the Gentiles was incorporated at three key places in the drama, in part as further validation of the mission to the Gentiles,[43] which is implied in action area one, authenticated in action area two, and demonstrated in action area three, and in part as an expression of Luke's anti-Jewish polemic. Certainly the words "Your blood upon your heads! I am cleansed of your guilt!" (18:6) are not likely to have been spoken by the same person who wrote Romans 9–11. Nevertheless, in popular Christianity and even in much Jewish thought, the apostle Paul is considered to have been almost doggedly anti-Jewish largely because of what is read in the Acts drama. Hence a careful and sensitive translation of the references to Jews also in 18:4–6 is necessary.

In 18:4b the sense of the reading is that Paul persuaded "some people who were of Jewish background and some who were of Greek." In 18:5 Paul's testimony was "mainly to Jews" that Jesus should be recognized as the Messiah. In 18:6 it is obviously "many (but not all) of them" who opposed him and spoke out against him. The remainder of 18:6 could be relegated to a footnote as a Lukan anti-Jewish bias. Without this portion in the vernacular text, the Lukan writer's characterization of Paul appears less inconsistent in continuing to work within synagogue settings and less out of accord with the Paul of the epistles, as well as much less anti-Jewish.

Acts 18:12–17: *The scene of the accusation against Paul presented to the proconsul Gallio.* The skill of the Lukan playwright is remarkable in this scene. The basis of the account—the reign of Gallio as proconsul of Achaia during this period—is historically verifiable from nonbiblical sources. It is plausible that mid-first-century Jews would say regarding Paul that this man is trying to persuade people to worship God in a way that is contrary to the Torah. Conceivably a Roman provincial head would refuse to rule on an intrareligious matter. The violence suffered by Sosthenes (18:17) has the appearance of an eyewitness report.

Nevertheless, there are indications that this is a literary composition intended in part to portray the ideal conduct of a Roman government official during the second half of the first century.[44] The playwright has the Jews present their accusation in concert but ambiguously, to try to induce Gallio to act against the Christians, but the Roman official is too clever to permit himself to be manipulated in this way. Paul is shown to be no enemy of the Roman government. He is a Roman citizen by birth, and in Acts 19:31 it is even stated that some of the Asiarchs of Ephesus were friends of his. The Christian audience—and any Roman officials who might read a copy of the drama in order to be able to report all evidence of activity subversive to the state—should see that the followers of Jesus are peaceful and certainly not disloyal to the Roman government;[45] it is their theological opponents, the Jews, who are demonstrably violent and vengeful. These opponents of the Christians should be driven from the presence of the Roman official just as Gallio is said to have driven them. If in their frustration they want to become self-destructive, the government should let them destroy each other.[46]

In our translation and use of this account, *hoi Ioudaioi* in 18:12 should become "the enemies of Paul," which is what those who would act together to attack Paul would be. Luke's "the Jews" is here again a gross generalization, since Paul and many of his friends are also Jews. In 18:14 *pros tous Ioudaious* should be "to Paul's accusers," and *ō Ioudaioi* should be left untranslated, since the nature of the persons addressed is already known. The entire scene is interesting, but hardly of immense theological significance for us today.

Acts 18:19–21: *The short visit of Paul in the synagogue at Ephesus.* For the fourth time (Acts 17:2, 17; 18:4, 19) the form of *dialegomai* employed in the Greek text should be translated as "he held discussions" with the Jews rather than as "he argued" with them. In 18:20 they are depicted as hospitable and perhaps even receptive to Paul.

Acts 18:28: *The comment about Apollos's forensic skill against the Jews in Corinth.* This text is merely cited as one more example of an anti-Jewish line provided for the "stage manager" character in this Lukan drama. It adds to the impression that Luke was nearly as anti-Jewish as he was pro-Christ.

Acts 19:8–10: *Paul among Jews and Greeks in Ephesus.* This is a typical description of the work of Luke's Paul. While the next scene is being readied, the "stage manager" speaks briefly about the most productive period of Paul's labors. Although Paul had already made two of his three announcements in this drama that he was going to leave the Jews alone and turn to the Gentiles, once more Paul is said to have entered the synagogue in Ephesus, which according to 18:19–21 he had promised to try to visit again.

The tension between the three announcements of turning from work among the Jews to the mission to the Gentiles and the reported continuation of Paul's activity in the synagogues in so many of the Acts accounts raises the possibility that either the three announcements or the reported activity of Paul in the synagogues may have been added by a redactor who did not adjust where necessary to remove the tension. It is conceivable, of course, that the Lukan playwright was that "redactor." From the 18:6 scene—the least developed of the three announcements accounts—Luke may have constructed the more complex parallels that were to become 13:46–49 and 28:25–29. The redactor's hand may be seen also in the resemblance of the Paul depicted here to the Jesus of the Gospel accounts. Luke's

Paul enters the synagogue (19:8), presumably taking along his disciples (19:9), who numbered "about twelve" (19:7), and, like the Jesus of the Synoptic Gospels, Paul's discussions and persuasive actions are concerned with "the kingdom of God" (19:8).

Typically, Luke's Paul presents his position in the synagogue, encounters opposition, and withdraws. He speaks boldly, discussing *(dialegomenos)*, not arguing, and attempting to persuade those who are in the synagogue to accept Paul's position regarding the kingdom of God. But since some of them hardened their hearts (something that in a sense God does as God had done to the Pharaoh and to the Egyptians) and refused to believe as Paul believed, even speaking evil about the Christian way in front of the large number of people who were present there,[47] Paul withdrew from the synagogue and took his disciples with him. Thus one more time Luke demonstrated the withdrawal of the church from the synagogue. Paul then held discussions (again *dialegomenos*) daily in the school of Tyrannus. Within two years in this academic setting Paul was able to reach all who were living in the province of Asia, Jews as well as Greeks, with the word of the Lord. (The highly partisan audience will gladly excuse the Lukan exaggeration here. The playwright is preparing the ground for the big Artemis of the Ephesians scene, which is soon to be enacted.)

There is not much that can be done by way of sensitive interpretative translation to reduce the anti-Jewish polemic of this short descriptive presentation. Perhaps what we can do is to try to envisage a similar situation today in which we might be involved.[48] Let us suppose that a group that is to a great extent a spin-off from Christianity, the followers of Sun Myung Moon, were to prepare and present for the education and edification of their young adherents a literary drama that would depict their successes contrasted sharply to the "hardness of heart" of Christianity, Christian congregations, and the Christian parents of teenagers and young adults who had been captivated by this new sect. Would their drama differ basically from the drama of our New Testament Acts?

Acts 19:11–20: *Jewish exorcists attempt unsuccessfully to imitate the miracles that God was doing through Paul.* The similarities between Luke's glorified Paul during Paul's most productive period in Acts and the Jesus of the Gospel accounts continues here. As Haenchen comments with regard to Acts 19:11–12, "He (Luke's Paul) lives no longer in the sphere of the cross but in that of glory."[49] But Luke was not satisfied merely to depict Paul as a great miracle worker in whom the power of God was operative as it had formerly been in Jesus. The occasion will not pass without the inclusion of a measure of anti-Jewish polemic in the drama. The exorcists, who are depicted as going around trying to get some of this power by using the name of Jesus as Paul had been using it, are said to be Jewish. When the seven sons of a Jewish high priest named Sceva tried this, the attempt misfired with disastrous consequences, which provided a delightful scene for the partisan audience for which Luke prepared this literary drama.

In this instance some sensitive interpretative translation and usage can be employed. In 19:13 the exorcists can be said to be "of Paul's own background," and in 19:14 there is no necessity for specifying in our translations and usage that the high priest named Sceva was Jewish.

Acts 19:33–34: *Alexander, the spokesman for the Jews, is shouted down by the mob in Ephesus*. Again, as in the Acts 19:11–20 scene just considered, a bit of anti-Jeweish polemic is included in the larger scene. What Luke seems to be demonstrating is that the Jews of Ephesus wanted to distinguish themselves from the accused Christians in order that they themselves might be spared the wrath of the mob, but that the Jews of Ephesus were so unpopular in that city that the mob merely responded by intensifying its chant. It was not Alexander the Jew but the Ephesian town clerk who quieted the mob. The message of the town clerk as delivered in this dramatic scene is that the mob should not act against the Christians, since the Christians are committing no irreverent actions against Artemis nor speaking blasphemously against her.

The anti-Jewish polemic of this account is relatively innocuous because of the lack of clarity regarding the purpose of the Jews and the content of Alexander's defense.

Acts 20:1–3: *Comments regarding Paul's travel arrangements and a plot by the Jews*. Just as Jesus is represented in the Gospel accounts as carrying on a ministry of exhortation and encouragement of his disciples in certain parts of Palestine, particularly around the Sea of Galilee, so also Paul here in these brief comments by the Lukan "stage manager" carries on a ministry of exhortation and encouragement of his disciples in certain parts of the Roman Empire, particularly around the Aegean Sea. Here also the Lukan "stage manager" has an opportunity to demonstrate the malicious enmity of "the Jews," who are said to have made a plot against Paul. Mention of this plot by the Jews helps to set the stage for mention of the "plots of the Jews" in Paul's speech to the elders of the church at Miletus in 20:19.

In our translations and popular usage *tōn Ioudaiōn* in 20:3 should be represented as "enemies of Paul," since even if there may be a historical basis for this remark, not all of the Jews would have plotted against him. Furthermore, any group of people that would be plotting against Paul would be "enemies of Paul." The other possibility would be to relegate this segment to a footnote in our translations as a Lukan anti-Jewish bias.

The listing of the seven companions who traveled with Paul (20:4) forms a transition to the second "we" portion of the drama. The Lukan playwright appears to have done relatively little editorial redaction of this first-person-plural travelogue source. It is noteworthy that except for one place in Acts 21:11, which is probably a Lukan redaction of the travelogue,[50] there is no anti-Jewish polemic in the "we" portions identified here as 16:10–17; 20:5–15; 21:1–18; and 27:1–28:16. Theologically, the first-person-plural travelogue source appears to be an expression of a variety of Jewish Christianity that meets in settings other than in the Jewish synagogues. In 16:13 it is said that on the Sabbath prayers and discussions were held outside the gate along the riverside. The days of Passover (Unleavened Bread) are cited in 20:6. In 21:5 prayers of farewell are spoken on the beach at Tyre. The brethren in Jerusalem gladly welcomed the groups repre-sented in the "we" portion (21:17), and on the following day Paul went in "with us" to James and all the elders were also present (21:18). The people of the "we" portions are almost always sailing somewhere, and they ap-pear to have "brethren" in nearly every port.[51]

Acts 20:17–38: *Paul's speech to the elders of the church of Ephesus at Miletus.* It comes as no surprise that in this major address by the Lukan playwright's Paul, the apostle has a line in which he speaks about tribulations that came upon him because of "the plots of the Jews." As in 20:3, the "Jews" here are really "all who have opposed Luke's Paul," and should be translated as "my enemies."

Acts 21:11: *The words of Agabus in the Agabus scene.* As noted above, the words of Agabus that are used to explain the significance of Agabus's symbolic act are probably a Lukan redaction of the travelogue.[52] With these words Luke provides a preview of what will happen to Paul in Jerusalem. Almost the identical things that according to the Gospel accounts had been done to Jesus will be done to Paul. But Paul, like Jesus, goes to Jerusalem in spite of everything. Luke explicitly blames "the Jews" for the Lukan Paul's passion and will provide the dramatic scenes with which to enact this for the benefit of the audience. Just as the message of Jesus continued even though he was delivered over into the hands of the Gentiles, so also the message of Jesus through Paul will be shown to continue even though "the Jews" deliver Paul in a similar fashion.[53]

In our translations and usage of 21:11, it would be appropriate to ex-press *hoi Ioudaioi* as "the enemies of Paul" in Jerusalem or simply "enemies of Paul" in Jerusalem. It will still be apparent from the context that Luke was writing about Jews at this point, because a few words later there is mention of Paul's being delivered over into the hands of the Gentiles. Since it is probable that the description of Agabus's symbolic act in the Jewish Christian travelogue prior to the Lukan redaction read something like this, "Thus shall the owner of this belt be bound and delivered over in Jerusalem," the translation "enemies of Paul" is to be preferred if we wish to provide in the vernacular a New Testament in which anti-Jewish polemic is recognized and dealt with in a sensitive and responsible manner. With this translation there is no loss of sense in the "we" portion in question. Indeed, it then reads more consistently with the other travelogue portions in Acts.

Acts 21:27–36: *The scene in which the arrest of Paul is depicted.* Those who precipitate the mob action that culminates in the arrest of Paul by the Roman military tribune are said to be "the Jews from Asia," who are now conveniently present in representative fashion. This entire section can easily be pictured on the "stage" of one's imagination. A few actors can represent "the Jews from Asia." A dozen stagehands can run on and off the stage to convey the impression that the entire city was aroused. Some of these can seize Paul and drag him from the temple area at one side of the stage to the platform front and center, where they can go through the motions of trying to kill him. Other Thespians dressed and acting as temple officials can close the gate to the temple area from the inside. The tribune can be summoned from the other side of the stage, command that Paul be arrested, interrogate the crowd, order that Paul be taken up the steps, and so on. The steps provide the ideal platform for Luke's Paul, undaunted and unharmed by all of the theatrics of the stagehands, to deliver the oration that the Lukan playwright has prepared for him.

In our translations and usage of this material today there is no need to emphasize that the primary villains in this Lukan scene are Jews. Therefore, *hoi apo tēs Asias Ioudaioi* in 21:27 should be "enemies of Paul from the province of Asia," and *andres Israēlitai* in 21:28 can be expressed as "All of you!" Even with these steps to deemphasize the Jewish identity of the villains, the scene will remain inherently anti-Jewish, with the false charges of Paul's accusers that he had brought Greeks into the temple and defiled the holy place and with the attempts by the mob to kill Paul. In spite of these steps, those who read or view this scene will still consciously or subconsciously picture Paul's opponents as Jews and see the relationship between this scene and the accounts of the arrest of Jesus in the Gospel texts. Thus, if we use this scene, Luke's purpose will be accomplished through us.

Acts 21:37–22:29: *Paul's speech to the people.* In a continuation of the previous scene, Paul addresses the people, and his detractors on the stage become silent. Luke's Paul delivers the speech that Luke has prepared for him, testifying to his impeccable background as a Jew from Tarsus, educated at the feet of Gamaliel in Jerusalem, but called from a life in which he had persecuted those who followed the Christian way to one in which he would be a witness appointed by "the God of Our Fathers" to share what he had seen and heard about "the Righteous One." By employing an autobiographical method to demonstrate the manner in which the Christian way supersedes and is superior to its antecedent, the speech is thoroughly anti-Jewish. Also anti-Jewish is the portrayal of the reaction of the mob, depicted in 22:22–23 as interrupting Paul's speech, defying the attempt of the Roman official to provide a measure of Roman justice, and viciously demanding the death of Paul.

The speech and its context provide further evidence of Luke's theological position with regard to the Jews. For Luke "the Jews from Asia" who opposed Paul with such vehemence, because Paul turned at the command of Jesus and of "the God of Our Fathers" to the Christian way and to sharing the Christian way with the Gentiles, are comparable to the opponents of Jesus as they are depicted in the Gospel accounts. In each instance those who retained their former ways when God had spoken in a new way to Jesus and to Paul were now so demented that they were actually opposing God. In Luke's opinion, when "the Jews" opposed and persecuted Paul and the church they were actually persecuting Jesus, whom God had vindicated by raising him from the dead.

Because this particular scene is so thoroughly permeated with anti-Jewish polemic, neither sensitive interpretative translation nor selective pruning of a few segments to footnote status can effectively reduce or repudiate unnecessary and destructive anti-Jewish material. What we can do is to recognize and to teach within the church that this material is a literary drama, not a documentary of history. When we use this material, we can and should use it as a drama and in a drama form, not as a reading in which the impression is given that this is a demonstration of exactly what happened. Beyond that, there are several places in which increased sensitivity and careful attention to context can result in a few reductions of the anti-Jewish polemic inherent in the scene.

For example, in 21:39 the pleonastic *anthrōpos . . . Ioudaios* in this context can be translated as "a Jewish national," which is what Paul apparently claimed to be even after he had become a major proponent of the Christian way among people both of Jewish and of non-Jewish background. In 22:3 there is a similar pleonastic construction, *anēr Ioudaios* ("a man, a Jew"). Paul is represented as making every effort at the beginning of his speech to identify completely with his audience in an effort to gain their support. Therefore, in 22:3 *anēr Ioudaios* can be rendered as "a Jew like you." More significant as a reduction of anti-Jewish emphasis would be the translation of *kata tas synagōgas* in 22:19 as "in one gathering place after another," departing from a literal rendering of *synagōgas*.

Acts 22:30–23:10: *The scene of the meeting of the Roman tribune, Paul, and the Jewish high council.* Again the Lukan playwright delights the audience with a scene that demonstrates the Jewish high priest's bitter hatred of Paul and of everything that Paul represented, the stupidity of the members of the Jewish high council in being led so easily by Paul into a violent internecine struggle, and the necessity of the Roman tribune to use military force to rescue Paul from the moblike actions of members of the highest court within Judaism. The account aptly indicates how actors in a drama—even in a literary drama—can succeed in doing for an appreciative audience many things that would be inconsistent in real life.[54] To anything other than either a highly partisan audience or a juvenile audience the scene is hardly a pleasant one. The confrontation between Paul and Ananias in 23:1–5 is especially distasteful. In its intent to show that even under these circumstances Paul was respectful of the Jewish Scriptures, more respectful than was the highest religious official of the Jews, it is also anti-Jewish. In this drama form Paul, who already twice had been said to have approved the mob action of stoning Stephen, could blandly state that he had lived his life in all good conscious before God until that day. The segment 23:1–5 is hardly to be recommended for young or for general audiences.

In our translation and usage of this account, *tōn Ioudaiōn* in 22:30 should be translated as "the enemies of Paul," in order to reduce the emphasis that it was "the Jews" by whom he was being accused.

Acts 23:12–35: *The scene of the plot to kill Paul in Jerusalem and how the plot was foiled.* Few scenes in Acts depict more vividly than this how insidious and evil are "the Jews" and how just and considerate are the Romans. Luke takes full advantage here of the playwright's license to exaggerate, to magnify the evil and the good in the building of the characterizations desired.[55]

The generalization "the Jews," so frequent in this drama, is in 23:12 modified in many Greek manuscripts to "some of the Jews." We would do well to modify it still further by circumlocution to "some of Paul's enemies." The inconsistency of generalizing about "the Jews" as collectively making this plot, when in the previous scene the majority group on the Jewish council, the Pharisees, are said to have declared Paul's innocence, should be apparent.

Similarly in 23:20 *hoi Ioudaioi* should be translated as "Paul's enemies." The nephew of Paul is himself a Jew, and if this line were a reminiscence of a conversation that had occurred exactly as we have it in this text, Paul's nephew would hardly have spoken about Paul's enemies as "the Jews."

At the beginning of the letter composed for Claudius Lysias to the governor Felix (23:27) *tōn Ioudaiōn* should be translated as "the natives," "some of the people here," or "an unruly mob." It would be less illogical for the tribune in this letter to refer to the people among whom he is stationed as "the Jews" than it would be for Paul's nephew or for Luke's "stage manager" to use that designation, but because of these associations of accusations, mob violence, and lynch murder, it would be proper for us in our translations and usage to employ some type of circumlocution here also.

Finally, in 23:14 it would be appropriate for us to translate *tois archiereusin kai tois presbyterois* as "some of their religious and political leaders," rather than more literally as "the chief priests and the elders."

Acts 24:1–27: *Paul under the jurisdiction of Felix.* Perhaps the basic core of what is "historically verifiable" behind these latter scenes of the Acts drama is that Paul was arrested in Jerusalem, detained in Caesarea, and taken to Rome as a prisoner. Most of the details can probably be attributed to Luke, who with some knowledge of Roman, Greek, and Jewish customs and literature and of various oral and written Christian traditions concerning Paul used a playwright's ingenuity to write these final scenes.

In the portion that has come down through time to us in which Paul is described as under the jurisdiction of Felix, special consideration should be given to the way in which we translate "the Jews," a designation that occurs four times.

1. In the oration of Tertullus the words *pasin tois Ioudaiois* (literally, "among all the Jews") in 24:5 should be rendered as "among us," or if we wish to make a distinction between the attorney and his clients as "among the people whom I represent." The distinction is hardly necessary, however, since at the end of 24:6 Tertullus is made to identify fully with his retainers by stating that "we arrested him."

2. Instead of the generalizing and inclusive "the Jews" in 24:9, we can use the information provided in 24:1 to translate *hoi Ioudaioi* here as "Ananias and the elders who were with him." They are certainly the ones who would act out this part on a stage.

3. In order further to reduce the multitude of pejorative references to the Jews in Acts, we should translate *tines de apo tēs Asias Ioudaioi* at the beginning of 24:19 as "But there were some of my own people from Asia," or ". . . some of my enemies from Asia."

4. Finally, *tois Ioudaiois* in 24:27 obviously does not mean all of "the Jews," but "Paul's enemies."

Acts 25:1-12: *Paul under the jurisdiction of Festus.* Here also Luke continues to emphasize the sense of justice displayed by the representatives of Rome. The characterizations of the tribune, Claudias Lysias; the governor, Felix; his successor, Porcius Festus in this section; and finally Agrippa, the puppet king, and his sister Bernice all are—with a few understandable lapses—reasonably good models of Roman justice. "The Jews," on the other hand, by contrast are presented as constantly plotting to thwart Roman justice by attempting an ambush of a Roman military escort with the sole purpose of killing Paul. In this particular account they are said to have added to the charges against Paul the accusation of a serious violation against Caesar—an echo of charges reported against Jesus in the Gospel accounts.[56]

The manner in which Luke developed Paul's appeal to Caesar appears to be rather strange.[57] Ordinarily one would not expect a jurist to ask a person under trial whether he would like to have change in venue. Neither is it easily understandable why Festus did not make a judgment on the accusation of an offense against Caesar. It would appear that the Lukan playwright had two principal items on the agenda to consider in this section. It was important to discredit and foil the Jews as much as possible, and it was essential that some explanation be provided as to how and why Paul's case was to be transferred to Rome. The addition of the implied accusation by the Jews of a serious violation against Caesar served both purposes, and Luke's Paul was enabled to dominate the entire scene. Festus was unable to do a favor for the Jews, Paul was later declared to be innocent by Agrippa the king (26:32), and authorization was given for Paul to be transported as a quite extraordinary prisoner to Rome.

Five times in this brief section "the Jews" are depicted as devious, sinister, and murderous. Partially to counter this exaggeration, the following suggestions for sensitivity in our translations and usage are offered:

1. In 25:2 *hoi archiereis kai hoi prōtoi tōn Ioudaiōn* should be expressed as "some of the religious leaders and other prominent officials there." This provides adequate identification without stressing that these people were "Jews." It also results in a more credible listing of who would have issued a report to Festus against Paul in such a situation.

2. In 25:7 the translation "those who had come down from Jerusalem," or "the enemies of Paul who had come down from Jerusalem" is sufficient for *hoi apo Hierosolymōn katabebēkotes Ioudaioi.* The Jewish identity intended here by the Lukan playwright is obvious from the context. Even from a purely literary perspective, the drama will be improved if "the Jews" are mentioned pejoratively less frequently.

3. Again from a literary point of view, as well as on the basis of theological sensitivity, "neither against the Torah nor against the temple" provides a pleasing alliteration in English for *oute eis ton nomon tōn Ioudaiōn oute eis to hieron* in 25:8, and certainly the Torah is "the law of the Jews" in this context.

4. In 25:9 the context suggests that "But Festus, wishing to do a favor for his constituents" would be appropriate as a translation for *ho Phēstos de thelōn tois Ioudaiois charin katathesthai.*

5. Since "the Jews" are "my accusers" to Paul in 25:10, *Ioudaious* can be translated in that manner.

Acts 25:13–22: *The scene in which Festus discusses Paul's case with the puppet king, Agrippa.* Luke required no informant or tape recorder planted in the residence of the Roman governor in order to record this conversation; the playwright simply wrote what it might be supposed that such officials would have said in such a situation. It afforded Luke an ideal opportunity to pay a compliment to Roman justice while reiterating and magnifying the complicity of the Jews.[58] Actually, it would hardly have been necessary for Luke to have specified for Festus in 25:15 that the chief priests and elders were "of the Jews." That would have been understood. In our translations and usage it would be proper to express *hoi archiereis kai hoi presbyteroi tōn Ioudaiōn* as "some of the most prominent religious leaders there."

The word *deisidaimonias* in the context of 25:19 should be rendered as "religion" rather than as "superstition," even though "superstition" could be appropriate for this word in other contexts. Mature Christianity has no necessity of labeling as "superstition" Jewish spirituality, which provided the context for the life and ministry of the historical Jesus, the earliest followers of Jesus, and the young man Paul. Nor is it likely that if this conversation had actually occurred, Festus would have described the Jewish religion as a "superstition" when he was talking with the Jewish puppet king.[59]

Acts 25:23–26:32: *The scene of Paul's audience with Agrippa and Bernice.* The beginning of this scene (25:23) provides for the reader's imagination a grand display of royal pomp and ceremony. It is further evidence that Acts is a literary drama about the early church and some of its heroes rather than a history of early Christianity.

Into the silence that follows the great processional, the prisoner Paul—for the audience "our hero" Paul—is summoned.[60] Festus is made to rise fully to the occasion in a broad expansive style replete with much exaggeration: "Behold this man, concerning whom the whole multitude of the Jews petitioned me, both in Jerusalem and here, shouting that it is not right for him to live any longer." In our translations of 25:24 the grandeur of the scene can be maintained even though we represent *tōn Ioudaiōn* not as "of the Jews," but as "of his own people."

In the speech of Luke's Paul as he made his defense before Agrippa, the following circumlocutions for "the Jews"[61] would be appropriate as suggested by the context in each instance.

1. In 26:2 "by my opponents" would be an accurate representation of *hypo Ioudaiōn.* "Opponents" is to be preferred to "enemies" in this setting, and even to Luke's "Jews," since Luke will soon in 26:5 have Paul claim to have lived as a Pharisee, within the most stringent party of "our" religion.

2. In 26:3 "among our people" would be desirable for *kata Ioudaious.* "Our people" links Paul and Agrippa together in a way which is more appropriate in this *captatio benevolentiae* (26:2–3) than is Luke's *Ioudaious.* In the speech itself Luke has Paul refer to "our religion" (26:5), "our fathers" (26:6), and "our twelve tribes" (26:7).

3. Again at the end of 26:4 *Ioudaioi* is best rendered as "my opponents." All of the Jews throughout the inhabited world would not have known about Paul's life-style before he became an advocate of the Christian way, but presumably all of his opponents would have known this.

4. In 26:7 *hypo Ioudaiōn* can be translated as "by my opponents," or passed over as understood without translation. The style of Paul's speech is improved if this instance of repetitiveness is ignored. It becomes apparent that Luke, who composed these speeches in Acts so skillfully, was at this point more interested in additional anti-Jewish polemic than in good style.

5. In the 26:21 context "my enemies" would be fitting for *Ioudaioi.* After all, those who "having seized me in the temple tried to kill me" are more than my opponents; they are my enemies! For Luke to have Paul speak about "the Jews" in this manner when Paul had just been made to declare that he had lived as a Pharisee is almost as absurd as if I, having lived all of my life as a citizen of the U.S.A., were to say that "the Americans" are out to get me. Here again Acts is improved if we through careful and sensitive interpretative circumlocution repudiate Luke's anti-Jewish polemic.

Finally, in 26:11 *kata pasas tas synagōgas* should be expressed as "in our various gathering places" in our translations and usage. *Synagōgai* are literally "gathering places," and there is no reason why those who hear Paul's speech in our time should be caused to associate what Luke's Paul is reported to have done with the synagogues in their own communities where their neighbors and friends gather for worship, study, and social enjoyment.

Acts 28:17–28: *The scene depicting Paul's contacts with the most prominent Jews in Rome.* This final scene in the Acts drama is one more indication of how important anti-Jewish polemic was for the Lukan playwright. This noteworthy final scene was used by Luke to demonstrate that also in Rome the Jews were divided and dissolute, just as they were in Jerusalem (23:6–10), in Antioch of Pisidia (13:14–51), and in Corinth (18:4–6). It is apparent that throughout the drama, including this final scene, it was considered to be more important to emphasize the negative polemic against the Jews than to stress the positive aspect of salvation for the Gentiles. How different this emphasis is from that of Paul in his letters!

In order to depict the stubborn depravity of the Jews one more time, the Lukan playwright was willing to construct a scene filled with illogicalities. Luke's Paul does not call together the leaders of the Christian communities in Rome about whom Paul had expressed so much concern in the Epistle to the Romans. Instead he is made to arrange an audience with the most prominent Jews in the city in order that he might set them up for a typically Lukan rejection from their own Scriptures. Luke's Paul is in chains because of the hope of Israel, but even those Jews who were convinced by what Paul said about the kingdom of God and about Jesus (28:23–24) were rebuffed along with the others in 28:25–28. Luke's Paul as a prisoner of the Roman authorities has no hostile Jews from afar at hand to bring charges against him, so he promptly offends and rebuffs the local Jews and causes them to become his enemies.[62]

For mature Christianity, some interpretative circumlocutions are appropriate in the translation of this scene also into vernacular languages for use today.

The expression "the Jews" is used twice in this scene, first by the Lukan writer's "stage manager" in 28:17 and then again by Luke's Paul in 28:19. In the former instance, a literal translation of the words *tōn Ioudaiōn* is to be preferred; "he called to himself the most prominent leaders of the Jews in Rome." The use of the expression is not pejorative at this point, and Paul is made to address them congenially. However, it is difficult to understand why Luke used the same words, *tōn Ioudaiōn*, with no further qualifier in 28:19 for persons depicted as rabid enemies of Paul. Even if sensitivity to the issue of anti-Jewish polemic were not a factor, the context in 28:19 clearly indicates that *tōn Ioudaiōn* should not be rendered woodenly as "the Jews," but by something such as "my enemies among my own people."

The similarities between the unjust treatment of Jesus and of Paul in Luke–Acts and the attempts of Luke's Jesus and of Luke's Paul to show from the Torah and from the prophets that Jesus is the Christ are apparent in this final scene. If Paul was bound with a chain because of the hope of Israel, the Lukan writer made it unmistakably clear in this same scene that for Israel there was no hope, unless Israel is redefined[63] as the Jewish people who rejoice in proclaiming the kingdom of God as proclaimed by Christians and in teaching the things that Paul taught about the "Lord Jesus Christ" openly and unhindered, as Luke's "stage manager" put it in closing this scene, the third action area, and the entire drama.

Conclusions regarding Anti-Jewish Polemic in Acts

Anti-Jewish polemic is a motif of major proportions in this Acts drama. The only parts of the document in which anti-Jewish polemic is not a significant factor are the "we"-section travelogues. These travelogues are also the only parts of the document in which the drama genre is not apparent.

This raises the possibility that the travelogues may have been derived from source material written by "Luke, the beloved physician and companion of Paul" (Col. 4:14; Philem. 24; 2 Tim. 4:11), whose name since the time of Irenaeus and the Muratorian Canon near the end of the second century has been associated with the entire Luke-Acts corpus. The principal writer of Luke-Acts, however, who skillfully moved into theological drama already in the Third Gospel and even more so in Acts and for whom anti-Jewish polemic was an important consideration, was probably a third-generation Christian of Gentile background whose historical name is unknown to us.

Even though anti-Jewish polemic is a motif of major proportions in the Acts drama, much of it can be removed by careful and sensitive interpretative circumlocution as we translate and use this material. Repudiation of anti-Jewish polemic such as that which is suggested within this chapter can be accomplished without damage to the theology of Acts. Actually, by deemphasizing the negative anti-Jewish polemic, these interpretative circumlocutions permit the positive aspects of the theology of the drama to receive greater attention. In many of the instances in which the Lukan playwright merely generalized regarding "the Jews," these interpretative circumlocutions also improve the style of Acts.

Notes

1. For a survey of the evidence and arguments, see Ernst Haenchen, *The Acts of the Apostles*, trans. B. Noble, G. Shinn, H. Anderson, and R. M. Wilson (Oxford: Basil Blackwell, 1971), pp 1–132, especially 116–21. See also C. K. Barrett, "Acts and the Pauline Corpus," *ET* 78 (1976): 2–5.

2. See Martin Dibelius, *Studies in the Acts of the Apostles*, trans. M. Ling and

P. Schubert, ed. H. Greeven (New York: Charles Scribner's Sons, 1956), pp. 1–25; Charles H. Talbert, *Literary Patterns, Theological Themes, and the Genre of Luke-Acts* (Missoula, Mont.: Society of Biblical Literature and Scholars Press, 1975).

3. Dibelius, *Studies in the Acts of the Apostles*, pp. 138–91. See also the considerations of method in the study of the speeches in Acts in Max Wilcox, "A Foreword to the Study of the Speeches in Acts," *Christianity, Judaism and Other Greco-Roman Cults*, ed. J. Neusner, Part One: New Testament (Leiden: E. J. Brill, 1975), pp. 206–25. Wilcox finds more indications of pre-Lukan material in the speeches than in the scenes within which the speeches occur.

4. Haenchen, *The Acts of the Apostles*, pp. 103–10.

5. As Johannes Munck, *Paul and the Salvation of Mankind*, trans. F. Clarke (Richmond, Va.: John Knox, 1959), p. 272, put it, it was a matter of winning Israel for the Gospel, and then by believing that Israel would become a light to the nations.

6. Jacob Jervell, *Luke and the People of God: A New Look at Luke-Acts*, trans. D. Juel, et al. (Minneapolis, Minn.: Augsburg, 1972), pp. 41–74.

7. For a survey of this type of Greek literary drama, see A. E. Haigh, *The Tragic Drama of the Greeks* (Oxford: Clarendon, 1896), pp. 428–29, 443–47.

8. The division into three major action areas here differs only slightly from the three-part outline of Dibelius, *Studies in the Acts of the Apostles*, pp. 193–94, which is simply: Acts 1–5 Jerusalem; 6–12 Judea and Samaria; and 13–28 to the ends of the earth. Dibelius further divided 13–28 into two parts, with the break coming either between 21:14 and 15 or 21:26 and 27. Other conjectures of the structural arrangement of Acts are, of course, possible. Ernst Haenchen, "The Book of Acts as Source Material for the History of Early Christianity," in *Studies in Luke–Acts*, ed. L. E. Keck and J. L. Martyn (Nashville, Tenn.: Abingdon, 1966), pp. 259–60, sees Luke as writing history by telling stories: "short, impressive, and dramatic scenes in relatively independent succession." Haenchen outlines Acts in four parts: 1:1–8:3; 8:4–15:35; 15:36–21:26; and 21:27–28:31. On p. 275 of his article Haenchen describes Luke as a dramatist who gets himself into a desperate situation when his hero, Paul, is arrested and put out of action before the last act.

9. As noted by Jacques Dupont, *The Salvation of the Gentiles; Essays on the Acts of the Apostles*, trans. J. R. Keating (New York: Paulist, 1979), p. 17, Acts 1:8 traces the great stages in the spread of the apostolic message and provides the general outline for the Acts document.

10. Careful attention to context suggests that *andres Ioudaioi* in 2:14 should not be translated as if it were a geographical designation "Men of Judea," but as a theological one, "Jews." Compare the vocatives in 2:22, 29.

11. If Judea in 2:9 and Cretans and Arabians in 2:11 were early additions to the Lukan listing, there were originally twelve geographical areas of Jewish Diaspora designated, which may have been intended as one for each of twelve apostles.

12. "Jews" (2:14) and "Israelites" (2:22), you nailed him to the cross and killed him, using non-Jews as your instruments of execution (2:23). "Therefore, let all the house of Israel know beyond a doubt that God has made him Lord and Christ, this Jesus whom you crucified" (2:36). As Eldon J. Epp, *The Theological Tendency of Codex Bezae Cantabrigiensis in Acts* (Cambridge: Cambridge University Press, 1966), has shown, the Codex Bezae text consistently increases the anti-Jewish polemic in Acts by introducing variant readings in which the Jews and their leaders are portrayed as even more hostile to Jesus and to the apostles of Jesus than they are in the Codex Vaticanus text.

13. Most notably Mark 12:35–37; Matt. 22:41–45; and Luke 20:41–44.

14. Acts 2:25–31 (but not 2:34–35) is included in the First Lesson recommended for the Second Sunday of Easter, Series A, which is Acts 2:14a, 22–32, in *Lutheran Book of Worship* (Minneapolis, Minn.: Augsburg, and Philadelphia: Board of Publica-

tion, Lutheran Church in America, 1978), p. 21. In this lectionary, Acts 2:34–35 does not occur. Acts 2:14a, 36–47 is recommended as the First Lesson for the Third Sunday of Easter, Series A. Acts 2:1–21 is the Second Lesson for the Day of Pentecost in all three series. (The use of Acts texts instead of Old Testament texts as the First Lesson for the great majority of the worship services during the Easter Season in this lectionary series is in my opinion unfortunate.)

15. Dibelius, *Studies in the Acts of the Apostles*, p. 178.

16. Even in its oblique reference to the siege and destruction of Jerusalem in 70 C.E., Luke 11:51 has been damaging to the human decency and sense of justice of Christians and to the well-being and the survival of Jews.

17. Haenchen, *The Acts of the Apostles*, pp. 211–12.

18. Along with the biblical text, perhaps also verse five of Samuel Crossman's Lenten hymn, "My Song Is Love Unknown," should be reworded.

19. See also the discussions of the kerygma in the speeches in Acts in Martin Dibelius, *From Tradition to Gospel*, trans. B. L. Woolf (New York: Charles Scribner's Sons, 1935), pp. 16–26, and Henry J. Cadbury, *The Making of Luke-Acts* (London: S.P.C.K., 1961), pp. 184–93.

20. The selection of verses to be read as the First Lesson recommended for the Second Sunday of Easter, Series B, Acts 3:13–15, 17–26, in *Lutheran Book of Worship* is particularly unfortunate. In these verses the bitter anti-Jewish polemic of 13b–15a and 26b is highlighted and the proclamation of the power of healing in Jesus' name (Acts 3:1–12, 16) is not included. Again on the following Sunday, the Third Sunday of Easter in the same Series B, the First Lesson is a brief selection in Acts 4:8–12, which includes the most damaging anti-Jewish polemic in Acts 4 with its memorable accusation that the Jews of Jerusalem and all the people of Israel rejected and crucified Jesus. For two Sundays in a row during the Easter festival season we are still proclaiming to the faithful Christian laypeople Luke's judgment that the Jews are "Christ-killers"!

21. Here a Levite is presented as a follower of Jesus. In the Lukan parable of the Good Samaritan a Levite is condemned for "passing by on the other side." The message in Acts 4:32–5:16 is that at one time there had been Levites who came forward and joined those who were followers of Jesus and became exemplary models among them.

22. Haenchen, *The Acts of the Apostles*, pp. 249–50.

23. Such license may include also the reference in Gamaliel's speech in 5:36 to the insurrection led by Theudas, a revolt that did not occur until 44–46 C.E., approximately ten years after the time this scene in Acts 5:17–42 would have occurred if it were taken as a precise record of certain historical events. Probably the Lukan playwright simply did not have accurate information about the date of Theudas's abortive revolt, an event that would have occurred as many as four decades prior to Luke's writing of Acts. See further in Dibelius, *Studies in the Acts of the Apostles*, pp. 186–87; C. S. C. Williams, *A Commentary on the Acts of the Apostles* (New York: Harper & Brothers, 1957), pp. 19–20; and Haenchen, *The Acts of the Apostles*, pp. 252–53.

24. Robert Maddox, *The Purpose of Luke-Acts* (Edinburgh: T. & T. Clark, 1982), p. 52, notes that the character of Stephen's speech differs from all of the other speeches in Acts in the way in which it is permeated by quotations from or allusions to the Septuagint, and in the fact that, unlike all of the other major speeches in Acts, Stephen's speech contains no positive affirmation of the possibility of salvation through Jesus.

25. *Lutheran Book of Worship*, pp. 22, 30–31. *Proclamation: Aids for Interpreting the Lessons of the Church Year, Easter, Series A* (Philadelphia: Fortress, 1975), p. 32, had limited the reading to Acts 6:1–7 on the Fifth Sunday of Easter, not the Fourth with

6:1–9; 7:2a, 51–60 as it subsequently has appeared in *Lutheran Book of Worship*. In *Proclamation, The Lesser Festivals 1*, 1975, pp. 8–11, on the festival of St. Stephen, Deacon and Martyr, only our Lutheran Lectionary includes the vitriolic, name-calling denunciations of 7:51–53 and the material concerning false charges brought against Stephen in 6:11–15. The Lutheran reading is 6:8–15; 7:1–2a, 51–60; the Roman Catholic 6:8–10; 7:54–59; and the Episcopal 7:55–60. Our Lutheran Lectionary selection currently being used, therefore, is the most anti-Jewish in this instance among the Christian groups sharing this lectionary.

26. On the form and role of commissioning accounts in Acts, see Terence Mullins, "New Testament Commission Forms, Especially in Luke-Acts," *JBL* 95 (1976): 603–14; Benjamin J. Hubbard, "Commissioning Stories in Luke-Acts: A Study of Their Antecedents, Form and Content," *Semeia* 8 (1977): 103–26; and Benjamin J. Hubbard, "The Role of Commissioning Accounts in Acts," in *Perspectives on Luke-Acts,* ed. C. H. Talbert (Danville, Va.: Association of Baptist Professors of Religion, 1978), pp. 187–98.

27. The anarthrous construction is to be preferred here, first on text critical grounds and second on theological ones.

28. Rom. 2:17–3:9; 3:27–4:25; 9:1–5; 11:1–2a; 2 Cor. 11:22; Phil. 3:3–6. Also, in Acts 21:39 and 22:3 even the Lukan playwright has Paul begin statements with the words, "I am a Jew."

29. See F. Lamar Cribbs, "The Agreements That Exist Between John and Acts," in *Perspectives on Luke-Acts,* ed. C. H. Talbert (Danville, Va.: Association of Baptist Professors of Religion, 1978), p. 59.

30. It is regrettable that *Die Gute Nachricht; Das Neue Testament in heutigen Deutsch* (Stuttgart: Bibelanstalt, 1967) in Acts 10:39b has "Die Juden brachten ihn ans Kreuz."

31. According to Haenchen, *The Acts of the Apostles*, p. 383, Otto Bauernfeind, *Die Apostelgeschichte* (Leipzig, 1939), p. 163, saw in the words "And the chains fell from his hands" in 12:7 a direct influence of the *Bacchae* of Euripedes.

32. The noun, though singular, in this construction has the sense of a plural in English because of its grammatical relationship with the collective noun *people*.

33. A. T. Kraabel, "The Disappearance of the 'God-fearers,'" *Numen* 28 (1981): 113–26, suggests that, since the archaeological evidence of synagogue inscriptions available to us provide no firsthand Jewish evidence of the existence of substantial numbers of devout Gentile "God-fearers" associated with the synagogues that have been excavated, it is possible—even likely—that the "God-fearers" in Acts are a Lukan literary symbol utilized by the Lukan writer in showing how Christianity had become a Gentile religion legitimately without losing its Old Testament roots. In Kraabel's words, "It is a tribute to Luke's dramatic ability that they (the God-fearers) have become so alive for the later Church, but the evidence from Paul's own letters and now from archaeology makes their historicity questionable in the extreme." P. 120.

34. Haenchen, *The Acts of the Apostles*, p. 422, notes that in these verses "we encounter Lucanisms at every turn: the vocabulary, turns of phrase and LXX formulae which Luke so loves to employ."

35. Also in 17:1, 10, 17; 18:4, 19, 26; 19:8.

36. W. F. Arndt and F. W. Gingrich, *A Greek-English Lexicon of the New Testament and Other Early Christian Literature* (Chicago: University of Chicago Press, 1957), p. 839.

37. See above, pp. 170–71, and Robert Brawley, "The Pharisees in Luke-Acts: Luke's Address to the Jews and His Irenic Purpose," Ph.D. dissertation, Princeton Theological Seminary, 1978 (Ann Arbor: University Microfilms, 1978), pp. 14–15.

38. Most of the English translations of the New Testament made since 1920,

including the majority of those enjoying the most popularity, replace pronouns and unexpressed subjects of verbs in the Greek text of Rom. 11:11–32 with the specific noun *Jews* or *Israel* in pejorative situations in from one to thirteen instances. See above, p. 70.

39. Arndt and Gingrich, *A Greek-English Lexicon*, p. 184.

40. See above, p. 228.

41. Jervell, *Luke and the People of God*, pp. 41–74.

42. Haenchen, "The Book of Acts as Source Material for the History of Early Christianity," in *Studies in Luke-Acts*, p. 260, thinks that Luke "writes not for a learned public which would keep track of all his references and critically compare them, but rather for a more or less nonliterary congregation which he wants to captivate and edify."

43. It is difficult to agree with Jervell (p. 64) that Luke merely "leads his readers to the threshold of the Gentile mission."

44. For this opinion, see also Conzelmann, *The Theology of St. Luke*, pp. 142–43.

45. Paul in Acts, but not in Paul's epistles, is repeatedly portrayed as a Roman citizen, even one by birth.

46. This is to assume that "all of them" in 18:17 are intended to be all of the Jews who acted against Paul in 18:12 and that the Western text reading "all the Greeks" is an interpolation. In either case, the Jews are treated pejoratively.

47. Again, just as "the multitude" is frequently the audience for Jesus in the Gospel accounts, "the multitude" is the audience for Paul here.

48. Note the helpful reconstruction of how events recorded in Acts might have been perceived from a late first-century viewpoint in Samuel Sandmel, *Anti-Semitism in the New Testament?* (Philadelphia: Fortress, 1978), p. 100. See also the review of Sandmel's book by the present writer in *Dialog* 18 (1979): 154–56.

49. Haenchen, *The Acts of the Apostles*, p. 563.

50. See below in the consideration of Acts 21:11.

51. For a more detailed analysis of the "we source" material, see Jacques Dupont, *The Sources of Acts* (London: Darton, Longman, and Todd, 1964).

52. For a discussion of this, see Haenchen, *The Acts of the Apostles*, pp. 601–5.

53. See the comparisons of Lukan patterns in the pertinent portions of the Third Gospel and Acts in Talbert, *Literary Patterns, Theological Themes, and the Genre of Luke-Acts*, pp. 16–20.

54. For a discussion of matters such as the tribune's embarrassment and concern that he had ordered a Roman citizen to be bound, his waiting until the following day to unbind Paul, Paul's temerity in addressing the council, the liberty that Ananias is reported to have taken in the tribune's presence, the unlikelihood that Paul would not have known that Ananias was the high priest, the ease with which Paul is reported to have stirred into violent action an august assembly whose members would have worked together on issues as difficult as this on many occasions, and the statement that Sadducees deny that there are angels when angels are mentioned in the Pentateuch, see Haenchen, *The Acts of the Apostles*, pp. 637–43.

55. Analysis of the great fifth-century B.C.E. Greek tragedies indicates this readily. It may be assumed that in stage productions skilled actors and directors will develop these characterizations even further, beyond that which is written into the script.

56. Talbert, *Literary Patterns, Theological Themes, and the Genre of Luke-Acts*, pp. 17, 22, compares the four trials of Paul in Acts 23; 24; 25; 26 (Sanhedrin; Felix; Festus; Agrippa) with the four trials of Jesus in Luke 22:26; 23:1; 23:8; 23:13 (Sanhedrin; Pilate; Herod; Pilate).

57. For a more extended discussion of this matter, see Haenchen, *The Acts of the Apostles*, pp. 668–70.

58. By having Festus state in this recapitulation of 25:2 that the chief priests and the elders (representing the entire Jewish council) requested the sentence of condemnation against Paul, Luke intensified the involvement of the Jews.

59. Kirsopp Lake and Henry J. Cadbury, eds., *The Beginnings of Christianity*, (London, 1933), 4:311.

60. Although Hermann W. Beyer, *Die Apostelgeschichte*, 4th ed. (Göttingen, 1947), p. 146, according to Haenchen, *The Acts of the Apostles*, p. 678, considers this scene to be historical, he nonetheless describes the bringing forward of Paul by Festus as "highly theatrical."

61. The various forms of *Ioudaioi* in Acts 25:10; 26:2, 3, 4, 7, 21 are nearly all anarthrous. According to Friedrich Blass and Albert Debrunner, *A Greek Grammar of the New Testament*, trans. and ed. R. W. Funk (Chicago: University of Chicago: 1961), p. 137, it was appropriate for the name of one's opponent to be anarthrous in Attic court speeches.

62. For a more detailed discussion of the difficulties inherent in this scene, see Haenchen, *The Acts of the Apostles*, pp. 726–32.

63. See Jervell, *Luke and the People of God*, pp. 41–74.

9

Anti-Jewish Polemic in John and in the Johannine Epistles

It has been fairly common in previous studies of anti-Jewish polemic in early Christian literature to find in the Fourth Gospel the greatest concentration and the most bitter intensity of anti-Jewish material in all of the New Testament. Eldon J. Epp, for example, in a brief survey of the Gospels and of the Pauline Epistles, discerns in the denigration of the Torah by Paul, the maligning of the Pharisees by the Synoptic writers, and the vilification of the Jews collectively by the Fourth Gospel writers three differentiated levels of anti-Jewish sentiment. According to Epp, the anti-Jewish material in all of this literature is deplorable, but the "baleful Fourth Gospel" is responsible for the pernicious consequences of this literature more than are the others, since Paul and the Synoptics at least "have certain redeeming characteristics when their attitudes toward the Jews and Judaism are assessed."[1]

On the other hand, there have been those who conclude that the Fourth Gospel is no more anti-Jewish than are the other Gospels, and that the term *the Jews* in John is merely symbolical, not a reference to the Jews in general.[2] Regardless of the meanings intended by the use of the term by the Fourth Gospel writers, however, to many persons, both Christian and Jewish, its portrayal of deep animosity between the Jesus of the Fourth Gospel and the Jews, together with the Johannine Jesus' emphasis upon the necessity of love for one another among his disciples, has caused this Gospel to be seen, as Kaufmann Kohler wrote many years ago, as "a gospel of Christian love and Jew hatred."[3] This anomaly of love and hatred challenges us to examine some of what appear to be the causes for anti-Jewish polemic in the Johannine Gospel before we attempt to recognize and suggest ways by which we can repudiate this aspect of the material.

A. Causes for Anti-Jewish Polemic in the Johannine Gospel

Perhaps the most significant advances in research on the Gospels during the past two decades, particularly with respect to Mark, Matthew, and

John, have resulted from the recognition that these Gospels, in part at least, are autobiographical of the communities for which they were written as well as of the persons who wrote them. We have seen from the work of H. C. Kee and others that to a considerable extent the Markan Gospel expresses within a ministry-of-Jesus vehicle the self-consciousness of the Markan eschatological community during a period of crisis. In this process, the Markan community and its writer(s) apparently evaluated the Jewish Torah traditions, assessed their own relationships with the Jewish and with the Roman authorities, and emphasized mutual responsibilities and support within the community.[4] A decade or more later, the Matthean community and its writer(s) utilized the Markan material, along with other written and oral sources, to express themselves theologically in a later model ministry-of-Jesus vehicle appropriate for their own religious and cultural setting. Apparently during approximately the same time period the Johannine community was operating within the same vein, so that the Fourth Gospel probably tells us as much or more about the community itself than about the Jesus of history.[5] It is within this "autobiographical" aspect of the Johannine Gospel that most of the reasons for its anti-Jewish polemic may be detected.[6]

The reasons for anti-Jewish polemic in the Johannine Gospel, therefore, lie primarily within the experiences of the people of that community and the experiences of the Jews spoken against during the period between the time of the crucifixion of Jesus and the last major writing or redaction of the document. Whatever tensions may have existed between the Jesus of history and other Jews would have been intra-Jewish tensions, and even if we had direct access to them, they would, as intra-Jewish tensions, fall outside the scope of this chapter and of this entire study. This is not to say, of course, that intra-Jewish tensions between the Jesus of history and other Jews would not have been remembered by his followers and would have no resemblance to what now may be described as anti-Jewish polemic in New Testament documents. It is only to say that there can be by definition no anti-Jewish polemic by early Christians and in early Christian documents until there is a separate, self-conscious, early Christian existence.[7]

It is probable that considerable time elapsed after the crucifixion of Jesus before there was a separate, self-conscious, early Christian existence in a Johannine community. In the opinion of Raymond E. Brown, careful analysis of the Fourth Gospel indicates that during the pre-Gospel period the origins of the Johannine community were in Jews of fairly standard messianic expectations and a relatively low Christology. Some of these Jews were, or had been, disciples of John the Baptist. Perhaps they were joined at some point by a second group of Jews who held peculiar anti-Temple views. Brown posits from John 4 that these latter Jews may have been instrumental in converting a number of Samaritans, who would have brought into the developing Johannine community substantial elements of Samaritan thought, including a non-Jewish mentality and self-consciousness, and a Christology not centered on Jerusalem and a Davidic Messiah. Furthermore, Brown suggests that the combination of a different Christology, opposition to the Temple cult, and the Samaritan elements probably was the catalyst that made the members of the Johannine community particularly obnoxious to the more traditional Jews and led to the break between the Johannine community and the synagogue. As the members of the community increasingly based their authority upon Jesus, as they now perceived Jesus, rather than upon Moses and the Torah, it is understandable that they would eventually claim that Jesus had preexisted since "the beginning," not merely of the community, but of time. In this way they were able to claim that their source of authority, the preexistent Jesus, antedated Moses and the Torah both in time and in substance. As happens so readily in religious polemic, in the heat of the controversy contestants will raise their authority symbols to the level of ultimacy. Accordingly, there is within the Fourth Gospel considerable evidence that at times—although not at all times—the members of the Johannine community claimed a oneness with God for their Jesus, producing a Christology so high that to traditional Jews the members of the Johannine community had become ditheistic, advocating a theology obviously untenable within Judaism. Proclamation of this high Christology could not be tolerated within the Jewish synagogues, and an institutional separation was inevitable. Either prior to, or following, or along with an official institutional separation, the Johannine community's Jesus was made to replace the Jerusalem Temple and through his presence to supersede the Jewish Sabbath and the Passover, Tabernacles, and Dedication festivals. According to the members of the Johannine community, "the Jews" had been the people of God by birth, but because they will not accept the authority of the preexistent Jesus of the Johannine community, they are now "children of the devil" and will die in their sins. The "real Israel" in present only among those who believe in the Johannine Jesus. "The Jews" have been superseded and replaced by a new religion,[8] which self-defensively affirms its position with chapter after chapter permeated with anti-Jewish polemic[9] in which the Johannine Jesus reflects the experiences of the Johannine community.

In retrospect, therefore, it was not so much the high Christology *per se* as it was the experiences of the members of the developing Johannine community that caused the anti-Jewish polemic of the Fourth Gospel.[10] The polemic was probably in part a response to the *Birkath ha-Minim*, the curse against heretics added to the Jewish Eighteen Benedictions *(Shemoneh Esreh)* in the revision of the synagogue liturgy under the leadership of R. Gamaliel II at Jamnia during the years 80–90 C.E. Expulsion of members of the Johannine community from Jewish synagogues would not in itself have been so significant, since Johannine Christians were probably reducing their participation there anyway, if it had not been for the political situation in which synagogue activity offered certain exemptions and pre-rogatives. The persecutions alluded to in John 16:2–3, including possibly the execution of some members of the Johannine community, were probably not direct actions by Jewish religious leaders, but more likely resulted from denunciations of Johannine Christians to Roman inquisitors, which left, as Raymond E. Brown puts it, "deep scars in the Johannine psyche."[11]

B. Recognition and Repudiation of Anti-Jewish Polemic in Specific Texts within the Johannine Gospel and Epistles

If the causes of the anti-Jewish polemic of the Fourth Gospel are deeply rooted within the experiences of the members of the Johannine community, how shall we proceed in our recognition of this polemic in specific texts and in our suggestions regarding repudiation of it in our translations and usage of the Johannine Gospel today?

Although many attempts have been made to identify a written "signs" source and possibly other pre-Fourth Gospel written materials utilized as primary sources in the composition of this Gospel,[12] there is not sufficient agreement about the reconstruction of such sources to warrant division of the Johannine material along such lines in this present study. Since the complete Gospel is now seen as in a sense autobiographical, analysis of anti-Jewish polemic as it occurs sequentially throughout the Gospel—and in the Epistles also, if it can be detected there—will be the procedure employed. There are certainly limitations, of course, to the use of the sequential procedure. Not only are the Prologue and chapter 21 probably additions during the final stages of development, but also the other segments were not always added at the end of the previously formulated portions. The sequential procedure appears to be less arbitrary, however, than an arrangement that would attempt to analyze polemic in a "signs" source, in a first edition by the "evangelist," in one or more revisions by the evangelist, and in one or more redaction stages would be.

Suggestions for sensitive translations and use will be made, in some instances including the pruning into footnotes of a few of the more vicious invectives, even though in the opinion of some,[13] purging the Fourth Gospel so as to offer the message of Jesus "without adulteration by hate and revulsion against the people of the Savior"[14] is out of the question because for the Christian church the Fourth Gospel is canonical Scripture.[15]

John 1:1–18: *The Prologue.* The polemic of the Prologue is "good" polemic, artful and many faceted, a model to be followed. The primary purpose of the Prologue is a positive one, to acclaim the person and work of the preexistent Logos of God, incarnate as Jesus the Messiah, a unique revelation of God. The polemic of the Prologue is negative, but clothed for the most part in what may have been a deliberate ambiguity. Only those who are looking for it will find offensive anti-Jewish polemic within the allusions to darkness, the world, the Logos' own people, the Torah, and Moses. Superiority and precedence over the Torah and Moses are claimed for the Logos and for the "children of God," but there are no vicious attacks upon "the Jews" or upon the Pharisees as such. If the entire Fourth Gospel were fashioned after this model, recognition of anti-Jewish polemic in it would be sufficient; repudiation of virulent anti-Jewish polemic would be unnecessary.[16]

The artful polemic of the Prologue is directed on the one hand against those who would follow the martyred John the Baptist as a Messianic figure and on the other against those who, in the opinion of the writer(s) of the Prologue and those who included the Prologue within the written Gospel, were allied too much with this world.[17] The polemic of the Prologue is directed also against those who ascribed deity to the preexistent Logos but denied that the Logos had ever "become flesh" and "lived among us."[18] Only in the assertion in 1:17 that the Torah was given through Moses—that is, within the limitations of space and time and human endeavor—while grace and truth were manifested in Jesus the Messiah, the preexistent Logos of God, is the polemic directed specifically against the Judaism of the post-70 C.E. rabbinic leaders.

The high Christology of the Prologue ("The Logos was God" 1:1c, "Apart from the Logos not one thing came into being" 1:3b, and "that unique Son[19] who is, was, and always will be in the bosom[20] of the Father, that one has shown to us the invisible God" 1:18) is unacceptable to Jewish theology. A religious community, however, which by its theology and by its actions separates itself from its primary parent religious community and sets its course into its own future is entitled to make its claims of superiority and supersession and even of precedence over its parent as it competes for the allegiance of the people of its milieu. It should be expected to show good taste in this process, especially in the literature that eventually in the development of the community becomes sacred Scripture for it. The Prologue of the Johannine Gospel exhibits that good taste.[21]

John 1:19–34: *The testimony of John the Baptist.* Ostensibly, the purpose of this testimony of John the Baptist is to reveal Jesus and the significance of Jesus to Israel. However, if the Fourth Gospel is in some respects an autobiography of the experiences of the Johannine community, this text (along with 3:22–4:3; 5:32–36; and 10:40–42) is also an indication that some disciples of John the Baptist remained separate from the Johannine community and that apologetic against the Baptist as a competing Messianic figure was thought to be necessary.[22]

Israel in the Fourth Gospel is the name used in describing those who come and follow the Johannine Jesus when that Jesus is revealed to them.[23] We see this in the testimony of the Baptist in 1:31 and in the Nathaniel account in 1:47–49. Those who come to the Johannine Jesus as Nathaniel is reported to have come will see greater things than they have anticipated. It is stated that "the Jews" and "the Pharisees," along with their priests and Levites, do not know the "Lamb of God who takes away the sin of the world." Even Nicodemus, although he is called a ruler among the Jews, must know and accept and receive much more before he can qualify as the teacher of Israel (3:1–13). Along with many other New Testament and early church documents, the Johannine Gospel shares the practice of preempting the name Israel, thus contributing to the anti-Jewish displacement of Judaism theology of the New Testament and of the church. Polemic against the Jews is not blatant, however, in this testimony-of-John-the-Baptist text. It may, as Brown suggests, indicate autobiographically that during an early period the Johannine community was sectarian in many respects but not yet militantly anti-Jewish.[24] To describe a man as one who "takes away the sin of the world" (1:29) would be to give power to a human being that in Judaism is reserved exclusively for God.

John 1:35–51: *Andrew, an unnamed person, Simon Peter, Philip, and Nathaniel follow the Johannine Jesus.* The Jewish Scriptures (Moses in the Torah and the prophets) are said to have been written about Jesus the son of Joseph, the one who is from Nazareth (1:45). The christological titles Messiah, Son of God, King of Israel, the Son of man are all ascribed to Jesus the son of Joseph, the one who is from Nazareth (1:41, 49–51), so that the totality of the Christology of the Synoptic Gospels is in effect gathered together here within a few verses at the beginning of the account of the ministry of the Johannine Jesus. Thus the claim is made that the Jewish expectations have been fulfilled in this Jesus. From the perspective of the Johannine community, the entire world, Jewish and Gentile alike, should have followed the Johannine Jesus at this point. Since it did not, it remains in darkness and is condemned.

John 2:1–11: *The Johannine Jesus puts "the good wine" into the Jewish ritualistic containers and supersedes "the inferior wine" of the Jewish cult.* What we have here is the Johannine Jesus commanding that water be poured into the Jewish ritualistic containers. In this first of the "signs" accomplished by the Johannine Jesus, by his creative word he produced "the good wine," which surpasses and supersedes "the inferior wine" of the Jewish cult and its institutions. Prior to this action the inferior wine had been acceptable. It had been the only wine that had been available. But the inferior wine in its inferiority failed. It fell short. It ceased to exist!

In this text we see one of the principal themes of John 2–10, the theme of the replacement of Jewish institutions and religious views.[25] By merely speaking the creative word the Johannine Jesus brings forth the good wine and brings it forth abundantly. In doing this he manifested his glory and his disciples believed in him, not merely that he could perform miracles but that he could supersede the Jewish institutions and religious views. The good wine is available now from the Johannine Jesus and in great abundance. Within three days after his temple is destroyed, the Johannine Jesus will raise it up and remain alive as the focal point of worship for his disciples forever (2:13–22). It is not sparingly out of a measuring scoop but abundantly that he gives the Spirit (3:34). Whoever drinks from the living water that he will give will never thirst again, because the water that he will give will become in that person a spring of water gushing up into eternal life (4:10–15). Since the Johannine Jesus had come as Messiah, worship of the Father at Gerizim and at Jerusalem has been replaced in him (4:20–26). Throughout John 5–10 the "true" meaning of important Jewish holy days is found in the person of the Johannine Jesus.

This theme of replacement of Jewish institutions and religious views using the symbolism of abundant new wine corresponds to the symbolism of Mark 2:22 that no one puts new wine into old wineskins, since the new wine will burst the old wineskins. Also, the end of the supply of the inferior wine in John 2:3 may be compared to the rejection of the purification practices of the Pharisees in Mark 7:1–23.

Although the claim of superiority of the new wine that Jesus supplies is clearly stated in this text, the anti-Jewish polemic involved in John 2:1–11 is not blatant or openly defamatory. In our usage of this text it is important that we emphasize the positive aspects of "the good wine" that Jesus supplies without detracting from that by making disparaging comparisons to what the Fourth Gospel tradition considered to be "the inferior wine," which was insufficient both in quantity and quality at the marriage feast that Jesus attended.

John 2:13–22: *The Johannine Jesus claims the temple as his Father's house and predicts the resurrection of "his temple."* The Fourth Gospel account of Jesus' disruption of the practice of supplying certified sacrificial animals and approved temple coinage within the outer court of the temple differs from the Synoptic accounts in numerous ways. Not only is the action placed near the beginning of the ministry-of-Jesus account in John, but also the Passover is described as being "of the Jews." Moreover, Jesus is described as so full of zeal (quoting Ps. 69:9) that he makes and uses a whip of cords to drive merchants and merchandise from the temple area. Then he claims the temple as his Father's house. This brings the Johannine Jesus into question by "the Jews," who ask for some type of sign as a proof of Jesus' authority. Jesus' resurrection of the temple of his body will be the proof, but only his disciples will recognize it.

The controversy with the Jews is not marked by anger or intense hostility in this account. Although the claim of superiority of the temple of Jesus' body to the Jewish temple practices is implied, Jesus is also presented as one who is concerned about the Jewish temple as his Father's house. It is probable that the account provides an indication of the attitude toward the temple of members of the developing Johannine community. Soon, however, they would reach the point at which Jesus' body would be the new holy place for them.

In our translation and usage of this pericope, we can note that "of the

Jews" is tautologous with "the Passover" in 2:13, and that to describe Jesus' questioners as "the Jews" in 2:18, 20 is theologically anachronistic. All three usages of "the Jews" probably have their origin in the Johannine community at a time when the people of the community clearly defined themselves as separate from "the Jews" and from their influence. Our retention of these designations in the Greek editions of John and in older translations of this pericope into vernacular languages can suffice to retain a historical record in this text of the conflict between the members of the Johannine community and some Jews who lived during the latter decades of the first century. In our translations intended for popular usage, "of the Jews" is unnecessary in 2:13 and *hoi Ioudaioi* in 2:18, 20 can be rendered as "some people in the temple" in 2:18 and simply as "they," the unexpressed subject of the verb *eipan*, in 2:20. Since the account is expressed in a ministry-of-Jesus vehicle, these translations bring us closer to a Jesus-of-history incident than does the Johannine usage, which labels Jesus' questioners as "the Jews" even though the Jesus of history was obviously also a Jew.

John 3:1–21: *Instructing "Nicodemus."* In this first major discourse encountered in the Fourth Gospel, a teacher of Israel named Nicodemus is rather brusquely instructed in the way to the kingdom of God and eternal life. Whatever initiative Nicodemus may have had at the beginning of the discourse, he loses almost immediately. As C. K. Barrett notes, he "never even states the purpose of his coming."[26] After that, he can only ask sensory questions while the Johannine Jesus typically speaks in spiritual terms. The dialogue soon becomes a monologue, and Nicodemus apparently disappears into the darkness from which he had come.[27] He returns, however, in 7:50–52 to urge his fellow Pharisees to give Jesus' words and works a fair hearing and in 19:39–42 to join the Joseph of Arimathea of the Synoptic traditions in providing a proper burial for the body of Jesus in a new tomb.

From these sequences it can be seen that Nicodemus—whether there was a historical person by that name who did and said what is reported in the Fourth Gospel, or whether he was partially or entirely a Johannine construction—is portrayed as a teacher of Israel who was brought to the light of the far superior teacher descended from God. He was instructed successfully by the Johannine Jesus, all the way to the cross and to the grave.

As Christians we may be so enthralled by the beautiful good news of John 3:16 in this account that we fail to see the negative side of the passage. To a Jew it is a message of condemnation. As Samuel Sandmel wrote concerning it:

> (The import of the passage is that Christianity is the only way to God and that Jews have not understood this.) In the sequel (3:18) there occur these words: "He who does not believe is condemned already."[28]

Along with continuing the emphasis upon the positive, redemptive Gospel in this text, we can diminish its anti-Jewish impact through the use of sensitive translation. There is no loss to the Gospel if we translate 3:1–2a as "One night a prominent religious leader named Nicodemus came to him and said," and 3:10 as "Jesus answered, 'You are our teacher and you do not know these things?' " The account may even be enhanced if as a result of this translation we as Christians apply the text more self-critically.

John 3:25: *Those who discussed purification.* There appears to be little relationship between the discussion about purification mentioned in 3:25 and the 3:26–36 account that follows it. In addition, there is a division in the early manuscripts between the readings "a Jew" and "Jews" in 3:25. Because of the textual uncertainty and because the competition for disciples in 3:22–36 seems to be between John the Baptist and Jesus, various commentators have conjectured that the text originally read "Jesus" rather than either "a Jew" or "Jews" and that early copyists emended the text to read "a Jew" and from that to "Jews." The sense of the text is improved by the conjecture "Jesus." At any rate, the readings "a Jew" and "Jews" are both anachronistic at whatever stage they entered the text, since at the time of the activities of the Jesus of history and of John the Baptist presumably all who would have participated in a discussion such as this would have been Jews anyway. In view of these textual difficulties, the best translation of 3:25 might simply incorporate the textual variants "a Jew" and "Jews" into the reading "There was a discussion among the disciples of John concerning purification." The explicit translations "a Jew" or "Jews" do little more than maintain an anti-Jewish posture within an account that otherwise is concerned about the relative prominence of Jesus and John.

John 4:1–3: *A reason for leaving Judea.* These rather awkward transitional verses cite the Pharisees as having heard that Jesus was making and baptizing more disciples than John was, and suggest that Jesus left Judea and went again to Galilee in part at least in order to get away from those particular Pharisees. This polemic, though mild, presents the Pharisees as a threat to Jesus for no significant reason other than possibly jealousy, since the context of 3:22–36 implies that the principal competition at this point in the ministry of Jesus and/or in the development of the Johannine community was the disciples of John. The segment of the text "that the Pharisees had heard" could be rendered simply as "that many people had heard" in a sensitive translation.

John 4:4–42: *With the Samaritan woman at Jacob's well.* Because the Samaritan woman addresses Jesus as a Jew in this drama (4:9) and becaus Jesus informs her that "we know what we worship because salvation is from the Jews," there may be evidence in this text that the Fourth Gospel here retained a primitive tradition in which antecedents of the Johannine community still considered themselves and Jesus to be Jews. This substratum of traditional material would then, as Raymond E. Brown has suggested,[29] have been formed into the "superb theological scenario" that we have, which employs misunderstanding (4:11), irony (4:12), quick changing of an embarrassing subject (4:19), staging on the front and back of the platform (4:29), and the Greek-chorus effect of the villagers (4:39–42). The account becomes anti-Jewish when Jesus as Messiah and Savior of the world says that the hour is coming when the current worship of the Father by Samaritans on Mt. Gerizim and by Jews in Jerusalem will be superseded by true worship of the Father in spirit and in truth (4:21, 23–24). It is anti-Jewish also when the Samaritans are depicted as having an understanding of Jesus' words and of Jesus' identity that is far superior to that of even those Jews in Jerusalem who believed in Jesus' name when they saw the signs that he did, and of Nicodemus, the Jewish ruler who came to Jesus by night. The account depicts a successful mission among the Samaritans that may, if Brown's postulation[30] has validity, indicate the presence of a second group with anti-Temple views who entered the Johannine community, brought Samaritans into their fellowship, accepted elements of Samaritan thought such as that of a Christology not centered on a Davidic Messiah, and became the principal catalyst in the break between the Johannine community and the synagogue. Whether this postulation is accepted or not, there can be no doubt that after chapter 4 the reader encounters a high Christology and sharp conflict with "the Jews," who object strenuously to the deification of the Johannine Jesus.

John 5:1–47: *The divine sovereignty of the Johannine Jesus over the Jews and over the Jewish sabbath.* The Synoptic miracles of healing that Jesus is reported to have accomplished on the Jewish sabbath are justified by the Synoptic Jesus on the basis of humanitarian concern and precedents of need shown within the Jewish Scriptures. We have seen a trajectory of development within the Synoptic tradition that resulted in the confessional statement that "the Son of man is Lord also over the sabbath."[31] Here as elsewhere the Fourth Gospel goes far beyond the Synoptics, confessionally and christologically. In 5:17 the Johannine Jesus says to "the Jews" who were beginning or continuing to oppress him that "My Father has been working from the beginning until this present moment, and so have I!" It is Jesus' preexistent divine sovereignty that is claimed here, so that in 5:18 we see the two levels in which the canonical account operates. There is what J. Louis Martyn[32] calls the *einmalig* level, "not only was he breaking the sabbath," as well as the level of the Johannine community, "but also he was saying that God was his own Father, making himself to be equal to God."[33]

The man who had been blind, lame, and paralyzed represents on the level of the Johannine community the Jew who even when helped by Jesus in the most basic way does not know the name of his benefactor, and after Jesus spoke to him the second time protected himself by informing against Jesus to Jesus' enemies. As soon as he has protected himself by informing against Jesus, this man drops out of the drama and attention turns to the claims of Jesus' divine sovereignty.[34]

It is the divine sovereign Jesus of the Johannine community who is oppressed and whose life is said to be threatened by "the Jews" contemporary with the Johannine community after the split with the synagogue and the bitterness of what John T. Townsend calls "a religious divorce."[35] It is the divine sovereign Jesus of the Johannine community who in that emotionally tense situation of "religious divorce" charges that "the Jews" have never heard the voice of the Father, have never seen his form, do not have his word nor his love abiding in them, do not seek the glory of God, and do not believe Moses, who accuses them (5:37–47).

The basic miracle account in 5:1–9a is similar in many ways to the Synoptic healing miracle texts. Beyond 5:9a, however, the high Christology and the anti-Jewish polemic are so thoroughly intertwined—probably because they developed simultaneously—that extremely delicate surgery is required to extricate one from the other. What we can do is to translate "the Jews" in 5:10 as "some of the religious leaders" and in 5:15, 16, 18 as "the religious leaders," and in our lectionary use confine ourselves to 5:1–36. The remaining segment (5:37–47) has a "historical museum type" of significance as evidence of the bitter controversy between the Johannine community and certain Jews during the latter decades of the first century, but along with similar material elsewhere in the Fourth Gospel, it should be bypassed in usage in favor of more edifying texts.

John 6:1–71: *The Johannine Jesus as the living (flesh-and-blood) bread from heaven.* The highly interesting questions regarding the composition and development of the chapter as a whole and of its parts cannot be entered into here. It is probable that the chapter developed as a somewhat separate unit through many stages and levels. Its polemic is directed against various groups outside the Johannine community. Our concern here will be limited to the anti-Jewish emphasis.

It is stated in 6:31–33 that the manna that our fathers ate in the wilderness did not come from Moses but it is the Father of the Johannine Jesus who gives the true bread from heaven. The Johannine Jesus is that life-giving bread (6:35–40). Throughout this portion of the account "the Jews" function somewhat as a foil to show the lack of understanding and to ask the questions that will most appropriately further the development of the thought to be expressed by the Johannine Jesus. This chapter, like others in the Fourth Gospel, can now be seen as—among other things—a brief autobiography of the Johannine community and its development. In the first segment of the chapter (6:1–24) Jesus is so popular as a bread-producing miracle worker that the people of Galilee want to make him accept the role of king over them. The Johannine Jesus rejects that role and enters into contention against them over their fixation upon physical bread (6:25–40). As the problems of contention against the Jews receded somewhat with the passage of time (6:41–59), new problems and issues caused by the departure from the community of what Brown calls the "Jewish Christians of inadequate faith in the Johannine Jesus"[36] arose (6:60–66). In this new struggle the "mainline" Christian groups represented by Peter and the twelve within the Synoptic communities are called in as allies, even though in the opinion of many members of the Johannine community they are not entirely trustworthy (6:67–71).

In our translations and usage, "the Jews" in 6:41, 52 should be rendered as "the people from Jesus' home area" in 6:41 and as "the people" in 6:52. This sensitive translation catches the sense of *hoi Ioudaioi* in each instance even better than a literal translation does and removes the edge from the anti-Jewish polemic with no loss of the meaning or content of the chapter.

John 7:1–52: *The Johannine Jesus as hated by the world and preparing to leave the world at the Jewish feast of Tabernacles.* The way in which relationships between the teachings of the Johannine Jesus and the Jewish festivals of the Sabbath, Passover, Tabernacles, and Dedication are developed in John 5–10 suggests that the movement of Jesus from place to place and season to season is motivated here also much more by the theological concerns of the Johannine tradition than by adherence to an itinerary and chronology of activity by the Jesus of history. As Brown has shown,[37] in John 5 the Johannine Jesus performs works that only God can do, in chapter 6 he gives himself as the true bread from heaven replacing the manna of the Exodus experience, in chapters 7–9 he replaces the water and light ceremonies of the Tabernacles celebration, and in chapter 10 he is consecrated in place of the Temple altar. More specifically, in chapter 7 he is a wanderer even to his own brothers, he is hated by the world, and he prepares to leave the world. He is a transient whose life is threatened, and he will be taken up as soon as his time has come. In these respects he is like and yet different from all others who celebrate the Tabernacles experience, and for his followers he will replace the Tabernacles observance.

Careful consideration of the context in the occurrence of the expressions *hoi Ioudaioi* and *hoi Pharisaioi* within this chapter permits us to translate in ways that will reduce emphasis upon the Jews as foils for the teachings of the Johannine community. From the context it is apparent that it was "the authorities there" who were seeking to kill Jesus (7:1); it was not all of the Jews or all of the people of Jerusalem.[38] It was "the authorities" who were looking for him at the feast (7:11). It was because of fear of "the authorities" that no one was speaking openly about him (7:13). It was "many people" who were amazed in 7:15 and who spoke to each other in 7:35. It is an unnecessary tautology to specify that the feast of Tabernacles was a feast "of the Jews" in 7:2. "The Pharisees" and "the chief priests and Pharisees" in 7:32, 45, 47, 48 are obviously "those who opposed him." Therefore 7:32 can be rendered accurately as "Those who opposed him heard the crowd whispering about him and sent attendants to seize him."

In lectionary readings 7:19–24 should not be used. The portions of the account that precede and follow these verses can be read together smoothly.

John 7:53–8:11: *The interpolation in which Jesus is asked to condemn a woman who was involved in adultery.* The credibility of the account as an incident from the experiences of the Jesus of history would have been improved if followers and admirers of Jesus rather than "the scribes and the Pharisees" had been said to have brought the woman to Jesus for his opinion, since presumably Jesus' friends rather than his opponents would have been interested in his ruling on such a matter. Because of the tendency of the early Christian tradition to transform a variety of types of incidents into controversy dialogues in which Jesus always emerges as the hero,[39] we are justified within a sensitive translation of the account to reverse this tendency slightly by rendering "the scribes and the Pharisees" in 8:3 as "some of the religious leaders." With this translation the account remains a *Streitgespräch* (controversy dialogue). If we also relegated to footnote status 8:6a ("They were saying this to test him, in order that they might have something with which to accuse him"), which is lacking in several of the ancient manuscripts, we could prune it back to the *Schulgespräch* (scholastic dialogue or teaching situation) that it may have been at an earlier stage in the development of the tradition.[40]

John 8:12–59: *The Johannine Jesus as "the light who gives life" engaging in an increasingly extended bitter controversy with those who do not accept his claims.* A reader coming to this harsh dialogue without the subjectivity of the Christian faith could readily conclude that the Jesus who speaks here was somewhat paranoid. It should be noted that the Jesus depicted here deliberately antagonized precisely those who according to 8:30–31 had believed in him. It was he, rather than his opponents, who suggested that they were seeking to kill him (8:37, 40). His opponents are remarkably restrained under the circumstances and not until the conclusion of the drama (8:59) do they, as they do at the conclusion of the Luke 4:16–30 drama, reach for the stones or seek the cliff. In spite of the positive, reassuring claims made by and for the Johannine Jesus and his followers in this account, objectively speaking the characterization of Jesus developed here is not an unsullied one.

As we attempt to come to terms with this dialogue, it is helpful to recognize that the harshest elements in Jesus' accusations, namely, that the Jews are children of the devil, liars, and murderers, are manifestations of Johannine dualism.[41] The motif is introduced in 8:44 and reiterated, for example, in 12:31; 14:30; 16:11; 17:15; and in 1 John 2:22 and 2 John 7 that the highest-level opponent of Jesus is the devil, the prince of this world, the evil one, the deceiver, the antichrist. The devil put the idea of betraying Jesus into the heart of Judas Iscariot (13:2), and when Judas received the morsel from Jesus in 13:27 it is said that Satan entered into him. According

to 1 John 2:22, whoever denies that jesus is the Christ is "the liar." Therefore, in Johannine dualism, whoever does not accept the claims of the Jesus
of John 8:12–59 is a child of the devil, a liar, and a murderer like the devil.

Even if everyone who reads or hears the words of John 8:12–59 becomes
aware of the polarities inherent in the Johannine dualism, however, the
extended, increasingly bitter invectives hurled at the Jews by the Johannine
Jesus in this chapter will remain and will continue to have their effect on
the psyche of Christians. But to limit the account to the positive, reassuring
christological statements of the Johannine Jesus would reduce it to little
more than verses 12, 18, 26, 28–29, 31b, 34–36, 50–51, 58—bits and pieces of
the whole.

A more conservative translation and usage of the account would employ,
therefore, careful circumlocution and selective lectionary choices. "The
Phraisees" in 8:13 can be rendered as "some of the people there," since
obviously not all of the Pharisees alive at that time would have addressed
Jesus simultaneously in one unified chorus. It is not necessary to specify
"the Jews" in 8:22; as elsewhere in that section of the account, "they" is
adequate. In 8:31 "the Jews who had believed in him" can be simply "those
who had believed in him," and in 8:48, 52, 57 "the Jews" can again be
"they." The account would be basically unchanged by these sensitivities in
translation, since the context makes it clear that Pharisees and other Jews
are being addressed. Their identity would merely not be reiterated every
few verses. With these minor adjustments the classic Lutheran lectionary
selection for Reformation Day (John 8:31–36) would become slightly more
applicable to our own time, with "Jesus said therefore to those who had
believed in him" as its introduction.

John 9:1–41: *A man who had never seen receives his sight and believes in and
worships the Johannine Jesus as the light of the world.* This "dramatic expansion
of a miracle story"[42] presents what can be considered the most elaborate
success story in all of the Four Gospel accounts. Only in the accounts of the
"conversion" of Saul-the-persecutor to Paul-the-apostle in Acts is there a
success story of greater magnitude and implications. In this John 9:1–41
account a man who had never seen anyone sees the Johannine Jesus so
clearly that he worships him. In the Fourth Gospel this is the only person
who is said to have worshiped Jesus.

This Johannine drama with its many scenes, along with other Johannine
dramas, is therefore in part autobiographical of the Johannine community.
Consequently, anti-Jewish polemic is again an important factor. In it the
man who had never seen anything now sees Jesus completely as the one to
be worshiped, and the Pharisees who supposedly should have seen Jesus
best of all are told that they have missed the point completely and their sin
remains.

Because this chapter is a favorite within Christianity,[43] it is particularly
important that the anti-Jewish polemic within it be handled with sensitiv-

ity. The miracle story itself (9:1–7) as it may have circulated orally and as it is written here is not specifically anti-Jewish. Neither is the second scene (9:8–12), in which the neighbors and acquaintances of the fortunate man appraise the situation. In the third scene (9:13–17) "the Pharisees" are specified as skeptical because, as we are informed at this place in the drama, Jesus had performed the miracle on the sabbath, and in the final scene (9:39–41) "the Pharisees" are condemned. In the intervening scenes it is "the Jews" who at first do not believe the miracle and who later are said to cause the man's parents to be afraid because "the Jews" had agreed that anyone who acknowledged the Johannine Jesus to be the Messiah would be excluded from the synagogue.

The following suggestions involving sensitive translation and usage are offered as efforts to reduce the specifically anti-Jewish emphasis somewhat without decreasing the significance of the account. In 9:13 "the Pharisees" can be represented as "some of their religious leaders," and in 9:15 as "these religious leaders." In 9:16 "some from among the Pharisees" can become "some of them," and in 9:18 "the Jews did not believe" can be merely "they did not believe." (The context indicates that "the Jews" in 9:18–34 are basically the same group as "the Pharisees" in 9:13–17, 40–41.) His parents said these things in 9:22 because "they were afraid of the Jews" can be expressed as "they were afraid of some of their religious and political leaders," and "for the Jews had already agreed" later in the same verse can be "for these leaders had already agreed." (The Jewish identity of the leaders is still maintained by the use of "an excommunicate from the synagogue" in the same verse.) Finally, in 9:40 "those who were with him from among the Pharisees" can be simply "those who were with him from among the religious leadership."

John 10:1–21: *The Johannine Jesus claims to be the door of the sheep and the good shepherd.* If this section is intended to continue a conversation with the Pharisees/Jews of 9:13–41 as well as to point forward to the discourse at the feast of Dedication,[44] the "thief," "robber," and "stranger" designations were probably intended to be applied to the Pharisees/Jews depicted in 9:13–41, but many persons who read or hear the account would probably not understand it in this way. The "one-wayism" implicit in the door analogy would force not only Jews and participants of other religions, but also all Christians to enter into "salvation" through the door of the Johannine Jesus. The claim for the superiority of "the good shepherd" over "the employee shepherd" in 10:2–5, 11–18 also is an indication that parts of this polemic are directed against religious leaders among followers of Jesus who are not within the fellowship of the Johannine community, but the sharpest polemic is reserved for "the Jews." If we are sensitive to this and if we wish to represent this account as if it is ostensibly at least an incident in the life of the Jesus of history, it would be appropriate for us to render *en tois Ioudaiois* in 10:19 as "among the religious leaders" rather than "among the Jews."

John 10:22–39: *During the feast of Dedication the Johannine Jesus angers the Jews to the point of violence by claiming to be the Messiah, the Son of God, and one entity with the Father.* It is not implausible that the Jesus of history might have angered some of his fellow-countrymen to the point that they would have wanted to seize him or to stone him, but his opponents in that situation would not have been designated as "the Jews." Second, the Jesus who in this text claims to be the Messiah, the Son of God, and one entity with the Father is the fully extended Johannine Jesus, not the Jesus of history whose life-style and teachings are in part painstakingly reconstructed by extensive study and comparison of the early Christian traditions. For these reasons, good translations and usage of this account—even when there is no sensitivity to the issue of anti-Jewish polemic—will take these factors into consideration and translate each instance of *hoi Ioudaioi* in this text carefully, giving close attention to the context. When this is done, choices by which to express *hoi Ioudaioi* in this account will include in 10:24, 31 "some of the religious leaders" or "his enemies," and in 10:33 simply "they."

John 11:1–54: *The Johannine Jesus restores the decaying body of Lazarus to life and the enemies of Jesus plot his death.* Again in this chapter the sense of the account can be improved by careful attention to the context during each translation of *hoi Ioudaioi.* In 11:8 they are obviously "your enemies there." The geographical designation, "the Judeans," suggested by some, is much too general since there were Judeans such as Mary, Martha, and Lazarus who are depicted as close friends of Jesus. The same words *hoi Ioudaioi* are used in 11:19, 31, 33, 36, 45 in quite a different sense as acquaintances of Martha and Mary who had come to bring consolation to them in their grief as "their friends." Therefore, *hoi Ioudaioi* should be translated as "their friends" in these verses. Even here, however, *hoi Ioudaioi* as friends of Martha and Mary, and by association friends of Jesus, are not all presented in a positive way. Some of them believed in Jesus (11:45), but others went to the Pharisees and reported the things that Jesus had done (11:46). In 11:54 *hoi Ioudaioi* are again better represented as "his enemies," or perhaps here by the geographical "the Judeans." As in 2:13 and 6:4, "of the Jews" is unnecessary with the Passover in 11:55.

In 11:46 "the Pharisees" and in 11:47, 57 "the top-ranked priests and the Pharisees" are actually "some of the religious leaders," and should be translated accordingly, since obviously not all of the Pharisees and probably not all of the top-ranked priests were present to convene a Jewish council and plot for the death of Jesus.

John 12:9–11, 17–19: *The crowd of people who came to Bethany to see the Johannine Jesus and Lazarus.* It is likely that these verses were added at some point as an editorial framework to the basic entry into Jerusalem narrative of 12:12–16.[45] "The crowd, many from among the Jews, having known that Jesus was there" are presented as curious to see Jesus and to see Lazarus, whom Jesus had raised from the dead. Many from among this group are said to be going away and believing in Jesus. "The Jews" in 12:9, 11, therefore, are not opponents of Jesus. The context here makes it possible for us to translate "the Jews" more specifically as "Jesus' own people" in 12:9 and as "these people" in 12:11. "The chief priests" in 12:10 would more precisely be "some of the religious and political leaders." "The Pharisees" in 12:19 are from the context of 12:9–11, 17–19 "some of those who did not follow Jesus as a Jewish Messiah figure."

John 12:42–43: *Influential Jewish Crypto-Christians of a latter period.* Expulsion from participation in synagogue worship and study because of interest in Jesus as a Jewish Messiah figure during the time of the Jesus of history is highly unlikely. This is a place, therefore, in which by our translation we can begin to share with the general readers of the Fourth Gospel an awareness that conditions during a later period were influencing the writers of this Gospel. The departure of Jesus and his hiding himself from his followers and from the crowd standing there (including some Greeks who had come to worship at the Passover feast?) in 12:20–36 probably is a reflection of the experiences of the members of the Johannine community from whom Jesus had "departed and hidden himself" after the crucifixion and the initial resurrection-faith appearances. The Johannine Christians obviously identified with the sentiments expressed in Isa. 53:1 and 6:9–10. They were deeply frustrated when influential Jews were interested in Jesus but would not openly join with them in following and proclaiming the Johannine Jesus because the Pharisees of this later period had decided that those who proclaimed the oneness of Jesus with the Father could not participate in synagogue activities. A good, late twentieth-century translation of 12:42–43 that would reflect our knowledge of these events would be:

> However, even later there were many influential Jews who remained interested in Jesus, but they did not profess this openly because they did not want to be excluded from participation in the synagogues by the synagogue leaders of that time. To the followers of Jesus it appeared, therefore, that they desired the approval of their friends more than they desired the approval of God.[46]

John 13:33: *Just as I said to the Jews.* The reference apparently is to 7:32–36 and to 8:21–30. Since the use of "the Jews" here is anachronistic, indicative of a later period when the members of the Johannine community saw their own identity as distinct from that of the Jews, it would be appropriate to translate *tois Ioudaiois* as "to others" in this verse.

John 15:18–25: *They have hated me in order to fulfill the word written in their law.* In 15:18–19 "the world" depicts all who hate the Johannine Jesus and the members of the Johannine community.[47] In 15:20b–25, however, the polemic is directed more specifically at the Jews who reject the Johannine Jesus. If they "hate" the Johannine Jesus, they "hate" the Father also; they cannot reject one without rejecting the other. Their rejection of the Johannine Jesus is sin, a fulfillment of what is written in "their law," where in Ps. 35:19 and Ps. 69:5 (4) we read in psalms of individual lament: "They hated me for no reason."

John 15:18–25 is additional evidence of the deep animosity felt by the members of the Johannine community against their Jewish parentage, for although they identified their Jesus with Israelite personal-lament psalmists, concurrently they separated him completely from the Torah.[48] The animosity of the Johannine community and of the Johannine Jesus against late first-century Jews is well documented in the Fourth Gospel, but animosity of the Jesus of history against earlier first-century Jews is not. Because the members of the Johannine community expressed their strong anti-Jewish feelings not in their own name but in a words-of-Jesus and a ministry-of-Jesus vehicle, it is difficult for us as late twentieth-century Christians to make this distinction, especially because the distinction has not been made during the past nineteen centuries. It is a responsibility of sensitive modern translators, therefore, to assist in making this distinction.

Since the polemic of this section is explicitly anti-Jewish only in 15:25, our efforts should be concentrated on this verse. This Matthew-like fulfillment text in Johannine syntax appears to have been a relatively late addition to the 15:18–27 section, attached somewhat awkwardly to other statements of the Johannine Jesus. Perhaps sensitive modern translators can begin to reverse the process of attributing the sentiments of late first-century writers to Jesus by starting with this verse, which still has the trademarks of having been an addition.

A rather drastic option would be to remove the verse to footnote status in vernacular translations, with the explanation that it appears to have been added to statements by the Johannine Jesus as an interpretation by a late first-century Johannine scribe.[49] If it is retained in the text, it could be translated literally but placed within parentheses or brackets, or simplified in translation and attached to the preceding sentence as "in order that the words of the psalmists, 'They hated me for no reason,' might be fulfilled." I prefer this latter option, which retains the verse in the text but in translation edits out the questionable and anachronistic expression "their law" from the words attributed to Jesus.

John 16:2: *They will make you excluded from synagogues.* This and other references within the Fourth Gospel to expulsion from synagogues are useful to us in ascribing dates to portions of the Johannine composition and in reconstructing the development of the Johannine community. However, because our Jewish neighbors worship, study, and gather socially in places that are still called synagogues, and because this reference is followed by the more inflamatory prediction that the time is coming in which anyone who has killed you will think that he has offered a service to God, a sensitive translator could render *aposynagōgous poiēsousin hymas* as "They will exclude you from places where they gather for worship and study" with no loss of accuracy.

John 18:1–12: *The arrest of the Johannine Jesus.* As is often noted, only the Fourth Gospel specifically mentions Pharisees as participants in the arrest and trials of Jesus. A sensitive translation of the Johannine arrest scene would describe the chief priests and Pharisees in 18:3 as "some of the religious and political leaders." In 18:12 *hoi hypēretai tōn Ioudaiōn* should be expressed as "the representatives of the religious and political leaders" rather than as "the Jewish guards" or "the officers of the Jews." Such a translation accurately reproduces the sense of the Greek without emphasizing the participation of Jews in the action. There are reasons, of course, for the Fourth Gospel tradition and other early Christian traditions to stress the Jewish identity of some of these participants and not to stress the Roman identity of those who had the overpowering judicial and military control of the area, but those reasons do not apply to us during these latter decades of the twentieth century. Our motivations for sensitivity and for objectivity permit us to render the account for late twentieth-century readers in a way in which some of the prejudices of the late first-century Christians are blunted.

John 18:13–23: *The account of the hearing conducted by Annas the high priest.* In the parenthetical verse 14 there is another Johannine emphasis upon "the Jews" that is not necessary for the reader of our time. It would be sufficient for us to translate that "Caiaphas was the one who had suggested that it is expedient that one man die rather than that the entire people perish."

In the speech of the Johannine Jesus in 18:20 the Johannine "all the Jews" can be written today as "all of our people," a nuance that retains the Jewish identity of Jesus that the Johannine tradition systematically removed from him.

John 18:28–19:16: *The account of the trial conducted by Pilate.* The amount of anti-Jewish polemic in the trial-before-Pilate accounts in Matthew, Luke, and John is comparable. Each heightens the polemic in its own way over that which we have in Mark. Short of a major redaction and rewriting of these accounts we cannot appreciably reduce the polemic and its force. What we can do, however, is to note the instances in which the noun *Ioudaioi* is used pejoratively in the Johannine account and by careful attention to the context, translate it in ways that will accurately reproduce the Greek text while putting less emphasis on "the Jews" *per se.* Also, in private reading and devotion and in corporate worship, particularly during the

Lenten Season, we can use more "theology of the cross" texts from the Epistles of Paul and less of the Matthean, Lukan, and Johannine trial scenes. When we do use a trial scene, the Markan account should be given preference. Being less embellished by anti-Jewish animosity, Mark's trial scene is likely to be closer than the others to a report of what actually happened.

In 18:31 *hoi Ioudaioi* can accurately be rendered by the pronoun "they." The context of 18:36 implies that the Johannine tradition considered *tois Ioudaiois* to be understood as "my enemies." In 18:38 *tous Ioudaious* is written for "Jesus' accusers" and can be translated in that way. Again in 19:7 *hoi Ioudaioi* can be expressed by the pronoun "they," and in 19:12 as "his enemies."

Finally, in the response of Pilate in 18:35 "Your own nation and the chief priests" are actually "some of your own religious and political leaders," since the entire Jewish "nation" was obviously not involved in the arrest and trials of the Jesus of history.

John 19:21: *The request to change the inscription on Jesus' cross.* The words "of the Jews" can be omitted in a sensitive translation of 19:21 as tautologous and unnecessarily anti-Jewish. "The chief priests" would be more accurately "some of the religious and political authorities."

John 19:31–42: *Certification of death and burial of Jesus.* Again in 19:31 the use of "the Jews" is an indication of the situation much later in the first century when the members of the Johannine community considered themselves to be separate from the Jews theologically and politically. Since obviously not all of the Jews would have asked Pilate that the legs of the three men be broken, *hoi Ioudaioi* in 19:31 should be translated as "some of the religious and political authorities."

The expression "because of fear of the Jews" in 19:38 and in 20:19 also reflects the situation of the members of the Johannine community many decades later than the day of Jesus' crucifixion. On the day of Jesus' crucifixion Jesus and most of his followers were Jews, and it is not perspicacious to state that a particular Jew was afraid of "the Jews" on that day. Therefore, it would be more accurate to translate *dia ton phobon tōn Ioudaiōn* in 19:38 as "because he was afraid of Jesus' enemies." Joseph of Arimathea, cited in the Synoptic accounts, is joined in this Fourth Gospel account by the Johannine Nicodemus figure. Together they become prime examples of Crypto-Christians who dare to act, if not openly to proclaim the risen Johannine Jesus, at least as those who provide this final service for the crucified Jesus.

John 20:19: *The doors locked where the disciples were because they were afraid of the Jews.* The locked doors in this verse serve many purposes, both practical and theological. At one stage in the development of this account the emphasis may have been upon the ability of the glorified Jesus to enter an area even though the doors had been locked. At the canonical stage that is represented in the text the emphasis is on the doors having been locked in order to keep "the Jews" out. This suggests, as indicated above, a late stage in development when "the Jews" were perceived as an alien, threatening group by the Johannine community. A sensitive translation for use in our time might by apocopation simply render the expression as "because they were afraid," after the analogy of Mark 16:8.

As indicated above,[50] the polemic that is prevalent within the Johannine Epistles is basically not anti-Jewish polemic, but polemic by one Johannine faction against others that had separated themselves from the faction that produced the Epistles. As Brown has demonstrated,[51] the so-called secessionists are in the Johannine Epistles the primary representatives of the world and all that is evil and they, rather than "the Jews," are now castigated as children of the devil. Neither "the Jews" nor "Israel" are mentioned specifically in the Johannine Epistles, and although there are statements such as 1 John 2:22–23; 3:10; 4:3; 5:10–12; and 2 John 7 that can be considered offensive to Jews, the verbal spears of the Johannine Epistles are not aimed at them. Our translations of the Johannine Epistles— particularly of 1 John 2:19—should make it clear to the reader that the polemic of these documents is the result of an intra-Johannine schism.

Excursus: The "Beloved Disciple" as a Symbol of the Johannine Community in Its One-Upmanship over the Apostolic Christians[52]

The "Beloved Disciple" may indeed have been a historical person who had been a companion of the Jesus of history.[53] The "Beloved Disciple" may have been a disciple of John the Baptist, perhaps the unnamed disciple of John 1:35–40, who achieved his identity only in a christological context when at the hour of Jesus' glorification (John 13) he began to understand Jesus fully, as Brown suggests.[54] However, it is possible that the "Beloved Disciple," a figure who appears only in the Fourth Gospel, who is obviously the hero of the Johannine community, and who in many ways is the paradigm of the Johannine community in the Fourth Gospel just as Peter is the paradigm of the "Apostolic Christians," may be a symbol of the Johannine community itself. The "Beloved Disciple" may be "The Community of the Beloved Disciple,"[55] a symbol of the community at one stage in its development, a symbol that upstages Peter and the mainline followers of Jesus represented in the Synoptic Gospels.

This is not to say that the "Beloved Disciple" is purely fictional or only an ideal figure. The community was certainly not fictional to its members; it was real to its people. It is to say that analysis of the "Beloved Disciple" passages indicates that the term is used only in competitive "one-upmanship" contrast to Peter (five times explicitly: 13:23–26; 18:15–16; 20:2–10; 21:7; 21:20–23; and the sixth implicitly: 19:26–27), as Brown has shown.[56]

Even if the "Beloved Disciple" was a single historical person, it is helpful to see that in the Fourth Gospel it is also "The Community of the Beloved Disciple" rather than the Apostolic Christians that is in intimate contact with Jesus (13:23–26). It is the Johannine community that could accompany Jesus even into the dangers of the court of the high priest, whereas the Apostolic Christians could enter only with the help of the Johannine community (18:15–16). It is the Johannine community that is present at the cross and is given the privileges and responsibilities of being the son of Mary when the Apostolic Christians have denied Jesus and fled (19:26–27). It is the Johannine community that outruns the Apostolic Christians in a theological race to the empty tomb and that believes when it is not said that the Apostolic Christians believed (20:2–10). It is the Johannine community that theologically recognizes the risen Jesus standing on the shore of the lake and tells the Apostolic Christians who Jesus is (21:7). Finally, it is the Johannine community that the risen Jesus wishes to remain where it is theologically until he comes, and that will die and change only when he comes (21:20–23).[57]

Even if there was a historical person who was called the "Beloved Disciple" in several instances in the Fourth Gospel, the "Beloved Disciple" can also be seen as a symbol used in John in relatively friendly competition over against the Apostolic Christians with whom it is the hope and prayer of the Johannine community that there can be unity in the Father and in the Son. The "Beloved Disciple" is not a symbol used in polemic against "the Jews." It is not used in the Johannine Epistles.

If there was a single historical figure who was called the "Beloved Disciple" within the Fourth Gospel, why was he never said to have been engaged in polemic against "the Jews"? Why did the Johannine Epistles never appeal to his authority? Why is no awareness of him shown within the Synoptic Gospels? Why is there so little agreement among modern scholars as to his name? Perhaps we shall have a better understanding of the "Beloved Disciple" texts and of the Johannine traditions as a whole if we see this figure primarily as a symbol of the community itself, a symbol used in this way for only a brief period of time in its one-upmanship competition with the Apostolic Christians of the Synoptic traditions.

Summary

There is a considerable amount of anti-Jewish polemic in the Fourth Gospel. Much of it is hard, even harsh, polemic. But there is also much other harsh polemic in the Fourth Gospel and in the Johannine Epistles against groups that have been defined as Crypto-Christians, Jewish Christians, and secessionists, and gentler polemic against mainline Apostolic Christians of the Synoptic traditions. Perhaps because the Johannine community was engaged in polemic against so many different groups, its anti-

Jewish polemic is not sustained throughout the Fourth Gospel and the Johannine Epistles. In comparison to related New Testament literature it can be said that the anti-Jewish polemic in the Fourth Gospel is no more vicious than the anti-Jewish polemic in Matthew, not so subtle as the anti-Jewish polemic in Luke, and not so sustained as the anti-Jewish polemic in Acts. Within the New Testament the most anti-Jewish document is Acts.

The anti-Jewish polemic within the Fourth Gospel developed in part at least because of experiences of the members of that community. The high Christology of the members of the community was an important factor in the development of the anti-Jewish polemic and in its polemic against other groups, but the Johannine Epistles provide evidence that members of the Johannine community could have a high Christology and yet express themselves without engaging in polemic against the Jews.

Notes

1. Eldon J. Epp, "Anti-Semitism and the Popularity of the Fourth Gospel in Christianity," *CCAR* 22 (1975): 35–57. In Epp's quick survey, the sustained and devastating anti-Jewish polemic in Acts is sketched within a single footnote. Neither the viciousness of the polemic in Matthew nor the subtlety of the material in the Third Gospel is adequately represented. John Koenig, *Jews and Christians in Dialogue: New Testament Foundations* (Philadelphia: Westminster, 1979), pp. 131, 137, in his attempts to show that "the New Testament as a whole, when understood historically, offers more resources than obstacles to those who value Jewish-Christian dialogue today," reluctantly acknowledges that the uncritical public reading of the Fourth Gospel as Scripture in Christian churches has fanned the embers of hatred of Jews deep within the psyches of otherwise moderate and tolerant parishioners. See the review of Koenig's book by the present writer in *Dialog* 19 (1980): 148–50. See also Joseph Stiassny, "Development of the Christians' Self-understanding in the Second Part of the First Century," *Immanuel* 1 (1972): 32–34; Rosemary R. Ruether, *Faith and Fratricide* (New York: Seabury, 1974), pp. 111–16; Reginald Fuller, "The 'Jews' in the Fourth Gospel," *Dialog* 16 (1977): 31–37; and the carefully considered evaluation by John T. Townsend, "The Gospel of John and the Jews: The Story of a Religious Divorce," in *Antisemitism and the Foundations of Christianity*, ed. A. T. Davies (New York: Paulist, 1979), pp. 72–97. As Townsend concludes, our increased understanding of the historical circumstances which caused the anti-Jewish tenor of the Fourth Gospel "will not prevent the gospel from continuing to broadcast its anti-Jewish message unabated." Therefore I urge that we consider repudiation of this polemic along lines such as those suggested in the present study.

2. See W. W. Sikes, "The Anti-Semitism of the Fourth Gospel," *JR* 21 (1941): 23–30; E. Grässer, "Die antijüdische Polemik im Johannesevangelium," *NTS* 11 (1964): 77–90; and Reinhold Leistner, *Antijudaismus im Johannesevangelium?* Theologie und Wirklichkeit (Bern: H. Lang, 1974), 3:142–50.

3. Kaufmann Kohler, "New Testament," *Jewish Encyclopedia* 9 (1905): 251.

4. See above, pp. 96–102.

5. For a detailed application to Johannine studies of the thesis that the Fourth Gospel tells the story not only of Jesus but also of the community that believed in him, see J. Louis Martyn, *History and Theology in the Fourth Gospel* (New York: Harper and Row, 1968; rev. ed., Nashville: Abingdon, 1979).

6. Here the writings of Raymond E. Brown have been outstanding, particularly *The Gospel According to John*, The Anchor Bible 29, 29A (Garden City, N.Y.: Doubleday, 1966, 1970); "The Passion According to John: Chapters 18 and 19," *Worship* 49 (1975): 130–31; "Johannine Ecclesiology—The Community's Origins," *Interp* 31 (1977): 379–93; " 'Other Sheep Not of This Fold': The Johannine Perspective on Christian Diversity in the Late First Century," *JBL* 97 (1978): 5–22; and *The Community of the Beloved Disciple* (New York: Paulist, 1979).

7. See also Rosemary R. Ruether, "The *Faith and Fratricide* Discussion: Old Problems and New Dimensions," in *Antisemitism and the Foundations of Christianity*, ed. A. T. Davies (New York: Paulist, 1979), pp. 235–37.

8. Contrary to Daniel J. Harrington, *God's People in Christ* (Philadelphia: Fortress, 1980), who thinks that neither Matthew nor John yet sees the Christian community as a new religion apart from Judaism.

9. See the bibliography listed in n. 6 above, especially *The Community of the Beloved Disciple*, pp. 22–51, for Brown's exposition and the supporting evidence within the Fourth Gospel texts. J. Louis Martyn thinks that it was not the development of the heightened Christology that led to the expulsion of the members of the Johannine community from the synagogue, but the rapid numerical growth of these "Christian Jews" that was seen as a threat to the other Jews. Then the Christology of the Johannine community people was used by the synagogue Jews as the formal reason. Brown, on the other hand, sees the high Christology as the cause for the expulsion.

10. This observation has important implications for relationships between Jews and Christians in our own time. It is not necessary that our theology be harmonized. Actually, rich diversity in theology can be stimulating in theological discussions. What is necessary is that we refrain from hurting each other. This applies not only to relationships between Jews and Christians, but also to relationships within Judaism and within Christianity.

11. Brown, *The Community of the Beloved Disciple*, p. 23.

12. Among the most notable of recent efforts are the following: Jürgen Becker, "Wunder und Christologie," *NTS* 16 (1968–70): 130–48; Robert T. Fortna, *The Gospel of Signs: A Reconstruction of the Narrative Sources Underlying the Fourth Gospel* (Cambridge: University Press, 1970); W. Nicol, *The Sēmeia in the Fourth Gospel—Tradition and Redaction* (Leiden: Brill, 1972); Howard M. Teeple, *The Literary Origin of the Gospel of John* (Evanston, Ill.: Religion and Ethics Institute, Inc., 1974); and Sydney Temple, *The Core of the Fourth Gospel* (London: Mowbrays, 1975). See the critical analyses of these reconstructions in Robert Kysar, *The Fourth Evangelist and His Gospel: An Examination of Contemporary Scholarship* (Minneapolis, Minn.: Augsburg, 1975), pp. 13–37, and "Community and Gospel: Vectors in Fourth Gospel Criticism," *Interp* 31 (1977): 357–59.

13. Such as Reginald Fuller in his commendable article, "The 'Jews' in the Fourth Gospel," *Dialog* 16 (1977): 31–37.

14. As it is presented in the anonymous publication, *The Gospel According to St. John* (New York: Philosophical Library, 1967).

15. Fuller, "The 'Jews' in the Fourth Gospel," p. 37, states that "the only thing to do is to counteract the potential anti-Semitism by careful teaching, so that people may understand the original *Sitz im Leben* of the anti-Judaic material." Fuller recognizes that "there is the formidable problem of getting ordinary lay people to appreciate the literary form of the Johannine discourses, namely that they are not tape recordings of Jesus' *ipsissima verba*, but the meditations on the Jesus tradition and the application of that tradition to the evangelist's own situation, cast in the form of Jesus-dialogue." Consideration of specific texts in the section that now follows will attempt to do more than Fuller suggests, since the majority of the "ordinary lay people" will read or hear the Fourth Gospel without benefit of the kind of careful

teaching that Fuller and many of us would like for them. For further discussion of this issue, see also John T. Pawlikowski, *What Are They Saying About Christian-Jewish Relations?* (New York: Paulist, 1980), pp. 1–32, especially pp. 24–25.

16. The entire Fourth Gospel is not fashioned after this model, however, and, read within the context of the entire Fourth Gospel, even the artful polemic of the Prologue can be considered offensive.

17. The "world" in the Johannine Gospel is loved by God so much that God sent his own unique preexisting Son, but the people of the "world" would not receive him. For the writers of the Fourth Gospel, the people of the "world" were probably comprised of both Jews and Gentiles, all who would not believe in the Johannine Jesus, even though they might claim to follow him. See the discussion of the Johannine treatment of this group in Brown, *The Community of the Beloved Disciple*, pp. 62–66, and n. 47 below.

18. This type of polemic is prevalent in the Johannine Epistles. It is basically not an anti-Jewish polemic, but an intra-Johannine community polemic. See Brown, *The Community of the Beloved Disciple*, pp. 23, 93–144.

19. Even though "God" is much better attested, "Son" should be read here. After all, a reading has to make sense, and "Son" is congruent with Johannine usage in 1:14, 3:16, 18; and 1 John 4:9. See also C. K. Barrett, *The Gospel According to John* (London: S.P.C.K., 1955), p. 141.

20. Here in the Prologue the uniquely privileged and beloved "Son" is in the bosom of the "Father." Later in the Johannine Gospel the Johannine community, represented by the uniquely privileged and beloved "Disciple," is in the bosom of the "Son."

21. The addendum (chap. 21) of the Gospel also is not overtly anti-Jewish. Its polemical concerns address the intra-Christian issue of rival claims of the Johannine community represented by the "Beloved Disciple" symbol and the communities symbolized by Peter and the Twelve. See the excursus: "The 'Beloved Disciple' as a Symbol of the Johannine Community in Its One-Upmanship Over the Apostolic Christians" below, pp. 268–69.

22. See Brown, *The Community of the Beloved Disciple*, pp. 26–30, 69–71. Brown observes that for the Johannine community John the Baptist was only a lamp to show the way; Jesus is the light of the world.

23. See S. Pancaro, "The Relationship of the Church to Israel in the Gospel of St. John," *NTS* 21 (1975): 398–401.

24. Brown, *The Community of the Beloved Disciple*, pp. 27–31; Harrington, *God's People in Christ*, pp. 101–5.

25. For this, see also Brown, *The Gospel According to John* (AB 29), pp. cxliii, 104–5.

26. Barrett, *The Gospel According to John*, p. 169.

27. Brown, *The Gospel According to John* (AB 29), pp. 144–45.

28. Samuel Sandmel, *Anti-Semitism in the New Testament?* (Philadelphia: Fortress, 1978), p. 104.

29. Brown, *The Gospel According to John* (AB 29), pp. 172–85.

30. Brown, *The Community of the Beloved Disciple*, pp. 34–54.

31. See above, pp. 105–106.

32. Martyn, *History and Theology in the Fourth Gospel*, rev. ed., pp. 68–73.

33. See also the statement by the second-century C.E. writer Maximus Tyrius that Heracles must work without ceasing, since Zeus his father does the same, as cited in the *ergazomai* entry of Arndt and Gingrich, *A Greek-English Lexicon of the New Testament and Other Early Christian Literature*.

34. Martyn, *History and Theology in the Fourth Gospel*, rev. ed., pp. 71–72. See also Brown, "Other Sheep Not of This Fold," pp. 9, 11–12.

35. Townsend, "The Gospel of John and the Jews," pp. 72–97.

36. Brown, "Other Sheep Not of This Fold," pp. 9, 12–14.
37. See the outline provided by Brown, *The Gospel According to John* (AB 29), pp. 201–4.
38. Note the opinion of Brown, *The Gospel According to John* (AB 29), p. 307: "*fear of the Jews.* This is a clear indication that 'the Jews' are the Jerusalem authorities, for the crowds themselves were certainly Jewish and still they fear the Jews."
39. Arland J. Hultgren, *Jesus and His Adversaries* (Minneapolis, Minn.: Augsburg, 1979), pp. 39–52, demonstrates the manner in which traditionalists composed such stories by introducing opponents and formulating their questions by which they attempt unsuccessfully to trap Jesus. "They are simply described in the most general terms, usually by sect or office, and that is sufficient to set up the necessary polarity for the conflict dialogue" (p. 56).
40. Note the didactic setting in the introductory 8:2, the address "Teacher," the citation of the Torah regulation, and that apart from 8:6a the nature of the dialogue is not abrasive.
41. See Brown, *The Gospel According to John* (AB 29), pp. 363–66.
42. The terminology is that of Martyn, *History and Theology in the Fourth Gospel*, p. 26, who uses this as the primary account to demonstrate his thesis that the Fourth Gospel presents its witness to an *einmalig* ("once upon a time") event during the time of the Jesus of history as well as to Jesus' powerful presence within the experiences of the Johannine community. In Martyn's transposition of the chapter into dramatic form he "doubles" Jesus with an early Christian preacher-disciple.
43. In the *Lutheran Book of Worship*, for example, it is the Gospel reading for the Third Sunday in Lent, Series A.
44. As suggested, for example, by Brown, *The Gospel According to John* (AB 29), pp. 388–90.
45. Ibid., p. 456.
46. Every translation is also an interpretation, hopefully guided by the best information available. For those who would object to the interpretative nature of the translation given here, it should be stressed that the RSV, for example, interprets 12:42 by expanding *alla dia tous Pharisaious* ("but because of the Pharisees") to "but for fear of the Pharisees."
47. In this context Brown, *The Community of the Beloved Disciple*, pp. 63–66, defines "the world" as composed of all who reject the Johannine Jesus, both Jews and Gentiles. Brown concludes that by the time the Fourth Gospel had been completed, the Johannine community had experienced sufficient rejection by non-Jews to realize that many of them were no more likely to accept their view of Jesus than were "the Jews."
48. Perhaps their description of psalter material as Torah indicates composition during a late first-century period when the psalter and other writings were officially accepted as sacred Scripture by the rabbis.
49. Those who would choose this option will be vindicated if some day a late first-century manuscript of John 15:18–25 is discovered that lacks 15:25.
50. N. 18.
51. Brown, *The Community of the Beloved Disciple*, p. 97. See also Rudolf Bultmann, *The Johannine Epistles*, trans. by R. P. O'Hara, L. C. McGaughy, and R. W. Funk; Hermeneia Commentaries (Philadelphia: Fortress, 1973), pp. 36–37.
52. Here, as elsewhere, I follow Raymond E. Brown closely, but differ with him in his interpretation of John 21:20–24 and in his insistence that the Beloved Disciple was a historical person and a companion of Jesus. See Brown, *The Community of the Beloved Disciple*, pp. 31–34, 82–88.
53. Bultmann, *The Gospel of John*, p. 715, for example, affirms that in the contrast between Peter and the "Beloved Disciple" in 21:20–23 it is completely clear and

confirmed in 21:24 that both figures are understood as definite historical persons and not as the embodiment of principles or groups such as Jewish Christianity over against Gentile Christianity.

54. Brown, *The Community of the Beloved Disciple*, pp. 32–33.

55. R. A. Culpepper, *The Johannine School* (Missoula, Mont.: Scholars, 1975), p. 265, comes close to this conclusion when he states that the role of the "Beloved Disciple" is the key to the character of the Johannine community. I would say that it is the key to the character of the community only during one period of its existence.

56. Brown, *The Community of the Beloved Disciple*, pp. 82–83.

57. Why should 21:20–23 be interpreted as reporting distress in the Johannine community over the death of the "Beloved Disciple"? The "Beloved Disciple" and his witness lives and testifies concerning these things. The "Beloved Disciple" has written these things and "we" (the members of the community of the "Beloved Disciple") know that this witness is true (21:24).

10

Anti-Jewish Polemic in the Remaining New Testament Documents

Anti-Jewish polemic in the remaining New Testament documents can be discussed briefly, since in them there is not the direct opposition to contemporary adherents of the parent religion that is written into the Gospel accounts and Acts. We shall begin with the Apocalypse because of its association with the Gospel of John and the Johannine Epistles.

A. *The Apocalypse*

Description of anti-Jewish polemic in the Apocalypse usually focuses on the references to Jews and to the expression "synagogue of Satan" in 2:9 and 3:9.[1] The meaning that these two verses had for their writer is no longer apparent. They are contained within two of the most positive "letters" of Rev. 2:1–3:22. If the Apocalypse were a Jewish document, these comments in 2:9 and 3:9 could be interpreted as supportive of observant Jews who were being troubled by impostors who were claiming to be Jews. Perhaps these verses are an indication that the writer(s) of the Apocalypse relied rather heavily upon Jewish apocalyptic sources, which were not always reworked into a thoroughly Christian framework. Possibly the references are an indication of hostility against Jews during the turbulent years of the reign of Domitian, but since the writer(s) of the Apocalypse did not utilize the opportunities offered by the numerous references to the death of the Lamb to place the blame for the crucifixion upon the Jews we should be hesitant to label these references anti-Jewish within their context in the Apocalypse. However, because of the associations engendered by the expression "synagogue of Satan" in the minds of late twentieth-century Christian readers and hearers of the Apocalypse, in a sensitive translation of 2:9 and 3:9 we should express *synagōgē* as "a gathering place," which indeed it is.

Throughout the Apocalypse Jewish and Christian images are juxtaposed with relatively little (for the New Testament) insistence that the latter form of spirituality supersedes the former. For example, in 15:3 those who had conquered the beast sing the song of Moses and the song of the Lamb. In 21:12–14 the holy city Jerusalem coming down out of heaven from God has on its gates the names of the twelve tribes of the sons of Israel and on its twelve foundations the names of the twelve apostles of the Lamb.[2] In the letter to the church at Pergamum there is condemnation of those who cling to the teachings of Balaam, who taught Balak to put a stumbling block in front of the people of Israel (2:14). Granted that Jesus is said to be "the root and the offspring of David, the bright morning star" (22:16), the one hundred forty-four thousand certified for salvation come from every tribe of the people of Israel (7:4–8). The glory of God illumines the new Jerusalem and its lamp is the Lamb (21:23). The Lord God is the temple of the new Jerusalem and the Lamb is the temple (21:22). In each of these instances the Lamb is added almost as a gloss, to the basic thought, which suggests that in many respects the Apocalypse has a Christian veneer placed over a Jewish base. Even when the Isa. 1:10 reference to Jerusalem as "spiritually" called Sodom is used, it is the beast, not the Jews, that conquers and kills the followers of the Lord Jesus (11:7–8). Therefore we conclude that the Apocalypse is not particularly anti-Jewish in its polemic. Its polemic is primarily anti-Rome, quite different from the polemic in Acts.

B. Hebrews

It is natural for adherents of a new religion to claim superiority for their heroes and for their beliefs over the heroes and beliefs of their religious antecedents and competitors. In their zeal such adherents of a new religion use whatever arguments and methods they can muster to try to induce others to join with them or to persuade members of their group to remain. Most of what we have in written form as the New Testament document Hebrews has the appearance of such an extended persuasive speech, the most elaborate speech of this kind within our biblical account.

The technique employed in this speech involved lengthy *midrashim* (interpretations of earlier texts or ideas to suit one's purposes) interspersed by much shorter, pointed exhortations urging hearers to conform to desired beliefs and behavior. That Hebrews has a place within our New Testament collection is evidence that the speech succeeded, at least for many, in attaining its immediate objectives.

Hebrews includes eloquent rhetoric in which various Septuagint texts that vary considerably from the Hebrew Scriptures are utilized in argumentation against cultic practices that, by the time that Hebrews was delivered, had been reduced in value and importance for most Jews. Therefore the document is not a frontal attack upon late first-century Judaism as such. Its polemic is not viciously anti-Jewish nor defamatory.[3] Its viewpoint, as Samuel Sandmel has noted,[4] is that revelation from God, which began in ancient Israelite religion, reached its pinnacle in the figure of the Christian Christ. Nevertheless, it is anti-Jewish in that the ancient Israelite religion and religious practices are disparaged in the comparisons that abound in the work.[5] Because there is continuity between the people and the writings of the ancient Israelites and the Jews of today, Hebrews is anti-Jewish, at least on an academic level. Its anti-Jewish influence upon Christians has been much less, however, than that of the Gospels and Acts. Most Christians, particularly during the twentieth century, have had little interest in the involved "proofs" in the document, such as the proof of the superiority of the high priesthood according to the order of Melchizedek over the Levitical priesthood. Nor are these proofs likely to convince critical readers today.[6]

Much of the appeal that Hebrews retains for us as Christians lies in its exaltation of Jesus as the Christ,[7] within the same document Jesus is said to have suffered and been tempted just as we are, yet without sin.[8] One can surmise how much more Hebrews might be read by Christians and how much more influential it might be if in some of our translations intended for popular use we placed in smaller type the rather forced demonstrations from the Old Testament of what God purportedly said to Jesus and of what Jesus said within the Old Testament, as well as the detailed argumentation against cultic practices of the ancient Israelites.[9] There is biblical precedent for this kind of distinction in that Hebrews, along with most other portions of the New Testament, reveals how freely the early Christian writers adapted the biblical accounts as they knew them (the major portions of what we today call the Old Testament) to meet the needs of their communities and to serve their own purposes as writers.

In Heb. 4:12–13 "the word of God" is acclaimed as living and active, sharper than any two-edged sword, penetrating and discerning of every aspect of our lives. This is expressed, however, in a manner that clearly indicates that the reference is not specifically to the written biblical account. Rather, "the word of God" is a designation for God speaking forcefully to and through the prophets and by Jesus as God's Son. "The word of God" is heard in the proclamation of the apostles and in personal encounters in which every creature is naked and exposed to the eyes of the Creator. The biblical account, on the other hand, is designated in Hebrews as "the law," which commands and authorizes that which is allegedly inferior and imperfect (7:5–11). When there is a change in the priesthood, there is of necessity a metathesis (change) also in "the law" (7:12). A commandment given earlier is annulled because of its weakness and uselessness—for "the law" made nothing perfect—and a better hope is introduced through which we draw near to God (7:18). "The law" establishes men who have weakness as high priests, but the word of the oath, which comes after "the law" in time, establishes a son as perfected forever (7:28). The new covenant text from Jer. 31:31–34 is employed as evidence that the old covenant is obsolete and about to disappear, to be replaced by "laws" given directly into the minds of people and written upon their hearts. (8:1–13). "The law" has a shadow of the good things that are coming, but it is not the form itself of these activities (10:1). In popular Christianity we have been accustomed to thinking that "the word of God" as cited in Heb. 4:12–13 is the Bible and that "the law" in 7:5–12, 18, 28; 8:1–13; 10:1 refers to Jewish legalism. If instead of simply translating literally we were attentive to the context in which these words occur, we would express *ho logos tou theou* in 4:12 as "the voice of God" or "the command of God" and *ho nomos* in 7:5–12, 18, 28; 8:1–13; 10:1 as "the biblical account" or "the earlier biblical account," and note the similarity of Hebrews on this issue to Paul's view in 2 Cor. 3:6–7 and Rom. 7:6. Paul, the writer of Hebrews, and other early followers of Jesus apparently did not consider the Scriptures as they knew them to be immutable. When the living active voice of God came to them, the static written code was reinterpreted rather freely.

C. The Epistle of James

The so-called Epistle of James is probably the least anti-Jewish of all the documents within the New Testament collection. In it the Torah is *basilikos* ("royal") and obedience to every part of it is applauded[10] (2:8–11). It is also *teleios* ("perfect"), the Torah of *eleutheria* ("freedom"), and those who live in accord with it are truly free (1:25; 2:12). Those who believe that God is one do well, but they are justified when their faith is acted out in works of love, as illustrated by examples such as Abraham and Rahab in the Torah (2:14–26). The "Lord" is "the Lord of Sabaōth" (5:4), "compassionate and merciful" (5:11), whose imminent coming is anticipated (5:7–9). The Israelite prophets and Job are cited as models of suffering and patience (5:10–11).

The document is Christian in that its writer is said to be a servant not only of God but also of the Lord Jesus Christ (1:1). The hearers are admonished not with partiality to the rich to have the faith of "our Lord Jesus Christ of glory" (2:1). Therefore "the Lord" of 1:7; 3:9; 4:10, 15; 5:4, 7, 8, 10, 11, 14, 15 may also, in part at least, refer to Jesus as the Christian Lord. Most of all, the document is Christian because it is included within the New Testament canon.

If there is anti-Jewish polemic in the Epistle of James, it is in its supersessionistic association of Jesus with the Jewish concept of Yahweh as "Lord," and in the designation of the totality of the followers of Jesus as "the twelve tribes in the Diaspora" in 1:1. Possibly the writer selected the name *Iakōbos* to recall the father of the twelve tribes of Israel. There is no attempt, however, to preempt the name Israel; neither is there any mention of the Jews.

D. 1 Peter

Even though the Jewish Scriptures are frequently quoted in 1 Peter, the document was probably addressed primarily to followers of Jesus of Gentile background. They are exhorted to become holy, not conformed to the desires that motivated them formerly when they had not known God and Jesus the Christ as Lord (1:14). They are reminded that they have been ransomed from the futile life-style established for them by their fathers (1:18). By means of the word of God, which lives and continues forever, they have been given new life (1:23). Formerly they had not been a people, but now they are God's people; they had not been treated mercifully, but now they have been treated with mercy (2:10). Most of all, the time that has passed is said to have been sufficient for doing what the Gentiles desire (4:3–5). The value of the Torah and of Jewish life-style is not a significant issue. If it was primarily followers of Jesus of Gentile background who were originally being addressed, the verses just cited are not anti-Jewish; they are anti-Gentile.

The anti-Jewish polemic in 1 Peter is present in the quiet[11] displacement of those who do not believe, who reject the "living stone," who do not believe the word for which they were intended (2:4, 7–8). Those to whom the document is addressed are invited to come to the "living stone" and themselves, as living stones, to be built into a spiritual house that they might be a holy priesthood (2:4–5). They are a chosen lineage, a royal priesthood, a holy nation, a people for preservation, a people of God treated with mercy (2:9–10). Readers today who are familiar with these descriptions as designations previously applied to Jewish people within the Jewish Scriptures will sense the displacement polemic; those who have little understanding of the Jewish heritage will be relatively unaware of the polemic and will, it is hoped, concentrate on the positive aspects of these verses.[12]

E. Jude

The primary polemic of this little tractate, with its warnings of dire consequences for those who "by perverting the grace of our God into licentiousness deny the only Master and our Lord Jesus Christ," is directed not against Jews, but against the gnostic type of Christians who are said to be motivated by their own godless passions. Within the secondary polemic—which is mild by comparison—there are anti-Jewish elements in the reference to a people from the land of Egypt saved but later partly destroyed (Jude 5) and in the reference to the faith tradition (Jude 3, 20) which, as Gerhard Krodel has indicated,[13] has for the writer of Jude taken the place of the Torah. The anti-Jewish polemic is hardly noticeable, however, in the midst of the severe attacks upon the gnostic type of Christians.

F. 2 Peter

Comparison with Jude, which almost certainly was used in the composition of 2 Peter, shows that this somewhat lengthier document has a higher Christology but even less anti-Jewish polemic than does Jude. This is evidence that while there is considerable correlation between high Christology and sustained anti-Jewish polemic within the New Testament documents, the Christology of a New Testament document can be high even when its anti-Jewish polemic is virtually nonexistent. Furthermore, 2 Peter, although with difficulty, was included in the New Testament canon while uncompromisingly anti-Jewish writings such as the Letter of Barnabas, even though they had probably been written earlier than 2 Peter, were finally excluded.

The Christology of 2 Peter is higher than that of Jude[14] in that the "righteousness of our God[15] and Savior Jesus Christ" is cited in 1:1, and Jesus Christ is given the appellation of imperial divinity, "Lord and Savior," throughout the document. Within the concluding doxology (3:18b) it is to Jesus Christ as "our Lord and Savior" that glory is to be given both now and until the day of eternity.

In the use of Jude in 2 Peter the reference to a people from the land of Egypt saved but later partly destroyed because they did not believe (Jude 5) was not utilized. Neither were the references to the way of Cain and to Korah's rebellion (Jude 11). The purpose of passing over these examples of disobedience and of nonbelief was probably not to reduce anti-Jewish polemic, however, but to restrict the examples to those which project the certainty of divine judgment and retribution.[16]

At any rate, it is gratifying to be able to conclude this survey of anti-Jewish polemic in the New Testament documents with a writing in which anti-Jewish polemic is not a significant factor. The lack of anti-Jewish polemic in 2 Peter, along with the relatively minor anti-Jewish polemic throughout the Apocalypse, Hebrews, James, 1 Peter, and Jude, is an indication that the New Testament and the Christian religion can function effectively without being virulently anti-Jewish.

Notes

1. See, for example, the citation in the report of the 1974 *ad hoc* committee of The American Lutheran Church noted on p. 49 above, and the comments in Samuel Sandmel, *Anti-Semitism in the New Testament?* (Philadelphia: Fortress, 1978), pp. 122–23.

2. If supersession of Judaism had been a primary emphasis in this document, one would think that at least these two images would have been reversed, so that the tribes would be the foundation now hidden from view and the apostles would be the gates of entry into the heavenly city.

3. There is no attempt to castigate first-century Jews even when there were opportunities to do so, such as in 13:12, "Therefore, Jesus, in order that he might sanctify the people by means of his own blood, suffered outside the gate."

4. Sandmel, *Anti-Semitism in the New Testament?*, p. 120.

5. As Rosemary R. Ruether, *Faith and Fratricide: The Theological Roots of Anti-Semitism* (New York: Seabury, 1974), p. 107, summarizes it, "the mere finite, mutable and carnal" is contrasted to "the eternal, immutable and spiritual."

6. See the summary of the document's use of the Old Testament in Reginald H. Fuller, "The Letter of the Hebrews," in *Hebrews-James-1 and 2 Peter-Jude-Revelation*, Proclamation Commentaries, ed. G. Krodel (Philadelphia: Fortress, 1977), pp. 6–15.

7. According to John T. Townsend, "The Gospel of John and the Jews: The Story of a Religious Divorce," in *Antisemitism and the Foundations of Christianity*, ed. A. Davies (New York: Paulist, 1979), p. 90, apart from the Fourth Gospel, Heb. 1:8–9 is the only place in the New Testament in which it is certain that Jesus is called "God." (The expression "our God and Savior Jesus Christ" in 2 Peter 1:1 may be another example.) See also Raymond E. Brown, "Does the New Testament Call Jesus God?" *TS* 26 (1965): 545–73.

8. See the interesting discussion about the humanity and the deity of Jesus in John A. T. Robinson, *The Human Face of God* (Philadelphia: Westminster, 1973).

9. Portions that would remain in standard print could include, for example, Heb. 1:1–4; 2:5; 2:8b–11; 2:14–3:2; 3:12–14; 4:9–16; 5:7–9; 6:10–12; 7:23–8:2; 9:11–28; 10:12–13:25.

10. See Martin Dibelius, *James; A Commentary on the Epistle of James*, rev. H. Greeven, trans. M. A. Williams (Hermeneia; Philadelphia: Fortress, 1976), pp. 142–43.

11. Neither "the Jews" nor "Israel" is used in the document. The "living stone" is rejected simply by "men" (2:4). The "chosen exiles of the Diaspora" may be a phrase used to denote supersession of the Jewish people by the new people of God, who follow Jesus as the Christ and are sent by him, but it could also be an indication that by the time of the writing of 1 Peter the followers of Jesus had been scattered throughout most of Asia Minor for political, economic, and personal reasons. The document was probably written toward the end of the first century by someone who chose to utilize the name Peter as a pseudonym. There is far more evidence that Peter and Peter's name were used effectively as symbols within the early church than that Peter himself was a writer. See the careful presentation of reasons for considering 1 Peter to have been a pseudonymous writing in Gerhard Krodel, "The First Letter of Peter," in *Hebrews-James-1 and 2 Peter-Jude-Revelation*, Proclamation Commentaries, ed. G. Krodel (Philadelphia: Fortress, 1977), pp. 53–59.

12. John Koenig, *Jews and Christians in Dialogue: New Testament Foundations* (Philadelphia: Westminster, 1979), p. 171, notes that the writer did not use a definite article with any of the titles in 2:4–5, 9–10 and interprets this as an indication that the writer did not deny the ongoing validity of these titles for Jews who did not join the Christian movement.

13. Gerhard Krodel, "The Letter of Jude," in *Hebrews-James-1 and 2 Peter-Jude-Revelation*, Proclamation Commentaries, ed. G. Krodel (Philadelphia: Fortress, 1977), p. 97.

14. If *Iēsous* is read instead of *Kyrios* in Jude 5, as it is in some important early manuscripts, there is in Jude a high Christology of preexistent saving activity of Jesus at the time of Moses.

15. Some early manuscripts read "Lord" instead of "God" here, which would harmonize this reading with that of 1:11; 2:20; 3:2; and 3:18. A translation of

dikaiosynē tou theou hēmōn kai sōtēros Iēsou Christou that would separate "God" from "Savior Jesus Christ" ("the righteousness of our God and of our Savior Jesus Christ") is also possible.

16. See the discussion of this by Frederick W. Danker, "The Second Letter of Peter," in *Hebrews-James-1 and 2 Peter-Jude-Revelation* (Proclamation Commentaries, ed. by G. Krodel; Philadelphia: Fortress, 1977), pp. 89–90.

11

Conclusions, Implications, and Future Agenda for a Mature Christianity

It will be helpful at this point to classify the anti-Jewish polemic of the New Testament documents in three major categories. These three types of polemic are interrelated but sufficiently distinct that we can respond to them in three distinctly different ways.

The first type of anti-Jewish polemic within the New Testament can be called in the broad sense *christological*. It can be found on nearly every page of the New Testament and can be expressed in simple terms as: Then Yahweh was Lord, but now Jesus is Lord. Or to put it another way, for the followers of Jesus who produced the New Testament Jesus is to God *(Theos)* almost what Yahweh is to God *(Elohim)* within the Jewish Scriptures and Judaism. Although the Jesus of history was probably acclaimed as an actual or potential Jewish Messiah by most of the Jews who followed him, the crucifixion of Jesus by the Romans and the lack of evidence that the Messianic age of peace and happiness had come through him caused most first-century Jews who had known him to turn their attention elsewhere. However, some continued to tell stories about Jesus and to repeat sayings of Jesus. These followers of Jesus and their followers reflected about what Jesus was for them, particularly as they moved into a Hellenistic environment, and believed with increasing certitude that God had raised Jesus from the dead and that Jesus was with God and also present in many ways with them. As they continued to reminisce about things that he had said and as they repeated their stories about him, he became for them the Christian Messiah, or simply the Christ. In their new and changed situation, with their new identity, they no longer affirmed that Yahweh is Lord but that Jesus is Lord, or that Jesus the Christ is Lord. Somewhat as Jews understand God *(Elohim)* through Yahweh their Lord, they began to understand God *(Theos)* through Jesus their Lord, as has been normative for Christians ever since that time.

This christological essence of Christianity should be recognized within a mature Christianity. The Christology should be expressed by each new generation in new and dynamic ways. But this christological essence of Christianity should not be repudiated.

Relationships and dialogue with Jews and with other religious groups are improved and Christianity becomes more credible when more emphasis in Christian theology is placed upon futuristic eschatology, upon unfulfilled messianism. Such relationships and dialogue are further enhanced when we as Christians acknowledge that, although the way to God through Jesus as the Christian Messiah may be the only way to God for us from our standpoint, ultimately God cannot be limited nor access to God restricted by any of us. Only God can limit God's self. As Christians, we have access to God by clinging to Jesus' coattails, or I should say by clinging to Jesus' cross, but there has been access to God also in other times and in other cultures.[1] A mature Christianity can recognize this without repudiating its own christological essence or refuting its classical dogmas and creeds. Within mature religious systems antinomies, even theological antinomies, can exist alongside one another and be theologically stimulating, as is evidenced by the vitality of Hindu, Buddhist, and Jewish systems that permit this. There is a precedent for this even within Christianity, particularly in the acceptance of Jewish Scriptures into the Christian canon.

The second type of anti-Jewish polemic within the New Testament is *supersessionistic* polemic. This type of polemic, while not so widespread as the christological, to which it is related, is nevertheless present in most portions of the New Testament literature. Polemic of this type is to be expected within religious literature, particularly within religious literature that is developed during the formative period of a religious community when the leaders of the community are establishing their identity and their newness over against parent groups in competition with them. Since the principal parent of the religious community that produced the New Testament is Jewish, most of the supersessionistic polemic of the New Testament documents is anti-Jewish.

As a result of this supersessionistic polemic within the New Testament, most Christian proclamation and teaching has refused to acknowledge that Jewish faith is a valid and living form of spirituality. Jewish theological development and Jewish expressions of faith in God have been largely ignored by Christians, and Christian theological development and Christian expressions of faith have been of limited use to Jews. This theological isolation can be broken as Christianity matures and as theological conversation on an adult-to-adult level between Jews and Christians increases.

The supersessionistic polemic of the New Testament documents will be recognized within a mature Christianity. There will be an increased awareness within Christian proclamation and teaching of the historical situation during the latter decades of the first century c.e. and of the attendant development of supersessionistic polemic over against Judaism in Christian literature during the adolescent period of Christianity. Mature sensitivity is needed in our translation and usage of New Testament material that includes anti-Jewish supersessionistic polemic. The present study is an attempt to demonstrate such sensitivity in a reasonable and responsible manner.

The third and final type of anti-Jewish polemic within the New Testament—an outgrowth of the supersessionistic polemic—is *defamatory* polemic. This type of polemic is not present in all portions of the New Testament. Although it may be understandable in view of the situation during the latter decades of the first century, we should not continue to defame during these latter decades of the twentieth century because of problems encountered during the first century. The first century problems seem to have been of limited duration, as our study of the Johannine literature indicates. The Apocalypse, Hebrews, James, 1 Peter, Jude, and 2 Peter are proof that it was possible to have a high Christology and to be supersessionistic within the early church without being defamatory. Defamatory polemic is not essential to the Christian message nor to Christianity. It is negative and damaging to Jewish people and dehumanizing to us as Christians. The defamatory anti-Jewish polemic of the New Testament should be repudiated.

If we will take seriously the statements of Christian groups such as the World Council of Churches since 1948, the Lutheran World Federation and the House of Bishops of the Protestant Episcopal Church since 1964, the Second Vatican Council of the Roman Catholic Church since 1965, the Lutheran Council in the U.S.A. since 1971, and The American Lutheran Church since 1974,[2] we will repudiate the defamatory anti-Jewish polemic of the New Testament not only in word but also in deed. Under the guidance of the Spirit of God in translations of the New Testament intended for popular use, we will "prune" into footnote status its most viciously defamatory particles.[3] In other instances, in which the polemic is less virulent, we will use circumlocution and translation according to the sense of the text in order to reduce emphasis upon the Jews, Judaism, and the Pharisees. Third, we will be more selective in our choice of lectionary texts, providing readings that are less blatantly anti-Jewish.

Future revisions of the major cooperative translations of the New Testament that have broad popular usage should include these measures. More thorough self-criticism can be accomplished by individual translators or small groups of translators who will dare to be more innovative. The author of the present study has begun a new translation of the New Testament in which the guidelines developed here are being followed. Only when translations of the New Testament that recognize its defamatory anti-Jewish polemic and repudiate it in a sensitive and responsible manner are sold, used, and accepted within the marketplace of ideas will substantial changes in defamatory attitudes occur. Several generations—perhaps as many as two hundred years—will pass before a nondefamatory attitude over against Jewish people will be normative within Christianity. It is thrilling to be led by the Spirit of God to participate in this process, by which the word of God remains "living and active, sharper than any two-edged sword."

Notes

1. See the attempt to illustrate this visually in Appendix B: A Diagram of Our Access to God through Various Major Religious Systems Operative Today.

2. See above, pp. 48–50.

3. The New Testament material that has already been "pruned" to footnote status in translations intended for popular use since 1611 as a result of text-critical studies during the past three centuries is much greater in volume and in significance than are the few particles of viciously defamatory anti-Jewish material recommended for footnote status in the present study.

Appendix A:
An Illustrated Diagram of the History of the Synoptic Traditions and of the Relationships and Interrelationships of the Synoptic and Johannine Traditions as Perceived in This Study

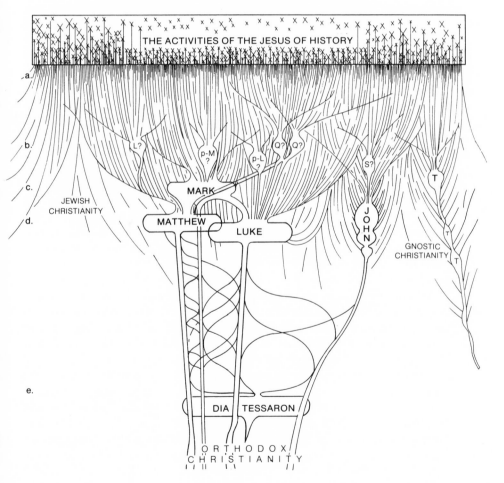

JEWISH CULTURE AT THE EASTERN EDGE OF THE ROMAN EMPIRE
IN AN AREA UNDER ROMAN MILITARY CONTROL

THE ACTIVITIES OF THE JESUS OF HISTORY

a.

b.

c.
JEWISH
CHRISTIANITY

d.

MARK

MATTHEW

LUKE

L?

p-M
?

p-L
?

Q? Q?

S?

T

J
O
H
N

T

GNOSTIC
CHRISTIANITY   T

e.

DIA | TESSARON

O R T H O D O X
C H R I S T I A N I T Y

a. Followers of the Jesus of history shared reminiscences about Jesus and sayings of Jesus. Many of these reminiscences were lost with the passage of time.

b. Stories about Jesus and sayings of Jesus were modified and shaped by the devotional, liturgical, kerygmatic, and didactic practices of developing communities of followers of Jesus. In this process new stories about Jesus and sayings of Jesus were sometimes developed to meet the needs and to validate the practices of the communities. Stories and sayings that were similar were associated with each other in oral tradition. As awareness of an existence apart from other Jewish groups grew, and as membership came to include larger numbers of non-Jewish persons in Greek-speaking lands, a few collections of stories about Jesus and sayings of Jesus were put into writing, some in Aramaic and some in Greek. These may have included the *Logia* of Matthew (L? in the diagram), pre-Markan written sources (p-M?), a proto-Luke (p-L?), "Q" or several "Q" documents (Q?Q), a Johannine "Signs" source (S?), and an early form of the gnostic Christian Gospel of Thomas (T). Large amounts of oral tradition remained and continued to develop. During this time antagonism against various Jewish groups was intensifying and different emphases among divergent groups of followers of Jesus were becoming more apparent.

c. Mark, the first "Gospel," was written within an extended eschatological community self-consciously establishing its own identity. To accomplish this, traditional stories about Jesus and sayings of Jesus were combined with small portions of the Jewish Scriptures which were synthesized, merged, and blended freely to express the proclamation and the parenesis of the Markan community in a ministry-of-Jesus vehicle. This new literary genre was later to become the basis and the model for the Gospels of Matthew and Luke.

d. Matthew was written by incorporating large portions of an early copy of Mark and utilizing one or more "Q" documents and other oral and possibly also written traditions. The Jewish Scriptures were used extensively in Matthew, but primarily for apologetical and polemical purposes. Luke was written, as its prologue stipulates, to provide a more orderly and more excellent account than was otherwise available. During this same general time period, a first and a second edition of John was formulated within the Johannine community from a mass of Johannine traditions. A writer-redactor later added substantial portions of oral Johannine tradition to the written Johannine account. During this time the writers and communities that had produced these four Gospels became increasingly aware of each other and of the Gospels being used within the other communities. Since each community had written rather freely, adapting whatever it wished from the oral and written sources available to satisfy its own needs and interests, each community quite naturally had the feeling that its own Gospel was superior to that of the others. The Johannine community in particular must have felt that its Gospel with its higher Christology of the preexistent Logos was of greater excellence than the others and probably would not have made extensive changes in its own format or have included much more of Mark, Matthew, or Luke even if it had them fully available, as it obviously did after some point in time.

e. During this period some harmonization of texts (such as providing a variety of post-16:8 portions for Mark) occurred within the Synoptic traditions, obscuring some of the distinctions otherwise apparent in the two-document hypothesis. There is evidence also of some harmonization involving the Fourth Gospel. As communication between the Synoptic communities and the Johannine community increased and as relationships improved, the Synoptic communities and their successors gradually accepted the higher Christology of the Fourth Gospel and the Johannine community and its successors gradually accepted the sacramental theology and other aspects of the Synoptic traditions. The result was the development of a Christian orthodoxy with an authoritative Four Gospel tradition. "Jewish" Christians were forced to choose between the religion of the Pharisees and the Christian emphases. "Gnostic" Christians were excluded and excluded themselves from fellowship. Tatian's *Diatessaron* was a notable attempt in the Syriac-speaking sector to combine the Four Gospels into one harmonious account. If one harmonized Gospel had gained favor throughout the Church, the Four Gospels of Mark, Matthew, Luke, and John might have been dropped from use and might not be available to us, just as no copies are extant today of the *Logia* of Matthew (L? in the diagram), possible pre-Markan written sources (p-M?), a proto-Luke (p-L?), "Q" or several "Q" documents (Q?Q), and a Johannine "Signs" source (S?). Eventually, however, the *Diatessaron* was discredited and the Four Gospels remained, with Mark, however, the earliest of the Four, in a subordinate position. As the written Gospels became generally accepted and used, oral tradition diminished.[1]

Note

1. In this appendix my indebtedness to the work of Raymond E. Brown, particularly in his *The Gospel According to St. John*, The Anchor Bible 29, 29A (Garden City, N.Y.: Doubleday, 1966, 1970), and " 'Other Sheep Not of This Fold': The Johannine Perspective on Christian Diversity in the Late First Century," *JBL* 97 (1978): 5–22, will be apparent to all who are familiar with the vast literature on this subject. See also Howard C. Kee, *Jesus in History*, 2d ed. (New York: Harcourt Brace Jovanovich, 1977).

Appendix B:
A Diagram of Our Access to God through Various Major Religious Systems Operative Today

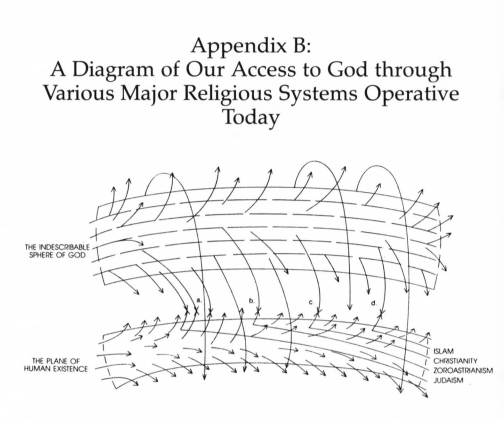

THE INDESCRIBABLE
SPHERE OF GOD

THE PLANE OF
HUMAN EXISTENCE

ISLAM
CHRISTIANITY
ZOROASTRIANISM
JUDAISM

Human existence, with its limitations, its freedoms, and its capabilities, is illustrated on the lower plane, which is broad and expansive, not merely a single line. Above it is an attempt to depict the far more extensive sphere of God, which we, theistically, postulate but can neither prove nor describe. Each of us can, however, within certain definite limitations, turn toward God, turn away from God, or attempt to live oblivious to God. This is illustrated on the diagram by the arrows turning up, down, and parallel to the human plane respectively. God, as creator, sustainer, and purifier of the human plane of existence and its environment, cannot be limited by us to any particular plane of existence and may indeed at all times operate not only above, but also below, beside, within, and all around us. When we with our limited freedom attempt to turn away from God or to live oblivious to God, God can if God wishes, choose to permit us to do so. When, however, we attempt to turn toward God and open ourselves to God, God

290

can if God wishes, choose to permit this also and to reveal God's self to us in special ways. Whenever this happens, we say that revelation or a revelatory experience has occurred. Such revelatory experiences are not restricted to one or to a few periods of time, but have occurred throughout human existence and continue to occur today. Some of these experiences are fleeting and momentary, with little lasting effect. Others, however, are deep and sustained.

Some individuals, such as a. Abraham, Moses, and the Israelite prophets, b. Zoroaster, c. Jesus, and d. Muhammad, depicted on the diagram above, have turned toward God with such intensity and persistence that a linkage between the human situation and God has been established that has remained until our present time. These individuals became the primary founders of major religions, and millions of other individuals during subsequent periods of time have benefited from their linkage to God. We, as Christians, who travel on the portion of the plane that has been characterized as Christian, affirm that our linkage to God is through Jesus. We recognize, however, that our contact with God is also through countless others within the Christian Church, and through other people of God, especially within the experiences of the Israelite people. Just as electrical current "flows" most readily through the most proximate and conducive conductors, so also the power that we receive from God comes to us via the means most readily available, which for us is Jesus as our Lord and Savior. Although as mature Christians we acknowledge that we cannot limit God and God's access to us and to other people, we enthusiastically invite others to join with us in our access to God through Jesus, and we remain open to other and continuing revelatory experiences.

Bibliography

Abbott, Walter M., ed. *The Documents of Vatican II.* New York: Guild, 1966.

Abrahams, Israel. *Studies in Pharisaism and the Gospels.* Vol. 1. Cambridge: Cambridge University, 1917.

Achtemeier, Elizabeth. *The Old Testament and the Proclamation of the Gospel.* Philadelphia: Westminster, 1973.

Achtemeier, Paul J. *Mark.* Proclamation Commentaries. Philadelphia: Fortress, 1975.

———. "The Lukan Perspective on the Miracles of Jesus: A Preliminary Sketch." In *Perspectives on Luke-Acts,* edited by C. H. Talbert. Danville, Va.: Association of Baptist Professors of Religion, 1978. Pp. 153–67.

Albright, W. F., and Mann, C. S. *Matthew.* The Anchor Bible. Garden City, N.Y.: Doubleday, 1971.

ALC-LCA Adult Augsburg Bible Studies, vol. 9, no. 4. Minneapolis, Minn.: Augsburg, 1976.

Anderson, Bernhard, ed. *The Old Testament and Christian Faith.* New York: Harper & Row, 1963.

Arndt, W. F., and Gingrich, F. W. *A Greek-English Lexicon of the New Testament and Other Early Christian Literature.* Chicago: University of Chicago Press, 1957.

Bacon, B. W. "Pharisees and Herodians in Mark." *JBL* 39 (1920): 102–11.

Banki, Judith H. "AJC Hails Liturgical Development." *Interreligious Newsletter: A Review of Trends and Developments in Interreligious Affairs* 1, no. 3 (May 1977): 1–2.

Banks, R. *Paul's Idea of Community: The Early House Churches in Their Historical Setting.* Leiden: E. J. Brill, 1979.

Barr, David L. "Toward a Definition of the Gospel Genre." Ph.D. dissertation, Florida State University, 1974.

Barr, James. *Fundamentalism.* Philadelphia: Westminster, 1977.

Barrett, C. K. *A Commentary on the Second Epistle to the Corinthians.* New York: Harper & Row, 1973.

———. "Acts and the Pauline Corpus." *ET* 78 (1976): 2–5.

———. *The Gospel According to John.* London: S.P.C.K., 1955.

Barth, Karl. *The Epistle to the Romans.* Translated by E. C. Hoskyns. London: Oxford, 1933.

Barth, Markus. *Ephesians.* 2 vols. Anchor Bible. Garden City, N.Y.: Doubleday, 1974.

————. *Israel and the Church.* Richmond: John Knox, 1969.

————. "Was Paul an Anti-Semite?" *JES* 5 (1968): 78–104.

Bauer, Walter E. "Some Observations on History, Historicity, and the Historical-Critical Method." *The Cresset* 40 (Sept.–Oct., 1977): 24–29.

Bauernfeind, Otto. *Die Apostelgeschichte.* Leipzig, 1939.

Baum, Gregory. *Is the New Testament Anti-Semitic?* New York: Paulist, 1965.

Baur, F. C. *Paulus, der Apostel Jesus Christi* (1845). *Paul, the Apostle of Jesus Christ.* Translated by A. Menzies. London, 1875.

Beach, Curtis. *The Gospel of Mark.* New York: Harper, 1959.

Beck, Norman A. "Efficacious Symbolic Acts of Jesus Christ during His Public Ministry." Ph.D. dissertation, Princeton Theological Seminary, 1967.

————. "Reclaiming a Biblical Text: The Mark 8:14–21 Discussion About Bread in the Boat." *CBQ* 43 (1981): 49–56.

Becker, Jürgen. "Wunder und Christologie." *NTS* 16 (1968–70): 130–48.

Benoit, Pierre, ed. *How Does the Christian Confront the Old Testament?* New York: Paulist, 1968.

Bertram, G. In the *Theological Dictionary of the New Testament* 9: 220–235.

Betz, Hans-Dieter. "The Cleansing of the Ten Lepers (Luke 17:11–19)." *JBL* 90 (1971): 314–28.

Beyer, Hermann W. *Die Apostelgeschichte.* 4th ed. Göttingen, 1947.

Black, Matthew. *An Aramaic Approach to the Gospels and Acts.* 2d ed. Oxford: Oxford, 1954.

————. *Romans.* London: Marshall, Morgan and Scott, 1973.

Blass, Friedrich, and Debrunner, Albert. *A Greek Grammar of the New Testament.* Trans. and ed. R. W. Funk. Chicago: University of Chicago, 1961.

Boers, Hendrikus. "The Form-Critical Study of Paul's Letters: I Thessalonians as a Case Study." *NTS* 22 (1975–76): 151–52.

Born, Adrianus van den. *De symbolische Handelingen der Oud-Testamentische Profeten.* Utrecht: Dekker en Van de Vegt, 1935.

————. *Profetie metterdaad; Een Studie over de symbolische Handelingen der Profeten.* Roermond: J. J. Romen en Zonen, 1947.

Bornkamm, Günther. "Der Philipperbrief als Paulinische Briefsammlung." In *Neotestamentica et Patristica, Freundesgabe für O. Cullmann,* 1962. Pp. 192–202.

————. *Jesus of Nazareth.* New York: Harper & Row, 1960.

————. *Paul.* Translated by D. M. G. Stalker. New York: Harper & Row, 1971.

Bornkamm, Günther; Barth, Gerhard; and Held, Heinz Joachim. *Tradition and Interpretation in Matthew.* Translated by P. Scott. Philadelphia: Westminster, 1963.

Braaten, Carl E. "Jesus Among Jews and Gentiles." *Currents in Theology and Mission* 10 (1983): 197–209.

Braun, Martin. *History and Romance in Graeco-Roman Literature.* Oxford: Oxford, 1938.

Brawley, Robert. "The Pharisees in Luke-Acts: Luke's Address to the Jews and His Irenic Purpose." Ph.D. dissertation, Princeton Theological Seminary, 1978.

Brown, Raymond E. "Does the New Testament Call Jesus God?" *TS* 26 (1965): 545–73.

———. "Johannine Ecclesiology—The Community's Origins." *Interp* 31 (1977): 379–93.

———. " 'Other Sheep Not of This Fold': The Johannine Perspective on Christian Diversity in the Late First Century." *JBL* 97 (1978): 5–22.

———. *The Birth of the Messiah.* Garden City, N.Y.: Doubleday, 1979.

———. *The Community of the Beloved Disciple.* New York: Paulist, 1979.

———. *The Gospel According to John.* Anchor Bible. 2 vols. Garden City, N.Y.: Doubleday, 1966, 1970.

———. "The Passion According to John: Chapters 18 and 19." *Worship* 49 (1975): 130–31.

Brown, Raymond E.; Donfried, Karl P.; Fitzmyer, Joseph A.; and Reumann, John. *Mary in the New Testament.* Philadelphia: Fortress, and New York: Paulist, 1978.

Brown, Schuyler. "The Role of the Prologues in Determining the Purpose of Luke-Acts." In *Perspectives on Luke-Acts,* edited by C. H. Talbert. Danville, Va.: Association of Baptist Professors of Religion, 1978. Pp. 99–111.

Bultmann, Rudolf. *The Gospel of John: A Commentary.* Oxford: B. Blackwell, 1971.

———. *The History of the Synoptic Tradition.* Translated by J. Marsh. New York: Harper & Row, 1963.

———. *The Johannine Epistles.* Translated by R. P. O'Hara, L. C. McGaughy, and R. W. Funk. Hermeneia Commentaries. Philadelphia: Fortress, 1973.

Burch, E. W. "Tragic Action in the Second Gospel." *JR* 11 (1931): 346.

Buren, Paul M. van. *Discerning the Way: A Theology of the Jewish Christian Reality.* New York: Seabury, 1980.

Burgess, Joseph. "Colossians." In *Ephesians, Colossians, 2 Thessalonians, The Pastoral Epistles.* Proclamation Commentaries. Philadelphia: Fortress, 1978. Pp. 41–71.

Burkill, T. Alec. "Anti-Semitism in St. Mark's Gospel." *NT* 3 (1959): 34–53.

Burridge, K. O. L. *New Heaven, New Earth: A Study of Millenarian Activities.* New York: Schocken, 1969.

Cadbury, Henry J. *The Making of Luke-Acts.* London: S.P.C.K., 1961.

Caird, G. B. *The Gospel of St. Luke.* Baltimore, Md.: Penguin, 1963.

Carre, H. B. *Studies of Early Christianity.* New York, 1928.

Cassidy, Richard J. *Jesus, Politics, and Society.* Maryknoll, N.Y.: Orbis, 1979.

"Controversial Long Island Churches Merge." *The Lutheran Standard* 18 (March 7, 1978): 22–23.

Conzelmann, Hans. *I Corinthians.* Translated by J. W. Leitch. Philadelphia: Fortress, 1975.

———. *The Theology of St. Luke.* Translated by G. Buswell. New York: Harper & Row, 1960.

Cope, D. Lamar. *Matthew: A Scribe Trained for the Kingdom of Heaven.* CBQ Monograph Series 5. Washington: Catholic Biblical Association, 1976.

Cribbs, F. Lamar. "The Agreements That Exist Between John and Acts." In *Perspectives on Luke-Acts,* edited by C. H. Talbert. Danville, Va.: Association of Baptist Professors of Religion, 1978. Pp. 40–61.

Crossan, Dominic M. "Anti-Semitism and the Gospel." *TS* 26 (1965): 189–214.

Culpepper, R. A. *The Johannine School.* Missoula, Mont.: Scholars, 1975.

Danker, Frederick W. *Jesus and the New Age According to St. Luke.* St. Louis, Mo.: Clayton, 1972.

———. *Luke.* Proclamation Commentaries. Philadelphia: Fortress, 1976.

———. "The Second Letter of Peter." In *Hebrews-James-1 and 2 Peter-Jude-Revelation.* Proclamation Commentaries. Philadelphia: Fortress, 1977. Pp. 81–91.

Davies, Alan T. *Antisemitism and the Christian Mind.* New York: Seabury, 1969.

———, ed. *Antisemitism and the Foundations of Christianity.* New York: Paulist, 1979.

Davies, W. D. "Israel, the Mormons and the Land." In *Reflections on Mormonism: Judaeo-Christian Parallels,* edited by T. G. Madsen. Provo, Utah: Religious Studies Center, Brigham Young University, 1978. Pp. 79–97.

———. *Paul and Rabbinic Judaism.* 2d ed. London: S.P.C.K., 1955.

———. *The Setting of the Sermon on the Mount.* Cambridge: University Press, 1964.

Deever, Philip. "Anti-Judaism of the New Testament in the Light of Its Biblical and Hellenistic Context." Ph.D. dissertation, Union Theological Seminary, 1958.

Dibelius, Martin. *From Tradition to Gospel.* Translated by B. L. Woolf. New York: Charles Scribner's Sons, 1935.

———. *James; A Commentary on the Epistle of James.* Translated by M. A. Williams. Hermeneia. Philadelphia: Fortress, 1976.

———. *Studies in the Acts of the Apostles.* Translated by M. Ling and P. Schubert. New York: Charles Scribner's Sons, 1956.

————, and Conzelmann, Hans. *The Pastoral Epistles.* Translated by P. Buttolph and A. Yarbro. Hermeneia. Philadelphia: Fortress, 1972.

Die Gute Nachricht; Das Neue Testament in heutigen Deutsch. Stuttgart: Bibelanstalt, 1967.

Ditmanson, Harold H. "Judaism and Christianity: A Theology of Coexistence." *Dialog* 16 (1977): 17–24.

Divine Principle. Washington: The Holy Spirit Association for the Unification of World Christianity, 1973.

Donfried, Karl P., ed. *The Romans Debate.* Minneapolis, Minn.: Augsburg, 1977.

Doty, William G. *Letters in Primitive Christianity.* Philadelphia: Fortress, 1971.

Drury, John. *The Gospel of Luke.* New York: Macmillan, 1973.

————. *Tradition and Design in Luke's Gospel; A Study in Early Christian Historiography.* Atlanta, Ga.: John Knox, 1977.

Dunn, James D. G. *Unity and Diversity in the New Testament.* Philadelphia: Westminster, 1977.

Dupont, Jacques. *The Salvation of the Gentiles; Essays on the Acts of the Apostles.* Translated by J. R. Keating. New York: Paulist, 1979.

————. *The Sources of Acts.* London: Darton, Longman, and Todd, 1964.

Easton, B. S. *The Pastoral Epistles.* London: SCM, 1948.

Eckardt, A. Roy. *Elder and Younger Brothers.* New York: Scribner, 1967.

————. "The Nemesis of Christian Antisemitism." In *Jewish-Christian Relations in Today's World,* edited by J. E. Wood. Waco, Texas: Baylor University Press, 1971. Pp. 45–62.

————. "The Theology of Antisemitism." *RL* 31 (1962): 552–62.

Eckart, K.-G. "Der zweite echte Brief des Apostels Paulus an die Thessalonicher." *ZTK* 58 (1961): 32–34.

Eckert, W., ed. *Antijudaismus im Neuen Testament? Exegetische und systematische Beiträge.* Abh. z. christl. jüd. Dialog 1. Munich, 1967.

Edwards, Richard A. *A Theology of Q: Eschatology, Prophecy, and Wisdom.* Philadelphia: Fortress, 1976.

Ellis, E. Earle. "Paul and His Opponents." In *Christianity, Judaism and Other Greco-Roman Cults,* Part One, Studies in Judaism in Late Antiquity, vol. 12, edited by J. Neusner. Leiden: E. J. Brill, 1975. Pp. 264–98.

————. *Paul's Use of the Old Testament.* Grand Rapids: Eerdmans, 1957.

————. *The Gospel of Luke.* London: Nelson, 1966.

Epp, Eldon Jay. "Anti-Semitism and the Popularity of the Fourth Gospel in Christianity." *CCAR* 22 (1975): 35–57.

————. "Jews and Judaism in the Living New Testament." In *Biblical and Near Eastern Studies: Essays in Honor of William Sanford LaSor,* edited by Gary A. Tuttle. Grand Rapids: Eerdmans, 1978.

————. *The Theological Tendency of Codex Bezae Cantabrigiensis in Acts.* Cambridge: Cambridge University Press, 1966.

Farrer, Austin M. "On Dispensing with Q." In *Studies in the Gospels,* edited by D. E. Nineham. London: Oxford, 1955, pp. 55–88.

Fischel, Henry. "Studies in Cynicism and the Ancient Near East: The Transformation of a Chria." In *Religions in Antiquity,* edited by J. Neusner. Leiden: E. J. Brill, 1968. Pp. 372–411.

Fischer, James A. "Pauline Literary Forms and Thought Patterns." *CBQ* 39 (1977): 209–23.

Fisher, Eugene. "Are the Gospels Anti-Semitic?" In *Faith Without Prejudice; Rebuilding Christian Attitudes Toward Judaism.* New York: Paulist, 1977. Pp. 54–75.

Fitzmyer, Joseph. "Anti-Semitism and the Cry of 'All the People.' " *TS* 26 (1965): 667–71.

————. "Qumran and the Interpolated Paragraph in 2 Cor. vi. 14–vii.1." In *Essays on the Semitic Background of the New Testament.* London: G. Chapman, 1971. Pp. 205–17.

————. "The Use of Explicit Old Testament Quotation." *NTS* 7 (1960–61): 319–21.

Fohrer, Georg. "Die Gattung der Berichte über symbolische Handlungen der Propheten." *ZAW* 64 (1952): 101–20.

————. *Die symbolischen Handlungen der Propheten.* Zürich: Zwingli-Verlag, 1953.

Fortna, Robert T. *The Gospel of Signs: A Reconstruction of the Narrative Sources Underlying the Fourth Gospel.* Cambridge: University Press, 1970.

Franklin, Eric. *Christ the Lord: A Study in the Purpose and Theology of Luke-Acts.* Philadelphia: Westminster, 1975.

Frey, Robert S. "Issues in Post-Holocaust Christian Theology." *Dialog* 22 (1983): 227–35.

Friedland, Eric L. "What of the Canaanites?" *JRJ* 27 (1980): 77–81.

Fuller, Reginald. "The 'Jews' in the Fourth Gospel." *Dialog* 16 (1977): 31–37.

————. "The Letter to the Hebrews." In *Hebrews-James-1 and 2 Peter-Jude-Revelation.* Proclamation Commentaries. Philadelphia: Fortress, 1977. Pp. 1–27.

————. "The Pastoral Epistles." In *Ephesians, Colossians, 2 Thessalonians, The Pastoral Epistles.* Proclamation Commentaries. Philadelphia: Fortress, 1978. Pp. 97–121.

Funk, Robert W. *Language, Hermeneutic, and Word of God.* New York: Harper & Row, 1966.

Furnish, Victor P. "The Place and Purpose of Philippians iii." *NTS* 10 (1963): 80–85.

Gager, John G. *The Origins of Anti-Semitism.* New York: Oxford University Press, 1984.

Gamble, Harry. *The Textual History of the Letter to the Romans: A Study in Textual and Literary Criticism*. Grand Rapids, Mich.: Eerdmans, 1977.

Geisler, Mary Jo. "Polemic in the Divine Principle." Unpublished paper. Texas Lutheran College, Seguin, Texas, 1978.

Glock, Charles Y., and Stark, Rodney. *Christian Beliefs and Anti-Semitism*. New York: Harper & Row, 1966.

Goulder, M. D. "Mark XVI. 1–8 and Parallels." *NTS* 24 (1977–78): 235–40.

———. *Midrash and Lection in Matthew*. London: S.P.C.K., 1974.

———. "On Putting Q to the Test." *NTS* 24 (1977–78): 218–34.

Grant, Michael. "Paul the Discontented Jew." *Midstream* (Aug.–Sept., 1976): 32–40.

Grässer, E. "Die antijudische Polemik im Johannesevangelium." *NTS* 11 (1964): 77–90.

Grassi, Joseph. "Are the Roots of Anti-Semitism in the Gospels?" In *Root and Branch*. New York: Roth, 1973. Pp. 71–88.

Hadas, Moses, and Smith, Morton. *Heroes and Gods: Spiritual Biographies in Antiquity*. New York: Harper & Row, 1965.

Haenchen, Ernst. "Matthäus 23." *ZTK* 48 (1959): 38–63.

———. *The Acts of the Apostles*. Translated by B. Noble, G. Shinn, H. Anderson, and R. M. Wilson. Oxford: B. Blackwell, 1971.

———. "The Book of Acts as Source Material for the History of Early Christianity." In *Studies in Luke-Acts*, edited by L. E. Keck and J. L. Martyn. Nashville, Tenn.: Abingdon, 1966. Pp. 259–60.

Haigh, A. E. *The Tragic Drama of the Greeks*. Oxford: Clarendon, 1896.

Hals, Ronald M. *Grace and Faith in the Old Testament*. Minneapolis, Minn.: Augsburg, 1980.

Hare, D. R. A. *The Theme of Jewish Persecutions of Christians in the Gospel According to St. Matthew*. Cambridge: Cambridge University, 1967.

Harrington, Daniel J. *God's People in Christ: New Testament Perspectives on the Church and Judaism*. Philadelphia: Fortress, 1980.

Hawkins, Robert M. "The Rejection of Israel: An Analysis of Romans IX-XI." *ATR* 23 (1941): 329–35.

Hengel, Martin. *Judaism and Hellenism*. 2 vols. Philadelphia: Fortress, 1974.

Hruby, Kurt. "The Future of Christian-Jewish Dialogue: A Christian View." In *Christians and Jews*, edited by Hans Küng and Walter Kasper. New York: Seabury, 1974/5.

Hubbard, Benjamin J. "Commissioning Stories in Luke-Acts: A Study of Their Antecedents, Form and Content." *Semeia* 8 (1977): 103–26.

———. "The Role of Commissioning Accounts in Acts." In *Perspectives on Luke-Acts*, edited by C. H. Talbert. Danville, Va.: Association of Baptist Professors of Religion, 1978. Pp. 187–98.

Hultgren, Arland J. "Interpreting the Gospel of Luke." *Interp* 30 (1976): 354–55.

———. *Jesus and His Adversaries.* Minneapolis, Minn.: Augsburg, 1979.

———. "The Double Commandment of Love in Mt. 22:34–40: Its Sources and Composition." *CBQ* 36 (1974): 373–78.

Idinopulos, Thomas A., and Ward, Roy Bowen. "Is Christology Inherently Anti-Semitic? A Critical Review of Rosemary Ruether's *Faith and Fratricide.*" *JAAR* 45 (1977): 193–214.

Isaac, Jules. *The Teaching of Contempt: Christian Roots of Anti-Semitism.* New York: Holt, Rinehart and Winston, 1964.

Jeremias, Joachim. *The Parables of Jesus.* Translated by S. H. Hooke. New York: Charles Scribner's Sons, 1963.

Jervell, Jacob. *Luke and the People of God: A New Look at Luke-Acts.* Translated by D. Juel, et al. Minneapolis, Minn.: Augsburg, 1972.

Jewett, Robert. "The Epistolary Thanksgiving and the Integrity of Philippians." *NT* 12 (1970): 40–53.

Johnson, Marshall D. *The Purpose of the Biblical Genealogies.* Cambridge: University Press, 1969.

Karris, Robert J. *Invitation to Luke.* Garden City, N.Y.: Doubleday, 1977.

———. "Poor and Rich: The Lukan *Sitz im Leben.*" In *Perspectives on Luke-Acts,* edited by C. H. Talbert. Danville, Va.: Association of Baptist Professors of Religion, 1978. Pp. 112–25.

———. "Romans 14:1–15:13 and the Occasion of Romans." In *The Romans Debate,* edited by Karl P. Donfried. Minneapolis, Minn.: Augsburg, 1977. Pp. 75–99.

Käsemann, Ernst. *Commentary on Romans.* Translated by G. W. Bromiley. Grand Rapids, Mich.: Eerdmans, 1980.

———. *New Testament Questions of Today.* Philadelphia: Fortress, 1969.

———. *Perspectives on Paul.* Philadelphia: Fortress, 1971.

Kee, Howard C. *Community of the New Age: Studies in Mark's Gospel.* Philadelphia: Westminster, 1977.

———. *Jesus in History: An Approach to the Study of the Gospels.* 2d ed. New York: Harcourt Brace Jovanovich, 1977.

Kelber, Werner H. *The Kingdom in Mark.* Philadelphia: Fortress, 1974.

———., ed. *The Passion in Mark; Studies on Mark 14–16.* Philadelphia: Fortress, 1976.

Kelly, J. N. D. *A Commentary on the Pastoral Epistles.* New York: Harper, 1963.

Kilpatrick, G. D. *The Origins of the Gospel According to St. Matthew.* Oxford: Clarendon, 1946.

Kirsch, Paul J. *We Christians and Jews.* Philadelphia: Fortress, 1975.

Knilka, J. "2 Cor. vi. 14–vii. 1 in the Light of the Qumran Texts and the

Testaments of the Twelve Patriarchs." In *Paul and Qumran*, edited by J. Murphy-O'Connor. Chicago: Priory, 1968.

Koenig, John. *Jews and Christians in Dialogue: New Testament Foundations.* Philadelphia: Westminster, 1979.

Koester, Helmut. *Introduction to the New Testament.* vol. 2. Philadelphia: Fortress, 1982.

———. "One Jesus and Four Gospels." *HTR* 61 (1968): 230–36.

Kohler, Kaufmann. "New Testament." *Jewish Encyclopedia* 9 (1905): 251.

Kraabel, A. T. "The Disappearance of the 'God-fearers.' " *Numen* 28 (1981): 113–26.

Krodel, Gerhard. "2 Thessalonians." In *Ephesians, Colossians, 2 Thessalonians, The Pastoral Epistles.* Proclamation Commentaries. Philadelphia: Fortress, 1978. Pp. 73–96.

———. "The First Letter of Peter." In *Hebrews–James-1 and 2 Peter–Jude–Revelation.* Proclamation Commentaries. Philadelphia: Fortress, 1977. Pp. 50–80.

———. "The Letter of Jude." In *Hebrews–James-1 and 2 Peter–Jude–Revelation.* Proclamation Commentaries. Philadelphia: Fortress, 1977. Pp. 92–98.

Kümmel, W. G. *Introduction to the New Testament.* Trans. H. C. Kee. Nashville, Tenn.: Abingdon, 1975.

Küng, Hans. *On Being a Christian.* Garden City, N.Y.: Doubleday, 1976.

Kysar, Robert. "Community and Gospel: Vectors in Fourth Gospel Criticism." *Interp* 31 (1977): 357–59.

———. *The Fourth Evangelist and His Gospel: An Examination of Contemporary Scholarship.* Minneapolis, Minn.: Augsburg, 1975.

Lake, Kirsopp, and Cadbury, Henry J., eds. *The Beginnings of Christianity.* Vol. 4. London, 1933.

Lane, William L. *The Gospel of Mark.* Grand Rapids, Mich.: Eerdmans, 1974.

Lapide, Pinchas. "Is Jesus a Bond or a Barrier? A Jewish-Christian Dialogue." *JES* 14 (1977): 466–83.

Leistner, Reinhold. *Antijudaismus im Johannesevangelium?* Theologie und Wirklichkeit. Vol. 3. Bern: H. Lang, 1974.

Lindars, Barnabas. *New Testament Apologetic.* London: SCM Press, 1961.

Lohse, Eduard. *Colossians and Philemon.* Translated by W. R. Poehlmann and R. J. Karris. Philadelphia: Fortress, 1971.

Lutheran Book of Worship. Minneapolis: Augsburg, and Philadelphia: Board of Publication, Lutheran Church in America, 1978.

Maddox, Robert. *The Purpose of Luke–Acts.* Edinburgh: T. & T. Clark, 1982.

Marshall, I. Howard. *The Gospel of Luke.* Grand Rapids, Mich.: Eerdmans, 1978.

Martyn, J. Louis. *History and Theology in the Fourth Gospel.* New York: Harper & Row, 1968; rev. ed. Nashville, Tenn.: Abingdon, 1979.

Marxsen, Willi. *Introduction to the New Testament.* Philadelphia: Fortress, 1968.

————. *Mark the Evangelist.* Nashville, Tenn.: Abingdon, 1969.

McNeile, A. H. *The Gospel According to St. Matthew.* London: Macmillan, 1915.

Metzger, Bruce M. *The Text of the New Testament; Its Transmission, Corruption, and Restoration.* 2d ed. New York: Oxford, 1968.

Mickelson, Arnold R., ed. *1974 Reports and Actions, Seventh General Convention of The American Lutheran Church.* Minneapolis, Minn.: Office of the General Secretary, The American Lutheran Church, 1974.

Minear, Paul. *The Obedience of Faith.* London: SCM, 1971.

Montefiore, C. G. *The Synoptic Gospels.* Vol. 1. 2d ed. London: Macmillan, 1927.

Mullins, Terence. "New Testament Commission Forms, Especially in Luke–Acts." *JBL* 95 (1976): 603–14.

Munck, Johannes. *Paul and the Salvation of Mankind.* Translated by F. Clarke. Richmond, Va.: John Knox, 1959.

Musurillo, H. A., ed. *The Acts of the Pagan Martyrs: Acta Alexandrinorum.* Oxford: Clarendon, 1954.

Nicol, W. *The Sēmeia in the Fourth Gospel—Tradition and Redaction.* Leiden: E. J. Brill, 1972.

O'Collins, Gerald. "Anti-Semitism in the Gospel." *TS* 26 (1965): 663–66.

Oesterreicher, John M. *Anatomy of Contempt: A Critique of R. R. Ruether's Faith and Fratricide.* South Orange, N.J.: The Institute of Judaeo-Christian Studies, Seton Hall University, Institute paper no. 4, 1975.

Okeke, G. E. "I Thess. ii. 13–16: The Fate of the Unbelieving Jews." *NTS* 27 (1981): 127–36.

Olson, Bernhard E. *Faith and Prejudice.* New Haven, Conn.: Yale University Press, 1963.

O'Neill, J. C. *Paul's Letter to the Romans.* Baltimore, Md.: Penguin, 1975.

Opsahl, Paul D., and Tanenbaum, Marc H., eds. *Speaking of God Today: Jews and Lutherans in Conversation.* Philadelphia: Fortress, 1974.

Pancaro, S. "The Relationship of the Church to Israel in the Gospel of St. John." *NTS* 21 (1975): 398–401.

Parkes, James. "Judaism and the Jewish People in Their World Setting at the End of 1973." Pamphlet distributed by the Canadian Council of Christians and Jews. Toronto, 1974.

————. *The Conflict of the Church and the Synagogue.* New York: Meridian Books, 1961.

Pawlikowski, John T. *What Are They Saying About Christian-Jewish Relations?* New York: Paulist, 1980.

Pearson, Birger. "I Thessalonians 2:13–16: A Deutero-Pauline Interpolation." *HTR* 64 (1971): 79–94.

Perrin, Norman. "Mark 14:62: End Product of a Christian Pesher Tradition?" *NTS* 12 (1965–66): 150–55.

Pollard, T. E. "The Integrity of Philippians." *NTS* 13 (1966): 57–66.

Rad, Gerhard von. *Biblical Interpretations in Preaching.* Translated by J. E. Steely. Nashville: Abingdon, 1977.

———. *Old Testament Theology.* Vol. 1. New York: Harper & Row, 1962.

Reumann, John. *Jesus in the Church's Gospels.* Philadelphia: Fortress, 1968.

Robinson, H. Wheeler. "Hebrew Sacrifice and Prophetic Symbolism." *JTS* 43 (1942): 129–39.

———. "Prophetic Symbolism." In *Old Testament Essays,* edited by D. C. Simpson. London: Charles Griffin, 1927. Pp. 1–17.

———. "The Hebrew Conception of Corporate Personality." In *Werden und Wesen des Alten Testaments,* edited by P. Volz, F. Stummer, and J. Hempel. Berlin: A. Töpelmann, 1936. Pp. 49–62.

Robinson, J. A. T. *The Human Face of God.* Philadelphia: Westminster, 1973.

Ruether, Rosemary Radford. *Faith and Fratricide: The Theological Roots of Anti-Semitism.* New York: Seabury, 1974.

———. "The *Faith and Fratricide* Discussion: Old Problems and New Dimensions." In *Antisemitism and the Foundations of Christianity,* edited by A. T. Davies. New York: Paulist, 1979. Pp. 235–37.

———. "Theological Anti-Semitism in the New Testament." *CC* 85 (1968): 191–96.

Salles, A. "La Diatribe anti-paulinienne dans le Roman Pseudo-Clémentin et l'origine des K II." *RB* 66 (1957): 526–51.

Sanders, E. P. *Paul and Palestinian Judaism.* Philadelphia: Fortress, 1977.

Sanders, Jack T. "The Transition from Opening Epistolary Thanksgiving to Body in the Letters of the Pauline Corpus." *JBL* 81 (1962): 348–62.

Sanders, James A. "From Isaiah 61 to Luke 4." In *Christianity, Judaism and Other Greco-Roman Cults,* edited by J. Neusner, Part One: New Testament. Leiden: E. J. Brill, 1975. Pp. 75–106.

Sandmel, Samuel. *Anti-Semitism in the New Testament?* Philadelphia: Fortress, 1978.

Schmidt, Daryl. "I Thess 2:13–16: Linguistic Evidence for an Interpolation." *JBL* 102 (1983): 269–79.

Schneider, Bernardin. "The Meaning of St. Paul's Antithesis 'The Letter and the Spirit.'" *CBQ* 15 (1953): 163–207.

Schoeps, Hans Joachim. *Paul: The Theology of the Apostle in the Light of Jewish Religious History.* Translated by H. Knight. Philadelphia: Westminster, 1961.

Schubert, Paul. *Form and Function of the Pauline Thanksgivings.* Beih. *ZNW* 20. Berlin, 1939.

Schweizer, Eduard. *The Good News According to Mark.* Translated by D. H. Madvig. Atlanta, Ga.: John Knox, 1970.

———. *The Good News According to Matthew.* Translated by D. E. Green. Atlanta, Ga.: John Knox, 1975.

Seesemann, H. In the *Theological Dictionary of the New Testament.* 5:163.

Shepherd, Massey H. "The Jews in the Gospel of John." *ATR* suppl. 34 (1974): 95–112.

Sikes, W. W. "The Anti-Semitism of the Fourth Gospel." *JR* 21 (1941): 23–30.

Sloyan, Gerard S. *Is Christ the End of the Law?* Philadelphia: Westminster, 1978.

———. *Jesus on Trial; The Development of the Passion Narratives and Their Historical and Ecumenical Implications.* Philadelphia: Fortress, 1973.

Smith, Jonathan Z. "Good News Is No News: Aretalogy and Gospel." In *Christianity, Judaism and Other Greco-Roman Cults,* edited by J. J. Neusner. Studies in Judaism in Late Antiquity, Vol. 12. Leiden: E. J. Brill, 1975. Pp. 21–38.

Smith, Morton. "Prolegomena to a Discussion of Aretalogies, Divine Men, the Gospels and Jesus." *JBL* 90 (1971): 174–99.

Stendahl, Krister. *Meanings: The Bible as Document and as Guide.* Philadelphia: Fortress, 1984.

———. *Paul Among Jews and Gentiles.* Philadelphia: Fortress, 1976.

———. "The Sermon on the Mount and Third Nephi." In *Reflections on Mormonism: Judaeo-Christian Parallels,* edited by T. G. Madsen. Provo, Utah: Religious Studies Center, Brigham Young University, 1978. Pp. 139–54.

———. "Towards World Community." In *Jewish-Christian Dialogue.* Geneva: World Council of Churches, 1975. Pp. 59–63.

Stiassny, Joseph. "Development of the Christians' Self-understanding in the Second Part of the First Century." *Immanuel* 1 (1972): 32–34.

Strachan, R. H. *The Second Epistle of Paul to the Corinthians.* New York: Harper and Brothers, 1935.

Strober, Gerald S. *Portrait of the Elder Brother: Jews and Judaism in Protestant Teaching Materials.* New York: The American Jewish Committee, 1972.

Suggs, M. J. *Wisdom, Christology and Law in Matthew.* Cambridge, Mass.: Harvard University Press, 1970.

Sundberg, A. C. "On Testimonies." *NT* 3 (1959): 272.

Talbert, Charles H. *Literary Patterns, Theological Themes, and the Genre of Luke–Acts.* Missoula, Mont.: Society of Biblical Literature and Scholars Press, 1975.

———. "Shifting Sands: The Recent Study of the Gospel of Luke." *Interp* 30 (1976): 381–95.

Tannehill, Robert C. "Tension in Synoptic Sayings and Stories." *Interp* 34 (1980): 145–46.

Taylor, Vincent. *The Gospel According to St. Mark.* London: Macmillan, 1966.

Teeple, Howard M. *The Literary Origin of the Gospel of John.* Evanston, Ill.: Religion and Ethics Institute, Inc., 1974.

Temple, Sydney. *The Core of the Fourth Gospel.* London: Mowbrays, 1975.

The Gospel According to St. John. New York: Philosophical Library, 1967.

Theissen, Gerd. *Sociology of Early Palestinian Christianity.* Translated by J. Bowden. Philadelphia: Fortress, 1978.

―――. "Wanderradikalismus: Literatursoziologische Aspekte der Überlieferung von Worten Jesu im Urchristentum." *ZTK* 70 (1973): 245–71. ET in *Radical Religion* 2, nos. 2 and 3. Berkeley, Calif., 1975. Pp. 84–93.

The Nag Hammadi Library. Translated by members of the Coptic Gnostic Library Project of the Institute for Antiquity and Christianity, James M. Robinson, Director. San Francisco: Harper & Row, 1977.

Tiede, David L. *The Charismatic Figure as Miracle Worker.* Missoula, Mont.: Scholars, 1972.

Tilborg, Sjef van. *The Jewish Leaders in Matthew.* Leiden: E. J. Brill, 1972.

Tillich, Paul. *Dynamics of Faith.* New York: Harper & Row, 1957.

Tödt, H. E. *The Son of Man in the Synoptic Tradition.* London: SCM, 1965.

Townsend, John T. "The Gospel of John and the Jews: The Story of a Religious Divorce." In *Antisemitism and the Foundations of Christianity,* edited by A. T. Davies. New York: Paulist, 1979, Pp. 72–97.

Tyson, Joseph B. "Source Criticism of the Gospel of Luke." In *Perspectives on Luke–Acts,* edited by C. H. Talbert. Danville, Va.: Association of Baptist Professors of Religion, 1978, pp. 24–39.

Vawter, Bruce. "Are the Gospels Anti-Semitic?" *JES* 5 (1968): 473–87.

Via, Dan O., Jr. *Kerygma and Comedy in the New Testament.* Philadelphia: Fortress, 1975.

Viviano, B. T. "Where Was the Gospel According to St. Matthew Written?" *CBQ* 41 (1979): 533–46.

Weber, Max. *Sociology of Religion.* Boston: Beacon, 1963.

Weeden, Theodore J. *Mark—Traditions in Conflict.* Philadelphia: Fortress, 1971.

―――. "The Heresy that Necessitated Mark's Gospel." *ZNW* 59 (1968): 145–58.

Westermann, Claus, ed. *Essays on Old Testament Hermeneutics.* Richmond, Va.: John Knox, 1963.

White, Ellen G. "One Seventh of Our Time Belongs to God." *These Times* 87, no. 5 (May 1978): 13–16.

Wiefel, Wolfgang. "The Jewish Community in Ancient Rome and the Origins of Roman Christianity." In *The Romans Debate,* edited by Karl P. Donfried. Minneapolis, Minn.: Augsburg, 1977. Pp. 100–119.

Wilcox, Max. "A Foreword to the Study of the Speeches in Acts." In *Christianity, Judaism and Other Greco-Roman Cults,* edited by J. Neusner. Part One: New Testament. Leiden: E. J. Brill, 1975. Pp. 206–25.

Wilder, Amos N. *The Language of the Gospel: Early Christian Rhetoric:* New York: Harper & Row, 1964.

Williams, C. S. C. *A Commentary on the Acts of the Apostles.* New York: Harper and Brothers, 1957.

Wilson, Bryan R. *Magic and Millennium: A Sociological Study of Religious Movements of Protest Among Tribal and Third-World Peoples.* London: Heinemann, 1973.

Wilson, R. McL. *Gnosis and the New Testament.* Philadelphia: Fortress, 1968.

———. "Slippery Words: II. Gnostic, Gnosticism." *ET* 89 (1978): 296–301.

Winter, Paul. *On the Trial of Jesus.* Studia Judaica I. Berlin: de Gruyter, 1961.

———. "The Markan Account of Jesus' Trial by the Sanhedrin." *JTS,* n.s. 14 (1963): 94–102.

Zeitlin, Solomon. *Who Crucified Jesus?* 5th ed. New York: Bloch, 1964.

Ziesler, J. A. "Luke and the Pharisees." *NTS* 25 (1979): 146–57.

Index of Scripture Passages

Index of Authors and Subjects